D1611798

Chrysler U.K.

Stephen Young
Neil Hood

The Praeger Special Studies program—
utilizing the most modern and efficient book
production techniques and a selective
worldwide distribution network—makes
available to the academic, government, and
business communities significant, timely
research in U.S. and international economic, social, and political development.

Chrysler U.K.

A Corporation in Transition

Praeger Publishers   New York   London

Library of Congress Cataloging in Publication Data

Young, Stephen, 1944–
    Chrysler U.K.

    (Praeger special studies in international business,
finance, and trade)
    Includes bibliographical references and index.
    1. Chrysler United Kingdom Limited. 2. Automobile
industry and trade—Europe. 3. International business
enterprises. I. Hood, Neil, joint author. II. Title.
HD9710.G74C488   338.4'7'62920941   76-24353
ISBN 0-275-23820-2

PRAEGER PUBLISHERS
200 Park Avenue, New York, N.Y. 10017, U.S.A.

Published in the United States of America in 1977
by Praeger Publishers, Inc.

789   038   987654321

Printed in the United States of America

CONTENTS

LIST OF TABLES

ix

LIST OF FIGURES

LIST OF ABBREVIATIONS

AMC	American Motor Corporation
BL	British Leyland
BLMC	British Leyland Motor Corporation
BLSP	British Light Steel Pressings
BMC	British Motor Corporation
BMH	British Motor Holdings
CKD	completely knockdown
CPRS	Central Policy Review Staff
cwt	hundred weight
DATA	Draughtsmen and Allied Technicians Association
ECGD	Export Credits Guarantee Department
EEC	European Economic Community
EEF	Engineering Employers Federation
EFTA	European Free Trade Area
EIU	Economist Intelligence Unit
EPTU	Electricians and Plumbers Trades Union
FFI	Finance for Industry
GATT	General Agreement on Tariffs and Trade
GM	General Motors
GNP	gross national product
gvw	gross vehicle weight
IDAB	Industrial Development Advisory Board
IDC	Industrial Development Certificate
IMF	International Metalworkers Federation
INIM	Iran National Industrial Manufacturing Company
IRC	Industrial Reorganisation Corporation
IVECO	Industrial Vehicles Corporation
KD	knockdown
MAA	Motor Agents Association
MEAL	Media Expenditure Analysis Ltd.
MSA	Metalurgica de Santa Ana
NEB	National Enterprise Board
NEDO	National Economic Development Office
NUVB	National Union of Vehicle Builders
PERC	Plant Employee Representation Committee
SLT	Stoke, Linwood, and Truck Plan
SMMT	Society of Motor Manufacturers and Traders
SMTA	Scottish Motor Trade Association
TGWU	Transport and General Workers Union
TUC	Trade Union Congress
UAW	United Automobile Workers

Christmas is coming, the goose is getting fat. Please
put £200 million in Chrysler's hat.

Mel Calman, The Sunday Times, December 14, 1975

We were considering writing a book on Chrysler before the crisis arose in the autumn of 1975. The company had been in the news
almost constantly for some time. Working virtually next door to the
company's Linwood plant, we were acutely conscious of the implications of the threatened closure of Chrysler for the immediate area,
for Scotland, and for the United Kingdom. As it happened, the speculation developed substance; the substance posed issues of importance
and concern for a wide range of interest groups in the United Kingdom. In turn, these issues led to debate as to why this had all happened to Chrysler in Britain. Commentators reached for their
"econo-medical" dictionaries to identify what strain of the British
disease was present. The pundits had a field day. The story mix
had a familiar ring: the British government had been weak again, a
multinational had once more used its bargaining strength to full effect. Where was the strategy for the British car industry now?
Above all, where was U.K.-industrial strategy? Sic transit gloria
mundi! It had lasted for all of two weeks. It was December 1975
and economic rationality was dead! Or was it?

It was in this context that the book was born. It was born of a
desire to analyze thoroughly before drawing conclusions. No problem of the magnitude of Chrysler U.K. emerges overnight, neither
can it be evaluated by an overnight study. We had been examining
the U.K. operations of Chrysler along with other U.S. multinationals
over an extended period, thus we found ourselves with the basic equipment to consider the 1975 crisis within a wider framework. We
shared much of the public distaste for the way the negotiations appeared to have been handled by the Chrysler Corporation and yet
were aware of the multidimensional nature of the problems faced by
corporation and government alike. These problems needed to be
documented, traced to their source, to have their natures analyzed
and to have the future assessed in the light of the 1975 rescue. In
that sense, this is, by definition, an interim report on Chrysler U.K.
The problems have not disappeared, the solutions posited are as yet
untested operationally. Any work on a live industrial organism will
require a reassessment as the future strategy develops. Chrysler is

far from having arrived at an optimum strategy for Europe. In that light, our objective has been to establish a base upon which further study could rest and to provide a measure against which future evaluation could be undertaken. If we are correct, the problems for Chrysler in Britain and Europe have hardly begun.

Essentially this book is a case study of a multinational enterprise. Our perspective is that of economists with strong managerial interests, especially in international business. The objective of the book is to provide an in-depth assessment of the operations of Chrysler U.K., and thereby draw out the implications of the case for the British government and British economic policy, for the Chrysler Corporation, and for the British and European motor industries. During the process of writing the manuscript we were asked by a top executive of Chrysler whether we were aware of the damage that such a book might have on Chrysler and therefore on the livelihood of many thousands of employees in the U.K. Our reply, that we were fully aware of our social responsibilities, and that we had no wish to do Chrysler U.K. or its future prospects any harm, still holds true. The tenets of social responsibility, however, could not be maintained without considering why the company failed miserably in the past in Britain.

The case of Chrysler U.K. incorporates a number of dimensions. The multinational dimension to the book is fundamental and recurs constantly. Chrysler behaved as a multinational in Britain. Therein lay many of its problems, ranging from its astonishing ability in labor matters "to set fire to the oil it had previously poured on troubled waters," to its blackmail of the British government at the time of the crisis. The ability of such an MNE to wield so much power over a government in one of the richer countries of the world is frightening to behold.

The multinational aspect means that the book is far from being merely a study of another "lame duck," to accompany famous names such as Rolls Royce, British Leyland, and the like. Yet the specifically U.K.-dimension of the study is very pertinent. It will be shown that in many ways the problems of Chrysler U.K. make it a micro cosm of the wider problems of the U.K. economy. The spirals of decline that Chrysler was experiencing regarding investment, productivity, labor relations, and profitability are all symptoms of the "British disease." If Chrysler is anything to go by, the restructuring necessary to restore British industry's international competitiveness is indeed horrendous in its enormity. On the other hand, it can be argued that by supporting Chrysler, as the "lamest duck in the pond," the prospects for this necessary restructuring faded that much further into fantasy-land.

The motor industry dimension to the book is equally important. Massive overcapacity seems likely to pertain in Europe for at least the rest of the decade, and Ford and Vauxhall find themselves competing in the United Kingdom against two state-supported companies, British Leyland, with potentially limitless access to funds, and Chrysler, with finance until 1979 but now tied in so closely to the government as to make further requests for aid perhaps impossible to refuse. It is against this background that this book attempts a serious analysis of the problems and prospects for Chrysler United Kingdom Ltd.

We openly and gratefully acknowledge the help of many individuals and organizations in the production of this work. We are indebted to the detailed help we received from: the Society of Motor Manufacturers & Traders, with special thanks to D. Dyster, C. Gallacher of the Scottish Motor Trade Association, the Statistics Department of the Motor Agents Association, M. Pecci-Boriani of the Statistical Office of the European Community, Media Expenditure Analysis Ltd., and Extel Statistical Services Ltd. While producing this book we sought and obtained active assistance from the staff in numerous libraries. Our special thanks are due to Tony Northeast of the Financial Times Library in London, and to the staffs of the Glasgow Herald and Mitchell Libraries in Glasgow. The efficiency with which Rosanna McLennan in our own Library at Paisley College handled our requests was remarkable and deserves special mention. Many individuals helped us considerably. These included Norman Buchan, M. P., Robert Rogers, Clerk to Trade & Industry Sub-Committee, John Carty, Convenor of Shop Stewards at Chrysler's Linwood plant, Bill Dewing, then chairman of the Chrysler Dealers Association, Alistair Cormack of James Ross & Sons (Motors) Ltd., Sandy Morrison, and other Chrysler dealers. We are grateful for the help eventually received from Chrysler U.K., especially since we constituted another burden during a period in which the company was under intense scrutiny from the MP's of the Expenditure Committee and management was fully committed to the restructuring of the company in line with the government plan. We are particularly grateful to Don Lander, at the time European vice-president of the corporation and managing director of Chrysler U.K.; Peter Griffiths, then joint deputy managing director of Chrysler U.K.; and to Colin Cook and John Bullock of the corporation's public relations staff. None of these individuals is in any way party to the conclusions expressed in this book, for these we alone accept responsibility. Our grateful thanks are due to our secretarial assistants, Jean Beggs, Ella Kininmonth, and Margaret Jamieson for their efficiency and patience throughout this whole project. Finally we acknowledge the support and encouragement of our wives, Anne and Anna, who suffered much.

Chrysler U.K.

1

THE MOTOR
INDUSTRY
IN EUROPE

Any study of the motor industry in Western Europe must be set in a context that not only identifies the structural changes within the industry but also emphasizes the role of the industry within the respective national economies. This chapter sets out to examine both these issues, concentrating principally on setting the European background for the detailed study of the Chrysler U.K. operation.

ORIGINS, GROWTH, AND NATIONAL IMPORTANCE

In any large industry as complex and diverse as the motor industry, it is almost impossible to quantify its true significance for the national economy. The interdependence of the individual parts of the industry—motor manufacturing, component production, and the distribution system—is reinforced by the scale of output, employment, exports, and investment. While the historic origins and relative rates of expansion within the major producing countries have varied, nevertheless, the motor industry plays a vital part in the growth and prosperity of the economies of all countries concerned. The welfare of the industry, moreover, has come to be regarded as a barometer of national economic health. Thus, it is not surprising that in recent years such matters as structural change, employment, ownership, and import penetration have become areas of both social and private concern. By whatever measure of national importance, the motor industry in Western Europe operates at the interface of private and social costs and benefits, and, as such, any foreign investor is likely to come under constant public scrutiny.

While the early developments in the motor industry in the United Kingdom had been mirrored, particularly in the 1920s and 1930s by parallel growth in Europe, the European industry had grown more slowly and on a more restricted basis. Subsequent war damage and disruption resulted in the vehicle market being largely controlled by U.S. and U.K. producers until the mid-1950s. Previously, expansion within Germany, France, and Italy was largely absorbed in meeting the pressures of excess demand in their respective domestic markets. This establishment of a secure domestic base may have been valuable to the German industry in particular, which began to grow rapidly from the mid-1950s and develop its export business. By 1960, the French and Italian manufacturers had completed their recovery, and together the European producers' commitment to export expansion began to erode British dominance in many markets. In production terms, output in these three countries expanded by a factor of 5 or 6 between 1950 and 1960. As is considered later in this chapter, subsequent expansion has only increased the relative importance of the industry.

Many parts of this study are dominated by considerations that stem directly from the size and importance of the motor industry. Thus, for example, the policies and attitudes of European governments toward the motor industry are unquestionably influenced by its relative importance. The remainder of this section considers some different measures of the size of the industry within the major producing countries in Europe.

The significance of the output of the car industry in terms of the gross national products (GNP) of the major producing countries is emphasized by the data in Table 1.1. While noting the inherent problems in obtaining comparable statistics, as between countries, the relative positions are clear. In both West Germany and the United Kingdom, the motor industry in general (NACE 35) accounts for between 5 and 6 percent of the GNP. This does not give the whole picture, however, since in the United Kingdom, for example, it has been estimated[1] that at least an equivalent proportion of the GNP is accounted for by output in other sectors of the economy, directly or indirectly affected by the motor industry. In France and Italy, the size of the industry's output is smaller in relation to the GNP, but this reduces rather than removes the effect of the motor industry on the economy as a whole.

In the United Kingdom, the importance of output is underlined by the export contribution made by the industry. Without question, the continuation of large positive trade balances has been a crucial factor in government involvement in the industry. Indeed, this contribution shows signs of increasing owing to the development of components and accessories trade, growing largely through the increased proportion of vehicles exported from the United Kingdom in kit or knockdown form (33 percent in 1960, 58 percent in 1974). Although export ratios are high in some European countries, the dominance of the balance of payments in the minds of U.K. policy makers places the U.K. export trade in a unique position within Europe.

TABLE 1.1

European Motor Industry: Output[a] as a Proportion of the GNP in
Major Producing Countries
(in percent)

	1968	1969	1970	1971	1972	1973	1974
NACE Activity 351[b]							
West Germany	3.87	4.25	4.29	4.26	4.15	4.02	3.50
France	2.61	2.51	2.88	3.16	3.19	3.15	3.01
Italy	n.a.	3.16	3.75	3.05	n.a.	2.74	2.04
NACE Activity 35[c]							
West Germany	5.52	6.07	6.25	6.19	5.92	5.87	5.33
France	3.77	3.85	4.21	4.54	4.59	4.55	4.24[d]
United Kingdom[e]	5.61	5.58	5.72	5.54	5.62	5.35	4.87

[a]In order to obtain approximately comparable figures, the following variables are employed in the numerator: West Germany, turnover (umsatz); France, sales before tax (vente hors taxes); Italy, production value (valore della produczione); United Kingdom, sale of goods produced and work done.
[b]Activity 351 includes manufacture and assembly of motor vehicles (including road tractors) and manufacture of motor vehicle engines.
[c]Activity 35 includes manufacture of motor vehicles and of motor vehicle parts and accessories.
[d]Estimates.
[e]Revised series from 1970.

Note: n.a. = data not available.

Source: Statistical Office of the European Communities (EEC), Luxembourg, 1976.

The motor industry output is particularly important because of the role it has played in economic growth and in year-to-year fluctuations in growth rates. It is, of course, hardly surprising that an industry that accounts for up to 10 percent[2] of total industrial production in major producing countries (taking into account the indirect impact of the industry in other sectors) is of crucial significance in influencing the rate of growth. Some estimates[3] for the United Kingdom in the early 1960s suggested that up to 25 percent of economic growth between the mid-1950s and the 1960s was accounted for by the expansion in the motor industry. While this growth almost certainly has decreased in the United Kingdom, and has only reached such high figures over limited periods in Europe as a whole, perhaps between 10 and 15 percent of growth is still accounted for by the industry. This stems directly from the high proportion of manufacturing investment accounted for by the motor industry. In the United Kingdom, for example, motor industry (Minimum List Heading 381) investment has varied between 5 and 10 percent of all manufacturing investment since the early 1960s. Such levels have been sustained in Europe by technological change and direct foreign investment in the industry.

The situation in employment is no less important, as Table 1.2 suggests. In the major producing countries, about 5 percent of industrial employment is involved in vehicle and accessory manufacture, and while the information presented for Italy indicates substantially smaller employment, this is only a reflection of the narrower base of these statistics. The relative increase in employment contribution from the industry in Germany and the United Kingdom contrasts with the comparative stability elsewhere. This is particularly important against a background of overcapacity in Europe as a whole. In the United Kingdom, the figures disguise the fact that the industry is employing an increased proportion of a reduced labor force in industrial employment. Moreover, the true significance of motor industry employment can only be fully appreciated when fluctuations in employment are considered. Estimates for the 1973–75 recession period suggest that potential unemployment by the latter year would exceed 20,000, reaching almost 40,000 in some European countries.[4] Clearly, the magnitude of job loss implied in these figures underlies much of the government involvement in the industry in Europe.

A comparison of the indexes of employment in Table 1.3 stresses the slightly different role that motor industry employment plays in the countries concerned. In Italy, expansion in motor industry employment has outstripped employment in manufacturing industry as a whole in recent years. Less dramatically, the French vehicle industry expanded consistently until the 1974 recession. The German situation is not dissimilar, although the expansion is less marked, while the sluggishness of the U.K. industry is reflected in its employment pattern.

THE STRUCTURE OF THE MOTOR INDUSTRY IN EUROPE

While within the overall objective of setting Chrysler into the European context, the specific aim of this section is to analyze the position of the car manufacturing industry in Europe. The particular matters that have been highlighted as of special importance are as follows:

TABLE 1.2

European Motor Industry: Employment as a Percentage of
Industrial Employment[a]

	1968	1969	1970	1971	1972	1973	1974
West Germany	4.3	4.5	4.9	5.1	5.0	5.2	5.2
France[b]	5.2	5.3	5.5	5.5	5.6	5.9[c]	5.4[c]
Italy	1.9	2.2	1.8	1.8	2.0	2.2	2.1
United Kingdom	4.1	4.2[c]	4.7	4.8	4.9	4.8	4.8

[a]Employment in NACE Activity 35, except in Italy where only
NACE Activity 351 figures are available. Total industrial employment
figures are the annual average on June 30 of each year.
[b]1968-71 French industrial employment figures are estimated
from manufacturing employment data.
[c]Estimates of motor industry employment.

Source: Statistical Office of the European Communities, Luxembourg. EEC General Statistics Monthly Bulletin, No. 12, 1975,
and EEC Social Statistics, No. 4, 1973, Statistical Office of the European Communities, Luxembourg.

1. The overall structure of the industry and its basic characteristics
    within each major producing country
2. The growth and development of the motor market in Europe, par-
    ticularly as it has adjusted with the progression of European eco-
    nomic integration
3. Long-term prospects for production and market growth
4. Competition policy and the European motor industry

Inevitably these aspects have interacted, combining to produce
15 years of change within the European industry and creating for an
incoming investor like Chrysler both an industrial structure and a
market in transition. Not only has the prediction of the nature and
character of demand been constantly difficult but the extent of the dramatic increase in business cooperation plans among European companies could hardly have been anticipated.

European Structure and National Characteristics

The overall structure of the European industry is shown in Table
1.4. In all countries, output is concentrated within a small number

TABLE 1.3

European Motor Industry: National Employment in Major Producing Countries

	1968	1969	1970	1971	1972	1973	1974
United Kingdom							
Manufacturing employment	101.1	100.8	100.0	96.7	97.0	99.2	99.6
NACE 35 employment	93.4	97.5	100.0	99.3	98.1	97.3	96.9
France							
Industrial employment	96.7	98.6	100.0	100.1	100.1	100.6	101.3
NACE 351 employment	91.7	92.4	100.0	101.4	103.6	107.3	99.5
NACE 35 employment	91.3	92.9	100.0	101.0	105.4	112.1	104.0
Italy							
Manufacturing employment	93.5	96.6	100.0	103.1	100.1	101.8	105.9
NACE 351 employment	99.6	118.8	100.0	103.4	108.6	121.0	121.8
West Germany							
Industrial employment	91.7	96.4	100.0	99.4	97.1	97.3	94.9
NACE 351 employment	81.4	90.6	100.0	104.7	102.8	105.2	101.3
NACE 35 employment	82.5	91.3	100.0	103.9	100.7	103.8	101.0

Source: European Economic Community and international financial statistics.

of producers, the Italian motor industry being the most concentrated and the West German the least among the major manufacturing countries. In comparison, however, the European industry is significantly less concentrated than that of the United States. For example, GM, Ford, and Chrysler produced 95 percent of the 1974 volume—total U.S. production being some 40 percent less than the combined output of the four major European producing countries.

In both the United States and Europe, vertical and horizontal integration is characteristic, but the reasons behind its development and timing are significantly different. In the United States, the historic acquisition policies adopted by Ford and GM, as well as the potential economies of scale in components production, led to the early achievement of self-sufficiency. In Europe as a whole, although not in the United Kingdom, there was little simultaneous development of an independent components industry, so that many manufacturers have had to establish supply points within their own plants. In the United Kingdom, by contrast, all the major vehicle producers are highly dependent on outside suppliers. This has several important implications, not least of which is the disruptive effect of production stoppages in components suppliers' plants, but also the fact that a high proportion of total unit costs per vehicle is outside the manufacturer's direct control. Paradoxically, profitability in components production invariably far exceeds that of the vehicle manufacturer.

The relative growth and development of motor output within the major producing countries is indicated in Table 1.4. Of the largest four vehicle manufacturing countries, the French output has grown most dramatically, increasing in the peak year of 1973 by 80 percent over 1967 output. This is closely followed by West German production with a 60 percent increase at the 1971 peak. The expansion in these two countries is in marked contrast to the relatively stagnant performance of the U.K. industry, which drifted from one crisis to another during the period. Italian production has been marginally better, but so closely tied to the performance of Fiat as to present a special case. To complete the overall view, the figures for Belgium and Spain are included. For different reasons, their production expanded significantly in the period. In the case of Belgium, the expansion of assembly from imported parts is in line with the general growth of the European market. The emergence of the Spanish vehicle industry is by far the more significant development, however, since it is part of a wider movement toward market expansion and low cost production, which will be discussed later in this chapter.

TABLE 1.4

European Motor Vehicle Industry: Production and Assembly by Manufacturer[a]
(percent of annual unit output)

	1967	1968	1969	1970	1971	1972	1973	1974	1975
West Germany[b]									
Audi-NSU Auto Union	1.6	2.2	3.3	8.2	7.1	7.8	10.4	8.6	6.4
Daimler-Benz	10.2	9.2	9.7	10.1	9.6	11.2	11.3	15.0	15.5
Ford	7.8	6.7	8.4	10.7	12.1	11.4	11.5	9.2	13.0
Opel	22.1	21.1	22.2	21.4	21.1	23.0	22.1	18.8	20.6
Volkswagen	46.8	49.9	45.5	42.2	43.1	38.7	37.1	40.0	35.2
Other	11.5	10.9	10.9	7.1	7.0	7.9	7.6	8.4	9.3
Total units (000)	2,482	3,107	3,605	3,842	3,983	3,816	3,949	3,100	3,186
France									
Citroen	24.9	22.2	20.6	19.6	22.0	22.1	20.9	19.9	20.9
Chrysler France	13.7	16.9	15.8	14.6	16.1	16.1	16.4	13.5	14.3
Peugeot	20.2	19.4	19.9	21.0	20.6	20.2	21.3	21.1	22.5
Renault	38.7	38.9	41.0	42.2	39.1	39.6	39.3	43.0	39.5
Other	2.5	2.6	2.7	2.6	2.2	2.0	2.1	2.5	2.8[c]
Total units (000)	2,010	2,076	2,459	2,750	3,010	3,328	3,596	3,463	2,861
United Kingdom									
British Leyland	46.0	44.3	46.6	45.8	48.2	45.3	46.7	44.5	44.8
Chrysler U.K.	10.9	9.7	9.4	11.9	14.0	12.4	13.5	14.8	14.9
Ford	27.6	29.7	30.6	28.1	22.2	29.6	27.2	26.6	27.8
Vauxhall	14.8	15.4	12.6	13.3	14.8	11.8	11.3	12.8	11.5
Other	0.7	0.9	0.8	0.9	0.8	0.9	1.3	1.3	1.0
Total units (000)	1,937	2,225	2,183	2,098	2,198	2,329	2,164	1,937	1,648

Italy									
Alfa Romeo	5.1	6.0	6.7	6.0	7.0	7.8	10.6	11.9	13.2
Fiat Group[d]	88.9	88.4	88.1	88.7	86.5	86.2	83.5	81.9	81.3
Innocenti[e]	3.0	3.0	3.0	2.7	3.4	3.4	3.0	3.4	2.3
Other	3.0	2.6	2.2	2.6	3.1	2.6	2.9	2.8	3.2
Total units (000)	1,543	1,664	1,596	1,854	1,817	1,840	1,958	1,773	1,459
Belgium (assembly)									
Ford	35.2	26.4	37.3	32.2	30.4	27.2	28.1	21.8	25.8
General Motors	17.1	25.0	23.0	25.1	28.8	28.4	29.0	23.3	25.0
Renault	14.6	14.7	13.4	14.0	12.0	12.3	10.8	17.4	17.5
Volkswagen	11.8	11.5	10.4	10.3	9.0	8.2	9.5	12.1	8.8
Citroen	8.0	5.6	4.7	5.5	6.4	7.4	6.8	8.3	7.3
Other	13.3	16.7	11.2	12.9	13.4	16.5	15.8	17.1	15.6
Total units (000)	520	652	828	842	972	993	1,052	836	858
Spain									
Chrysler Espana	10.1	10.1	9.5	7.8	6.2	9.8	11.4	10.1	9.0
Citroen Hispania	10.1	10.2	8.0	7.6	9.7	8.3	8.9	10.9	13.6
Fasa–Renault	20.0	8.0	18.7	18.3	20.7	19.9	22.1	21.9	25.3
Seat	44.3	45.8	48.9	52.6	48.0	48.7	43.9	43.6	40.8
Other	15.5	16.0	14.9	13.7	15.4	13.3	13.7	13.5	11.3
Total units (000)	362	393	454	539	532	695	822	837	814

[a] Includes cars and commercial vehicles.
[b] Excludes NSU before 1970.
[c] French figure not comparable with that for previous years. Comparable output figures (000s) for France for 1972-75 as follows:

1972	1973	1974	1975
3,017	3,218	3,075	2,861

[d] Includes Fiat, Autobianchi, and OM.

Source: Society of Motor Manufacturers and Traders, The Motor Industry of Great Britain, various issues.

9

Principal Characteristics of the Major Producing Countries

West Germany

The growth and expansion of vehicle production in the postwar period has resulted in Germany ranking third in the world after the United
States and Japan. Highly concentrated, Volkswagen still dominates
the market with around 40 percent, although its market share has
fallen continuously since the late 1960s. Four other manufacturers—
Opel, Daimler-Benz, Ford, and Audi-NSU—account for over half of
total output, having increased their share at the expense of Volkswagen and the smaller specialist producers, such as BMW. These
smaller producers have had mixed fortunes in recent years: Borgeward went into liquidation in 1961, while BMW absorbed Glas in 1967,
and in 1966 Mercedes sold its Auto Union subsidiary to Volkswagen.
Volkswagen also tried to remedy its declining market position by acquiring NSU in 1969.

The relative production growth of the U.S. multinationals, Ford
and GM (Opel), did not vary significantly from that of domestic manufacturers in the period from 1965, although a market share improvement
from 30 percent in 1967 to nearly 34 percent in 1973 did occur. This
was largely owing to the fact that Volkswagen production levels are
very dependent on the U.S. market,* which was particularly depressed
in 1973-74. The U.S.-owned companies' penetration has been more
significant in the smaller-sized car market segment, both Ford and
Opel having failed to attain a major share of the large and medium-
sized car market. Their failure in part may be due to a general mis-
conception of European car demand where engine size at the top end
of the market appears to be secondary to a positive desire for distinc-
tiveness as provided by many of the medium-sized companies.

There is little question that the German motor industry has not
yet reached its optimum structure and that the partial integration and
cooperation that exist among several of the key producers could well
result in formal merger agreements. In this context it is more than
possible that the existing BMW and Daimler-Benz cooperation could
lead to a three-way agreement incorporating Volkswagen. While the
competition policy of the European Economic Community (EEC)[5] provides actual and potential constraints on the car industry, the general
atmosphere should be more conducive to such rationalization in West

---

*In general, Volkswagen's export performance has been consistently
impressive: export sales of 8,365 million marks in 1968 (74.6 percent
of sales) increased to 11,805 marks in 1974 (69.5 percent of sales).
U.S. dependence, however, has increased home market vulnerability.

Germany than in the past. Any such moves would then, of course,
pose problems for the European development of both Ford and GM.

France

Production is concentrated in the hands of Citroen, Chrysler
France, Peugeot, and Renault. Over the period from 1967 the relative production shares of these major companies have remained substantially unchanged, although Renault has improved its position somewhat, mainly at the expense of Citroen. Output has increased significantly and, aided by the elimination of tariffs between member countries of the EEC, the improvement of some French companies' exports
has been dramatic. Between 1964 and 1974, Renault, for example,
moved from market shares of 2.9, 1.7, and 0.7 percent, respectively,
in West Germany, Italy, and the United Kingdom to 7.4, 6.2, and 8.9
percent.

Renault, which is state owned, and Peugeot form one closely
cooperating group; although financially independent they have undertaken numerous joint ventures in development since 1966. The links
between the major French companies were strengthened still further
when Peugeot took control of Citreon in April 1976. The struggle for
ownership of Citroen is an interesting one. Fiat purchased a 15 percent interest in Citroen in 1968 and increased its share to just under
50 percent by 1971. However, Fiat suffered in its attempts to take
ultimate control by the backlash from the French government over the
earlier Chrysler-Simca deal. Thus, although extensive cooperation
occurred, the venture never went as far as total absorption of Citroen
by Fiat. Indeed, subsequent events led in a different direction, with
a decrease in Fiat's holdings to 27 percent by 1973. Fiat indicated
a desire to retain its interest but, in effect, only as a sound investment. The change of direction in this case was probably as much due
to developments in Citroen as to those in Fiat, since the relative financial strengths of the companies changed from 1968 to 1973. With
the decrease in Fiat's holdings, Citreon regained some of its bargaining
power in components purchase, with few other long-term implications,
since there had been almost no progress toward common designs.

Citroen, however, continuing to perform below the expectations
of its major shareholder, Michelin, the tire manufacturer, moved under Peugeot management in December 1974. Peugeot took a 38 percent shareholding and Citroen received 1 billion francs in state loans.
As part of the deal, Peugeot was granted the right to take a majority
stake in the company, which it did in the spring of 1976, and its holdings were boosted to 90 percent. This left Chrysler France as the
only foreign manufacturer, having gained control of Simca in 1963 in
spite of vigorous protests from the French government. This was not

in fact Simca's first experience with foreign participation, for, until 1963, all Simca output was based on Fiat designs and Fiat still had a 29 percent stake in the equity.

Assuming that the close cooperation between Renault and the new Peugeot-Citroen Group continues, the long-term structure of the French industry is still difficult to predict. Suffice it to say that, in the French domestic market, Chrysler appears increasingly isolated, not only because of its foreign ownership but also because of its size. The two major indigenous groups now account for about 85 percent of output.

The general structure of the French industry is somewhat similar to that in the United Kingdom in the sense that a significant proportion of total car value is purchased from outside suppliers by the car manufacturer. Estimates suggest a figure of about 35 percent,[6] although the consistent French practice of trying to maintain more than one supplier has led to a smaller components manufacturing industry than in the United Kingdom. One notable characteristic of the French industry is the extent to which the system of motor taxation has influenced produce design. No truly large cars are being produced. Thus, over 50 percent of French car production is in the small to medium-small range, a factor of particular importance for export expansion to developing car markets and to the performance of the industry in the wake of the oil crisis.

United Kingdom

The relative position of the major U.K. producers is clear from Table 1.4, with the largest four companies, three of these American, accounting for 99 percent of unit production. Apart from the greater concentration of foreign ownership, the specialist car market is less important in the United Kingdom than in any other European country. While in 1973 and 1974, underproduction characterized most of the European car industry, this problem has been recurrent in the United Kingdom and is reflected in the slow and erratic growth of output. Structurally, there have been particular, rather than general, changes since the early 1960s, most of them related to the ultimate emergence of British Leyland backed by significant government support. Having acquired Standard-Triumph International in 1961 and to form British Leyland Motor Corporation Ltd. (BLMC). This merger was actively promoted by the U.K. government and the Industrial Reorganisation Corporation,[7] but it proved merely a token of the volume of long-term financial support required from 1975. Following the recommendations of the Ryder Report, the British government backed a recovery program for British Leyland (the name of the company having been changed from BLMC in August 1974), as the only major domestic manufacturer, to the tune of approximately £1,000 million.[8]

Of the U.S. companies, Ford has a successful European policy, whereas Chrysler and GM (Vauxhall) continue to struggle for a profitable formula. In light of the existing structure of the U.K. industry, any further integration would almost certainly involve British Leyland and either Chrysler or Vauxhall, with obvious employment and potential export implications. Indeed, U.K. government involvement with Chrysler as an independent unit in 1975 was atypical in a European context.

One of the most significant features of the U.K. industry is the very high dependence on outside purchases, estimated at between 65 and 70 percent of the material cost of cars.[9] This is up to a third higher than in the other major producing countries. Both U.K. and U.S. manufacturers display a similar dependence pattern, which has had important implications for cost control and security of supplies. It has often been alleged that the profit performance of the industry is influenced by its reliance on oligopolistic suppliers, and a number of the components manufacturing companies have been the subject of Monopolies Commission inquiries in recent years.[10]

Italy

In analyzing the motor industry in Italy, the outstanding problem is one of understanding the structure and policies of one company rather than the industry as a whole. Fiat provided 88 percent of employment in the Italian motor industry in 1973. Italy is unique within the major European producing countries for another reason, namely, the absence of U.S. investment in vehicle production. Apart from Fiat, Innocenti, primarily an engineering and machine tool company, was purchased by Alfa Romeo in 1971, and together they have accounted for 10 to 15 percent of total production in the recent past.

From a period of very rapid growth in the 1960s, overall output in Italy has not grown significantly in the 1970s. Within the total output, Fiat has suffered a fall in production in the last four to five years, a decline that was ultimately reflected in the company's first loss in 25 years in 1973. Officially, Fiat's results for 1973 showed a profit of 261 million lire, which in fact made a 65,000 million lire operating loss. Under Italian company law, a company must declare a profit if it wishes to pay a dividend. While the loss was the result of the combined problems of stagnating output and soaring costs, the company has made massive depreciation provisions in recent years in order to provide cash for reinvestment. For example, during 1969-73, 682,800 million lire was set aside for "depreciation," much of which would have counted as profit under the accounting practices of other countries.

As in other countries in Europe, the EEC has led to dramatic changes in the Italian trade pattern as tariffs applying to car trade

among member countries fell from 21 percent to zero between 1960
and 1961. For example, while previously Fiat had production and
market share dominance domestically, its market share was substantially eroded particularly after 1963. Fiat had up to 90 percent domestic market penetration in the 1950s, but by 1975 this was under 60
percent, even though it managed to reverse this trend for a period by
capacity expansion and government help. However, the importance
of this domestic market erosion has been reduced by the fact that Fiat
has taken a broader European view over a long period—probably the
major distinguishing characteristic of the company in comparison with
other domestic European manufacturers. The company adopted a policy of supplying the European market through part or complete ownership of factories outside Italy rather than through direct exports. In
this way, Fiat had financial interests in NSU in Germany, and, through
Seat, its Spanish licensee, gained close to 60 percent of the Spanish
market by the late 1960s.

This policy was only one expression of the company's declared
aim to spread its financial interests in Europe; and Fiat was one of
the earliest European companies to declare that it was specifically
motivated in its actions by a drive to prevent further U.S. penetration
in Europe. In the last ten years much of the structural change within
Fiat and its overseas markets has been directed to extending and developing sales and service networks. Such a program is in accord with
a longer term strategy of more stable distribution, as distinct from
the large-scale, self-contained ventures that the company has undertaken in the USSR and Eastern Europe.

Within the domestic market, the structure of Fiat also varies
from the European norm. From a background of being the largest
metal and engineering company within an underindustrialized country,
Fiat has developed a more integrated production complex for motor
manufacture than is common elsewhere in Europe. Balancing the obvious advantages of Fiat's position are the consequences for any
smaller company trying to gain entry into the industry. This has
clearly created problems for Alfa Romeo and others, but internal EEC
tariff removal and general reductions in external tariffs have opened
up markets elsewhere. In addition, government support expressed
inter alia in the expansion of Alfa Romeo into the Naples area has contributed to a marginal but sustained decline in Fiat's dominance.

Conclusion

While it has been necessary to analyze some of the essential
structural characteristics of the industry on a national basis, one of
the major trends within the last 15 years in Europe has been the increasingly international nature of the vehicle industry. This trend

is particularly reflected in the significant increase in the number of
agreements that have been developed outside the country of manufacture to pool interests in technology, marketing, and distribution. In
evidence this parallels the continuous extension of U.S. interests in
Western Europe, as both sets of producers have developed strategies
aimed at long-run profitability. Few of these policies have led directly to horizontal integration across national boundaries, but many
have been motivated by attempts to achieve economies of scale in
marketing.

Overall, from the U.S. manufacturer's viewpoint, the European
industry has shown a high propensity to develop mutually convenient
forms of intercountry cooperation.[11] This, together with the growing
concern of European governments with the maintenance of viable and
identifiable indigenous manufacturers, poses a formidable competitive
threat.

Growth and Development of the European
Car Market

The last decade has seen significant changes in the demand for
vehicles in Europe. Table 1.5 indicates that, while within the 1966-74
period vehicles in use in the major markets rose by an average of 58
percent, there were important differences among Italy, West Germany,
and the other major producing countries. The notable laggard was the
U.K. market with a low annual growth rate, only on one occasion reaching 5 percent. The importance attached to slow domestic market expansion as an explanatory factor in poor profit performance varies within
the motor industry. It is sufficient at this stage, however, to observe
that when European producers were increasingly regarding all Europe
as their domestic market, Chrysler found itself in Britain with a share
of the slowest growing domestic market in Europe, a market, moreover, that was subject to a major increase in foreign penetration.
France, with a 50 percent unit growth from 1966, was expanding, but
was still below the largest five-market average and experiencing the
full force of the impact of EEC trade liberalization. Once again there
was no easy opportunity for Chrysler, whose chosen strategy in France,
as in the United Kingdom, depended on volume.

The corresponding information on export dependence is presented
in Table 1.6. In the mid-1960s, West Germany exported about half
its output as compared with approximately one-third by the United Kingdom, France, and Italy. German motor industry expansion since that
time has been export-based, as Germany increased its export proportion significantly in comparison with its neighbors, although exports
also have grown faster than home market production in Italy and France.

TABLE 1.5

Vehicles in Use in Selected European Countries
(1968 = 100)

	1966	1967	1968	1969	1970	1971	1972	1973	1974	1975
West Germany	89.0 (11.7)	94.0	100.0	109.0	118.7	127.5	134.6	140.4	145.2	149.0 (19.6)
France	89.2 (11.6)	95.1	100.0	105.1	110.2	115.2	122.1	128.2	133.5	135.8 (17.7)
United Kingdom	92.0 (13.6)	97.6	100.0	102.1	103.5	106.5	111.4	117.0	118.9	120.9 (17.9)
Italy	78.6 (7.0)	89.6	100.0	109.9	124.1	137.3	150.6	161.6	170.9	180.8 (16.2)
Belgium	85.7 (1.8)	92.8	100.0	105.4	112.5	117.3	123.2	129.1	134.9	140.5 (2.9)

Note: Includes cars and commercial vehicles; figures in parentheses are in millions of units.

Source: Society of Motor Manufacturer and Traders, The Motor Industry of Great Britain, 1975.

TABLE 1.6

European Motor Industry: Principal Exporters
(thousands of units)

	1964	1965	1966	1967	1968	1969	1970	1971	1972	1973	1974	1975
United Kingdom												
Units of production	679	628	556	503	677	772	690	721	627	599	565	516
Percent of production	36.3	36.5	34.7	32.4	37.3	35.3	32.9	32.8	27.8	27.7	29.2	40.7
France												
Units of production	442	487	501	547	629	787	1,061	1,149	1,240	1,340	1,298	1,233
Percent of production	31.8	34.2	28.1	30.8	34.3	32.0	38.5	38.1	37.2	37.2	37.4	48.4*
West Germany												
Units of production	1,357	1,434	1,476	1,351	1,802	1,875	1,934	2,156	2,098	2,204	1,882	1,500
Percent of production	51.2	52.5	52.1	58.8	62.9	52.0	50.3	54.1	55.0	55.8	60.7	51.6
Italy												
Units of production	313	308	372	404	558	595	632	640	659	656	686	661
Percent of production	30.4	27.9	29.0	28.1	36.1	37.3	34.1	35.2	35.8	33.5	38.7	49.0
Japan												
Units of production	67	101	153	223	406	560	726	1,299	1,407	1,451	1,727	1,827
Percent of production	16.4	17.4	17.4	16.2	19.7	21.4	22.9	16.0	35.0	32.4	43.9	40.0

*1975 French figure not comparable with that for earlier years.

Note: Includes all exports of new cars only.

Source: Society of Motor Manufacturers and Traders, The Motor Industry of Great Britain, various issues.

While in general it is true that export growth is higher in countries where domestic demand has increased most rapidly, no causal
relationship can be inferred, since, for example, some of the largest
declines in exports (for instance, in West Germany between 1968 and
1969) have coincided with major home market expansion. U.K. performance is outside the pattern of Table 1.6, with the industry showing
distinct signs of becoming less export oriented overall.

It is not possible to view the export performance of European
producers without including Japan, since, as Table 1.6 shows, the proportion of its exported output has expanded dramatically in the period.
This trade, backed by systematic marketing and product development,
has had a particular impact on the United States and Europe, these
two markets having accounted for some 70 percent of Japanese car
exports in recent years. The impact, however, goes beyond these
markets, since it is arguable that the most significant long-term effect
of Japanese exports will be in Asia, Africa, and South America—areas
where the European industry is also looking for long-run growth to
solve some of its domestic capacity problems. Japan is no longer below the European norm in terms of its export-production ratio, and
has only turned to foreign markets in recent years in the search for
growth and in response to domestic demand fluctuations. Under the
special pressures of the lifetime employment of workers,[12] it is unlikely that the Japanese industry will be able to respond to demands
for export restraint.

It is clear that the overall performance of the European market
will be greatly influenced by the performance of the Japanese industry
in the next ten years. Figures for the first six months of 1975 confirm,
for example, that Japanese penetration into France and Germany is
still very low, under 1.5 percent of new registrations. Estimates have
suggested that if the Japanese gained 4 percent of the market in France
and Germany and 15 percent in the rest of Western Europe, this would
reduce potential demand for European produced cars by 500,000 units
in 1980.[13] On the basis of the penetration pattern adopted in the United
Kingdom, a lengthy period of distribution development will proceed a
major Japanese push in these markets. There are signs that such developments already have taken place on the Continent with promotional
preparation geared to a strong marketing effort by both Toyota and
Datsun.

Intra-European trade, of course, accounts by far for the largest
proportion of exports by the European manufacturers. Outside Europe,
export performance (Figure 1.1) is dominated by trends in the U.S.
market, although some two-thirds of these sales are accounted for by
Volkswagen. This U.S. trade has proven to be a problem in recent
years, showing almost no growth between 1965 and 1970 and a fall of
25 percent between 1973 and 1974. Nevertheless, the North American

FIGURE 1.1

Exports of European* Cars Outside the EEC and the European Free
Trade Area (EFTA), 1975
(in percent)

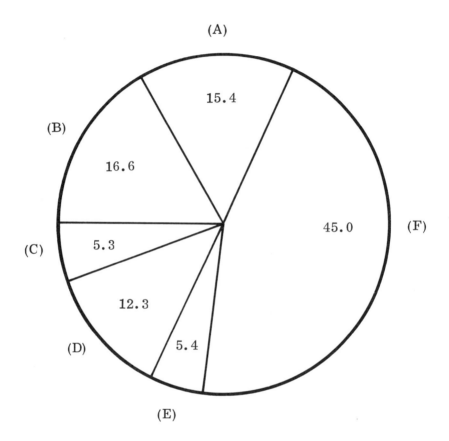

*United Kingdom, France, Italy, West Germany, and Sweden.

(A) Africa (including North Africa)
(B) Asia (including Middle East)
(C) Americas (excluding the United States and Canada) and un-
specified destinations
(D) Other European markets
(E) Australasia
(F) United States and Canada

Source: Society of Motor Manufacturers and Traders, The
Motor Industry of Great Britain, 1976.

market will continue to be of considerable importance for the foreseeable future.

   With market penetration of imports in the United States at 20 percent, lower than the Western European average, competition also is increasing, particularly through the production of domestic subcompacts. And evidence from the late 1950s and the 1960s indicates that the responses of U.S. manufacturers to imports have either halted or reduced their growth. Volkswagen is likely to be more affected by such developments than the exporters of more specialist cars, such as British sports models. Competition, market growth, and tariff barriers are all likely to make expansion in European sales to other markets more difficult in the next ten years.

   The growth of imports into selected European countries, as presented in Figure 1.2, provides another view of the market. From a general perspective, all four countries had reasonably comparable levels of market penetration of imports by the end of the period considered. They have, however, arrived at that pattern from different situations and display contrasting trends for the future. The French and Italian markets have been more stable since 1970, show signs of having gained net benefit from trade liberalization, and have captured a major part of their own domestic market expansion, as the comparison with Table 1.5 shows. In contrast, imports have expanded since 1965 in West Germany, although at a slightly slower rate in the last few years. The exception to the norm is again the United Kingdom, where, although neither domestic market nor export expansion has been comparable to those in other major European countries, imports have taken a growing proportion of the market from 1965. Thus, below the major market average in 1971, the U.K. propensity to import cars rose dramatically thereafter as a result of price, styling, and general marketing influences, combined with new trading arrangements through the EEC. From the viewpoint of the domestic producers in the United Kingdom, the timing of this structural change could scarcely have been less opportune.

   Table 1.7 brings together the net effects of some of the changes observed in the European car market since 1966. As such, it gives some indication of the relative movement of domestic market growth and home production, thereby pointing to the outcome of various changes in the structure of the industry and of government policies toward it. As would be expected, new registrations and home production do not move together, allowing for the impact of imports, exports, and stock changes. While in aggregate the West German domestic market has suffered more years of decline in new registrations, many of these have been small, and the most significant annual fluctuations in registrations have been in the United Kingdom and France. Consistent with the overall expansion of their domestic markets, Spain and Italy rarely

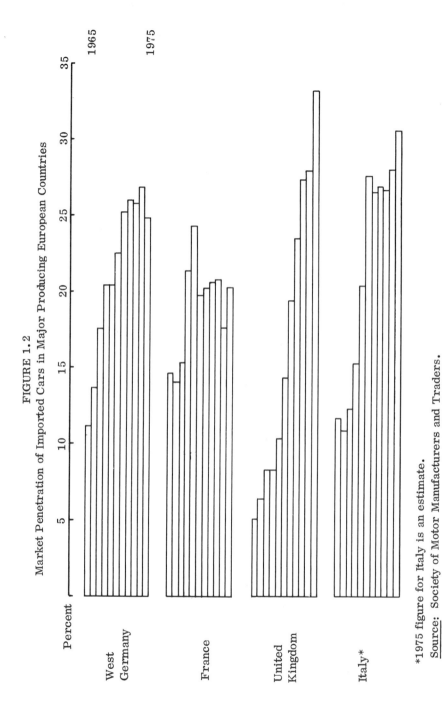

FIGURE 1.2

Market Penetration of Imported Cars in Major Producing European Countries

*1975 figure for Italy is an estimate.

Source: Society of Motor Manufacturers and Traders.

TABLE 1.7

Major European Producing Countries: Growth Rate of New Registrations and Home Production
(percent change over previous year)

	1966	1967	1968	1969	1970	1971	1972	1973	1974	1975
West Germany										
NR	-0.7	-10.4	+5.5	+28.4	+14.4	+1.8	-0.9	-5.4	-17.0	+23.0
HP	+2.5	-18.6	+25.2	+16.0	+6.6	+3.7	-4.2	+3.5	-21.5	+2.8
France										
NR	+13.7	+1.1	+1.7	+13.0	-5.3	+12.7	+11.3	-16.9	-11.8	-5.0
HP	+23.3	-0.7	+3.3	+18.5	+11.8	+9.5	+10.6	+8.0	-3.7	-7.0
United Kingdom										
NR	-4.3	+3.5	+0.8	-8.9	+6.1	+15.7	+24.0	+2.6	-23.3	-6.7
HP	-6.2	-5.2	+14.9	-2.0	-3.7	+4.7	+6.0	-7.1	-10.5	-14.9
Italy										
NR	+14.4	+15.4	+1.1	+4.4	+10.6	+4.5	+2.5	-1.3	-9.8	-18.2
HP	+16.0	+13.1	+7.8	-7.4	16.2	-2.0	+1.3	+6.5	-9.5	-17.7
Spain										
NR	+41.4	+13.3	+2.4	+16.7	+4.3	+6.4	+17.0	+17.3	-2.9	-1.5
HP	n.a.	n.a.	n.a.	n.a.	n.a.	-1.2	+30.6	+18.2	-1.9	-2.8

Note: n.a. = data not available.

Source: Adapted from Society of Motor Manufacturers and Traders, The Motor Industry of Great Britain, various issues.

21

have seen decline. The fluctuations in home production follow a different pattern. The United Kingdom has experienced continuous problems, with some of the instability, at least, attributable to government macroeconomic policies and to difficult labor situations. In six of the years considered, U.K. production has declined relative to the previous year, and while the degrees of decline have been less severe than in some other countries (especially West Germany), they have been more persistent than in any of the other European countries and have been cited by manufacturers as making a major contribution to profit loss.

In terms of the timing of overall fluctuations, it is not possible to make too many generalizations on a short series such as Table 1.7, but there is a tendency for boom and slump to coincide more closely as trade integration brings the industry closer together. This does not totally explain the coincidence of problems in 1974–75 when both indicators pointed to severe declines owing to wider world trade and general economic problems. From Chrysler's viewpoint, the position is again one of contrast, since in France the company has been in the most stable domestic production environment in Europe, whereas in the United Kingdom its production environment has been the most unsettled.

Long–Term Prospects for Production and Market Growth

The trends identified in the preceding section point to a European industry that will be under increasing competitive pressure in the long term. While the motor industry traditionally has been prone to cyclical demand patterns, the prospect of persistent underutilization of capacity within firms that have become financially weaker is a formidable one. Table 1.8 summarizes the severe impact that 1974 had upon the industry and the degree of underutilization of capacity that was experienced. Although 1973–75 was the worst period for the industry, there are signs that the future market growth will be damaging to the volume producer, who is particularly subject to penalty costs when operating below optimum capacity. As in 1973–75, the more specialist European manufacturers, such as Volvo, BMW, and Mercedes, are likely to be able to preserve margins. While indicating the extent of the overcapacity problem, Table 1.8 understates the position to some degree, since it is based on European shift working and productivity levels. Given pressures to improve productivity, the problem could increase. The drive to achieve profitability in such circumstances may be expressed in intensified price–led competition among producers for market share and renewed pressures for diversification among the indigenous manufacturers.

TABLE 1.8

Major Car Manufacturers' Utilization of European Assembly Capacity

Volume Car Manufacturers	1974 Profit After Tax* (000 pounds)	Two-Shift Capa-city	Pro-duc-tion in Best Year	Per-cent Capa-city Utili-zation	Actual Pro-duc-tion in 1974	Per-cent Capa-city Utili-zation
BL (including Belgium)	-11.0	1,190	916	77	738	62
Chrysler U.K. and France	-25.8	900	780	86	647	72
Fiat	-13.7	1,850	1,514	82	1,206	65
Ford U.K. and Germany	-31.1	1,450	1,428	98	807	56
General Motors (Vauxhall, Opel)	-20.8	1,400	1,116	80	715	51
Peugeot-Citroen	-85.4	1,570	1,263	80	1,127	72
Volkswagen (including Audi-NSU)	-168.7	1,800	2,032	113	1,436	80

*Before extraordinary items.

Source: Central Policy Review Staff, The Future of the British Car Industry (London: HMSO, 1975).

In light of the prevailing circumstances, numerous estimates have been made of the possible prospects for the industry, two of which are shown in Tables 1.9 and 1.10. The likely combined effects of a change in the balance between domestic and foreign trade is shown in Table 1.9. Although no complete agreement can be found, reliable estimates suggest that the car demand in Europe is unlikely to be in excess of 10 million units by 1980, with the EEC market reaching 9.5 million by that date and growing slightly less rapidly than the European average.[14] Even allowing for optimistic export forecasts and assuming the ability to better the import penetration suggested in Table 1.9, spare capacity is unlikely to be less than 25 percent in 1980. In view of this, it is difficult to see how rationalization, mergers, and integrated model policies (especially for U.S. producers) will not be constant themes.

Table 1.10 introduces a new dimension to the long term, since the future of the European industry cannot be viewed separately from

TABLE 1.9

Market Prospects for the Western European Car Industry
(millions of units)

	1974	1980	1985
Sales of new cars in Western Europe	8.0	9.6-10.9	11.3-12.6
Imports of new cars into Western Europe	0.4	1.0-0.6	1.1-0.7
Exports of new cars from Western Europe	2.1	1.1-1.7	1.1-2.0
Production of new cars in Western Europe	9.6	9.7-12.0	11.3-13.9
Capacity in Western Europe	14.1	14.8	14.8
Spare capacity (percent)	32	34-19	24-6

Source: Central Policy Review Staff, The Future of the British Car Industry (London: HMSO, 1975).

that of the world in general in view of the increasing importance of nontraditional production locations. Several issues raised by these figures are particularly important for this study. The predicted decline in the European share of world production is significant, but marginal compared to the relative decline of the United States as a car producer. While for Ford, General Motors, and Chrysler the 1985 situation may be recouped by external production (see Table 1.11) from new supply points, their success in these often troublesome ventures will become increasingly important as an extension to domestic production. The figures in Table 1.10 are inevitably based on assumptions that may prove invalid in light of events since 1973. For example, relative shares within Europe do not reflect the long-term impact of financial and structural changes during and following the weak markets of 1974-75. Nevertheless, the principal expectations are clear, and the impact of Japanese and emergent producers is predictably large in terms of production share and possibly much more significant in terms of obtainable market shares.

European producers have not been unaware of the long-term potential competitive advantage to be gained by siting in emerging markets. As Table 1.11 shows, however, their operations to date are relatively small, and some have been motivated by the necessity to produce within the country to gain access to the market on competitive

TABLE 1.10

World Car Production Forecasts by Country,[a] 1973-85
(percent)

	1973	1985
Benelux[b]	0.6	0.5
France	9.7	8.9
Germany	12.4	9.7
Italy	6.2	5.8
Britain	5.9	6.5
Enlarged EEC	34.8	31.3
Spain	2.4	3.5
Scandinavia	1.1	1.2
Total Europe[c]	38.3	36.0
United States-Canada	36.9	24.6
Total Europe plus United States-Canada	75.2	60.6
Latin America	3.2	5.5
(Argentina	(0.7)	(1.0)
Brazil)	(1.8)	(3.1)
Africa	—	0.8
Asia	0.2	0.4
Japan	15.1	20.4
Australia	1.1	1.3
Total Western world	95.0	89.0
Communist bloc	5.0	11.0
(Soviet Union)	(3.1)	(6.8)
Total	100.0	100.0

[a]Country production includes output of domestic and foreign-owned plants.

[b]Benelux production includes all DAF production and that part of Ford Genk for Belgian market; the remainder of Ford Genk production in Ford Cologne.

[c]Includes other Western European countries.

Source: "Euroeconomics Forecasts," quoted in Vision, February 1975.

TABLE 1.11

Car Production: Emergent Producing Countries
(thousands of units)

	Spain	Brazil	Australia	Argentina	Mexico	South Africa
European						
Fiat	358	190	—	60	—	—
Renault	166	—	—	40	—	—
Volkswagen	—	325	—[b]	—	67	28
Leyland	40	34	32	—	75	13
Citroen	45	—	—	16	—	—
Peugeot	—	[a]	—	26	—	—
United States						
Ford	[a]	110	101	40	26	30
General Motors	[a]	95	135	14	35	37
Chrysler	63	34	45	19	45	16
Total	672	565	313	216	173	125
Share of market leader (percent)	53.3	57.5	43.1	27.8	38.7	24.6

[a]Planning to enter market.
[b]Withdrawn from market.

Source: Financial Times, May 1, 1974.

terms rather than to view such developments as a long-term supply
point for other markets. Such European moves, of course, are coun-
tered by Japanese production in several European countries that are
not traditionally in motor manufacturing, such as Portugal, Finland,
and Switzerland. This Japanese investment and the related development of distribution systems in Europe, together with the actual and
potential investment by U.S. manufacturers in Spain, are probably the
two factors that will influence the structure and performance of the
European industry most directly in the short to medium term. The
planned Spanish capacity is in excess of 1.6 million units per year,
and, although export ambitions are high and the long-term EEC response to Spain as a major exporter (almost tariff free) in the Community uncertain, there is little comfort for European manufacturers.

Competition Policy and the European Car Industry

The aim of this section is to summarize some of the developments in competition policy that have affected the motor industry within
the recent past in order to complete the overall view of the structure
of the industry and its markets. These developments fall into several
categories, including trends in EEC competition policy as they have affected the industry, and a range of issues stemming from external de-

THE MOTOR INDUSTRY IN EUROPE

cisions on dumping, market access, and so on. While these do not necessarily affect the present structure of the industry, they are constraints on development.

By the terms of Articles 85 and 86 of the Treaty of Rome, the EEC has potentially wide powers in monopoly and restrictive practices. As these powers have began to be utilized, several car producers have come under examination. For example, in late 1974, the EEC Commission ordered BMW to modify its distribution system to comply with Community rules on selective distribution. The commission formulated a ruling, with implications for all European manufacturers, that while it was accepted that limiting the number of distributors of a firm's vehicles and spare parts was in the interests of the consumer inasmuch as it encouraged good after-sales service and safer vehicles, BMW was not entitled to give distributors exclusive sales territories. This ruling was considered to eliminate effectively competition among distributors in various parts of the Community. BMW was not allowed to oblige its distributors to sell only BMW cars when "objective reasons" for selling other makes were given, and the distributors were to be allowed to use non-BMW parts of equal quality in the repair of BMW vehicles if they desired.

While this judgment was temporary (to the end of 1977) and applied to a relatively small producer, it has much wider implications, if upheld and sustained over the long term. Indeed, the Commission stated on making the ruling that the decision could be considered as a general guide to motor manufacturers that operated with similar distribution agreements. Other producers have not escaped attention. For example, GM Continental, the GM Belgian subsidiary, was fined under Article 86 of the Rome Treaty for having abused a dominant position, as the sole importer of GM cars into Belgium, in the issue of "certificates of conformity" for Opel vehicles. GM appealed this action and won. While this represents a fairly minor issue, it is characteristic of the pressures that are likely to continue to be placed on industry within the EEC as policy develops.

Commission activity has extended into other car industry affairs. One of the particular recurring problems concerning European producers has been the persistent difficulties in tackling the Japanese market. Tariff barriers to entry are not in themselves high, but allegations[15] of the existence of "other nontariff barriers" abound. In late November 1975, the EEC sent a "note verbale" to Japan to obtain an easing of vehicle testing procedures so as to facilitate expansion of European car exports to Japan. In effect, the request was for a standardization of Japanese testing procedures and for Japanese agreement to the testing of European cars for export to Japan at the factories of the European manufacturers. Many other issues also have been raised, including the fact that Japanese vehicle regulations have only been translated in part and that the practice of giving only six months notice of changes in regulations was contrary to the European norm of two to three years, making planning extremely difficult.* At this stage, however, although the Japanese market offers potential export prospects for European producers, European penetration will be difficult and slow. Conversely, of course, pressure is building up in Europe for retaliatory action against imports of Japanese cars.

One of the continuing difficulties in external trade has been the persistent allegations of dumping by European producers in the United States. Various pressure groups renewed calls for antidumping legislation in early 1975 when imports had gained a record 21 percent of the U.S. market and domestic car sales were 18 percent down on 1974. Allegations were made that European (and Japanese) cars were sold at lower prices in the United States than in Europe and that such practices were in violation of the GATT (General Agreement on Tariffs and Trade) antidumping code of practice. While all manufacturers were included, British Leyland, Volkswagen, and Fiat came under particular scrutiny. The EEC vigorously defended the pricing policies of the European producers. Indeed, price may not be at the root of the importer's success in the United States, since, for example, in 1975 the Volkswagen Rabbit cost $500 more than the Ford Pinto. Fuel economy in particular has led to volume expansion and to the resultant major shift in U.S. product policy. It is more than likely that the actions of U.S. producers, whose medium-term plans are estimated to result in 80 percent of U.S. cars being below standard size by 1980,[16] will be more effective in reducing imports than any antidumping legislation. This is particularly important for Volkswagen and the other indigenous European producers that would wish to seek further U.S. expansion for volume production. Some of the European subsidiaries of the U.S. producers would appear likely to compete for U.S. market share, although Ford with a mini from Europe is the only one with announced plans in this direction.

THE EXPANSION OF U.S. FIRMS IN EUROPE

Some of the principal forces influencing the structure and performance of the European industry are a direct result of the entry and expansion of U.S. multinationals within the last 30 years. By 1975, the Big Three—Chrysler, Ford, and General Motors, accounted for

---

*By late February 1976, for example, only about 25 percent of the 150 foreign models selling in Japan had passed the new emission control tests that became effective in April 1976.

25 percent of all cars registered in the EEC. This contrasts with the impact made by European car exports to the United States, which, although over half of all imports, currently account for under 10 percent of the U.S. domestic market. It is likely that such relativities will become increasingly important politically, as both indigenous and U.S. firms strive toward optimal levels of penetration and profitability within Europe.

Comparative Strategies for Entry and Expansion

Europe, particularly the EEC, is the most important base for the multinational operations of the Big Three outside the United States, whether measured in terms of numbers of supply points, investment, or size. From the early stages of the expansion of volume production within the United States, producers have looked for European bases where local production stragegies could be worked out. The overall effect of the location policies adopted is shown in Table 1.12.

Both General Motors and Ford undertook early direct investment in Europe. From the 1920s, Ford was established in the United Kingdom and thereafter progressively established major manufacturing facilities in West Germany and later opened assembly plants in Belgium and the Netherlands. Ford is unique among the Big Three in having opened a plant (in France) and then closed it in the 1950s. Ford's strategy was based on the establishment of new plants from the beginning, and this has developed in recent years to a policy designed to take advantage of an emerging single European domestic market, while, at the same time, searching for new production locations. The latter was expressed in the decision in 1973 to invest in a new plant in Valencia, Spain, to commence production of a front wheel drive mini in 1976.

General Motors adopted an equally early strategy toward Europe but by a different entry route. By acquiring Vauxhall Motors in the United Kingdom in the early 1930s, GM took over an established producer in the largest single European market at that time and developed its activities from that base. At a later date, GM extended the application of the entry model by acquiring Adam Opel AG in West Germany, the company's largest manufacturing unit outside the United States, thereafter generally expanding by opening assembly units, initially in Belgium and Denmark. Like Ford, General Motors has continued to look for expansion in southern Europe, and took over the British Leyland Authi plant in Pamplona in 1974.

Chrysler's timing and method of entry contrast with those of the other two major producers. Entering in the 1960s, Chrysler came much later into Europe, but the rate of expansion of its international

operations as a whole since that period has resulted in a growth rate
outside the United States far exceeding that of GM and Ford. Chrysler's
method of approach was, in effect, a variation on the GM model and
involved the acquisition of a substantial interest in first a French
(Simca in 1963) and then a U.K. producer. Specific policies, designed
toward eventual control, were pursued in both cases, although complete ownership did not follow until the early 1970s. Again, looking
for an extension into underdeveloped European markets, Chrysler
enlarged Simca's Spanish production facilities and complemented that
business by the acquisition of the Barrieros commercial vehicle manufacturing operation.

Production and Market Shares

The relative effect of these strategies on production in the major
European nations is shown in Table 1.13 over an extended period of
years. By far the largest individual share of production is Ford's in
the United Kingdom with around 28 percent, GM in West Germany being
the only other member of the Big Three to have one-fifth of a domestic
market. The relative shares of the Big Three in aggregate again points
to the special case of the United Kingdom where, unique among the
major European countries, all are represented in manufacturing (although all three are now manufacturing in Spain). Additionally, pro-

TABLE 1.12

Principal European Manufacturing and Assembly Operations of the
Big Three

	Production	Assembly
Chrysler	Chrysler U.K.	Eire, Malta, Portugal
	Chrysler France	
	Chrysler Espana	
Ford	Ford U.K.	Belgium, Eire, Netherlands
	Ford West Germany	
	Ford Spain	
General Motors	Vauxhall U.K.	Belgium, Denmark, Eire
	Opel West Germany	
	Spain	

Source: Economist Intelligence Unit, Motor Business, no. 83,
1975.

TABLE 1.13

U.S. Subsidiaries: Share of Production of Cars and Commercial Vehicles in Major European Countries
(percent)

U.S. Share of	1950	1960	1967	1970	1975
U.K. production					
Ford	18.2	27.9	27.6	28.1	27.8
MG (Vauxhall)	11.1	13.5	14.4	13.3	11.5
Chrysler	—	—	10.9	11.9	14.9
Total United States	29.3	41.4	52.9	53.3	54.2
West German production					
Ford[a]	9.7	10.4	7.8	10.7	13.0
GM (Opel)	23.7	18.0	21.8	21.4	20.6
Total United States	33.4	28.4	29.6	32.1	33.6
French production					
Ford	5.6	—	—	—	—
Chrysler	—	—	13.8	14.6	14.3
Total United States	5.6	—	13.8	14.6	14.3
EEC[b] and U.K. production					
Ford	12.2	12.2	10.9	9.7	9.5
GM	10.1	10.5	10.0	10.4	9.3
Chrysler	—	—	5.9	6.2	7.1
Total United States	22.3	22.7	26.8	26.3	25.9

[a]Ford Werke only.
[b]West Germany, France, and Italy only.

Source: Society of Motor Manufacturers and Traders, The Motor Industry of Great Britain, various issues.

duction shares of the Big Three in the United Kingdom consistently
have exceeded 50 percent in recent years. The growth of the U.S.
share in the United Kingdom is also exceptional and reflects both the
degree of penetration of the U.S. manufacturers and the use of the
United Kingdom as a supply point for an emerging EEC market. Elsewhere, with the exception of Italy with no U.S. investment, U.S.
shares have grown less dramatically, Ford and GM suffering particularly badly in the 1974 recession (see Table 1.8) compared with the
larger indigenous producers.

There are increasing signs that within the overall production
shares outlined, the Big Three are developing production programs
for Europe as a whole, in a direct attempt to consolidate their positions within the European markets. Table 1.14 summarizes their
relative shares within the EEC car markets. In examining the companies' performance, it has to be remembered that 1975 was still a
fairly exceptional year and the results should be interpreted with
caution. Nevertheless, the relative positions are clear and some important conclusions follow. Within the largest four markets, the Big
Three have been able to exceed a 30 percent share only in the United
Kingdom and West Germany, the two countries where there is extensive manufacturing capacity and where product policy is more market
centered. In contrast, U.S. producers have been least successful in
Italy, the fastest growing volume market in Europe, although Chrysler
has done marginally better than the other two. The French market
share is also low, with Chrysler's penetration, at around 19 percent,
being the only one approaching respectability. Clearly, given the
search for volume, there is considerable potential for expansion in
both France and Italy for U.S. producers, but, as has been observed
earlier, it has to be gained in the face of entrenched local producers
with implicit or explicit state funding.

Looking at the comparative performance of the components of the
Big Three, it is clear that Chrysler and GM have some hard decisions
ahead for their U.K. capacity, since the evidence would point to Simca
and Opel being better placed than Chrysler U.K. and Vauxhall for
genuinely European developments. Ford, on the other hand, has gone
farther in rationalizing its range.

Since 1967, when Ford of Europe was formed, there has been an
extensive program aimed at concentrating components production
within the group and at coordinating the design, production, and marketing of a number of related products in both U.K. and West German
plants. These policies were motivated by a desire to gain long production runs, as well as to avoid design failures such as had occurred in
the Consul Classic and Mark 4 Zephyr/Zodiac range. Starting from
the Escort, which was designed for production in both the United Kingdom and West Germany, the range has been modified to maximize

TABLE 1.14

Market Share of Ford, General Motors, and Chrysler in the Major EEC Passenger Car Markets, 1975[a]

(percent)

	West Germany	France	Italy	United Kingdom[b]	Total, Four Countries	Total EEC[c]
Ford Germany	13.5	3.3	2.4	—	6.1	6.5
Ford U.K.	—	[d]	[d]	21.6	4.4	3.9
Total Ford	13.5	3.3	2.4	21.6	10.5	10.4
Opel	18.1	1.8	2.7	0.9	7.7	7.8
Vauxhall	0.1	[d]	[d]	7.3	1.5	1.4
Total GM	18.2	1.8	2.7	8.2	9.2	9.2
Chrysler France	2.7	8.9	5.5	1.4	4.5	4.9
Chrysler U.K.	[d]	[d]	0.1	6.6	1.4	1.3
Total Chrysler	2.7	8.9	5.6	8.0	5.9	6.2
Total Big Three	34.4	14.0	10.7	37.8	25.6	25.8

[a] West Germany, France, Italy, and United Kingdom.
[b] For individual companies, registration data refer to GH/Ireland; for total market, data refer to United Kingdom.
[c] In this column each company's market share in the EEC as a whole (including Belgium/Luxembourg, Denmark, and the Netherlands) has been calculated.
[d] Less than 0.05 percent.

Source: L'Argus de L'Automobile, June 1976.

33

common elements and to preserve variety only where volume can be attained (for example, in the middle of the range where the Cortina is produced for the United Kingdom and the Taunus for West Germany). Higher up the range Ford has pushed the development of large sedans and has tended to concentrate manufacture in West Germany.

In contrast, GM not only has a wider, less coordinated range of 13 body styles, it also started late to produce cross-links in components. This operation has gathered momentum in recent years but largely involves Opel components and parts for Vauxhall cars in line with an emerging policy of concentration on Opel as the European base.[17] As to whether or not the recent introduction of the Vauxhall Cavalier, based on an Opel model, proves to be the beginnings of a policy to phase out a separate Vauxhall range is a matter that time will confirm or deny. Although with only half of the German market share held by Volkswagen, the Opel range has been of consistently high quality and the company has performed closer to GM objectives than Vauxhall. Vauxhall's U.K. position has declined steadily, having had few successful models since the early 1960s and having failed to develop a credible range for the U.K. market. Models have tended to lag behind the market on several occasions, notably when competitors began to introduce larger versions of their small and medium-sized cars in the early 1970s. In addition, the larger engined models, available since the mid-1960s, are in need of replacement. The widening of the range in 1975 by introducing the Chevette at the small end is unlikely to stop the general trend toward a redundant Vauxhall range.

While Chrysler's product strategy is dealt with in detail in Chapter 4, it is important to observe here that Chrysler, too, has had difficulties in achieving a European range in the mode of recent years. The Simca range has been revised frequently, and by gaining a reputation for quality control, the company has had good success in Europe, particularly with the 1301 and 1501 range. The first joint venture between the British and French plants was the Chrysler 180, designed in Britain and produced in France from 1970, and this was followed up with the Alpine in 1975. However the degree of integration achieved to date is very limited.

In summary, for U.S. producers there is little cause for confidence except in the case of Ford. The company has sizable market shares and thus can still achieve economies of scale by producing the same model in two manufacturing locations. Ford also has a product base sufficiently advanced to perform above the European norm. Chrysler and GM would still seem to face some basic problems of strategy on the dual problems of which brand to develop and which facility to expand, given that volume expansion is to be profitably achieved. Unlike Ford, the market shares achieved by GM and Chrysler are such that profitable production for any model will only be obtained by concentrating output at a single location.

A COMPARATIVE ASSESSMENT OF THE PERFORMANCE
OF U.S. AND INDIGENOUS FIRMS

The principal purpose of this section is to summarize some of
the comparisons of performance between European and U.S. producers.
At this stage, the main concern is to draw broad comparisons between
U.S. and European companies, many of the more detailed aspects of
performance being examined in the Chrysler context in Chapter 5.
It must be emphasized that the normal, and considerable, problems
of intercompany comparisons are compounded by the presentation of
data derived from different accounting traditions in different countries,
as well as the particular difficulties arising from performance measurement in subsidiaries of international enterprises. It is against
this background therefore that tentative conclusions are drawn from
the tabulations provided.

Table 1.15 is based on the 1970-73 period, which was reasonably normal for the car industry and without the special circumstances
of 1974 (see Table 1.8). Whether or not comparisons are made between
U.S. and European or among European companies, a varied record of
profitability is characteristic. Three different measures are used as
a guide in Table 1.15. By the criterion of return on shareholder's
funds[18] and accepting 8 to 12 percent as a minimum rate of return,
only certain of the European operations of the Big Three managed to
provide reasonable performance. Particularly sharp contrasts exist
in the rates of return for Opel versus Vauxhall and Simca versus
Chrysler, confirming the problems noted in the previous section.
On the measure of return on capital invested,[19] the best performances
were recorded by Opel and Ford of Germany and by some of the more
specialized European producers. A number of the less successful
firms are those with high or total public sector control. Finally, the
use of the measure of return on trading assets[20] is important since it
avoids some of the more obvious anomalies arising from using different accounting standards. Only six of the fourteen European producers
achieved a minimum trading return during this period, as did GM and
Ford in Germany, alone of the six U.S.-owned companies. Overall,
therefore, U.S. subsidiary performance has been very mixed. By
any criterion, Chrysler U.K. and Vauxhall lag far behind most European and Japanese producers. While, as a general principle, U.S.
companies have been able to establish themselves relatively easily in
Europe and apparently more harmoniously than in the few cross boun-
dary mergers between European companies, there is no evidence to
suggest that their technology transfer has been reflected in consistently
better performance than in indigenous firms.

Much of the debate on comparative performance within the industry has centered around differential rates of investment in recent

TABLE 1.15

Comparison of Car Manufacturers' Profitability
(average: 1970-73)

Return on Shareholders' Funds (percent)		Return on Capital Invested (percent)		Return on Trading Assets (percent)	
Opel	19.1	Opel	28.1	Toyota	39.3
Peugeot	18.4	Daimler-Benz	26.2	Opel	37.4
Ford-Werke	17.9	Ford-Werke	22.3	Ford-Werke	37.4
Nissan-Datsun	15.5	Toyota	21.6	Daimler-Benz	35.3
Toyota	15.4	BMW	21.3	Peugeot	30.7
Volvo	15.0	Peugeot	20.7	Fiat	30.5
Daimler-Benz	11.6	Volvo	17.6	BMW	30.4
Minimum required	8-12		8-12		25-30
Simca	7.2	Volkswagen	11.2	Volkswagen	23.1
Ford U.K.	5.9	Simca	11.0	Ford U.K.	21.6
British Leyland	5.6	British Leyland	10.6	Nissan-Datsun	21.2
Volkswagen	4.2	Ford U.K.	10.2	British Leyland	19.6
Fiat	(-1.5)	Renault	6.1	Volvo	19.1
Renault	(-3.6)	Fiat	2.6	Simca	18.6
Citroen	(-5.5)	Citroen	2.4	Vauxhall	13.7
Vauxhall	(-8.4)	Vauxhall	0.6	Renault	12.9
Chrysler U.K.	(-9.6)	Chrysler U.K.	0.5	Citroen	12.1*
				Chrysler U.K.	8.1

[a]Estimated.

Source: Central Policy Review Staff, The Future of the British Car Industry (London: HMSO, 1975).

years. This has been particularly topical in the United Kingdom where explanations for low productivity have been constantly sought. Figure 1.3 presents some of this information and permits some general comparisons to be drawn. There is an obvious asset gap between U.K. and European manufacturing in the figures given, but a four-year period is a limited time over which to make such a measurement. The position of the U.S. companies is particularly important. In terms of gross fixed assets relative to sales and value added, the Big Three's capital intensity and inherent need for volume production are obvious.

FIGURE 1.3

Comparison of Asset Base and Capital Expenditures of U.K. and
Continental Car Manufacturers

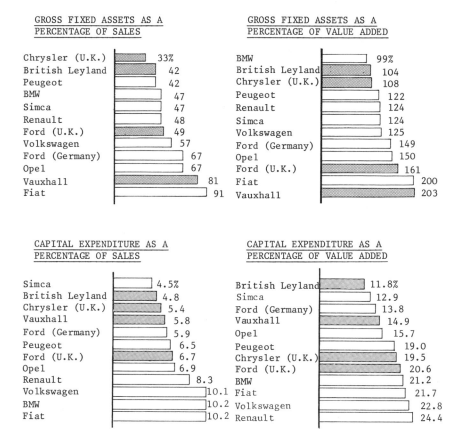

GROSS FIXED ASSETS AS A
PERCENTAGE OF SALES

Chrysler (U.K.)	33%
British Leyland	42
Peugeot	42
BMW	47
Simca	47
Renault	48
Ford (U.K.)	49
Volkswagen	57
Ford (Germany)	67
Opel	67
Vauxhall	81
Fiat	91

GROSS FIXED ASSETS AS A
PERCENTAGE OF VALUE ADDED

BMW	99%
British Leyland	104
Chrysler (U.K.)	108
Peugeot	122
Renault	124
Simca	124
Volkswagen	125
Ford (Germany)	149
Opel	150
Ford (U.K.)	161
Fiat	200
Vauxhall	203

CAPITAL EXPENDITURE AS A
PERCENTAGE OF SALES

Simca	4.5%
British Leyland	4.8
Chrysler (U.K.)	5.4
Vauxhall	5.8
Ford (Germany)	5.9
Peugeot	6.5
Ford (U.K.)	6.7
Opel	6.9
Renault	8.3
Volkswagen	10.1
BMW	10.2
Fiat	10.2

CAPITAL EXPENDITURE AS A
PERCENTAGE OF VALUE ADDED

British Leyland	11.8%
Simca	12.9
Ford (Germany)	13.8
Vauxhall	14.9
Opel	15.7
Peugeot	19.0
Chrysler (U.K.)	19.5
Ford (U.K.)	20.6
BMW	21.2
Fiat	21.7
Volkswagen	22.8
Renault	24.4

Note: Average for four years 1970-73.

Source: Central Policy Review Staff, The Future of the British
Car Industry (London: HMSO, 1975).

In terms of the other measures of capital expenditure on sales
and value added, their lower rates are equally clear. In some ways,
Figure 1.3 presents a summary of the U.S. companies' strategic
dilemma in attempting to recoup meaningful profits from heavy long-
term investment within a highly competitive European market. Para-

doxically, within their overall performance, some of the most modern plants are giving poorer returns. This is certainly the case when the record at the modern Vauxhall plant at Ellesmere Port is compared with the comparable Opel plant at Bochum. It is equally true of Chrysler at Linwood versus Simca. Overall, it is not possible to make direct comparisons between low productivity and capital investment in the industry in Europe or to conclude that profits performance can be explained by this one variable. It is sufficient to indicate at this point that U.S. producers generally have invested above European norms for the industry but have not been able to achieve results to match the investment.

During the years in question, many of the European companies, while not producing returns to satisfy longer term criteria, were viable in that they were able to provide enough funds from current operations (via retained profits, depreciation, and other reserves) to finance their capital expenditures. The imponderable aspect of this, however, is whether or not the continued decline in profitability reduces capital expenditure programs to such an extent that the funds allocated will do no more than keep business moving. As far as is possible to detect anything in the four years to 1973,[21] U.S. producers were among the lowest spenders of capital, Vauxhall and Chrysler U.K. being the only two operations requiring external investment funds.

Comparative performance, however, has not been only a matter of investment activity. Indeed, some of the most apparent influences within the European market can be attributed to the complex adjustments in trading relationships that have stemmed from currency parity changes. There are two distinct parts to this problem, both of which influence the U.S. subsidiaries directly. The first is the intra-European parity changes, which can lead to important departures from planned pricing policies and are particularly important when all European car companies are under pressure to improve their basic cost structures. This effect can be even more serious for the U.S. producers, which, as observed earlier, often have to rely on a European market since they have a small part of the domestic base market in Europe. It also leads to specific locational costs unforeseen at time of entry. One illustration of the extent of this effect between France and West Germany since 1968 is shown in Figure 1.4. Some manufacturers, such as British Leyland, started with a stated policy of not adjusting prices because of currency changes, on the basis that parity adjustments merely compensate for differential rates of inflation. On the other hand, Renault in 1973, for example, increased its British prices because price controls had prevented the company from recouping cost increases in the domestic market.

The second, and in this case potential, effect is the possibility that U.S. manufacturers may progressively face so severe problems

FIGURE 1.4

Effects of Parity Changes on the Import Price of a Passenger Car[a]

Unfavorable effect on the import of a German passenger car entering France

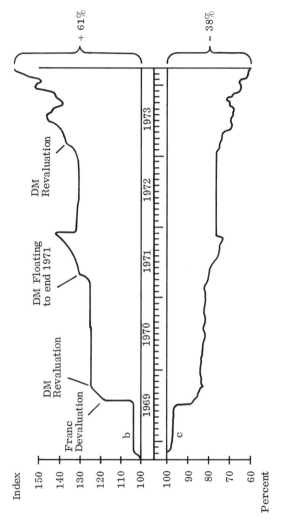

Favorable effect on the import of a French passenger car entering West Germany

[a] Assuming an unchanged manufacturer's price in terms of domestic currency.

[b] Export tax of 4 percent applying December 1968–November 1969.

[c] Import relief applying December 1968–November 1969.

Source: Daimler–Benz Aktiengesellschaft accounts, 1973.

with direct manufacture in Europe that direct exporting to exploit dollar devaluation may become an increasingly attractive strategy. Various estimates[22] would suggest that such policies applied at selective sectors of the market in Europe could have significant results. This could be done, for example, by selling subcompacts (for example, Ford Pinto) to attack the Renault 5/Opel Kadett sector of the market in Europe; alternatively, the Chevrolet Camaro could be marketed competitively as a quality substitute for the bottom of the BMW range. Such a policy would require a growing detachment to developing European capacity but may yet prove to be a way of recouping partially the decline in returns from Europe.

In the longer term, one important aspect of the performance of U.S. producers in Europe is to be found in both the structure and ownership of their main European competitors. For a considerable period of time, some of the major manufacturers in Europe have accepted the logic of the performance situation and have initiated programs to diversify into other activities. Two particular examples, Renault and Fiat, are indicated in Table 1.16. Renault, in the public sector, and Fiat, as a private company, have both made some progress toward their respective targets of only 50 percent turnover in cars by 1985 and 1980, respectively. Volvo provides another example, where, in addition to

TABLE 1.16

Renault and Fiat Diversification, 1974
(percent turnover)

Renault		Fiat	
Engineering	0.4	Steelmaking	4.52
Machine tools	0.5	Machine tools	0.37
Rubber, plastics	0.6	Engines	1.4
Steelmaking	3.2	Aeronautics	1.94
Parts and bearings	3.9	Tractors	6.8
Engines (marine and		Industrial vehicles	18.84
industrial)	1.3	Other products	1.9
Agricultural equip-		Motor cars	64.23
ment	2.3		
Industrial vehicles	10.4		
Motor cars	77.5		
Declared targets			
Motor cars	50.00 (1985)	Motor cars	50.00 (1980)

Source: Company accounts.

buying a majority holding in DAF cars (a Dutch producer whose range complemented its own), the company has invested in nonautomotive products, such as boats, sporting goods, and industrial and forestry machinery. Clearly, the relative importance of these moves for the Big Three in Europe depends on the degree to which diversification brings profitability and on the role that car margins will be expected to play in funding growth elsewhere. In either event, competition from efficient European producers will increase. There is nothing within this trend to suggest long-term problems for Ford or GM, given a desire to rationalize where required; for a weakened Chrysler, however, the potential threat is more serious.

One of the most uncertain effects is not structure but ownership, since it is too early to predict how the Big Three performance will be affected by the growth in numbers of major producers coming under public ownership or strong public control. European governments always have been able to exert considerable indirect influence on motor manufacturers. The advent of more direct involvement has come by various routes, including poor profits performance, the need to stabilize employment, the desire to sustain exports, or an obligation to give financial guarantees. Thus, while Renault and Alfa Romeo have been state owned for a long period of time, British Leyland has been added since 1974; Volkswagen is 40 percent owned by the regional government and there are increasing signs that Fiat will come under such pressure in Italy to move into the public sector. In addition, government investment interest has grown considerably, for example, in France through loans to Peugeot to rescue Citroen and in the United Kingdom through the Chrysler support plan. Already disquiet is being expressed over the prospect of break-even strategies in the growing public sector in Europe.[23] The overall ownership position is shown in Figure 1.5, which readily shows the relative size of public sector operations in France and the United Kingdom. A wholly owned Volkswagen and a government-sponsored Fiat would further change the environment for the Big Three in Europe.

In conclusion, the factors discussed in this chapter point to an industry seeking a long-term solution. Given the present or predicted state of the world car markets and current technology, the capacity, structure, and number of companies in Europe are far from optimum. That the car industry plays a major role in the Western European economy makes the situation more complex. It has drawn governments into a position of partial or total commitment to an overcapacity industry whose shape by 1985 is likely to be dramatically different from that of today and whose members are unlikely to exceed five or six indigenous producers.

FIGURE 1.5

Principal Motor Manufacturers of Western Europe: Ownership and Production Volumes, 1975

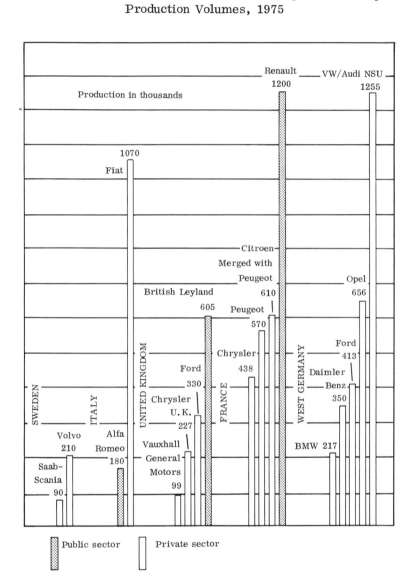

Note: The majority ownership only is shown. Peugeot took control of Citroen in April 1976. Black stars indicate estimates of 1975 production. Gray bar : public sector; white bar: private sector.

Source: Economist Intelligence Unit, European Trends, February 1976.

NOTES

1. National Economic Development Office, The Effects of Government Economic Policy on the Motor Industry (London, 1968), pp. 6-7.

2. Ibid., p. 6.

3. A. G. Armstrong, "The Motor Industry and the British Economy," District Bank Review, no. 163 (September 1967).

4. Manpower and Labour Relations in the Car Industry 1970-85 (Paris: Eurofinance), as quoted in Daily Telegraph, December 31, 1974.

5. See, for example, European Economic Community, Third Report on Competition Policy (Brussels, May 1974).

6. D. G. Rhys, The Motor Industry: An Economic Survey (London: Butterworth, 1972), p. 138.

7. For a detailed discussion of the circumstances, see G. Turner, The Leyland Papers (London: Eyre and Spottswoode, 1971).

8. British Leyland: The Next Decade, HC 342 (London: HMSO, April 1975).

9. Fourteenth Report from the Expenditure Committee, Session 1974-75, The Motor Vehicle Industry, HC 617 (London: HMSO, August 1975), p. 19.

10. Illustrated in The Supply of Electrical Equipment for Mechanically Propelled Land Vehicles, Monopolies Commission (London: HMSO 1963); Electrical Wiring Harnesses for Motor Vehicles: A Report on Whether Uneconomic Prices are Quoted, Monopolies Commission (London: HMSO 1966).

11. This had already gathered momentum from the late 1950s. See, for example, "Changes in the Ownership of the European Motor Industry," Economist Intelligence Unit, Motor Business, no. 36 (October 1963), which summarizes some of the changes in investment portfolios of European producers between 1953 and 1963.

12. See, for example, The Economist, March 23, 1974, for a discussion of this problem.

13. Central Policy Review Staff (CPRS), The Future of the British Car Industry (London: HMSO, 1975), p. 42.

14. Ibid., p. 52. See also World Vehicle Production and Sales Forecasts to 1985 (Paris: Eurofinance, 1975).

15. As, for example, in some of the reported comments of the president of the U.K. car manufacturers association (Society of Motor Manufacturers and Traders) in Financial Times, October 29, 1974.

16. "Lessons to Learn," The Economist, July 5, 1975, pp. 81-82.

17. For a more detailed discussion of GM strategy in Europe, see "The Big Three Vehicle Manufacturers of the U.S. in the EEC,"

Economist Intelligence Unit, Motor Business, no. 83, 1975, pp. 23, 24.

18. As used in the CPRS report, op. cit., p. 53. This is defined as profits after interest and tax dividend by shareholders' investment in the company.

19. Ibid., defined as profits before interest and tax on the total capital employed in the business.

20. Ibid., defined as trading profit before interest and tax plus depreciation divided by net assets less cash, bank deposits, and trade investments.

21. Ibid., Chart 16, p. 54.

22. "Threats to Europe," The Economist, October 13, 1973.

23. See, for example, "The European Motor Industry: Integration or Disintegration," Economist Intelligence Unit, European Trends, February 1976, p. 24.

2

THE CHRYSLER
CORPORATION
IN EUROPE

The decision to expand the Chrysler Corporation into Europe was always an important one. From the corporation's viewpoint, it involved major financial commitments; from the host's viewpoint, it represented capital injection, possibly some transfer of technology, and certainly a diminution of national control in the motor industry. Few, however, could have foreseen that some of the problems of the company in the United States were also being exported to Europe and that the cumulative impact of these, and subsequent distinctly European difficulties, would be such as to raise many basic economic, management, and political issues regarding the effectiveness of multinational companies in Europe. As part of the framework for the more detailed analysis of Chrysler U.K., it is therefore necessary to examine the origins of the decision to expand in Europe, as well as the background of U.S. performance of the corporation while the European policy was being implemented. In addition, some of the strategic alternatives open to Chrysler are considered as part of the analysis of the expansion route chosen by the corporation.

PERFORMANCE OF THE CHRYSLER CORPORATION
IN THE UNITED STATES

There is little doubt that the European operations of Chrysler have been at least influenced, and at most dictated, by developments in the U.S. market. The exact pattern of cause and effect between the United States and Europe is not easy to determine at any one time. However, it is reasonable to assume that corporate performance in the United States was of particular importance at the point of entry and expansion in Europe and at major breakpoints in the clarification of

European strategy, involving extension of equity participation, changes in model programs, large-scale capital investment, and so on.

By 1958, when Chrysler took its first tentative but direct step toward becoming fully involved in Europe by purchasing a 15 percent interest in Simca, the corporation was in a period of serious decline. In terms of shares of U.S. production, Chrysler declined from its 1957 peak of 20 percent to a 1962 low of just over 10 percent (see Table 2.1). Consequently the corporation's returns on its U.S. activity were far below the norms for the industry (Table 2.2)—a reflection of cumulative problems in the design, production, and marketing of a model range that was not always in line with the rapid changes in the U.S. market.[1] As indicated in Table 2.2, the sales volume fluctuations on the domestic market were particularly damaging to a company of Chrysler's size, and the growth and volume potential of Europe began to appear attractive.

The initiative for averting a serious crisis and planning recovery came from the appointment of Lynn Townsend as chairman in 1961. His development package was sweeping and far-reaching, based on aggressive marketing in the United States and the expansion of the company into Europe. At home, the program commenced with extreme cost reduction, and 7,000 office workers were released within six weeks of his appointment. The program included an aggressive pricing policy in the volume fleet and leased car business, the expansion of warranties on new cars to five years or 50,000 miles on costly power train components (a move reluctantly followed by competitors four years later), and the rebuilding of the dealer network.

Abroad, the policy was one of finding a formula to benefit directly from European market expansion. At that time, the only Chrysler manufacturing plant in Europe was Dodge Brothers (Britain) Ltd. at Kew in the United Kingdom, a small-scale commercial vehicle operation producing an estimated 4,500 trucks in 1961,[2] with some vehicles being assembled at the Chrysler International S.A. plant at Rotterdam in Holland. The corporation, therefore, had the choice of either establishing a new plant and facilities as part of a program of designing and manufacturing vehicles for the Western European market, or, alternatively, pursuing the more immediate policy of purchasing an existing vehicle producer. The expense and delay of constructing a new manufacturing plant seemed to preclude the former alternative, and the rejection of this approach was reinforced by the competitive problems that small European vehicle manufacturing units were facing at the time. The logic of the domestic strategy demanded purchase and entry to Europe as quickly as possible, so the decision was purchase.

The period from 1963 to 1968 was one of recovery and profit improvement for Chrysler. The domestic policies were reflected in

TABLE 2.1

Big Three Shares of U.S. Production

Year	Percent Shares of Production		
	General Motors	Ford	Chrysler
1956	52.8	28.8	15.0
1957	46.1	30.9	20.0
1958	51.1	28.7	13.7
1959	45.7	31.2	13.2
1960	47.7	28.3	15.2
1961	49.4	30.6	11.8
1962	53.9	27.9	10.3
1963	53.4	25.7	13.7
1964	51.1	27.7	16.1
1965	53.0	27.5	15.7
1966	51.7	28.2	16.9
1967	55.6	22.9	18.4
1968	51.9	27.1	17.9
1969	53.8	26.3	16.9
1970	45.5	30.8	19.4
1971	56.6	25.3	15.3
1972	54.1	27.2	15.5
1973	54.3	25.8	16.1
1974	48.8	30.2	16.1
1975	54.8	26.9	13.4

Source: Ward's Automotive Yearbooks (Detroit: Wards), various issues.

an expansion of market share (Table 2.1) and by 1969 the European program had led to the ownership of at least 77 percent of Rootes in the United Kingdom, 77 percent of Simca in France, and 86 percent of Barreiros in Spain. While the corporation's profit situation (see Table 2.3) was strong until 1968, there were two trends in this period that subsequently proved to be highly significant for Chrysler. The first, in the domestic U.S. market, was the rise in import sales from a 1962 low to 10.5 percent in 1968. Chrysler was not alone among the Big Three in the almost passive reaction to this expansion of imported small car sales led by Volkswagen. The difference was that, by 1968, GM, Ford, and American Motors Corporation (AMC) had all realized that this was an important development, and in that year announced

TABLE 2.2

U.S. Car Producers: Sales, Profits, and Dividends, 1958–62

	GM	Ford	Chrysler	American Motors
Consolidated Net Sales (millions of dollars)				
1958	9,522	4,130	2,165	470
1959	11,233	5,357	2,643	870
1960	12,736	5,238	3,007	1,058
1961	11,396	6,709[a]	2,127	876
1962	14,640	8,090[a]	2,378	1,056
Operating Income as Proportion of Net Sales (percent)				
1958	10.9	3.1	-3.5	5.5
1959	14.9	14.2	-0.5	11.4
1960	15.0	12.5	2.2	9.2
1961	14.5	12.2[a]	0.9	5.1
1962	18.6	12.4[a]	5.2	6.1
Cash Dividends per Share (dollars)[b]				
1958	2.00	1.00	1.50	nil
1959	2.00	1.40	1.00	0.40
1960	2.00	1.50	1.50	1.15
1961	2.50	1.50	1.00	1.20
1962	3.00	1.80	1.00	0.80

[a]Not strictly comparable with the years 1958–60.
[b]Adjusted for bonus share issues.

Source: Economist Intelligence Unit, Motor Business, no. 34, 1963.

their respective plans for a new line of small cars costing under $2,000. Chrysler was much later in trying to cope with these market changes in U.S. manufacture, and under its agreement with Mitsubishi, planned to supply the market with Japanese small cars. A different Chrysler strategy toward small cars at that time could well have allowed the corporation to build more profitably on the solid base of 1962–68.

The second important trend was in the European market. In spite of the investment in Europe by the Big Three, the share of the

TABLE 2.3

Chrysler Corporation and Consolidated Subsidiaries: Operating Data
(millions of dollars)

	1966	1967	1968	1969	1970	1971	1972	1973	1974	1975
Net sales	5,583	6,136	7,354	6,942	6,887	7,893	9,641	11,667	10,860	11,598
Passenger cars and trucks (000 units)	2,134	2,246	2,610	2,432	2,434	2,663	3,028	3,402	2,763	2,476
Research and development	129	152	161	168	174	174	171	178	182	124
Earnings (loss) from continuing operations	199	209	310	107	—	92	226	266	(41)	(207)
Net earnings (loss)	194	203	303	99	(8)	84	220	255	(52)	(260)
Cash dividends paid per share (dollars)	2.00	2.00	2.00	2.00	0.60	0.60	0.90	1.30	1.40	—
Net earnings as percent of sales	3.5	3.3	4.1	1.4	(0.1)	1.1	2.3	2.2	(0.5)	(2.2)

Source: Chrysler Corporation, Annual Report, 1975.

total market taken by their European affiliates did not increase. Indeed, in the EEC, the share of the Big Three affiliates declined slightly
from 24.4 percent in 1963 to 23.1 percent in 1968. The facts of this
situation were clearly known by Chrysler,[3] but the implications were
not. As a latecomer, Chrysler's need for an overall European product and marketing policy was immediate, particularly when long-established competitors were finding real expansion difficult to achieve.
There were obviously some executives within Chrysler who read the
signs, appreciated the implications of transferring U.S. model policy
to Europe, and saw that the U.S. model differentiation conventions
might not produce results. As one person observed, "Such a response
to an increasingly demanding, knowledgeable and fragmented public
[in Europe] may no longer be adequate. The U.S. automobile industry may now be beginning to appreciate this fact."[4] The corporation's
particular interpretation of these two trends within this period of relative prosperity was important for corporate progress in later years.
Paradoxically, therefore, when the basis for European expansion was
being laid and corporate profit performance was good, the seeds of
future problems were being sown.

Chrysler's consolidation of the takeover strategies in Europe
coincided with a marginal fall in sales but dramatic loss of profitability
in the United States in 1969 and 1970. This occurred at a time when
the corporation as a whole was expecting a marked profit improvement
following the completion of a $1.7 billion five-year capital improve-
ment program.[5] By mid-1969, operations were being cut back severely and company stock was under serious pressure. The corporation placed much of the responsibility for its situation on the existing
economic climate in the United States. Townsend indicated that "because of uncertainty in the economy, including the high rate of interest
and anti-inflationary measures in general which seems to be holding
down expected increases in the total car market, Chrysler management has thought it prudent and move to defer some longer range expansion programs until the economy returns to a more normal growth
pattern."[6]

While Chrysler saw this crisis largely in terms of macroeco-
nomics, perhaps the underlying issue was, as it had been so often before, product policy. By 1969, the corporation had seriously drifted
away from industry product trends in the United States. Reflecting a
combination of public concern over the deterioration in the trade balance in motor vehicles and parts and of private concern over erosion
of market shares, the other manufacturers introduced a new generation of subcompacts.[7] GM, for example, announced its version, the
XP887, in 1968, an unprecedented two years before the car was introduced, and Ford launched the Maverick in the spring of 1969, following its successful entry into the subcompact market with the Mustang
five years previously.

Chrysler, however, did not develop a subcompact at this time, nor did the company try to build up imports from Rootes and Simca. The total U.S. sales of Simca early in 1968 were 42 percent below those of 1966 and those of Rootes 8 percent under 1966, although part of the reason for this derived from difficulties in meeting federal safety standards. Chrysler, in fact, seemed less than convinced that the European products had an immediate contribution to make to U.S. volume, and made minimal use of its established U.S. dealer network for Rootes and Simca vehicles.* One Chrysler executive was quoted as saying that there was "no point in changing our distribution and marketing system until we've got some hot products to sell. When the new designs from France and Britain start arriving we expect demand for the two lines to climb substantially . . . and it will be relatively easy to convince our dealers to carry the import lines."[8] In the event, the European cars were rejected in favor of sales of the Mitsubishi Colt from 1970 onward, with the knowledge that Japanese imports were making dramatic strides in the U.S. market. In 1968, for example, Toyota and Datsun accounted for 11.1 percent of import registrations in the United States (including Canadian production). While Chrysler did in fact modify this policy and introduced a subcompact in 1971, it was too late to bring immediate assistance to profits.

Some of Chrysler's problems in 1969 and 1970 stemmed more directly from difficulties with the European subsidiaries. While acknowledging the problems, Chrysler executives were viewing these almost as temporary aberrations: "We've been down and almost counted out many times in the past, but we've always managed to bounce back. I think we'll do the same with Rootes and Simca."[9] Although Erwin Graham, the vice-president for Europe, expressed concern about the Rootes situation, he stated that "it is virtually inconceivable that we would decide to pull out of Rootes."[10]

For a variety of reasons, the financial position of the corporation was weakened in this period. This weakness was expressed in a deterioration into a loss situation and in an increase in borrowing requirements that, even in good years such as 1968, had proportionately far exceeded those of Ford and GM. Subsequent attention directed to this debt burden led to the chairman being forced to deny in mid-1970 that the corporation was going bankrupt and to confirm that short-term obligations were well covered by unused bank lines and cash in hand.[11] Other symptoms of the financial market's view of Chrysler at this time

---

*In early 1968, Chrysler had 6,500 dealers in the United States. Of these, only 389 were handling Simca and 98 handling Rootes cars. In contrast, of the 7,400 Ford dealers, 802 sold Cortinas; while of 14,500 GM dealers, 1,500 sold Opels.

were the stock price fall and removal of prime credit rating in the spring of 1971, owing to the value of outstanding commercial paper.[12] It is difficult to conceive of a less opportune background against which to develop and implement the necessary rational, long-term plans for Europe than that that existed in Chrysler between 1968 and 1971.

By 1971, Chrysler's investment in Europe had almost reached $300 million (Table 2.4) and had produced a situation where the production contribution from Europe was, as the bottom half of Table 2.4 shows, comparable to that achieved by Ford and GM. Allowing for the fact that this was based on recent acquisition and control, Chrysler was already overdependent on Europe and in a position where success or failure in Europe would materially affect corporate performance. This overdependence was further evidenced in the fact that Chrysler had committed proportionately more of its overseas net investment to Europe than Ford and GM, and that some of the companies involved were of questionable financial stability.

As Table 2.3 indicates, 1971 marked for Chrysler the beginnings of a profit improvement that was to last until the severe recession dramatically affected the figures in 1974 and 1975. By the end of 1972, the company was reporting the elimination of its short-term domestic debt and the existence of substantial cash reserves. Nevertheless, overseas borrowing was still relatively high and the company remained very vulnerable to any turndown in the economy as profit margins were still low. Chrysler benefited from the Nixon administration's Phases One and Two anti-inflation controls, which helped to hold down the domestic costs that had been cited by all of the Big Three as having a crucial effect on sales pre-1972.[13] However, much of the corporation's improvement came from internal policy changes, including a 30 percent reduction in the number of models offered in the United States compared with two years previously, the dropping of its mini car for the U.S. market, and the holding back in rotary engine development. Some of these measures were proven later to be short-sighted, particularly in the light of Detroit's switch to smaller cars during the fuel crisis of 1973-74. The overseas operations were beginning to produce marginal profits at $5 million in 1971 compared with a loss of $7.6 million in 1970. These represented totally unacceptable returns on capital employed, but added to the general feeling of recovery until 1974.

Chrysler's accelerating losses in 1974 and 1975 were, in common with the industry as a whole, sudden and swift since it was a fall from the 1973 peak year for car sales. While it is true that Chrysler was less capable of withstanding such losses, its relative decline was no more dramatic than that of the other major producers. Between the end of 1973 and October 1975, the corporation's worldwide sales fell by 27.2 percent (Table 2.3). Although it could in no way offset the effect of the general turndown, Chrysler's market share in the United

TABLE 2.4

Net Investment and Total Production of the Big Three U.S. Producers and Their Consolidated Subsidiaries Outside the United States and Canada, 1971

Net Investment as of December 31, 1971 (millions of dollars)

Net investment (before reserve for foreign operations) in

General Motors		Ford		Chrysler	
Western Europe	355	United Kingdom and other sterling area countries	685	Europe	298
United Kingdom, Australia, New Zealand, and South Africa	498	Continental Europe	440	Far East and Africa	178
Other (largely Mexico and Latin America)	244	All other (largely Latin America)	179	Latin America	150
Total net investment (before reserve for foreign operations)	1,097		1,556*		626

Production of European Subsidiaries, 1971

	General Motors	Ford	Chrysler
Total production (million units)	7.8	4.9	2.7
Of which percent produced outside United States and Canada	19.3	32.1	34.0
Percent of production in			
West Germany	54.8	48.5	—
United Kingdom	22.0	32.0	33.0
France	—	—	48.1
Europe as percent of total production outside North America	76.8	80.5	81.1

*Total includes $252 million representing excess of cost of investments over equities in net assets.

Source: Economist Intelligence Unit, Motor Business, no. 72 (1972).

States held well and, early in the recession, shared in the benefits arising from the problems of GM. This happened in spite of a minimal contribution from European imports in 1973 and no contribution in 1974, when the corporation depended solely on Mitsubishi for a captive import source.

It was in this atmosphere that Chrysler had to evaluate its European strategy and the future of its U.K. operation in particular. By mid-1975, the corporation had been activating policies of severe retrenchment for well over 18 months. These policies included major cost and project pruning and finally the closing of five of the six U.S. car assembly plants for a period of six weeks from November 1974. Institutional and stockholder criticism was continuous. The short-term prospects offered no improvement in the United States in that factory sales of passenger cars in the first five months of 1975 were 21.7 percent below the 1974 figure, with the commercial vehicle situation even worse at 30.6 percent down. Some major new initiative was required to begin to offer a way ahead. The U.K. operation was a source of continuous financial drain and was an obvious area in which to attempt to cut losses.

CHRYSLER EXPANSION IN EUROPE

The International Context

As a background against which to examine in detail the Chrysler European entry strategy, the wider global development of the corporation is summarized briefly in this section. The information presented in Table 2.5 highlights the expansion that took place, from the limited base in the early 1960s toward the 1971 position where over 80 percent of the corporation production outside the United States and Canada took place in Europe. Consistent with the development of international policy and the growth of the individual markets concerned, the period was also one of transition from substantial dependence on assembly abroad to the establishment of manufacturing units that dominated overseas production figures. Assembly plants remained in some of the developing South American markets, South Africa, and the Philippines, many of which were inherited from Rootes' and Simca's overseas operations (see Table 2.6). By 1971 the ownership transition also had largely been completed except in a few cases, and the corporation had moved from a position of having a portfolio of interests in car manufacturing and assembly in Europe to one of substantial ownership, with consequent control and responsibility for initiating strategy.

Table 2.7 demonstrates the result of Chrysler's international expansion program over the last ten years. As such, it provides a glo-

TABLE 2.5

Chrysler Corporation: International Operations (Manufacturing and Assembly), 1962, 1965, 1971

	1962	1965	1971
Europe			
	United Kingdom (Dodge)	United Kingdom[a] France Greece	United Kingdom France
	Netherlands	Netherlands Spain[b]	Spain[b]
Americas (except United States)			
	Canada	Canada	Canada
	Mexico	Mexico	Mexico
	Argentina	Argentina	Brazil
	Venezuela	Venezuela	Argentina
			Colombia
			Peru[c]
Africa			
	South Africa	South Africa	South Africa
			Morocco[d]
Australasia and Far East			
	Australia	Australia	Australia
		Philippines	Japan[e]
			Philippines
Other			
	Turkey	Turkey	Turkey

[a]Dodge plus Rootes, as an associated company in which Chrysler had a 30 percent interest.

[b]Production in Barreiros in which Chrysler had a 40 percent interest.

[c]Chrysler Peru S.A. was 51 percent controlled by the government.

[d]Through a 15 percent interest in Mitsubishi Motor Corporation.

[e]Through its associated company Somaca.

Source: Economist Intelligence Unit, Motor Business, various issues.

TABLE 2.6

Models Produced by the Chrysler Corporation, 1964

	United States	Argentina	Australia	Brazil	Canada	France	Greece	Mexico	Morocco	Netherlands	Philippines	Rhodesia	South Africa	Spain	Turkey	United Kingdom	Venezuela
PASSENGER CARS																	
Imperial	●																
Chrysler	●		◐		●												●
Plymouth	●				●					●	●						●
Valiant	●	●	●		●		○			●	●		●				●
Barracuda	●				●		○						●				●
Dodge	●	●			●		○			●	●		●				●
Dart	●						○			●	●						●
Simca 1000						●			○		●		●				
Simca 1300						●			○								
Simca 1500						●											
Simca Verdett			○														
Hillman		○										○	○			○	○
Sunbeam																○	○
Singer		○														○	
Humber		○											○			○	○
TRUCKS																	
Dodge	●	●	●		●			○		●	●		●		●		●
Fargo		●			●					●					●		
De Soto		●													●		
Kew		●								●	●		●		●	○	
Farmobil							●										
Commer		○										○	○		○	○	○
Karrier		○											○			○	
Barreiros														○			
Unic						○											

●   Chrysler consolidated companies
○   Chrysler associated companies

Source: Economist Intelligence Unit, *Motor Business*, no. 45, 1965.

bal view of many of the issues that will be studied in this and later chapters. In focusing attention upon the movements of sales from France and the United Kingdom, it reflects the importance of the prosperity of these two operations for the whole overseas policy. In the only remaining overseas production unit of size, namely, Japan, the corporation is dependent on gaining some of the benefits of Japanese penetration into the U.S. market. After Japan, the best long-term

TABLE 2.7

Chrysler Corporation and Consolidated Subsidiaries: Unit Sales of Cars, Trucks, and Trailers

Area of Manufacture	1967	1968	1969	1970	1971	1972	1973	1974	1975
United States									
Passenger cars	1,376,594	1,570,675	1,384,411	1,287,352	1,320,535	1,394,319	1,571,743	1,187,646	980,127
Trucks	142,172	172,741	165,049	177,295	207,025	326,660	315,293	346,152	327,681
Canada									
Passenger cars	188,198	212,286	206,370	237,752	232,099	264,950	258,823	219,174	257,802
Trucks	16,147	17,169	15,650	11,273	18,652	27,541	24,155	29,313	30,340
Total United States and Canada	1,723,111	1,972,871	1,771,480	1,713,672	1,778,311	2,013,470	2,230,014	1,782,285	1,585,950
France	256,340	315,177	354,211	368,457	439,543	494,019	546,779	412,137	424,601
Britain	197,092	204,858	180,504	217,527	269,776	264,693	289,087	201,049	135,010*
Japan	—	—	—	4,347	51,323	59,003	58,171	105,881	100,318
Spain	2,512	43,237	44,039	46,954	39,095	54,820	80,135	73,979	78,286
Mexico	—	—	—	—	—	44,594	48,548	61,555	63,273
Australia	47,818	50,972	56,018	52,054	49,731	46,830	69,863	55,322	33,748
All other	18,710	22,901	25,229	31,387	34,738	50,783	79,816	70,634	54,411
Total outside United States and Canada	522,472	637,145	660,071	720,726	884,206	1,014,742	1,172,399	980,557	889,647

*Prior years restated to exclude unassembled vehicle component parts (comprising approximately 60 percent of a vehicle) sold by Chrysler U.K. to Iran.

Source: Chrysler Corporation, Annual Report, 1975.

57

prospect would appear to be in Spain, although increased investment in car production in that country may diminish the potential domestic market share available to Chrysler, leaving it as a base for Middle East and African exports. In short, finding a correct solution within the European market has been, and remains, vitally important for Chrysler if it is not to face many of the old competitive pressures and problems of scale in the United States without the flexibility that could come from foreign sources of revenue and captive imports.

TOWARD A EUROPEAN EXPANSION BASE:
THE CHRYSLER EXPERIENCE

Prior to 1958, when Chrysler first invested in Simca, the corporation's ownership of a small truck producer in the United Kingdom and an assembly plant in Rotterdam hardly constituted any serious recognition of Europe as a major growth market. Chrysler's presence was token, vulnerable to the process of European integration through the EEC and scarcely credible to U.S. stockholders. This section assesses the method of expansion chosen, the nature of the European partners themselves, and the national response to Chrysler participation, ownership, and, ultimately, control. Since the purchase of Rootes and its sequel are the principal concerns of this study, it is examined in its own right in Chapter 3. Simca and Barreiros are thus the main topics at this stage.

While Chrysler undoubtedly was both looking for, and making preliminary offers to, other manufacturers in Europe before 1963, the company's first success in establishing a car manufacturing interest came with the purchase of 15.2 percent of the Simca shares from Ford in 1958. Ford, as will be discussed later, was more anxious to sell (because of its French experience) than Simca was to have Chrysler as owners of an important block of shares. In spite of its shareholding subsequently rising to 25 percent, Chrysler did not find it easy to exert strong influence over Simca partly because of the fact that Fiat reportedly still owned 30 percent of the equity of the company and was actively involved in joint ventures with Simca.[14] As indicated in Chapter 1, Simca had been under Fiat influence since its founding by Pigozzi in 1934. After 1958, Simca was caught between Chrysler and Fiat in what at times took the shape of a power struggle for control. Chrysler undertook to assemble partly completed Simca cars in its U.K. plant at Kew and took over the sales and distribution of Simca as of June 1958. A few months later Simca and Fiat concluded a sales arrangement whereby Simca was to sell Fiat cars in France and vice versa in Italy. This deal, the common aim of which was "to meet British and German competition in our countries" was

TABLE 2.8

French Car Industry Performance, 1957-61

	Simca[a]	Citroen	Panhard	Peugeot	Renault
1957					
Output (units)	151,405	139,706	37,991	126,902	265,522
Export ratio (percent)	34.5	18.1	10.3	28.0	40.3
Profit margins (percent)[b]	1.0	n.a.	0.34	2.9	1.9
1958					
Output (units)	189,010	178,879	34,784	145,346	363,924
Export ratio (percent)	40.1	18.3	15.8	36.4	43.5
Profit margins (percent)	1.1	n.a.	0.24	2.4	1.5
1959					
Output (units)	225,897	213,162	24,427	154,729	457,944
Export ratio (percent)	52.7	25.0	27.4	44.9	63.6
Profit margins (percent)	0.16	0.87	nil	2.2	1.1
1960					
Output (units)	204,213	231,736	34,050	173,571	464,122
Export ratio (percent)	38.2	26.0	28.8	45.2	56.0
Profit margins (percent)	0.13	0.78	loss	2.1	0.01
1961					
Output (units)	201,621	250,662	29,746	193,338	309,744
Export ratio (percent)	28.4	27.0	23.1	40.3	55.4
Profit margins (percent)	0.13	0.73	nil	2.1	loss

[a]The division of the company into Simca Automobiles and Simca Industries took place in 1960. Figures are for cars only in 1960 and 1961.

[b]Profit margins shown as a percentage of turnover.

Note: n.a. = data not available.

Source: Economist Intelligence Unit, Motor Business, no. 35 (1963).

ironic and scarcely a policy that could readily be subscribed to by
their multinational shareholder. The sales arrangement between
Chrysler and Simca was subsequently abandoned when it was announced
in January 1962 that Simca would be taking over its own sales distribution in the United Kingdom. Chrysler's justification at the time
was that it "must concentrate on those commercial vehicle products
for which we are primarily organized to produce and market."[15]
For whatever reason, therefore, some of these initial links proved
problematic.

Table 2.8 gives some indication of the financial background of
Simca before the advent of Chrysler majority early in 1963. Although
in profit until 1963, profit margins on Simca's car operations were low
compared with the other major French producers. The company went
into a loss position in 1963 largely owing to a change in depreciation
practices and the costs involved in launching the new 1300 and 1500
models. In spite of the two new models, Chrysler did not take over
many product advantages, for, by 1963, over 60 percent of Simca production was of the 1000 model and sales of a number of the remaining
cars in the range were showing distinct signs of decline. The lack of
investment funds for product development was expressed in the fact
that the company had introduced only four basically new models in the
previous 12 years, and the company was operating well under capacity,
which was estimated at 330,000 vehicles in 1962.[16] Export performance
had fluctuated considerably—over 40 percent of output was exported in
the best year compared with 23 percent in 1961. Chrysler was later
to develop the company's exports considerably from this position, but
it did not start with a particularly favorable base as compared to
Renault and Peugeot at that time.

Another significant feature of Simca was that it was managed in
a particularly autocratic style by its founder, Pigozzi, who was, for
example, strongly resistant to national unions in his plants. Pigozzi
resigned from the management of car production five months after
Chrysler took over. In summary, Simca, at the time of takeover,
displayed many of the characteristics of a company open to acquisition
and required several basic investment decisions on both models and
markets.

Between Chrysler's initial investment and its takeover of Simca,
the French attitude toward U.S. investment changed considerably.
For example, in July 1959, Prime Minister Michel Debré declared
that it was desirable that U.S. companies establishing themselves in
the EEC should do so in France rather than in the other member countries.[17] In general, during the first four years of Charles de Gaulle's
presidency (mid-1958 to the end of 1962), the French government judged
U.S. investments on the basis of their economic contribution to French
stabilization policy, with reliance being placed, where necessary, on

the use of exchange controls to limit foreign investment. The short-comings of this regulation were shown by Chrysler's acquisition of control of Simca through the purchase of dispersed shareholdings held in Switzerland and beyond the reach of French exchange controls. Chrysler thus announced in January 1963 that it had gained majority control with 63.8 percent of the equity and that Fiat was to retain 20 percent of the equity. While this heralded the end of the sales agreement with Fiat, liaison was to continue through agreement between Fiat and Someca (Simca's tractor division) to establish a plant in Algeria for tractors and agricultural equipment.

The Chrysler announcement that it had attained control aroused a storm of political protest, which is important in the context of the subsequent French attitude toward the company. The widespread chauvinism that underlay the comments made has had a continued effect on government long-term policy toward the car industry in France.* The reasons behind the French reaction were complex and varied. The size of the company—the third largest car manufacturer and, in sales terms, the fifth largest company in France—was undoubtedly important. The dependence of the French economy on the car industry and the fact that Chrysler then employed 20,000 Frenchmen were both significant. The timing, too, focused particular attention on Chrysler, which might credibly have considered that it was taking a low profile approach to acquisition by purchasing shares largely held by foreign investors outside France. The announcement was made four days after De Gaulle had vetoed Britain's entry into the EEC for reasons that included the undesirability of Anglo-American economic influence, and came at a time when both layoffs and extension plans had been announced by a number of other U.S. companies.[18] The general political background can be understood by the comments of Valéry Giscard D'Estaing (then minister of finance), who indicated "it is not desirable that important sectors of the Common Market's economy depend on outside decisions"[19] and that of Maurice Duverger, a professor at the Sorbonne, who contended "these [U.S.] investments are the true Trojan horses for Europe."[20] Chrysler might be forgiven for thinking that it was not welcome in France.

Subsequent events led to a tempering of attitudes, as the delays and rejections of applications under the 1965 selective investment policy actively discouraged some major projects. The U.S. car manu-

---

*These protests were important largely because the issue appeared to unite many disparate groups, including the conservative protectionists; the Gaullists with aspirations for economic (and military) independence; French economic planning mandarins, and the Marxists with their neocolonialist critique.

facturers featured in these developments, and the Ford decision to
establish a new factory on the German side of the border at Saarlouis
caused particular concern. By 1966, Georges Pompidou and Debré
had begun wooing Ford, and after another meeting in 1969, Ford established an automatic transmission factory in Bordeaux. Chrysler
remained the only U.S. car manufacturer in France and bought an additional 38 percent interest in Simca in 1969. While the fluctuations
in French government attitudes did not seriously affect Chrysler in the
short term, the consistent viewing of the industry as "sensitive" has
led to continued influence being exerted on the structure and investment plans of the French companies. There are grounds for arguing
that the French government's control objectives were clarified by
Chrysler's purchase of Simca. Since then, the government has pursued a well-planned policy of support for domestic manufacturers,
vetoing structural change where desired (including De Gaulle's intervention to stop Fiat from taking a blocking minority share in Citroen),
and has thereby arrived at a more rational structure for the industry
than several of the other European countries. Such restructuring, of
course, was detrimental to Chrysler's expansion in the French market,
and pointed more clearly to the need for European policies.

The immediate impact of Chrysler's influence on Simca was reflected in the vigorous application of marketing techniques and the introduction of a range of models in the 1- to 1.5-liter size. While production at Simca increased by over 10 percent in the first two years,
the preacquisition plant capacity was still not fully utilized. On the
returns side, the company was restored to a profit-making position
after 1963, but the profit on turnover in the following five years continued very much as before with only marginal improvements in 1966
and 1967. These years saw a major capital investment program in
Simca, capital expenditure peaking in 1967 at 15.3 percent of turnover. In spite of the relative success of Simca after the Chrysler
takeover, the problem of the identity of the company remained and
was expressed in such comments as "Renault la populaire, Peugeot
la bourgeoise, Citroen l'inventive . . . et Simca, quel est aujourd'hui
son visage? Simca, hier; Simca-Chrysler, maintenant Simca l'apa-
tride. Comme un voyageur sans bagage, la firme de Poissy soufre
d'une identite imprecise. Americaine ou Francaise."[21] These comments, long after the name changed to Chrysler France in 1970, are
symptomatic of the French market's perception of the company.

In its Spanish venture, through the purchase of an initial 40 percent interest in Barreiros Diesel S.A. in 1963, Chrysler was buying
into a different type of situation and a company of very different origins. Starting as a small repairing business after the Spanish Civil
War, the company's first phase of expansion was based on the modification of Russian gasoline engines, which they mounted on secondhand

chassis. Protected by high tariffs, the company developed rapidly and by the early 1960s was engaging in large-scale barter deals with the Middle East, particularly Egypt, exchanging vehicles and spares for cotton. In 1961, Barreiros entered into a licensing agreement with the British heavy truck manufacturer AEC, Ltd. to manufacture bus chassis to AEC design, incorporating Barreiros' engines. By this time, however, the company appeared to have developed an over-diversified product line, with some of its component parts well below optimum size. In addition, Barreiros had a financial structure that was not sufficiently strong to be able to resist long-term competition from its state-controlled competitor, ENASA, whose heavy vehicles were providing serious domestic challenge. ENASA also benefited from technical and some financial involvement by British Leyland. The Chrysler offer of becoming a minority partner included the intro-duction of a production line of Dodge Dart and Simca cars. For the Barreiros family, it was an opportunity offering financial support and the attraction of a volume car line for the Spanish market; for Chrysler, the arrangement gave entry to a developing market and the prospect of a base on which to extend Simca capacity.

Chrysler took majority control of Barreiros in 1967, moving to ownership of 77 percent of the equity. At that time, Chrysler appor-tioned $20 million to the company and made a declaration in principle to invest another $35 million in ensuing years. During the transition period, domestic and foreign sales had performed indifferently, and it was anticipated that the company would concentrate more on commercial and agricultural vehicles. In 1968, Barreiros sales were down almost 11 percent from the 1966 peak and almost all the exports of the com-pany were to the Middle East, with some parts being sent to Simca. By that time the reorientation of the company's facilities to car production had progressed significantly, trucks, buses, and diesel engines being only 15 percent of production in 1968. The integration between Simca and Barreiros was a good example of transnational policy operating under special government constraints. Simca shipped kits to Barreiros, which, in turn, supplied engines and transmission parts for Simca cars. By agreement with the Spanish government, the body stampings sent to Spain were made in France from specially imported Spanish steel. Similar considerations regarding the Spanish balance of payments in-fluenced the production and exporting of Simca components at Barreiros. Chrysler thus was constrained by political pressures in the implemen-tation of its policies for Barreiros. The corporation was, of course, also subject to the requirement to obtain government approval before obtaining a majority holding in Barreiros.

In buying into Barreiros, Chrysler found itself with persistent financial problems. By 1968, the accumulated losses were considered to be $15 million,[22] and a corporation spokesman was quoted as saying

that "Barreiros has never made any money."[23] In 1969, Chrysler's
share of the equity in Barreiros rose to 86 percent and the family interest of the Barreiros family was bought out by a Spanish bank. Later
that year, Chrysler presented a recapitalization plan to the Spanish
stockholders that required additional financial commitments. As part
of the developments of June 1969, the four Barreiros brothers resigned,
openly criticizing the Chrysler style of management and alleging that
the commitments made in 1967 regarding parts and car exports had
not been fulfilled, since they had slumped from the 1964-66 peak.

It is more than possible that Chrysler was caught between the
pressures of trying to obtain entry into Spain and those of developing
an integrated policy between Simca and Barreiros such as to build a
more stable financial base for the future. However, there are some
signs that the base for expansion has now been established in Spain in
spite of continued poor returns. Chrysler rid itself of the Barreiros
coach-building interests in 1972, receiving government permission to
sell its Zaragoza plant to a Belgium firm, Van Hool. The situation
had improved sufficiently by 1974 for Chrysler to announce major expansion plans for the heavy commercial vehicle side of the business,
involving a doubling of production by 1978 (from 7,000 in 1973).[24]
Car production, still less profitable, has continued to rise, but, at
62,000 units in 1973, the operation in Spain remains a better prospect
for the long term than the short.

Toward a European Expansion Base: The Ford
and GM Experience

Chrysler was not alone among the Big Three in finding that it is
one thing to set profitable European expansion as an objective and quite
another to find the appropriate formula for its implementation. Unlike the others, Chrysler had neither the time to be able to try various
approaches in Europe nor the benefit of moving into a market at the
time of Ford's or GM's entry when the U.S. management, and possibly
technical, advantage was significant. In this section, the GM and
Ford experiences are reviewed from two viewpoints: one to focus
upon some of the operational problems found by the other two major
U.S. producers in their search for an acceptable formula for Europe
and the other to review the stage of development of GM and Ford
strategies toward Europe by the early 1960s when Chrysler entered
the market. Both of these aspects are relevant to making an objective
assessment of Chrysler's particular problems and subsequent performance.

The differences in approach adopted by GM and Ford have been
summarized in Chapter 1, leaving this section to emphasize the oper-

ational difficulties. While GM saw the development opportunities in
Europe very early, it did not manage to implement its buy-in strategy
at the first attempt. Having tried to acquire Citroen in 1919 and Austin in 1925, GM finally managed to purchase Vauxhall in the United
Kingdom in 1925 and Opel in Germany in 1929. It was widely recognized that Vauxhall was by no means the ideal initial European purchase for GM since it was so small (1,500 cars per year in 1925),
although it did give the company the opportunity to gain experience in
operating overseas. Perhaps the major influence on GM attitudes toward Europe was the anticipation of rapid overseas market growth after the war, an issue stressed in the Overseas Policy Group report
in 1944, which was based on the belief "that during the 20-year period
following the war, the overseas markets for cars and trucks will at
least equal the market in the United States and Canada."[25]

Following the logic of this forecast, and only after many years
in Europe, GM expanded the range of passenger cars produced in
West Germany and the United Kingdom from one that served only part
of the market to full-line production. Although GM had actively sup-
plemented the European-produced range by the assembly of U.S. models at GM Continental in Antwerp, its caution in product expansion in
Europe is significant, and the final decision to move to full-line production was not made until 1960. Thus, while GM took this step after
evaluating in situ the manufacturing economies and marketing efficiency
of such operations in Europe, Chrysler had no such advantage. Neither
did it inherit information from well-planned local companies that would
have been a proxy for its own experimentation. Thus, in the areas
where GM showed caution through real or anticipated operational problems, Chrysler was required to reduce dramatically the time span and
find the correct strategy almost immediately after entry.

The net effect of the GM advantage was that at the time when
Chrysler was entering Europe, the GM policy of moving into the rapidly
expanding 1-liter market had been implemented by the introduction of
the Opel Kadett in 1962 and the Vauxhall Viva in 1963. Both models
were to provide formidable competitors to the products inherited by
Chrysler later in the 1960s. They were the outcome of a product policy that, although not European in the transnational terms of the 1970s,
was mature and rooted in European domestic conditions.

In examining the emergence of Ford strategy in Europe, it is
even more obvious that it took time to find the correct base for future
operations. By the 1930s, Ford had operations in all the European
countries in which Chrysler is now represented. Both France and
Spain subsequently were abandoned in the 1950s, only for Ford to return to France with an engine plant in 1969 and to recommence manufacture in Spain in 1976. The early Ford experience in France, of
course, is particularly pertinent to the Chrysler strategy, since it is

in itself a part of Chrysler's inheritance from Simca. Following the Ford model, Chrysler entered two of the most difficult European countries in which to establish rapidly a solid base.

In the mid-1930s, Ford in France entered into its only significant venture with a foreign car producer. Apart from giving Ford SAF a temporary French appearance, the corporation's experience with Mathis was "a fiasco, leading to financial difficulties, management quarrels and litigation."[26] Postwar progress in Ford SAF was persistently disappointing and policy ultimately fundamentally misdirected. The continued production of poor results from France did not appear to surprise the U.S. senior staff, since, with the apparent exception of Henry Ford II, most of them had absorbed the GM philosophy that "you can't do business in France."[27] In spite of three major injections of capital in the postwar period, the situation in Ford SAF deteriorated dramatically. By October 1952, Ford seemed to have taken the decision in principle to merge or liquidate, both of which strategies required better results. A general manager came from the United States in 1953, and the turnaround accomplished was used as the base for the sale of the Ford SAF plant, staff, and dealer organization to Simca in 1954. In return, Ford obtained a 15.2 percent share in Simca equity. This dramatic exit clearly took the French organization by surprise and was particularly final in that it involved the dealer network. One dealer expressed his feelings at having been sold "comme le mouton."

The Ford failure in France is particularly unusual because of the company's long period of establishment in the market and seemed to stem directly from problems of product strategy. Resulting from the considerable freedom in product policy given by Ford U.S. to its European companies, the French firm did not develop models for the low-priced volume market. In fact, there are analogies between the situation of rundown that Ford experienced in France in 1954 and those of Chrysler in the United Kingdom in 1975. Against a background where significant cash injections had been absorbed in keeping Ford SAF operational, it was estimated that between $50 million and $100 million was required to develop a smaller four-cylinder car. Even if this were developed, success would have had to be in the face of strong domestic competition. In addition, the difficulties coincided with shortage of design capacity in Dearborn, Michigan, an issue that confirmed the rejection of a product-based solution. Apparently, at the time, Ford considered the possibility of purchasing an existing French company with a small car, but found no willing vendors. Thus, Ford, from a strategy of using France as a supply point, ended the 1950s with a residual presence in France in a marketing company. At the same time, it held the equity in Simca that was to be sold to Chrysler in 1958.

In its Spanish experience, Ford came under government constraints that violated its policy of ownership. Thus, while an assembly operation started in 1920, it came under growing pressures in the
postwar period from a government that wanted a national industry and
a controlling interest in any joint venture. The Ford assessment was
that such a policy was unworkable given the small Spanish home market, and the Ford stake in the Spanish operation was sold in 1954. By
taking the initiative in this situation, Ford was able to withdraw from
assembly in Spain and then reconsider the Spanish market at a later
date. It is doubtful whether any advantage would have accrued to Ford
in persisting with its Spanish investment in the intervening period,
since both income and attitudinal changes were required before take-
off in the domestic market and the company was, in any event, represented in southwestern Europe from 1963 through its Portuguese
assembly facilities.

Although the French and Spanish activities of Ford are illustrative of the initial difficulties of Ford in Europe, these were in the past
and any lessons were assimilated into strategy long before Chrysler's
entry. Thus, by the early 1960s, Ford had experienced a period of
years when its European operations had performed above U.S. norms
and where European production was over 30 percent of the U.S. total.
By profit, product, and performance criteria, Ford strategy was tried
and tested in Europe by the early 1960s.

AN INTERPRETATION OF CHRYSLER
STRATEGY IN EUROPE

The timing and entry routes adopted by the Big Three in their
approach to Europe now reviewed, this section will try to establish
the principles that could have motivated Chrysler policy toward the
European market. Inevitably, there are problems in attempting to
impute strategy from observed behavior. It is not apparent, nor
would it be expected, that the strategy be dominated by one simple
objective, established in the early 1960s. However, as a framework
for subsequent analysis of the corporation's performance in Europe,
it is necessary to try to assess the various ways in which Chrysler
could have perceived its European operation. Each of these objectives,
had it been exclusively pursued, would have led to a different emphasis in operational plans.

1. Maximize market penetration and profitability in the European countries with the largest or fastest growing markets within the
constraints of suitable partners being available. In terms of this
strategy, individual European countries would be seen as separate en-
tities. Plans to integrate subsidiaries through the production of com-

mon components and so on would be strictly limited. To gain full advantage of this strategy, a company such as Chrysler would have to look for the purchase of volume producers in Europe. This would be reinforced by the logic of avoiding the spread of management resources over a large number of specialist companies. Success in such a strategy, applied singly, would be in terms of sustained (and then expanded) market share, maximizing domestic market connections through product and distribution policies and improving profit performance.
Against this strategy was the knowledge, based on U.S. experience, of the market size required to achieve production and marketing economies.

2. Enter Europe to maximize ex-U.S. sales and profitability, but with the dominant aim of denying increased market shares in Europe to Ford and GM. Chrysler was the smallest and most vulnerable of the Big Three in the United States, both of which factors were accentuated by Ford's and GM's presence in the large European market. A similar presence by Chrysler would be necessary if the company were to be able to compete on equal terms in the United States. Again, Ford and GM had a flexibility that Chrysler lacked to use their European subsidiaries as U.S. import supply points where necessary.

As a subsidiary point, Chrysler had to be in Europe if the corporation was to be credible to U.S. stockholders as one of the largest companies in the world, and remain a truly international force in vehicle production. Success would be expressed in gaining entry with companies that would provide a basis to build for the future after they were controlled and redirected. A capability to sustain growth and be employed as a future expansion base for subsequent developments in Europe was thus an essential ingredient.

3. Move into Europe, consolidate, but, above all, be there. Since major changes in the world car business were ahead, they must be anticipated and some of them are going to stem directly from European manufacturers. The situation in Europe was changing rapidly and the door to foreign participation in the car industry was rapidly closing as domestic merger activity increased. Government interest in car production was increasing, which might lead to a rise in state-funded competition, but that risk had to be taken. If this aspect of strategy was emphasized, success criteria could inevitably only be judged in the long term.

4. Move into Europe to develop an integrated car and commercial vehicle facility that would anticipate EEC development and expansion, creating a European home market on the U.S. scale. Chrysler's lateness of entry and the intensity of competition and structural changes taking place within the industry in Europe indicate that this would have been the most nearly optimum strategy. It was perhaps the only way to obtain the required economies of scale, given that it was almost im-

possible to obtain a large enough market share in any one European country. An effective implementation of this strategy required rapid purchase and a clear program of assimilation. Ideally, this strategy also required the purchase of companies that were relatively free of political pressures in employment, investment transfer, product base, and so on. Success in this strategy, which would have to have been viewed over a five- to ten-year period, would be seen in a common European model range, plant complementarity, centralization of design and development, and so on. However, since the process of European integration was only just beginning in the 1960s and the United Kingdom was still outside the EEC, the criteria for establishing an integrated production and marketing operation were difficult to establish. Furthermore, the costs of implementing a unified European strategy would always have been difficult to forecast.

5. Enter Europe experimentally, gradually taking over some significant suppliers, and gaining experience of Europe via the outgoing management. This strategy theoretically was also highly suitable, since an entrant company would have little technological advantage compared with European-based manufacturers. It would allow the differences between the U.S. and European markets to be appreciated, documented, and interpreted in company policy; and while at the same time it did involve a high break-in cost of purchase, the subsequent investment demand was capable of being regulated. Such a policy, of course, depended for its effectiveness on the acquisition of at least moderately successful firms in that the U.S. entrant would require both reasonable performance and good advice and information in the early years when initial investment decisions were being made. Against this strategy, long-term "European" policies would still be necessary if the individual companies were not to suffer problems of lack of scale. Integration could also be more difficult the longer it was delayed.

6. Buy into Europe, invest up to or close to U.S. standards, manage the plants on U.S. experience, and await results. This strategy would assume management advantage and attribute much to the effective application of transplanted control procedures. It would leave little flexibility for policy change if the initial assessment of the problems were misjudged. It assumes implicitly that European market development can be interpreted within a U.S. framework and has no unique characteristics of its own. The logic of this policy would be to lead to the concentration of resources on plants meeting established criteria with inevitable problems for the parent company with the residual parts of the operation that continually fail to meet objectives and become potential write-offs. Methods of testing for the application of this strategy would include the pattern of allocating resources among plants, the existence of extended lags in product and investment planning, and so forth.

Inevitably, these strategic alternatives do not always represent mutually exclusive choices. However, on the basis of the information presented on Simca and Barreiros, and without yet considering the corporation's acquisition of Rootes, it is clear that Chrysler could have expected severe difficulties in any attempt to implement certain of these strategic options. The choice of locations would have permitted any of the first three strategies to be pursued: the United Kingdom and France were both large markets although competition was also fierce; the United Kingdom was an obvious choice for another reason, namely, its cultural similarity with the United States, while France and Spain were free from GM and Ford domestic production. However, the political situation in both France and Spain undoubtedly posed formidable problems for any Chrysler attempt to pursue an integration strategy, and the experimental approach was constrained by the fact that the performance of Simca and Barreiros had not been entirely satisfactory prior to Chrysler's involvement.

Chrysler was clearly aware of its inherited difficulties in Europe. In 1968, Lynn Townsend, when questioned regarding the performance of the European subsidiaries, indicated that his company had had to be realistic when it invested in Simca, Rootes, and Barreiros, since financially healthy companies were not for sale.[28] The existence of substantial majority interests in the initial years of Chrysler's involvement was not always conducive to the implementation of optimal policies. Thus Chrysler's management style is a pragmatic one, which tends to fluctuate between the centralization of Ford and the decentralization of GM. This has given both flexibility and instability to its European management, based initially in Geneva and later in London from 1970. From 1970, policies toward Europe were to become more integrated. Outlining his aim, John Riccardo, the corporation's president, indicated that the company was taking steps to centralize styling, product planning, and engineering functions under the basic objective of coordinating European products to have the same models no matter where they were to be built.[29] As part of this overall philosophy, Chrysler's U.S. policy of enforcing a single name and brand image was transferred to Europe, resulting in the names of the three operating subsidiaries being changed from July 1970 to Chrysler France, Chrysler U.K., and Chrysler Espana. As will be shown, however, the corporation's integration policy never proceeded beyond the name changes.

NOTES

1. See J. White, The Automobile Industry since 1945 (Cambridge, Mass.: Harvard University Press, 1971). This was, in fact, the third

time that Chrysler cars had met serious market resistance. In 1953-54, its cars were shorter and in styling very much out of line with its competitors, leading to sales falling from 20.3 percent of the market (1953) to 12.9 percent (1954), with profits declining from $200 million to $21 million. Similarly, the 1958 models, with an emphasis on large fins, led to a slump in market shares from 18.3 in 1957 to 11.3 in 1959; correspondingly, pretax profits of $252 million in 1957 changed to losses of $73 million (1958) and $10 million (1959).

2. United States Motor Manufacturers and the Common Market, Economist Intelligence Unit, Motor Business, no. 31, 1962.

3. See William Reiber (then director of sales and marketing, Chrysler France) in "The European Automobile Market: Sophistication in High Gear," Columbia Journal of World Business 5, no. 5 (1970): 41.

4. Ibid., p. 44.

5. Lynn Townsend, quoted in Wall Street Journal, February 27, 1968.

6. Times (London), July 14, 1969.

7. "The U.S. Passenger Car Market: The Sub Compacts and the Imports," Economist Intelligence Unit, Motor Business, no. 59 (1969).

8. Sunday Times (London), January 14, 1968.

9. Quoted from a Chrysler vice-president in Harlow Unger, "Rocky Road for Rootes and Simca in the States," Sunday Times (London), January 14, 1968.

10. Times (London), July 14, 1969.

11. Financial Times, June 25, 1970.

12. Ibid., March 27, 1971, reported Dun & Bradstreet action reflecting the $1,000 commercial paper outstanding.

13. For a comment on this situation, see H. A. Stark, ed., Ward's Automotive Yearbook (Detroit, 1971); and L. Szeplaki, "Structure, Conduct and Performance in Modern American Automobile Manufacturing," South African Journal of Economics 40, no. 3 (1972). These included two related aspects, namely, the high cost of labor and materials in the United States that opened the market to imports and the program to meet "social obligations" (emission requirements, safety, and so on) that involved significant cost increases.

14. This was claimed by a Chrysler executive (Financial Times, October 12, 1959), although it was subsequently denied by Simca.

15. W. S. Clough, managing director of Chrysler Motors, quoted in Financial Times, January 2, 1962.

16. "A Financial and Economic Analysis of the French Motor Industry," Economist Intelligence Unit, Motor Business, no. 33 (1963), p. 26.

17. R. Hellman, The Challenge to US Dominance of the International Corporation (New York: Dunellen, 1970), p. 126.

18. For a detailed summary of these reasons, including the lay-offs at the GM refrigerator factory at Gennevilliers, those at the Remington factory at Lyons, and the Libby McNeill canning factory proposals for Langvedec, see A. W. Johnstone, American Investment in France (Cambridge, Mass.: Massachusetts Insitute of Technology Press, 1965), chap. 2.

19. Le Monde, January 1, 1963.

20. Ibid., January 10, 1963.

21. Ibid., March 20, 1973.

22. Financial Times, June 20, 1969. At that time it was reported that Chrysler was considering an offer by Ford to take over Barreiros. Estimates suggested that up to $50 million in additional funds would be required to improve the financial position and allow the production of cars cheap enough to compete in export markets.

23. Wall Street Journal, June 3, 1969.

24. Financial Times, September 23, 1974.

25. Quoted in F. G. Donner, The World Wide Industrial Enterprise (New York: McGraw-Hill, 1967), p. 27.

26. M. Wilkins and F. E. Hill, American Business Abroad: Ford on Six Continents (Detroit: Wayne State University Press, 1964), p. 426.

27. Ibid., p. 393.

28. "Les Grandes Voix de l'Automobile," l'Equipe, April 1968.

29. International Management, October 1971.

3

CHRYSLER'S
INHERITANCE
FROM ROOTES

While it is not within the scope of this chapter to undertake a detailed historic study of the Rootes Group, it is clear that both the character and performance of Chrysler U.K. are related in some measure to the Rootes Group. This is particularly so when it is remembered that the initial Chrysler investment in Rootes in 1964 and the advent of majority in 1967 are both recent events, particularly in the time scale of rectifying poor business results in the car industry. Thus, it is essential to highlight some of the principal issues of the past that realistically can be seen to have influenced Chrysler U.K.'s policy alternatives.

These issues include the origins, structure, and organization of the component parts of Rootes. This consideration encompasses the degree to which the company was close to optimum size and location in its various operations. It is also necessary to examine the extent to which growth and rationalization had been accomplished successfully in the latter days of the independent Rootes amid the competitive pressures of the early 1960s.

In addition, the particular circumstances surrounding the Chrysler investment in and subsequent takeover of Rootes come within the scope of this contextual review. Clearly, some of the conditions established in 1967 and many of the political nuances that underlay them could be said to have structured Chrysler's attitude toward its investment in the United Kingdom in more ways than one. To give focus to this aspect, the initial Chrysler policy changes are considered to indicate exactly how they ranked the problems of Rootes.

The pre-Chrysler record of performance is also of major importance in evaluating subsequent events. In this area, attention is drawn directly to matters of productivity, labor relations, and profitability, although the objective is to set the general scene before 1964 by utilizing a number of performance criteria.

To complete the setting, it is essential to examine Rootes' policies in selected key areas of business activity, particularly those where historic decisions take a considerable time to reverse. Particular emphasis is placed on marketing policy and the implications of Rootes' investment strategies. These concerns form the basis of Chapter 4 where the marketing aspects of the inheritance are examined in detail.

ORIGINS

The critical dates in the beginnings of the Rootes enterprise can be summarized as follows:

1898 William Rootes established a motor business selling cars in Hawkhurst, Kent.

1913 The business was transferred to Maidstone, Kent. In the same year his son (William Rootes) became an apprentice in the Singer Motor Company. Subsequently, he and his brother Reginald went into their father's business.

1926 The beginnings of the many Rootes acquisitions and the initiation of the major character change from purely servicing the motor industry. That year the company acquired Thrupp and Maberley, a long-established company of coach builders.

1932 Humber and Hillman were merged into the group. These two companies had cooperated since the end of World War I, although they had maintained separate identities. This gave Rootes an entry to both car production and commercial vehicle manufacture since Humber controlled Commer Cars Ltd., a commercial vehicle producer since 1905.

1934 The acquisition of Karrier Motors Ltd expanded the Rootes' commercial vehicle capacity.

1937 The Sunbeam Motor Company and Clement-Talbot Ltd were bought, being salvaged from the collapsed Sunbeam-Talbot combine.

All three initial acquisitions were companies that were either facing bankruptcy or already in receivership. Rootes was thus able to buy into the manufacturing sector relatively cheaply, realizing that reorganization and capital restructuring would not in themselves produce profitable performance, but that the strategy from the outset must be one of growth and expansion. It has been estimated that the combined annual car output of all of the companies acquired at this stage was of the order of 5,000 to 6,000 units before the group was formed.[1] The short-term benefits of reorganization and standardization were beginning to be realized by 1939 when total sales from the same companies had grown by close to 600 percent, giving Rootes 10 percent of the U.K. car market.[2]

1937   Rootes acquired British Light Steel Pressings (BLSP), a purchase that was to prove advantageous owing to the growing pressures on body supplies that developed in the late 1930s and became acute post-World War II. This situation, of course, was aggravated by the numbers of vehicles on offer. It is estimated that two-thirds of the models of the largest six manufacturers had sales of less than the 5,000 units regarded as the critical output of the "popular" class.[3]

BLSP, founded in 1930, was a producer of a wide range of pressings for almost every industry but the motor industry. Its initial Rootes activity was the making of body shells for Sunbeam, but it rapidly extended its range to include suspension units, gasoline tanks, and many small pressings.

With the preparation for war, Rootes plants became involved in 1936 with the government's Shadow Factory Scheme for volume manufacture of airplanes and aeroengines. By 1945, estimates showed that the group had made over 14 percent of the bombers, 60 percent of the armored cars, and 30 percent of the Scout cars produced in the United Kingdom during the war.[4] In addition, a significant amount of repairing and assembling of imported vehicles was undertaken. The Rootes brothers themselves were closely involved in the war effort and were knighted in consequence: William as chairman of the Shadow Industry Scheme and head of the Supply Council of the Ministry of Supply and Reginald for his work in managing the war production in the plants.

Postwar Rootes, in common with other manufacturers, faced a world lacking cars such as to ensure a seller's market until the mid-1950s. The major difficulties of the period were shortages of materials (especially steel) and skilled labor. Such were the shortages that return to prewar levels of output was delayed until 1949. In sharp contrast to the 1930s, concern was more with output and volume than with model price competition as Rootes attempted to gain the economies of volume production. Eventually, the shortages ended and the industry as a whole raised output by 30 percent and reduced costs by 20 percent in the 1950-54 period alone.[5]

The pressures were on Rootes to grow and integrate group facilities sufficiently rapidly to retain and expand its share of the market. Clearly, this objective motivated model rationalization and subsequent acquisition by Rootes in the 1950s. It did, however, leave Rootes with a particular coincidence of problems, namely, having to act positively to rationalize several plants and companies while knowing that the group as a whole did not have the market share required to ensure that the benefits of rationalization would be fully realized.

It was this search for market share that motivated the extensive Rootes postwar drive for exports. It had established one of the first sales organizations in Latin America in 1931 and established the first Australian car plant in 1946. Subsequently, manufacturing and sales networks were established abroad, including Rootes Motors, Inc. in New York and Rootes Motors (Canada) Ltd. in 1947. Before 1948, the group had its own trading company in Belgium and another in Brazil. As a whole, Rootes was sensitive to the market opportunities offered by the postwar shortages. Consequently, in an industry in 1949 where the export average was 20 percent of production, Rootes was exporting 30 percent of Humber and Hillman production. [6]

1950 The acquisition program continued with the purchase of Tilling-Stevens Ltd., a commercial vehicle producer originally established at Maidstone in 1897. The company had taken over Vulcan Motors just before World War II. Rootes clearly did not intend to develop these names and quickly switched the facilities for general group production. Its new role was to specialize in engine production and make a particular contribution to the manufacture of the new Rootes two-stroke, three-cylinder diesel engine.

1955 In the Singer takeover, from the Rootes viewpoint, one of the major interests in Singer was its property assets, since, at the time of acquisition, the output of Singer cars had fallen to about 50 per week. This said however, the shareholders accepted the Rootes offer with the assurance that the name and reputation would be maintained. Indeed, the day after the takeover, late in December 1955, a brief was given to designers to develop a new model, introduced nine months later as the Singer Gazelle. [7]

1956 Rootes acquired a controlling interest in Tempair Ltd., a company manufacturing air-conditioning equipment with a wide range of applications.

1963 Production commenced in the new 1.6 million square foot plant at Linwood in Scotland. Having been refused permission to expand in its heartland area at Ryton because of the government's Industrial Development Certificate policy, the group decided to expand 250 miles north of its nearest plant.

In many ways the Linwood development was a watershed in the history of the Rootes enterprise. In terms of the product planned to be manufactured at Linwood, this was a new venture for Rootes in the small car market. Its subsequent inability to realize sales objectives proved to be one of the dominant factors affecting the pre-Chrysler profitability of the company. Furthermore, the location of the plant and problems of manpower, production facility, and logistics were a continuing source of friction in government-company relations. They were to remain so under Chrysler. Indeed, the recurrence of Linwood as a political pawn at several stages in the company's subsequent progress is in itself another facet of the watershed hypothesis. Linwood has influenced ownership, attracted and repelled capital, directly and indirectly affected the actual (and perceived) performance of the group, and has featured in all government deals since.

CHRYSLER'S TAKEOVER OF ROOTES

At least in part, the interest of the Chrysler Corporation in European expansion stemmed from the significant improvement in company performance in the period following 1962 and extending to 1968. Internal reorganization and U.S. market growth combined to raise the company's share of the U.S. market from 10 percent in 1962 to over 18 percent in 1968. This was reflected in the general strategy adopted toward Europe, which aimed at sustaining expansion. While the European strategy has been explored fully in Chapter 2, the particular concern of this section is to examine the detailed circumstances surrounding Chrysler's attempts to develop in the United Kingdom through Rootes.

Chrysler's courting of Rootes was apparently not its first effort to establish a manufacturing foothold in the United Kingdom. As early as 1956 Chrysler approached Standard, then an independent producer, to develop a new small car for the European market on its behalf. Again, in 1961, new approaches were made to Standard, various proposals being examined, and, in the same year, with Leyland Motors. The latter efforts culminated in Chrysler's unsuccessful attempt to buy a share in Leyland in 1962. All of these efforts reveal a consistent determination to become directly involved in the U.K. industry, efforts that failed for a range of reasons, including relative strength of the parties and preferred future relationships with other U.K. and U.S. companies. Rootes was not the first approach, nor the first choice.

It was not so much that Chrysler had come too late to look at the establishment of a profitable manufacturing operation in the United Kingdom, since some significant merger arrangements postdated Chrysler's entry (for example, 1966 Leyland Motors acquiring Rover, 1967 British Motor Holdings, formed a year earlier from the British Motor Corporation, and Leyland Motors combining to form British Leyland Motor Corporation). Rather, it was that the scale on which Chrysler could acquire demanded an integrated European strategy (with Simca and Barrieros) that could begin to make sense of the ailing

Rootes package. Chrysler perhaps was not big enough or did not have sufficient funds to be able to undertake the outright acquisition of a major European producer. Thus, the collection of a series of European activities that could be integrated into a Chrysler-directed whole seemed the optimal solution.

In order to understand the political attitudes underlying both the government and Chrysler positions in the 1975 crisis, it is essential to examine the two main periods of takeover activity involving Chrysler and Rootes, first in 1964 (Chrysler already had a limited base in the U.S. vehicle manufacturing industry through its joint venture, Chrysler-Cummins Ltd., with Cummins Engine Company and its own Dodge activity) and then in 1967. Therefore these two events and the immediate outcome are examined in some detail in this section.

Takeover: 1964-65

As late as May 26, 1964, Lord Rootes was denying rumors of a takeover bid for the company by Chrysler or, as rumor had it, by BMC.[8] On June 4, 1964, it was announced that Chrysler had undertaken to acquire 30 percent of the ordinary (voting) shares and 50 percent of the "A" (nonvoting) ordinary shares in Rootes Motors Ltd. Chrysler was to purchase the voting shares at 24/6d. and the "A" shares at 21/-. On the day of offer these shares closed at 12/- and 7/9d., respectively, and the offer value was placed at approximately £12.3 million, Rootes' total assets in the latest previous balance sheet (7/31/63) being £66.2 million. As part of the initial announcement, the Chrysler Car and Dodge truck operations in the United Kingdom were to be combined with the Rootes Group as soon as possible. In addition, shareholders were informed immediately of development and expansion plans for the United Kingdom and abroad, Rootes intending to offer an issue to shareholders within the ensuing 18 months to raise up to £15 million. In any such arrangement, Chrysler would take up its shares and any proportion unsubscribed.

The political reaction to the deal instantly polarized into, on the one hand, vigorous government reassurances of the maintenance of the autonomy of Rootes and potential benefits of the Chrysler link, while the Labour party, in opposition, was highly critical of the whole principle and, in particular, of further foreign dominance in the car industry. Speaking in Glasgow, Edward Heath (then minister for industry) reassured workers that it was in the best interest of all to have the connection with Chrysler because of its size and experience and that there was no question of the Americans dominating the U.K. motor industry, since Chrysler would only have one-third of the voting power in Rootes.[9] Presenting his perspective on the matter, Lord Rootes, interviewed in New York the day after the announcement, indicated that it was completely untrue that Rootes was under financial pressure or that the need for additional funds had motivated the deal.

From the Chrysler viewpoint, I. J. Minnett, vice-president for international operations, claimed, as part of the announcement on the implications, that Rootes' marketing operations would be strengthened by the association and that no drastic policy changes were anticipated. Sales of Simca and Rootes cars were to be coordinated and some Chrysler dealers abroad would probably add Rootes cars to their lines. Clearly, Chrysler was under considerable pressure at that stage to maintain a low profile in the Rootes arrangement, and the official statements in no way reflected the extent of the reorientation and development that it must have realized was essential to its prosperous future in Europe.

There was also some anxiety expressed at the time[10] over the potential effect on Rootes sales to the United States, which at 7,000 in 1963 and 13,000 in 1964 were growing significantly as part of the beginning of large-scale foreign car importing.[11] Chrysler strongly denied any suggestion that there would be limitations put on Rootes sales to the United States, Minnett stressing that the Chrysler bid was not a bid to take over the management of the company.[12] There would be, Chrysler claimed, little exchange of personnel, but manufacturing and marketing cooperation would occur, perhaps involving the supply of Chrysler equipment to Rootes and vice versa.

While expressing disappointment, the motor industry generally appeared to see the relationship as understandable as far as overseas distribution was concerned and hoped that Rootes' access to Chrysler's research and testing facilities would speed up new model introduction. This raises the fundamental question that is discussed elsewhere as to what extent Chrysler had, and used, its technological advantage in its subsequent involvement with Rootes. Indeed it was on this type of issue that some of the most particular defense was made. Replying to Harold Wilson's question of the guarantees in the agreement against conversion to majority, Edward Heath argued that the overall Labour Opposition attitude was a major threat to bringing foreign investment into the country.[13]

In defense of the criticism of the deal, Rootes consistently claimed that there was no analogy with the Chrysler interests in Simca cars in France as the relative shareholdings were completely different, and the company was confident that there would be no change of control. It was the matter of the erosion of control that proved to be the focus of persistent criticism. Reginald Maudling, then chancellor of the exchequer, told Parliament that he would rather see Chrysler investing money in the United Kingdom than with "our Continental competitors."[14] In the same debate, the Opposition pressed Heath to appoint

an inspector to ensure that the acquisition did not, in fact, give Chrysler effective control of Rootes. The government refused this, but did
acknowledge that Exchange Control consent was required on two counts:
to ensure that the price was not artificially low and that the deal would
be reflected fully in the country's currency reserves. This consent
was in fact given by the Treasury on July 29, 1964, and Chrysler, as
part of the arrangements, was required not to increase its holdings
without consulting the U.K. government. In accepting this condition,
Minnett anticipated the future development of the Rootes–Chrysler relationship by indicating that Chrysler would appreciate an assurance
from Maudling that, in considering whether or not to give its agreement in such circumstances, the British government would take into
account the interests of a prosperous and viable development of the
motor industry in general and of the Rootes business in particular. [15]

      The Rootes major shareholders list at the time of the Chrysler
offer is presented in Table 3.1. It indicates the significance of the influence of the Rootes family, associates, and trusts in the ordinary
(voting) holdings. This in itself caused political questions. For example, James Callaghan pressed the chancellor to appoint an inspector
to investigate the beneficial shareholdings of the company to make
certain that share ownership could not be dispensed through the family
trusts, thereby giving Chrysler effective "back door" control. [16]

      The formal offer details forwarded to shareholders on August 10,
1964 and the related statement from Lord Rootes provide an important
perspective on the anticipated benefits of the deal from the Rootes viewpoint. Lord Rootes declared that, in welcoming the Chrysler approach,
the association would give obvious benefits in research, technical advances, production, and other techniques and would facilitate overseas
development in many ways, including dealer development. In addition,
it would be particularly advantageous in certain markets where overseas government action demanded increased local manufacture and
large capital expenditure. This inevitably poses the question about the
optimal size of Rootes as it existed, finding itself unable to cope with
the next generation of exports via local manufacture in the way it had
succeeded in direct exporting in the 1950s. By late September 1964,
the Chrysler offer became unconditional and the final arrangements
made.

      An attempt to make an objective assessment of subsequent de-
velopments in the relationship faces the problem of distinguishing
Chrysler's preferred strategy from that actually adopted in the face
of recurrent serious financial troubles in Rootes. As was anticipated
in some of the earlier statements, Chrysler realistically recognized
the need to reserve the right to protect its large, and rapidly growing,
investment in Rootes, and most probably saw the desirability and perhaps inevitability of being the first obvious source of finance and man-

TABLE 3.1

Rootes Motors Ltd.: Major Shareholdings as of Chrysler Bid, 1964
(thousands of shares)

	Ordinary	"A" Ordinary
Cooperative Insurance Society	25	108
General Trust and Securities (of the Bahamas)	2,285	2,743
A. L. Goate and another	15	435
R. W. Hammond and another	—	375
Lady Nancy W. Rootes	2	66
Sir Reginald Rootes	179	774
Sir Reginald Rootes and others	10	67
Sir Reginald Rootes and others	—	405
Sir Reginald Rootes and others	104	416
Lord Rootes	60	518
Timothy D. Rootes and another	—	100
W. G. Rootes and another	—	100
S. P. Angel Nominees	—	141
Tay Trust	15	225
Field Nominees (of Bermuda)	87	1,254
Lloyds Bank Grosvenor Nominees "A" Account	20	80
Pearl Assurance	25	100
Prudential Assurance	474	2,650
Royal London Mutual Insurance	—	120

Note: The list amounted to 66 percent of ordinary and 53 percent of "A" shares as of December 1963. Total shareholders at the time were approximately 15,000. Issued equity capital was 5 million ordinary and 20 million "A" ordinary 4/- shares.

Source: Financial Times Library.

agement expertise in time of need for Rootes. However, if some aspects of the short-term impact of the deal are examined, the following two-month sample is characteristic of the type of structural modifications undertaken in late 1965:

October   Rootes to sell Chrysler Simca in Germany.
           Production stepped up by one-third at Linwood and Coventry.
           High performance Imp model announced.

December   Rootes' reorganized Car Sales Division to get full advan-
           tage of increased production at Coventry and Linwood.
           Chrysler to sell Rootes cars in the United States, assum-
           ing full responsibility for sales in that market.
           Deal announced covering Simca and Rootes outlets, in-
           volving 100 sales and service centers in France for
           Rootes and up to 120 Simca outlets in the United Kingdom.

These changes took place after a further modification in the relationship, since in May 1965 Chrysler was allowed by the (now Labour)
government to increase its holdings in Rootes to 45 percent of the ordinary (voting) shares and 66 percent of the "A" (nonvoting) shares.
As part of the general package, Rootes at that time acquired Dodge
from Chrysler and combined it with its existing commercial vehicle
activity in Commer-Karrier. Much of the money received in the sale
was used to purchase the Linwood Pressing Plant as part of an "in
sourcing" drive. Money also came from the sale of the Australian
manufacturing facilities to Chrysler. The financial situation at that
time is well summarized elsewhere.[17]

Takeover: 1966-67

As the Chrysler relationship developed during 1966-67, it became
clear that the Rootes loss situation was incapable of short-term solution. Following the £2.1 million loss in the year ending July 1965,
losses increased steeply to £3.6 million in 1966. The seriousness of
the Rootes problem again featured in political debate late in 1966.
The Labour government, having opposed the deal when in opposition,
began to take active steps to find a "national" solution. These steps
apparently included active examination at cabinet level as to whether
or not it would be practicable to bring Rootes into partnership with
the U.K.-controlled section of the car industry. Wedgewood-Benn
(then minister of technology) held discussions with key figures in the
car manufacturing sector and was reported as concluding that the difficulties in pursuing that particular option "were insuperable."[18] The
chairmen of both BMC and Leyland Motors were involved in these discussions as the government attempted to find a formula to secure a
continuing U.K. interest in Rootes and to maintain a measure of employment stability within the company.

Several major issues seem to have precluded a national solution
in the form of participation from within the industry. One undoubtedly
was that neither BMC nor Leyland had the capital required, and it became certain that the government would have had to provide over 90
percent of the finance. It was here, yet again, that the government

was caught in what was later to prove the crucial pincer movement in 1975, between open-ended financial commitment and employment. It was impossible to have production rationalization with Rootes and another U.K. producer without very significant cuts in employment, but, at the same time, it was also impossible to obtain a guarantee that either BMC or Leyland would continue to operate the Linwood plant in its politically sensitive location.

Any Rootes solution, however interim, was inevitably going to involve further government participation.

It is important in light of subsequent events to understand the apparent attitude of the U.K. government at the time. Under the pressure of persistent questioning in Parliament, Wedgewood-Benn clearly indicated that the government "did not believe that Rootes by itself was a viable organisation with or without Government money, owned or not by a British company."[19] Superficially, this might be interpreted as implying either that the U.K. government was skeptical about any future for the Rootes organization or that it had become convinced that the solution lay in a transnational solution rather than a national one. In fact, to imply that any consistent business strategy was accepted, or even understood, by the government is to give credit where none is due. When pressured to explain why Chrysler had wanted to acquire the company if the outlook was so bleak, the minister explained the action as protecting the 1964 investment and proceeded to draw an analogy between the U.S. and U.K. car industry. The moral of this episode was that it was unlikely, in the eyes of the U.K. government, that the United Kingdom would be able to sustain three large American corporations as well as an indigenous one.

It was this type of analysis that apparently led the government to reject nationalization in 1967, although its view was often expressed in a somewhat different form. In cross-examination by his own supporters, Wedgewood-Benn claimed that "if we had nationalised Rootes we should have been left, even then, with a company which, in technological terms, was not on a scale which could survive at a critical time."[20] He went on to indicate that this was so because the expansion plans of Rootes "depend entirely" on being integrated with Chrysler technology, marketing, management, and finance. Indeed, "the act of nationalisation would have severed the link with the company upon which the future of Rootes currently depends."

In 1967, Rootes was obviously an embarrassment to the government. A deal it had opposed in opposition had developed and had proved to be the only possible, let alone practicable, route to rescue jobs. Chrysler was to hand; it was becoming locked in in order to protect its own investment and therefore seemed to offer the only prospect for continuing the company.

Throughout this period, Chrysler, understandably, was making it clear to all concerned that it would not proceed with any further in-

vestment in Rootes without voting control. The immediate background
to the crisis was the acceleration of losses from the predicted loss
of £4.75 million in the first six months of the 1966/67 fiscal year.
(This was in fact realized and the total annual loss exceeded £10 million in 1966/67.) By that time, Chrysler had invested £27 million and
was prepared to provide an additional £20 million (£10 million of which
was required urgently in early 1967 as working capital) and to commit
additional capital provided permission to take control was forthcoming
from the government. The Chrysler investment to that date had been
in equipment changes in Linwood and Coventry, and the acquisition of
Pressed Steel at Linwood cost £14 million. This was part of a program to produce more major parts within the organization, a program
that extended, for example, to renting a plant at Baginton, adjacent
to the Ryton factory, to produce interior trims employing female labor.

The Chrysler proposals for rescue were finally put to the Treasury for approval on December 12, 1966 and approval was granted
by January 17, 1967, without reference to the Monopolies Commission
being required. While the offending of monopoly legislation was not
in question in this case, it was, in any event, within a time in the
United Kingdom when considerable reliance was put on mergers and
rationalization as a solution to problems of industrial profitability and
investment. The corollary to this was the government's desire to
avoid extreme changes in industrial concentration, and together they
made up the elements of the classic antitrust dilemma. The Rootes
case, in spite of questions being raised regarding the validity of a
foreign takeover solution, was not, by 1967, open to other solutions.

Chrysler thus increased its voting interest in Rootes to 66 percent by exercising its rights to a new Rootes issue of voting shares.
In replying to vigorous criticism by Labour members of Parliament,
Wedgewood-Benn indicated that a government takeover would have involved putting massive sums of public money into "an insolvent private
enterprise company without any guarantee that in this way it would
remain viable."[21] The lack of government confidence is apparent in
this type of comment, as Chrysler was given access to a chronically
sick enterprise for political expediency. Indeed, there are grounds
for arguing that, given that economies of scale are difficult to achieve
in current car production in the United Kingdom, this support action
has had fundamental repercussions for the whole industry and for the
subsequent British Motor Holdings and Leyland merger (in 1967) in
particular.

As part of the 1967 package, Chrysler agreed to certain conditions, made public (see the Appendix). The undertakings are in themselves interesting and reflect some of the critical aspects of the underlying negotiations. One or two of them were innocuous from Chrysler's
viewpoint and were not unsubtle window-dressing exercises. Others

highlight the dual importance of the employment-export dilemma of the
U.K. government over the whole car industry, a debate still unresolved in an overcapacity industry in 1976. Political forces were even
more overt in the undertakings regarding Linwood.* The government's
desire for a national solution devolved ultimately into the newly formed
industrial Reorganisation Corporation (IRC) making its first investment
and acquiring 48.7 percent of the Rootes total equity capital. (The
difference between expectations and reality in this affair is further emphasized in the IRC claim in May 1968 that participation in the arrangements for reconstituting the financial structure of Rootes was at the
request of the government and that "Rootes is making good progress
towards recovery and profitability."[22])

Although at the time this seemed a minor, symbolic gesture of
overt government participation in the restructured organization, in
some ways it proved to be of greater significance. One of the items
that did not appear in the balance sheet of near-bankrupt Rootes in
1964 was the degree to which U.K. government was prepared to go to
support a backer for this organization. Although, as has been pointed
out, Rootes was not at the optimum commercial size, it was proven
to be beyond the optimum political size. Too small to make money,
it was always too large to close down. Employment constraints were
to be a constant dimension within any government policy toward the
company. It remains to be seen whether or not Chrysler was aware
of this additional unquantified and, at times, beneficial inheritance
from Rootes.

Takeover: Post-1967

As subsequent events have proved, this was the beginning rather
than the end of direct involvement of the U.K. government with Chrysler. It is difficult to consider, however, that the government was
naive enough to regard this as the final way out in a problem of this
scale. While 1964 and 1967 arrangements saw both entry and control,
they were the major events pre-1975.

There were, however, two additional technical watersheds in
Chrysler's acquisition program, namely, 1972 and 1973. Based on
the agreement of January 1967 between Chrysler and the IRC, the
government exercised the right to require the Chrysler Corporation

---

*There were questions in Parliament on January 24, 1967 as to
what these undertakings meant for Linwood. Benn indicated that employment would rise there by 4,000 to 5,000 over about a five-year period. A Rootes spokesman subsequently claimed that such figures were
purely speculative.

to purchase at par, plus accrued dividends and interest, over 7.5 million preferred ordinary shares (20 p) and the outstanding unsecured loan stock (1981) subscribed by IRC in 1967. This was the move to almost total ownership, giving Chrysler 96.8 percent of the preferred ordinary shares and 99.4 percent of the "A" preferred ordinary shares, 65.4 percent of the ordinary shares, 79.2 percent of the "A" ordinary shares, and all the 1981, 8 percent unsecured loan stock. Early in 1973 Chrysler bought out all other shareholdings for about £6 million, thus gaining complete control by government agreement. In so doing, the company indicated that this would permit "improved coordination" of all its European operations. By that time, the debate on ownership, control, and national sovereignty was over as far as the future of Rootes was concerned, although inevitably the same principles re-emerged in the 1975 crisis, as discussed in Chapter 9.

ROOTES PERFORMANCE PRE-CHRYSLER

Rootes in Perspective

Since Chrysler chose to expand into Europe through acquisitions, the whole setting of the merger is governed by the performance of Rootes, particularly in the ten years before U.S. involvement. The pre-Chrysler performance is important for other reasons, including the extent to which Rootes' record precluded anything other than take-over given Chrysler's desire to be a serious force in the car industry in Europe. Furthermore, the continued poor performance of Rootes perhaps sucked Chrysler into the situation more rapidly than expected, given initial involvement as a minority shareholder but in cognate manufacturing activity. Moreover, the events that followed 1967 and that continue to develop inevitably have some of their origins in the Rootes performance in this period. Rootes pre-1964 acts as a kind of benchmark for the analysis of Chrysler's performance discussed in Chapter 5. Inevitably, only a limited number of criteria have been chosen to highlight the size and performance of Rootes and to compare the company with its closest competitors.

As events have developed, there are grounds for arguing that the relative size has proven to be as serious a problem as the relative performance from Chrysler's viewpoint. Three important issues dominate the 1950-64 period: structural change, output growth, and sustained demand.

As far as the industrial structure within which Rootes was operating was concerned, this was the beginning of a period of accelerating concentration of production. For Rootes, the major period of acquisi-

tion had passed; for others the drive for rationalization was only beginning. The first major example of this was the creation in 1952 of
the British Motor Corporation by the merging of Austin and Morris
interests, producing in 1954 a group with 38 percent of the U.K. market. (The main aim of BMC was marketing economies of scale, especially in exports, but it apparently solved the problem of a successor
to Lord Nuffield, who as William Morris had founded Morris Motors
in 1877.[23]) There was also the reemergence of significant foreign interest in the industry with the abortive takeover attempt in 1957 for
Standard-Triumph by the Massey-Harris Group from Canada, which,
as Massey-Ferguson in the United Kingdom, was keen to have its own
production capacity. Rootes, of course, was itself still involved in
acquisitions, with the Singer deal early in 1956. But while the Singer
acquisition did give much needed capacity, it was not reflected in an
increased market share for the company.

In the 1950s, a very significant increase in output occurred in
the U.K. car industry, production rising from about 0.5 million cars
in 1950 to 1.3 million in 1960 and 1.9 million in 1964. This was made
possible by the extensive expansion programs implemented in this period in both traditional manufacturing areas and new locations. It
was a period when the mass producers extended their market dominance and increased their share of the market at the expense of the
smaller specialist producers. Lee Francis and Jowett, in 1954, and
Armstrong-Siddeley, in 1960, were examples, and, although Singer
was a different type of company, it went under through the same pressures. For Rootes, while output grew, it was generally a period when
expansion and development were required simply to stand still. The
company both started and ended the period too small.

As Table 3.2 shows, Rootes continued to be at the smaller end
of the U.K. Big Five. The formation and consolidation of BMC and
the expansionism of Ford, particularly after the U.S. takeover of its
minority shareholders in the U.K. company in 1960, had made them
dominant market influences. Within its own league, Rootes lost
ground in both cars and commercial vehicles in the period.

It was the drive for production that motivated the use of the
government's "carrots" to direct new investment to the regions and
that also, particularly in the early 1950s, led to extensive backward
integration to ensure body supplies. The latter was expressed both
in Ford's purchase of Briggs Motor Bodies and in BMC's takeover
of Fisher and Ludlow in 1953. Rootes, almost continuously suffering
from financial strains, had to await Chrysler-sourced funds in 1965
before finally consolidating body supplies.

Finally, the period was one of sustained demand for cars in the
U.K. home market and abroad. In exports, however, the market emphasis changed significantly between 1955 and 1964, with a marked de-

TABLE 3.2

Production by U.K. Leading Firms, 1955-64
(percent)

	1955	1960	1961	1962	1963	1964
Cars						
BMC	39.0	36.5	38.5	37.5	38.5	37.0
Ford	26.5	30.0	32.5	29.5	31.5	28.5
Vauxhall	8.5	11.0	8.5	11.5	10.0	13.5
Rootes	11.5	10.5	9.5	11.5	10.5	12.0
Standard-Triumph	9.5	8.0	6.5	6.0	6.5	6.5
Other	5.0	4.0	4.5	3.5	3.0	3.0
Number of cars produced (000)	898	1,353	1,004	1,249	1,608	1,868
Commercial vehicles						
BMC	32.5	30.5	40.0	39.0	35.0	33.5
Ford	19.0	21.5	17.5	20.0	20.0	19.5
Vauxhall	19.0	23.0	20.5	17.5	21.0	22.5
Rootes	7.0	8.5	6.5	7.0	6.0	6.5
Standard-Triumph	3.0	3.0	1.0			
Leyland*	5.5	4.5	4.5	6.0	6.0	5.5
Land Rover	9.0	7.5	7.5	8.0	8.5	9.5
Other	4.5	1.0	2.0	2.5	3.5	3.0
Number of commercial vehicles produced (000)	341	458	460	425	404	465

*Leyland figures include Associated Commercial Vehicles, Ltd. (ACV), Scammell, and Albion.

Source: A. Silberston, "The Motor Industry 1955-64," Bulletin of Oxford University Institute of Economics and Statistics 27, no. 4 (1965), Table A10.

cline in dependence on the sterling area, as in the early 1950s, being offset by expansion in the United States and Europe. The European market accounted for 14 percent of total exports in 1955 but 36 percent in 1964, while exports to the United States rose as a percentage of the total from 9 to 17. At home, overall demand was consistently good, with minor peaks, for example, in 1955, 1960, and 1964. While attempting to expand as rapidly as possible to meet domestic demand, Rootes started this period with a particular emphasis on exports, expressed, for example, in Lord Rootes' dictum that the U.K. car industry's role was to provide the second car of the family, especially in the North American market. [24]

Production and Productivity

It is within this general background that Rootes must be assessed. Since the company started as a sales and service organization, there was perhaps a tendency from its foundation to emphasize variety and choice to a degree that was destructive of economies of scale.* While the excesses of the 1930s were soon corrected under the pressures for rationalization and efficiency in the postwar period, the philosophy ruling at the origins of the group is basic to understanding the subsequent history of the company, particularly since it was run in the style of a family business until Chrysler became involved. This was further complicated by the absence of a clear, long-term policy for the brand names in the 1959-64 period, the group apparently never being sure of which to develop or which to drop. Thus, in spite of very significant technical advances and automation,[26] Rootes never tried to become a one-product company to which its overall size pointed and where more optimal product costings would have been achieved.

The superficial position of comparability shown in Table 3.3 belies the fact that, for its size, Rootes was a diverse company even at the end of the rationalization between its component parts. A comparison of Tables 3.2 and 3.3 clearly indicates, for example, that, using the rough measure of car output per body type, Ford's performance was 56 percent greater than Rootes' in 1955 and 42 percent greater in 1964. By this type of comparison, Rootes emerges as a company conscious of the need to rationalize but caught with scale and diversity problems at a time when all the pressures from automation were on cost and price reduction.

---

*H. G. Castle[25] estimates that in the early stages of the Rootes Group, it manufactured 54 vehicle types, 22 engines, and 42 car body types.

Performance in the period was inevitably affected by some of the fundamental motor industry problems stemming from the cost structure of the industry. Clearly, at low production levels, heavy fixed costs prove punitive, but, as others have observed, a change in variable costs can be extremely serious, since at optimum output levels variable costs are much more important than fixed costs.[27] Estimates (for 1968) indicate that they could amount to 84 percent of total costs, with a very significant amount being purchased materials (between 40 and 70 percent of total variable costs).[28] Undoubtedly, the scale of the company and its lack of integration as a total car producer did not help Rootes in the period in question, and the company on several occasions was particularly badly hit by supplier strikes. It is interesting to note that the development of in-house supplying was one of the first production areas to be tackled by Chrysler after control in 1967.

The relative position of leading Rootes models in 1964 is shown in Table 3.4. The scale of the Rootes operation is clear from the output of the two main models, the Imp, emerging only in 1963 and being produced in a plant that in 1966 was still at 50 percent of capacity, and the Minx, after years of development and refinement as the basic model from which many Rootes derivatives stemmed, with a volume comparable to other models that were near the end of their production. In product terms, Chrysler inherited neither a model that was clearly established in a growth sector of the U.K. market nor one with extensive development potential. While it was too early in 1964 to judge the

TABLE 3.3

U.K. Big Five: Number of Car Bodies and Engines Produced,
1956 and 1965

	Bodies		Basic Engines	
	1956	1965	1956	1965
BMC	7	8	3	2
Ford	3	4	2	2
Standard-Triumph	2	2	2	2
Rootes	3	3	3	2
Vauxhall	1	3	1	2
Total	16	20	11	10

Source: A. Silbertson, "The Motor Industry 1955-64," Bulletin of Oxford University Institute of Economics and Statistics 27, no. 4 (1965), Table 5.4.

TABLE 3.4

U.K. Big Five: Model Concentration of Production, 1966

	Leading Model			Two Leading Models			Total Output (000s)
	Model	Production	Percent of Total	Model	Production	Percent of Total	
BMC	1100	209,335	34.6	1100	384,610	63.5	604
Ford	Cortina	342,371	52.1	Cortina and Anglia	353,834	76.0	466
Vauxhall	Viva	88,857	51.6	Viva and Victa	151,027	87.7	173
Rootes	Minx	104,473	61.2	Minx and Imp	151,727	88.9	172
Standard–Triumph	Herald	42,536	35.7	Herald and 2000	65,967	55.4	121

Source: J. M. Loiseau, "The British Motor Industry and Europe" (D.Phil. thesis, Oxford University, 1969), Table 38.

final sales volume performance of the Imp, it was already obvious that it was late (by three to five years) and was being produced in a plant that was having more than a few startup problems and that was likely to be at undercapacity for the following two or three years.

As Table 3.4 indicates, the Rootes product problem was not solely expressed in terms of the variety of cars produced but also in the fact that the sales of the two main models amounted to almost 90 percent of 1966 output, while, for example, comparable production figures for BMC accounted for just over 60 percent of its output. Even as late as 1966, Rootes was more reliant on one basic model than any other leading producer. Clearly, any company taking over Rootes required both products and production.

Table 3.5 provides a perspective on the production performance in 1965 and gives some limited impression of how Chrysler viewed productivity in Rootes. Although these figures should not be taken too literally in view of the many problems associated with different vehicle types and the range of activities included in each company, some conclusions can be drawn about the Rootes position. The low output per worker in Rootes reflected the absence of economies of scale and also

TABLE 3.5

Comparison in Leading U.S. and U.K. Manufacturers of Vehicles Produced per Employee, 1965

United Kingdom		United States	
Rootes	7.0	Chrysler	15.1
Vauxhall	10.1	General Motors	12.1
Ford	10.9	Ford	15.9
BMC	8.9		
Leyland	3.1		
Average for companies selected	8.3		13.5

Note: Includes tractors and different types of vehicles made by the different companies, hence exceptionally low figures for Leyland owing to a high proportion of heavy vehicle production. Figures are for 1965 or nearest year.

Source: Adapted from A. Silbertston, "International Comparison of Labour Productivity in the Automobile Industry, 1960-65," Bulletin of Oxford University Institute of Economics and Statistics 29 (1967), Table 10.

suggested that degrees of standardization were far from U.S. norms. While these facts are equally applicable to all U.K. companies at the time, the Rootes relative position is clear. Indeed, it was this type of measurement that underlay much of Chrysler's investment and product strategy after acquisition.

Although a detailed examination of labor relations is not within the scope of this chapter, no background to the financial performance of Rootes pre-1964, or for that matter of the U.K. motor industry as a whole in any time period, would be complete without some brief examination of strike activity. Table 3.6 provides a summary background of the situation in the 1962-65 period. The causes behind the problems in these years were varied and complex, with important differences among the companies. At Ford, for example, where time rate was the basic pay system, shift working was a common source of contention. At BMC, stoppages were largely attributable to disputes over piecework. At Rootes, many of the problems were associated with bonus payments and were to recur later in the Chrysler era. Table 3.6, by showing the recurrent problems at Pressed Steel, emphasizes an important part of Rootes' difficulties at this time. Indeed, in 1961, Rootes had a 13-week shutdown caused by a strike at one of Pressed Steel's London plants—a strike that had most serious consequences on short-term production and market share (see Table 3.2) and turned the 1960-61 profits into losses in the following year. The timing of this dispute was critical for Rootes in its drive to increase production to catch a buoyant U.K. market, and the consequences were a reflection of the company's dependence upon outside suppliers for main parts.

Table 3.7 shows the relative position of Rootes in terms of hours lost per unit of production. The general labor malaise of the industry in the period is indicated. Care, however, should be exercised in interpreting these figures, since the full significance of strike disruption is not reflected in the table. Furthermore, the fact that Rootes' record was better than those of some competitors has to be considered in the light of other performance variables. When viewed on the basis of financial performance of the company, the total impact of these lost hours is clear. While not having the most serious losses (see Table 3.7), they further eroded the diminishing margins Rootes was earning and exacerbated production logistics.

Financial Performance

This section examines the results of the interplay of the various performance criteria examined. The period 1950-64 straddles fundamental changes in the profitability of car production for the U.K. in-

TABLE 3.6

U.K. Motor Industry: Strike Record, January 1962–October 1965

Company		1962 Strikes	1962 Man-Hours-Lost	1963 Strikes	1963 Man-Hours Lost	1964 Strikes	1964 Man-Hours Lost	1965 (to October 31) Strikes	1965 (to October 31) Man-Hours Lost	Total Strikes	Total Man-Hours Lost
AEC	a	n.a.	187,550	nil	nil	nil	nil	nil	nil	nil	187,550
	b	nil	nil	nil	nil	nil	nil	nil	nil	nil	nil
	c		187,550	nil	nil	nil	nil	nil	nil	nil	187,550
BMC	a	263	2,943,232	302	1,684,643	387	1,942,727	340	5,003,573	1,292	11,574,175
	b	n.a.	78,056	n.a.	283,197	n.a.	223,130	11	984,664	11	1,569,047
	c	263	3,021,288	302	1,967,840	387	2,165,857	351	5,988,237	1,303	13,143,222
Ford	a	58	793,011	7	34,201	22	76,997	25	185,905	112	1,090,114
	b	nil	nil	nil	nil	nil	nil	nil	nil	nil	nil
	c	58	793,011	7	34,201	22	76,997	25	185,905	112	1,090,114
Jaguar	a	n.a.	n.a.	n.a.	n.a.	n.a.	53,026	4	15,375	4	69,401
	b						122,696	1	7,500	1	130,196
	c				n.a.		175,722	5	22,875	5	198,597
Pressed Steel	a	74	454,732	89	199,605	116	74,424	148	881,432	427	1,612,193
	b	15	121,247	30	198,369	59	252,188	57	452,803	161	1,024,607
	c	89	575,979	119	397,974	175	328,612	205	1,334,235	588	2,636,800
Rootes	a	41	223,003	58	45,933	79	88,963	96	85,567	274	443,466
	b	1	6,286	4	48,614	10	10,634	12	401,592	27	467,126
	c	42	229,289	62	94,547	89	99,597	108	487,159	301	910,592
Rover	a	33	246,178	45	140,861	92	282,975	126	412,327	296	1,082,341
	b	2	29,666	1	27,000	2	76,729	3	103,167	8	236,562
	c	35	275,844	46	167,861	94	359,704	129	515,494	304	1,318,903
Standard	a	n.a.	n.a.	n.a.	237,700	n.a.	199,500	107	1,267,921	107	1,750,121
	b				74,000		175,850	nil	nil	nil	249,850
	c				311,700		375,350	107	1,267,921	107	1,954,971
Vauxhall	a	1	17	4	5,202	24	nil	17	202,636	46	244,161
	b	nil	nil	nil	nil	nil	36,306	nil	nil	nil	nil
	c	1	17	4	5,202	24	36,306	17	202,636	46	244,161
Total	a	470	4,847,723	505	2,348,145	720	2,756,918	863	8,054,736	2,558	18,007,522
	b	18	235,255	35	631,180	71	861,227	84	1,949,726	208	3,677,388
	c	488	5,082,978	540	2,979,325	791	3,618,145	947	10,004,462	2,766	21,684,910

Note: a = strikes within the company; b = effect of strikes outside the company; c = total of a and b; n.a. = data not available.

Source: Royal Commission on Trade Unions and Employers' Associations, Minutes of Evidence no. 13 (London: HMSO, 1966), Appendix A.

94

TABLE 3.7

U.K. Motor Industry: Man-Hours Lost per Unit of Production,
1962–64

	1962		1963		1964	
	a	b	a	b	a	b
Rootes	1.3	1.3	0.2	0.5	0.3	0.4
Ford	1.7	1.7	0.06	0.06	0.13	0.13
Vauxhall	0	0	0.02	0.02	0.1	0.1
BMC	4.7	4.8	2.2	2.6	2.3	2.6

Note: Includes cars and commercial vehicles. a = strikes
within the company; b = items in a plus effects of strikes outside the
company.

Sources: Royal Commission on Trade Unions and Employers'
Associations, Minutes of Evidence no. 13 (London: HMSO, 1966),
Appendix 4; and Society of Motor Manufacturers and Traders, The
Motor Industry of Great Britain, various issues.

dustry in general. In the early 1950s, profits per unit of output were
continuing to rise and, in general, rise faster than profits measured
relative to turnover. It has been estimated that until 1953, while the
gross profits per vehicle were rising in absolute terms (by up to 70
percent), the rise in production costs eroded gross margins considerably.[29] In consequence, the trading profits on turnover of the largest car producers fell progressively from 1950 until 1955. For many
companies this was a period of changing product mix, with sales of
small cars falling considerably in the late 1940s, then rising, and only
reaching the 1947 level in 1955. It may be that the rise in costs would
have been steeper had the market not moved toward smaller cars.
The upward pressures on costs at this time were being offset by dramatic volume increases (52 percent increase between 1950 and 1955)
and the resultant scale economies. There was, however, no way of
offsetting fully the underlying trend.

For Rootes, this was particularly serious, and already by 1952
(by the measure of net profits to net tangible assets), the rate of return on capital had turned from its upward trend. Profitability in the
car industry is notoriously variable at any time, largely owing to the
dramatic profit falls that can follow fairly minor drops in capacity
utilization. No company needed Rootes' particular structural and historic problems in addition to the normal concerns of the industry. In

the period to 1955, Rootes' rates of return on capital were already
beginning to drop more severely than those of its competitors. From
a peak of 40 percent, it gradually declined to 30 percent by 1954 and
20 percent in 1955. This set up the origins of Rootes' vicious circle
of industrial deprivation in the early 1960s. Low sales, low returns,
and low investment were the first ingredients in the Rootes-Chrysler
mix; time was to add products, distribution, and labor to complete the
circle.

In spite of this, Rootes was not a highly geared company in the
mid-1950s and although it had gone to the market for long-term capital
in 1949 and 1954, it was not particularly unique in this. In 1954-56,
all the major producers (except Morris and Ford) had gone through the
same process. Another indicator of the relative position of Rootes in
the mid-1960s is given by G. Maxcy and A. Silberston in their study
of changes in net asset value up to 1956.[30] Again, Rootes does not
come out unfavorably, with an increase in net assets ranking third in
the major producers (behind Standard and Ford) over the period 1947-
56. At this time Rootes could have been expected to be in a good position, having consolidated its earlier acquisitions, benefited from the
postwar excess demand, and, above all, its Singer properties. In
general, at this time, although rates of return were declining, the
industry was to fund most of its growth through retentions of (albeit
decreasing) profits and raising capital in the market.

From the late 1950s onward, the U.K. industry was beginning
to show signs of moving from being a marginal loss maker to a marginal profit maker, with few exceptions (notably Ford). While Rootes
was farther advanced in the process of decline and in the stage of serious profit erosion, others (as Tables 3.8 and 3.9 show) were not in
recurring loss. However, by 1960, many were experiencing reduced
rates of return that were becoming more serious in the new situation
of the 1960s. The exceptional character of the Rootes problem, measured by any criteria, is obvious from these tables. There were, as
always, individual explanations underlying particular figures. The
plunge from the 1960 record level of profits was attributable to the
very serious strike in 1961, and was not helped by the general industry
trends in the 1962 recession. By this stage, on a knife-edge Rootes'
powers of recovery had been weakened seriously. This limited normal commercial alternatives in other areas of Rootes activity, for
example, in the price competition of the early 1960s. In these circumstances, minor price variations made the company more vulnerable
to any abnormality in labor supply, consumer credit, or supply limitations. These, within a context of the heyday of stop-go macroeconomic policies in the United Kingdom, created a vacuum when Rootes
needed an oxygen tent.

TABLE 3.8

U.K. Motor Industry: Rates of Return on Capital, 1954-63

	1954	1955	1956	1957	1958	1959	1960	1961	1962	1963
BMC	32	29	17	11	26	20	28	11	4	15
Ford	44	25	13	24	25	28	24	15	11	21
Vauxhall	43	28	14	-2	4	23	22	12	16	16
Rootes	23	17	9	-2	10	17	14	4	-8	1
Standard-										
Triumph	23	24	5	6	13	18	9	—	—	—
Leyland	16	19	22	17	15	15	24	12	7	15
Average	34	26	14	12	19	22	23	12	8	16

Note: Net profits (pretax) as percent of net assets.

Source: A. Silberston, "The Motor Industry 1955-64," Bulletin of Oxford University Institute of Economics and Statistics 27, no. 4 (1965), Table 6.6.

Moving to the last few years of pre-Chrysler investment in the United Kingdom, the industry was showing some of the effects of variations in profits and both variation and decline in returns on capital. As is common in an industry with long-term structural problems, increased reliance was placed on depreciation provision to provide cash flow in a time of falling net earnings.[31] This was undertaken in the hope that the competitive 1960s, when it was more difficult to pass on cost rises as price increases, would give way to a more stable environment. Neither was there any short-term possibility for Rootes of improving sales volume in exports. The contrary, in fact, happened since, as company accounts show, the percentage of unit sales exported fell from 45 in 1960 to an average of 32 between 1961 and 1964 —this at a time when Ford was averaging 47 percent and falling, Vauxhall 50 percent and falling, and BMC 36 percent and rising. Although, as has been seen, Rootes was early and aggressive in exporting post-World War II, this advantage had long passed by 1964 as the company faced the need to extend both distribution and assembly abroad on negligible aggregate earnings.

INITIAL ACTION AFTER 1967

While certain changes occurred in the Rootes organization at Chrysler instigation after 1964, these were necessarily limited in ac-

TABLE 3.9

U.K. Motor Industry: Pretax Profits
(millions of pounds)

	1958	1959	1960	1961	1962	1963	1964	1965	1966	1967
Rootes	3.4	3.9	4.4	2.9	-0.89	-0.25	1.8	-0.2	-3.1	-10.5
BMC	21.0	15.7	26.9	10.1	4.2	15.4	21.8	23.3	21.8	-3.28*
Ley-land	6.4	5.3	9.2	6.9	5.5	11.0	18.2	20.5	16.4	18.0
Ford	24.7	32.2	33.7	22.2	17.0	35.0	24.0	8.9	7.4	25.4
Vaux-hall	1.1	13.5	14.1	14.5	16.0	16.3	17.9	17.7	13.7	12.0

*British Motor Holdings.

Source: Company accounts.

cord with their shareholding at the time. It was, therefore, after 1967 when the major reorganization took place in Rootes. The objectives of the brief summary of initial changes in this section and those in the marketing area incorporated in Chapter 4 are to assess the way in which Chrysler perceived the major problems it had inherited from Rootes. This is not to imply that Chrysler was not constrained after 1967, since there were obviously corporation and government influences on its priorities and methods of achieving them. The situation, however, was much clearer and the circumstances of the takeover gave Chrysler a stronger hand politically.

Structure and Personnel

Changes in structure and top personnel came early. The 26 U.K. subsidiary companies belonging to Rootes, many being used as product names, were consolidated into two: Rootes Motors and Rootes Motors Scotland. As part of the reorganization of production logistics, three London-based plants (Acton, Kew, and Cricklewood) were closed in 1967, while, abroad, the Australian and South African plants were sold to Chrysler (for £5.5 million) as were subsequently some European activities (in Switzerland and Portugal) and the Venezuelan organization. There were also conscious attempts to try to accelerate interplant contact and begin to absorb Rootes into the complex. There is some evidence, however, that this never was pursued with particular vigor or went very far.

As part of the standardization, Chrysler rapidly introduced its own reporting methods, reinforced by a Chrysler financial comptroller being appointed at each plant. There was also an extensive recruitment of middle managers, many coming from Ford U.K.'s plants. As anticipated, some key senior executives were appointed, with Chrysler nominating five of the eleven members of the main board. Half of the old Rootes board, including all members of the family, with the exception of Lord Rootes, resigned. Control was effectively and quickly vested in an administrative committee, meeting monthly, with only two Rootes directors as members. This committee was empowered to make almost all decisions (excluding matters such as dividend policy and major capital projects) within the parameters set by Detroit. It is difficult to interpret the initial Chrysler action in personnel and organization in any way other than that, having had the opportunity to assess the situation from 1964, Chrysler considered the Rootes management deficient in many ways. At the same time, it has to be accepted that any similar corporation in acquiring a weak company would have acted with the same speed to impose its own style and controls, whatever it thought of the management. All things considered, Chrysler was widely regarded as having been severe and uncompromising in its management changes.

Plant Facilities and Investment

In common with most of the U.K. industry, Rootes plants were concentrated in the Midlands and southeast of England. The company thus was represented in both of the major manufacturing cluster areas, Birmingham-Coventry and Northwest London, although it was not always clear that maximum agglomeration economies were guaranteed by the locational pattern of Rootes, whose supply lines were longer than those of other U.K. manufacturers. This was in part derived from the jigsaw means by which the group had been put together over time from the remnants of decaying companies. This pattern was not made more rational by the Linwood expansion under the political pressures placed on all major manufacturers between 1960 and 1963.

Within a relatively short period, Chrysler had committed upward of £25 million in major reinvestment for each of the Linwood and Coventry plants. At Ryton (Coventry) three separate assembly lines that had been geared for three different vehicle types were replaced by a single track. In the Stoke plant, the main manufacturing facilities were tight for space and subsequently were extensively redeveloped to produce the power train for the new Avenger introduced in 1970. In addition to adding a paint shop and body-building shop at Ryton, major facility rescheduling was planned. This included, for example,

rationalizing the relationship between Linwood and the other plants
by transferring all Arrow production to a redeveloped Linwood, which
would then supply Ryton with body stampings for the Avenger. Linwood,
in 1966 operating at one-third capacity on a mixture of Imps (ten variants), Hunters, and Vogues, when it had been constructed with the Imp
in mind, was one of the obvious high loss areas requiring urgent rationalization. While the changes were less dramatic in the other
plants, they did include, for example, modifications in the commercial
vehicle production at Dunstable into a two-track system (one for up to
7-ton commercial vehicles, the other for the heavier Commers and
Dodges).

The capital program was directed toward rationalization, "in-
sourcing," new model introduction, and, above all, volume. In the
latter, the clearly defined target[32] was a theoretical capacity of
300,000 cars annually (divided approximately evenly between Coventry
and Linwood) and 40,000 commercial vehicles in addition. G. Foster
emphasized the extent of the volume problem, noting that in fiscal
year 1967/68 only 216,000 units were produced, including 26,000
commercial vehicles.[33] While it is difficult to make completely accurate unit comparisons, this suggests that output had not markedly
increased from that of the early 1960s before Linwood was operational.
Chrysler's capital program essentially assumed volume to reduce unit
costs and flexibility to enable product mix to alter with market variations.

Figure 3.1 shows the functions of the reorganized plants in 1974,
after over six years of restructuring and investment.

In spite of reorganization, Chrysler was still influenced by the
immobility of the plants inherited from Rootes and by having three
centers. While minor closures, such as in North London, were possible, the company was in no position, financially or politically, to concentrate production in one central area. Thus, rationalization could
not finally resolve fundamental locational disadvantage, an issue
that will be discussed in the context of the impact of regional policy
on Chrysler U.K.'s operations.

While labor relations are the concern of another chapter, it is
important to note that within the implementation period for this capital
program, Chrysler was expressing concern over the future. In March
1969, a spokesman in Geneva was indicating that labor troubles at
Coventry and Linwood could jeopardize the long-term investment program and that there was a "certain nervousness" in the United States
about the British labor situation.[34]

FIGURE 3.1

Chrysler U.K. Plant Locations and Employment, 1974

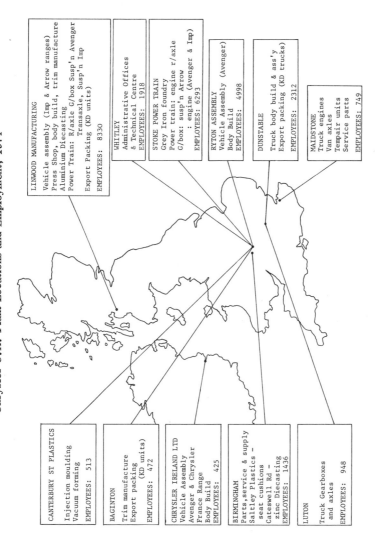

LINWOOD MANUFACTURING

Vehicle assembly (Imp & Arrow ranges)
Press Shop, body build, trim manufacture
Aluminium Diecasting
Power Train: R/axle G/box Susp'n Avenger
                      Transaxle, Susp'n Imp
Export Packing (KD units)
EMPLOYEES: 8330

WHITLEY
Administrative Offices
& Technical Centre
EMPLOYEES: 1918

STOKE POWER TRAIN
Grey Iron foundry
Power train: engine r/axle
G/box: susp'n Arrow
          : engine (Avenger & Imp)
EMPLOYEES: 6293

RYTON ASSEMBLY
Vehicle Assembly (Avenger)
Body Build
EMPLOYEES: 4998

DUNSTABLE
Truck body build & ass'y
Export packing (KD trucks)
EMPLOYEES: 2312

MAIDSTONE
Truck engines
Van axles
Tempair units
Service parts
EMPLOYEES: 749

CANTERBURY ST PLASTICS
Injection moulding
Vacuum forming
EMPLOYEES: 513

BAGINTON
Trim manufacture
Export packing
          (KD units)
EMPLOYEES: 472

CHRYSLER IRELAND LTD
Vehicle Assembly
Avenger & Chrysler
France Range
Body Build
EMPLOYEES: 425

BIRMINGHAM
Parts,service & supply
Saltley Plastics –
    seat cushions
Cateswell Rd –
    zinc Diecasting
EMPLOYEES: 1436

LUTON
Truck Gearboxes
    and axles
EMPLOYEES: 948

Source: Fourteenth Report from the Expenditure Committee, session 1974–75, The Motor Vehicle Industry, HC617 (I) (London: HMSO, August 1975), p. 192.

APPENDIX: CONDITIONS GOVERNING 1967
CHRYSLER-ROOTES AGREEMENT

Letter from Mr. I. J. Minett, Chrysler Corporation, to the Rt.
Hon. Anthony Wedgwood Benn, M.P.

Dear Minister,

We refer to your letter of 16th January 1967 in connection with
Rootes Motors Lts. (Rootes) and confirm our Undertakings as follows:—

(i)   Chrysler will not initiate any action to impair either the
       home or overseas operations or the management and direc-
       tion of Rootes as a British Company in its relations with
       the Government, labor, its British shareholders, and the
       public.

(ii)   Chrysler undertakes to maintain a majority of British direc-
       tors on the Board of Rootes.

(iii) Chrysler confirms the plans of expansion covering develop-
       ment work at various factories and especially at Linwood
       in Scotland where the major development will take place
       and where it is planned to increase employment by several
       thousands; these plans are essential if Rootes is to remain
       competitive, achieve its proper share of exports and return
       to reasonable profitability.

(iv)   Chrysler plans to achieve a progressive increase in the ex-
       port of Rootes products without restriction to all practicable
       markets and to continue to make available its full interna-
       tional organization for this purpose. They note that, in the
       view of Her Majesty's Government, the test of the fulfill-
       ment of this undertaking would be that the export percentage
       of the products of the Rootes Group should be at least as
       high as the average for the British Motor Vehicle Industry
       as a whole.

(v)   Chrysler will nominate a Rootes Director (British) to each
       of the Boards of Simca S.A. and Chrysler International
       S.A.; and it is understood that a Simca Director (French)
       will be nominated to the Board of Rootes.

(vi)   Chrysler confirms its intention to leave at least 15 percent
       of the entire equity capital (Ordinary, "A" Ordinary and
       Preferred Ordinary) in the hands of shareholders other than
       Chrysler, provided that in calculating this 15 percent Chrys-
       ler may take into account any shares held by the Industrial
       Reorganisation Corporation (IRC) or put by IRC to Chrysler
       (in accordance with Undertaking (vii) below).

(vii)   Provided that Chrysler acquires Preferred Ordinary Shares
in excess of its rights entitlement of £6,263,686 nominal,
it will make available to IRC at par up to £1,512,228 nominal of such excess, i.e., up to 15 percent of the total Preferred Ordinary Shares, of £10,081,519 on condition that
IRC participate to the same percentage in Chrysler's undertaking to subscribe up to £10,000,000 Unsecured Loan
Stock. IRC will have the right on 1st January, 1972 to put
these securities to Chrysler at par plus any accrued but un-
paid dividend or interest.

(viii)   IRC will have the right to nominate one Director on Rootes
Board as long as it owns all the securities mentioned in
Undertaking (vii) above.

We agree that these Undertakings may be made public.

Yours faithfully,

IRVING J. MINETT,

for Chrysler Corporation.

16 January 1967.

Source: Fourteenth Report from the Expenditure Committee,
Session 1975-76, The Motor Vehicle Industry HC 617 (I) (London:
HMSO, August 1975), pp. 223, 224.

NOTES

1. G. Maxcy, in P. I. Cook, Effects of Mergers, Sect. 5 on
the Motor Industry (London: Allen & Unwin, 1957), p. 374.
2. L. Rostas, Comparative Productivity in British and American Industry, National Institute of Economic and Social Research
(NIESR), Occasional Papers 13 (Cambridge, England, 1948), p. 17.
3. The Economist, April 16, 1938.
4. The Rootes Group, A Survey of a Great Enterprise (mimeo.,
1961). Obtained from London: Business Archives Council.
5. Estimates made by G. Wansbrough, "Automobiles: The
Mass Market," Lloyds Bank Review, October 1955.
6. H. G. Castle, Britain's Motor Industry (London: Clerke
and Cocheran, 1950), p. 218.
7. The Rootes Group, The Singer Story (mimeo., 1956). Obtained from London: Business Archives Council.

8. Financial Times, May 26, 1964.

9. Ibid., June 6, 1964.

10. Richard Crossman asked the chancellor if he were satisfied that the export franchise of the company would be retained since this had not always happened in similar cases. In reply, Maudling cited both Ford and Vauxhall as evidence of the use of the U.K. as an export base. Weekly Hansard, House of Commons, Parliamentary Debates (London: HMSO, p. 42.

11. An issue developed by D. F. Chandler, noting at the time (post-1970) when Japanese and German manufacturers enjoyed a boom in car exports (especially to the United States) British exports from Vauxhall to the United States were stopped completely and neither Chrysler nor Ford had sold many British small cars in the United States. He concludes that the maximization of their own advantage as practiced by the U.S. car companies did not appear promising for the long-term development of the British industry. D. F. Chandler, The Strategy and Structure of British Enterprise (London: Macmillan, 1973), p. 109.

12. Financial Times, June 6, 1964.

13. Ibid., June 8, 1964.

14. Weekly Hansard, House of Commons Parliamentary Debate, no. 696 (London: HMSO, 1963-64), p. 38.

15. Financial Times, July 30, 1964.

16. Weekly Hansard, House of Commons Parliamentary Debates, no. 696, p. 36.

17. "The Cost of Keeping Rootes British," Statist, June 18, 1965.

18. Times (London), January 18, 1967.

19. Weekly Hansard, House of Commons Parliamentary Debates, no. 739 (London: HMSO, 1966-67), p. 39.

20. Ibid., p. 43, reply to Michael Foot.

21. Weekly Hansard, House of Commons Parliamentary Debates, no. 739, p. 38.

22. Industrial Reorganisation Corporation, First Report and Accounts, H.C. 252 (May 1968), p. 9.

23. G. Turner, Leyland Papers (London: Eyre and Spottiswoode, 1971).

24. "Motor Industry; Export Achievements," The Statist, October 30, 1948, p. 3.

25. Castle, Britain's Motor Industry, p. 170.

26. See, for example, E. Woodbridge, "The U.K. Motor Vehicle Industry," Institute of Petroleum Review, February 1959.

27. G. Maxcy and A. Silberston, The Motor Industry (London: Allen & Unwin, 1959), p. 65.

28. D. G. Rhys, The Motor Industry: An Economic Survey (London: Butterworth, 1972), p. 277.

29. Maxcy and Silberston, The Motor Industry, p. 167.

30. Ibid., p. 178.

31. National Economic Development Office NEDO, Motor Industry Statistics, 1959-68 (London: HMSO, 1969).

32. G. Foster, "Rough Road for Rootes," Management Today, July 1969, p. 93.

33. Ibid., p. 93.

34. Joint Union Delegation of Shop Stewards and Staff Representatives, Chrysler's Crisis: The Workers Answer (mimeo., 1975). This was a submission to the U.K. government by Chrysler shop-stewards at the time of the company's difficulties in 1975.

4

THE MARKETING POLICY OF CHRYSLER U.K.

As with most other aspects of policy, Chrysler's desired marketing policy was inevitably severely constrained by the products being marketed at the time of the takeover, the model names used, and so on. The takeover of a loss-making firm had a further constraining effect in this regard. Thus, any independent marketing policy required new models, which, in turn, assumed an ability to generate the cash flow to invest in such new products or, alternatively, required a substantial capital inflow from the Chrysler Corporation. While these points have already been raised, they are of crucial importance in the motor industry given the long lead time and heavy investment requirements for new products. It is within this context that Chrysler's marketing policy is examined.

PRODUCT POLICY

In the car market, product strategy encompasses a wide area and includes such aspects as the product range, model names, styling, model and style change, performance, quality and reliability, range of accessories, warranty plans, and so on.

Manufacturer/Model Names

A successful model name can be of immense value to a manufacturer, representing as it does an accumulated store of customer goodwill that can be exploited profitably. The name in this sense may be that of the manufacturer or it may be a model name. In Chrysler's case, arguably some of the most important but unquantifiable advan-

tages it acquired on buying into the U.K. market were manufacturer
and model names. When taking over Rootes, Chrysler, from a marketing viewpoint, was acquiring not only the Rootes name itself but
also the Hillman, Humber, Sunbeam, and Singer names—companies
bought by Rootes between 1932 and 1956. Each of these companies
had a distinct tradition and a particular brand characteristic within
the U.K. market, which had been developed further within the Rootes
marketing philosophy. At the same time, model names, such as the
Minx, Snipe, Hawk, and Rapier, all conjured up their particular product associations.

Space does not permit a lengthy discussion of the ways in which
Rootes utilized these manufacturer and model names in its marketing
strategy, but some basic principles are necessary in order to assess
the subsequent policies of Chrysler. Essentially, the Hillman name
occupied the central position in the Rootes strategy. Cars sold under
this name were intended for the mass market and were associated with
conventional mechanics and style leadership. The Humber name was
essentially used by Rootes to market large, durable quality cars, such
as the Snipe and Hawk, although a serious attempt was made to develop
the quality image in the medium range car market with the Humber
Sceptre in 1964. Sunbeam, on the other hand, was viewed by Rootes
as a brand name with a sports association, and seems to have been
used to try to preserve margins in the performance sector of the market. Singer Motors was the most recent of the Rootes acquisitions
(1956). The inherited Singer name was least valuable from a marketing viewpoint, but by using the name for deluxe versions of basic
Hillman models, Rootes again was trying to develop a quality association with the name. It was aimed to reinforce this through separate
model names (and thus the Singer Gazelle was merely the deluxe derivative of the Hillman Minx) but also through separate dealer networks. Apart from these names, Chrysler also inherited the Rootes
name itself, which the company had used quite openly to support the
other brands in the group.

As can be seen from Figure 4.1, most of these traditional names
have been maintained, at least in principle. It is probably fair to say
that the earlier connotations associated with the names have largely
disappeared, although this may be primarily a function of the elimination of many models in the range. The phasing out of the big Humbers
in 1967, for example, was a reflection of a market trend away from
larger cars. By 1968, the only car in the Chrysler range with the
Humber brand was the 1.7-liter Sceptre, by then a prestige version of
the Hillman Hunter. There is little question that by this action Chrysler was removing a potential source of development up-market in the
United Kingdom that could have been used to aid product differentiation.
While the Humber brand name was not associated with volume business

and was unprofitable as it stood, the association of the quality image could have proved valuable support for the characterless Chrysler 180.

Undoubtedly, Chrysler's aim is to eliminate the traditional names associated with Rootes, but to date, at least, the company seems to be content to do this as new models are introduced on to the market. The Simca 1307, for example, was introduced to the U.K. market at the very end of 1975 as the Chrysler Alpine. The Rootes policy of over-lapping, if not directly competing, names and models could be criticized first, because it confused customers, second, because it increased the stock requirements of dealers, and third, because it was uneconomi-cal in terms of marketing effort. Some rationalization therefore was necessary and inevitable. Whether the building of a distinct Chrysler name and image represents either a more efficient or more effective strategy is a moot point.

Product Range

In establishing a product range, a company with aspirations as a mass market producer would wish to cover a number of market seg-ments, while aiming at strongest representation in the fastest growing sectors. The limitation on such a policy obviously is the need to secure adequate volume so as to minimize production costs and thereby permit the firm to price competitively. An inability of a company to secure adequate market penetration would then require it to pursue an alternative marketing strategy, which, via product differentiation, avoided direct competition in the mass market and allowed higher prices to be charged.[1]

Rootes policy, at least until 1963, was closest to the latter. The company's range focused on the market for medium-sized cars, and tried to exploit this to its maximum through name, performance, and design variations on the Hillman Minx. The Humber cars provided an additional niche in the up-market segment, while the two and a half seater Sunbeam Alpine provided representation in the sports market. The most radical change in this product range came in 1963, when the Imp was launched to compete in the small car market with the Leyland Mini. This was a considerable gamble, not only because Rootes was attack-ing the strongly established Mini, launched in 1959, but also because by launching an unashamedly mass market car the company was gam-bling that its quality image would be unimpaired. As of 1966, the com-pany's product range appeared as in Figure 4.1, of which cars in the Minx range accounted for 61 percent of output and the Imp an additional 28 percent.[2] The Hillman Hunter was launched in 1966 in an attempt to rejuvenate Rootes' central range. The Humber took over the cru-

FIGURE 4.1

Major Model Changes for Rootes and Chrysler

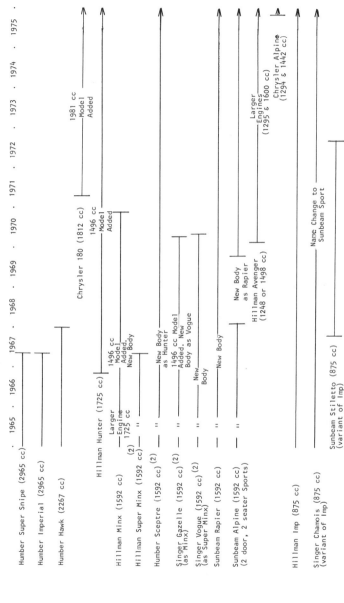

[1]Essentially, a body design similar to that of the Minx, until the launch of the Hunter. Thereafter, body design was based on the Hunter.

Source: Parker's Car Price Guide (London: Parker's Price Guides Ltd.), various issues.

109

cial role in the Rootes range previously occupied by the Minx and the
body shells of the remainder of the family were subsequently replaced
accordingly. Eventually, under Chrysler, the family name became
the Arrow range.

By the date of the Chrysler takeover, the Rootes range had become very disjointed, possibly as a result of pressures for limited
standardization in some cases. By giving the Minx-Hunter family
larger 1.7-liter engines in 1965, the company had moved slightly out
of the fastest growing medium car segment, while in the luxury class,
the products were in need of replacement. Finally, in the mini class,
Imp sales never achieved their targets.

The decisions taken during 1967 to offer smaller 1,500 cc engines for the Minx and Gazelle and to cease production of all the Humber cars except the Sceptre were presumably ongoing, but the impact
of the Humber decision in particular, without a replacement in sight,
was to reduce the breadth of the range quite considerably. This, together with the gaping void in the sector between 1 and 1.5 liters in
which the bulk of the British sedan car sales were made, posed enormous problems for Chrysler: "All Rootes had to offer here was a
hole in its range."[3]

The Avenger concept had been initiated and developed from 1964
onward under Rootes management, and the vehicle was launched as
the first completely new car from Chrysler early in 1970. It was conceived as a bread-and-butter car and was aimed directly at the market
in which all of the other three major U.K. manufacturers already had
representation—Ford with the Escort, Leyland with the 1100/1300
series, and Vauxhall with the Viva. To avoid head-on confrontation
with the other models, the Avenger was available initially in four-door
form only and the size was slightly bigger than that of the competition.
Even so, the degree of product differentiation between the models was
small, and became smaller when Leyland launched the Triumph Toledo
in August 1970 and the Marina in the spring of 1971. Body designs of
the competing models were so similar that Autocar remarked caustically
that all "were as alike as packets of detergent."[4]

Apart from the Avenger, the only two completely new cars to be
introduced to the U.K. market were both built in France: the Chrysler
180/2 liter and the Chrysler Alpine (although the Alpine is being assembled in Britain from 1976). After the demise of the large Humber cars
in 1967, Chrysler for three years had no bigger car to sell than the
top end of the Hunter range, an undoubted sore point with dealers since
it eliminated the possibilities of trading up. It was to fill this gap that
the Chrysler U.K. design office started development on the first of the
so-called "C" cars, following on the "B" car Avenger. With what appeared to be some rationalization of Chrysler's European activities,
the U.K.-designed engine was dropped and the chassis transferred to

Chrysler France where the car was built incorporating a new French-designed engine. The newest car in the Chrysler range, the Alpine, only really became available in the United Kingdom at the start of 1976. This car was designed in England and is available with 1,300 and 1,500 cc engines.

The full range of Chrysler U.K. and Chrysler France cars on sale in the United Kingdom at the beginning of 1976 and the ranges of the three leading U.K. manufacturers and chief importers are shown in Figure 4.2. The extremely restricted line of cars actually manufactured by Chrysler in the United Kingdom is immediately apparent. Of these, the Imp has been produced without major body or engine changes for 14 years; the Hunter (Arrow range) for ten years, with the only major change being the addition of a smaller engine version in 1970; and the Avenger for 6 years. The multinational nature of Chrysler, however, invalidates this superficial condemnation of the product range. For companies the size of Chrysler in France and the United Kingdom, both too small to match such European giants as Ford individually, a rationalization of the product lines to maximize production runs would be necessary. By inspecting the whole product range, including the French-produced cars, the range looks much less dangerously restricted, although the criticism of the U.K.-manufactured cars in terms of their antiquity still applies.

A number of other problems are also apparent. In the first place, neither Chrysler nor, for that matter, any of the U.K. manufacturers is represented within what may be termed the second-generation minicar segment (typified by the Renault 5 as better equipped and much roomier versions of the original mini concept). Between 1973 and 1975, as a result of the fuel crisis, this segment of the market had grown from 11.5 percent to 16 percent of the total following a long period of decline.[5] In fairness to Chrysler, the oil crisis could hardly have been forecast, but the development of a replacement for the Imp might have been logical. It was reported that there were plans for a new front wheel drive Imp at one stage, but that Chrysler dropped these, reflecting partly at least the U.S. view of the car.[6] One American at Rootes is quoted as saying that it was a "damned poorly designed automobile" and, most importantly, "it was not designed by people with high volume production at the back of their heads."[7]

Finally, Chrysler seems to have withdrawn completely from the very top end of the market and has not even tried, as other manufacturers such as Ford have done, to stretch existing models to cover this segment. In view of the potential margin contribution, this seems unfortunate, and, when considered with the lack of success of the Chrysler 180, is even more disturbing.

It is self-evident that the establishment and development of a product range require money, and Chrysler's problem in this regard

FIGURE 4.2

Manufacturers' Product Ranges

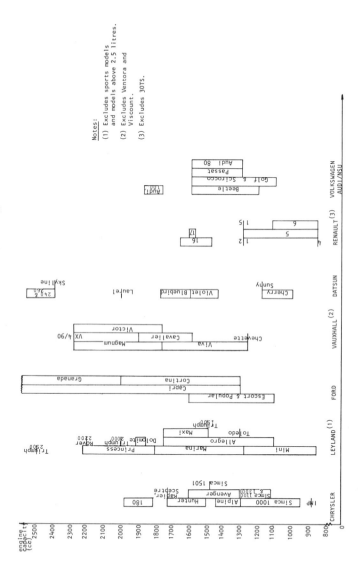

Source: Parker's Car Price Guide (London: Parker's Price Guides Ltd.), various issues.

was mentioned at the start of the section. The fact, therefore, that models have not been launched to produce a viable and integrated range is not of itself an adequate basis for condemning Chrysler policy in this area. Consideration needs to be given first to the extent to which design and development work has been proceeding in those market segments where deficiencies are apparent. This is considered in the Appendix.

At this stage, the only point that needs to be mentioned is the relationship of company policy to its product range. Clearly, the important inference is that Chrysler views its European subsidiaries as mass market producers with adequate representation in the various market segments. This is highly relevant to the argument that will be considered later in the production context that the company is too small ever to become a successful volume producer. Conversely, the possibilities of developing via differentiated products, building perhaps on Rootes' quality brand names, apparently were never contemplated.

Other Aspects of Product Policy

The policy of all manufacturers has been fairly similar with respect to their intramodel ranges, except perhaps in the extent to which certain accessories are standard. As an example, excluding accessories, the Avenger is available in 29 versions, derived from only two different body shells and two basically different engines, with prices at the end of 1975 ranging from £1,558 to £2,329. Chrysler departed from tradition on the launch of the Avenger since only a four-door version was available initially, unlike the models of its competitors. The two-door Avenger was only added three years later, which was somewhat surprising since its addition was estimated to increase total Avenger sales by between a quarter and a third.

Alone of the manufacturers in Britain, Chrysler has gone in for product competition through "limited editions." The Imp Caledonian, Avenger Tiger, Avenger Top Hat Special, and Hunter Topaz are examples of limited edition versions. Basically, such models provide a wide range of accessories plus greater individualization of trim than on standard models at budget prices. At the end of 1975, Chrysler, in its advertising for the Caledonian and Topaz versions, was claiming savings of over £166 and £230, respectively, on recommended retail prices. Effectively, such a plan is the equivalent of short-term price cutting, but, by maintaining unchanged list prices, the belief is that the risks of retaliatory action by competitors are reduced.

The year 1975 saw the reemergence of other forms of product competition in the U.K. car industry, with Chrysler leading the way with longer and less limited warranty plans. Warranty plans varied in the industry, but a 12-month or 12,000-mile guarantee was fairly usual. Toward the end of 1975, Chrysler extended its guarantee to unlimited mileage, with the additional guarantee of the replacement of selected worn-out (as opposed to defective) parts. Additionally, for the Imp, Chrysler offered free service for one year. Leyland replied a week later with its Supercover plan and the other U.K. manufacturers are presently offering unlimited mileage guarantees.

As with the limited editions that appeared during 1975, Chrysler's Protector plan was again a policy of trying to improve short-term competitiveness as well as to maintain customer confidence in Chrysler cars. Chrysler had extended the warranty period once before, but only continued with the plan for a year or so. It seems unlikely that the present move is again anything other than a short-term expedient, particularly given the costs that such plans can incur.* There is also a considerable potential for disputes that exist with high-mileage fleet users. Additionally, the positive effects of the move have also been reduced or eliminated by the responses of other manufacturers.

PRICING

There are essentially two aspects to pricing policy in the car industry: the question of how and the level at which prices are set, a long-run pricing problem; and the more short-run question of how prices change.

Short-Run Price Competition

Price variation, as a short-run marketing strategy, has not been used frequently in the U.K. car industry. In the majority of cases where price adjustments do occur, it is usually in response to changes in input prices that affect all producers.

During the 1960s there were some examples of aggressive price cutting. The Rootes group cut the price of the Hillman Minx by £41 in August 1961 on a basic price of £539, with smaller reductions on

*It has been suggested by dealers that warranty costs on Chrysler cars might amount to as much as £50 per vehicle. While there is no way of testing this, a CPRS report quoted an "illustrative" warranty cost for U.K. manufacturers of £35 per vehicle, which it suggested is on average 30 percent above Continental levels.[8]

some other models in the Hillman and Singer ranges. The aim was
to raise sales and market share profitably by increasing capacity
utilization from the then level of around 50 percent. Although the company was profitable in 1960/61 but made losses the following financial
year, this cannot be directly associated with the impact of the price-
cutting strategy, since the company was also hit by a disastrous three-
month strike during 1961. A second example of price cutting occurred
in 1964 when Ford reduced the price of the Anglia by £30, passing on
to the customer the results of cost reductions associated with moving
to a larger scale plant and the writing off of some tooling costs. [9]

Chrysler's first attempt to challenge the status quo in the U.K.
car industry came during the last week of October 1968. All the basic
prices of cars in the Imp range were reduced: the Imp deluxe from
£488 to £467 and the Super Imp from £526 to £502, with smaller reductions on the Imp California and Singer Chamois. It was unfortunate that some of the public relations impact might have been lost by
government tax increases on cars a couple of months later. But even
so, the effect of the cuts on the price differential between the Imp and
its long-standing, seemingly ageless, competitor, the Mini, were quite
significant.

This challenge to the market leaders was followed up in July
1969 by price cuts on most other models in the company's range, *
the total effect being to raise sales by 2.5 percent in a year when
total U.K. registrations dropped by over 12 percent. However, it
has been estimated that the increased revenue produced by the price
cuts was insufficient to cover the rise in total costs, [10] and certainly
company losses increased further in 1969/70. Whether or not because
of this, similar moves have not been apparent from Chrysler since
then. Of course, circumstances have changed quite dramatically.
With accelerating cost inflation through 1975, a short-run strategy
aimed at changing established price differentials between competitive
models would not require a company to cut prices. A mere holding of
prices at a time when competitors were making regular upward adjustments would produce exactly the same effect.

Inevitably in these conditions, the question of collusion and price
leadership arises. Figure 4.3 suggests that, in the main, the two
smaller U.K. manufacturers, Chrysler and Vauxhall, do not instigate
price increases. Rather they are content to follow, within a fairly
short period of time, the announced price changes of their larger competitors. In this way the responsibility for determining the "proper"

---

*The bout of aggression was followed fairly soon by two longer
term strategic moves: the launch of a basic Imp in October 1969 and
then the Avenger launch in February 1970.

new price levels is shouldered by the larger firms. The first price increases during 1975 were announced by Ford and Leyland, just before the start of the new year, followed two weeks later by Chrysler and Vauxhall. The next round was begun by Ford, but neither Chrysler nor Vauxhall announced any increases until after the new Leyland price lists were available. In general, it seems that it is the price announcements of Leyland rather than of Ford that influence the price decisions of the two smaller American subsidiaries. At Motor Show time toward the end of the year, however, it is not unexpected for all manufacturers to announce increases together since this follows the normal pattern in the industry.

It must be emphasized, of course, that the prices on which the inferences of noncompetitive short-run pricing behavior are based are list prices only. No account is taken of discounting by dealers. While no information was available on this latter aspect, it would be surprising if the discounts offered by Chrysler dealers during 1975 and 1976 were not at least greater than those of competitive dealerships. Whether or not, as has been suggested, a Chrysler franchise has become a "discount franchise" is much more open to question.

Long-Run Price Competition

A smaller mass market manufacturer such as Chrysler would be expected to have little flexibility in the level at which prices are set in relation to competition. In spite of this, Chrysler seems to pursue a long-run pricing policy to undercut competitors, even though this must have adverse effects on profits per unit sold. The most obvious example of this came with the launch of the Avenger in 1970. Compared with the other four-door models in its class, the Avenger Super was £26 cheaper than the Escort 1300 Super, £19 cheaper than the Viva deluxe, and £6 cheaper than the Austin/Morris 1300 Super. It was reported that "the other manufacturers were dubious, and perhaps surprised, concerning the efficacy and validity"[11] of this pricing policy, but, not surprisingly, retaliatory price cutting did not occur. It is interesting that when Leyland launched the Marina 1300 about 13 months later, the Super version cost £14 more than the Avenger. Although it had a slight edge in performance, this at least provides some evidence to support the manufacturers' view that the Avenger may have been underpriced.

There is no doubt, however, that the price fixed for the Avenger was viewed as a long-run price, rather than as, say, a penetration price, where low prices are chosen only for a period immediately following the market launch. By the end of 1975, the price differential between the Avenger and its rivals had increased in both absolute

FIGURE 4.3

Price Movements During 1975

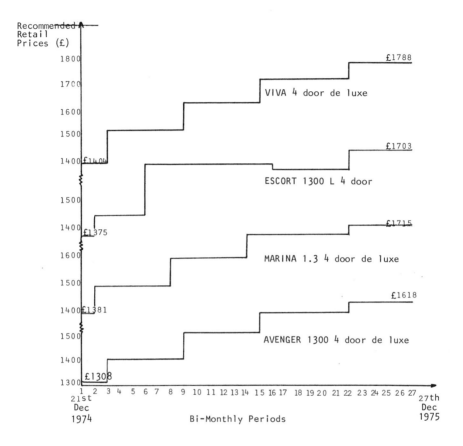

Source: Autocar (London: IPC Transport Press Ltd.), various issues.

and percentage terms, and this applied whether one considered basic or more up-market versions of the car.[12] Of course, the Avenger was designed from the start as a vehicle with low manufacturing costs, being technically conventional and straightforward, but how far the price reflected production costs compared with lower unit profits is not known.

Chrysler pursued a somewhat similar strategy with respect to the Imp. When the Hillman Imp was launched in 1963, the two models most nearly competitive with the Mini were the deluxe and super versions. However, both were more expensive than either the Mini Saloon or the Mini deluxe. At the beginning of 1967, for example, the relative prices were as follows: Imp deluxe Saloon (850 cc), £549; Mini Saloon (850 cc), £478; Super Imp Saloon (850 cc), £576; and Mini deluxe (850 cc), £524. This situation continued into 1969, although the relative position of the Imp had been improved toward the end of the previous year by the price cuts noted earlier. The events of October 1969 were, nevertheless, much more significant, representing a good example of what has been termed "long-run model price competition."[13]

Chrysler launched the Basic Imp at a price of £570 (thereby becoming the cheapest car on the U.K. market at the time), £26 below the the price of the Mini Saloon, while Leyland launched a 1,000 cc version of the Mini. By the middle of 1970, the comparable prices were Imp Saloon, £606; Imp deluxe Saloon, £651; Super Imp Saloon, £698; Mini 850 Saloon, £619; and Mini 1000 Saloon, £702.

The Hunter was launched before the Chrysler takeover, but all the other U.K. manufacturers subsequently have produced new models for this market segment, so that Chrysler has had ample opportunity to review its long-run pricing strategy for this car also. Once again, price competitiveness has been a crucial element in the strategy. At the time of the launch of the Leyland Marina in the spring of 1971, for example, comparative prices of some competitive models at the top end of their ranges were Morris Marina TC 1800, £1,177; Hillman Hunter GT (1,725 cc), £1,164; Ford Cortina 2000 GXL, £1,338; Renault 16 TS, £1,359; and Vauxhall VX 4/90, £1,333.[14]

Given the brand image Rootes tried to portray, this discount pricing policy was not an inherited one. Moreover, it cannot be deemed to be the natural fate of second division U.K. manufacturers, since Vauxhall has not pursued this price-cutting strategy. The policy does, of course, fit in with Chrysler's aspirations to be a volume producer.

ADVERTISING

It has been seen that price reductions have been used only very infrequently by Chrysler U.K. as a short-run marketing strategy, in line with generally prevailing policies in the industry. Because of this, company advertising could be viewed as a more aggressive tool in the marketing mix, a pattern that frequently has been observed in other oligopolistic markets.[15]

Advertising data are by no means comprehensive and do not extend back on a consistent basis for many years. In the following tables only press and televesion advertising expenditures are analyzed, with numerous other media omitted (for example, cinema, posters, and commercial radio) that may be important in car advertising. Furthermore, the data only relate to expenditure by the manufacturers, excluding spending by franchised car dealers. Even with these provisos, the data are revealing. In 1968, Chrysler was second only to Leyland in its advertising expenditure (Table 4.1), but, while spending rose in absolute terms, the company's share of total spending dropped sharply. To some extent this merely reflects the aggressive advertising policies pursued by the importers in support of their successful assault on the U.K. market, and all domestic manufacturers' shares of advertising declined during the period. (The sharp fall in the case of Ford in 1974 is somewhat misleading and seems to have been related to company policy, which aimed at minimizing the effects of inflation on car prices at this time.) But, in addition, as Table 4.2 shows, Chrysler's falling share of expenditure was related closely to its product policy, the phasing out of the Rootes model names, and the failure to introduce replacements.

The year 1968 was still a transition period for Chrysler, both in a policy sense and in the sense that some of the advertising that appeared may have been committed much earlier. In that year, the Imp and its variants were advertised both under the then company name and under the Hillman, Singer, and Sunbeam model names separately—hardly, perhaps, a very cost-effective policy. As both the names and many of the models were withdrawn, advertising was left to support only the four cars in the range and one of these, the Chrysler 180, is produced in France. Reflecting the narrow range of cars produced by Chrysler U.K., expenditure on Simca cars rose from just over £13,000 in 1968 to £166,000 in 1974.

The changeover from the Rootes to the Chrysler name is also evidenced in the advertising data. By 1974, advertising spending in support of the name and the company's range (including Simca) was substantial. Its purpose seems to have been not only to introduce the car-buying public to the Chrysler name but also, by linking Simca cars within the range, to draw attention away from the paucity of models produced by Chrysler in the United Kingdom.

The advertising data of competitive models (Table 4.3) permit some assessment of the promotional strategies of the companies. Expenditure on the Mini rose sharply after Leyland's launch of the Mini 1000 and Clubman versions at the end of 1969 and increased significantly again in the wake of the oil crisis. Chrysler was phasing out advertising support for the Imp until 1974, when a big campaign was launched to support the Imp as a gas saver. The effectiveness of this strategy was evidenced by the fact that sales rose from 15,200 to 16,600 cars at a time when demand for the Mini declined by 7,000 units (-7 percent).

TABLE 4.1

Shares of Press and Television Advertising Expenditure on Cars
(percent)

Make of Car	1968	1969	1970	1971	1972	1973	1974	1975
Chrysler	18.3	12.5	9.5	8.2	5.7	6.6	7.6	8.1
Simca	0.3	0.6	1.7	2.4	0.5	0.5	1.5	0.6
British Leyland	23.8	30.0	29.7	32.3	18.9	18.2	20.7	27.4
Ford	15.0	14.3	12.2	7.0	10.3	7.2	4.1	9.4
Vauxhall[a]	12.1	10.7	14.6	10.8	11.6	8.3	9.7	8.1
Subtotal	69.5	68.1	67.7	60.7	47.0	40.8	43.6	53.6
Citroen	0.9	0.9	0.8	1.1	3.4	2.4	2.6	2.1
Datsun	0.4	1.1	0.3	0.7	3.0	4.1	5.7	1.6
Fiat	4.3	2.8	5.0	5.0	5.5	8.8	8.1	4.3
Peugeot	0.3	0.3	0.2	2.2	2.5	2.6	3.8	3.7
Renault	4.2	5.8	5.7	3.9	5.8	5.3	5.1	6.5
Toyota	0.5	0.5	0.4	1.0	3.6	2.6	2.7	3.0
Volkswagen[b]	5.5	6.6	4.5	7.2	10.9	15.9	7.6	6.6
Other	14.4	13.9	15.4	18.2	18.3	17.5	20.8	18.6
Total	100.0	100.0	100.0	100.0	100.0	100.0	100.0	100.0
Pounds (000)	4,360.2	5,233.9	4,314.0	5,986.8	8,969.6	11,818.6	11,119.9	18,152.5

[a]Includes Opel
[b]Includes Audi and NSU.

Source: MEAL (London: Media Expenditure Analysis Ltd.), various issues).

TABLE 4.2

Breakdown of Chrysler Press and Television Advertising Expenditure
(thousands of pounds)

Model	1968 Total	1968 Television	1968 Press	1970 Total	1970 Television	1970 Press	1972 Total	1972 Television	1972 Press	1974 Total	1974 Television	1974 Press
Chrysler Range	—	—	—	—	—	—	84.8	0.2	84.6	261.2	234.0	27.1
Chrysler 180	—	—	—	—	—	—	126.5	76.6	49.9	96.4	18.2	78.2
Chrysler Valiant	10.7	—	10.7	19.4	—	19.4	—	—	—	—	—	—
Rootes Range	4.2	—	4.2	12.2	—	12.2	—	—	—	—	—	—
Rootes Imps	342.3	198.6	143.7	—	—	—	—	—	—	—	—	—
Hillman Range	15.7	—	15.7	—	—	—	27.5	—	27.5	0.7	—	0.7
Hillman Avenger	—	—	—	356.8	128.6	228.2	231.1	67.6	163.5	259.2	90.2	169.1
Hillman Hunter	101.2	—	101.2	50.6	—	50.6	39.7	—	39.7	89.1	—	89.1
Hillman Imp	5.9	—	5.9	2.4	—	2.4	1.0	—	1.0	134.4	23.1	111.3
Hillman Minx	102.4	—	102.4	—	—	—	—	—	—	—	—	—
Humber Sceptre	21.1	—	21.1	1.8	—	1.8	—	—	—	—	—	—
Singer Chamois	21.7	—	21.7	—	—	—	—	—	—	—	—	—
Singer Gazelle	25.4	—	25.4	2.4	—	2.4	—	—	—	—	—	—
Singer Vogue	35.7	—	35.7	3.7	—	3.7	—	—	—	—	—	—
Sunbeam Alpine	—	—	—	—	—	—	—	—	—	—	—	—
Sunbeam Imp	17.3	—	17.3	—	—	—	—	—	—	—	—	—
Sunbeam Rapier	53.0	—	53.0	6.3	—	6.3	—	—	—	—	—	—
Sunbeam Stiletto	5.7	—	5.7	—	—	—	—	—	—	—	—	—
Dealer promotions	37.3	—	37.3	—	—	—	—	—	—	—	—	—
Total	799.6	198.6	601.0	455.6	128.6	327.0	510.6	144.4	366.2	841.0	365.5	475.5
Total including Simca	812.9	198.6	614.3	538.5	128.6	409.9	558.2	144.4	413.8	1,007.0	400.7	606.3

Source: MEAL (London: Media Expenditure Analysis Ltd.), various issues.

TABLE 4.3

Press and Television Advertising Expenditure on Selected Models Competing with Chrysler

(thousands of pounds)

Manufacturer and Model	1968 Total	1968 Television	1968 Press	1970 Total	1970 Television	1970 Press	1972 Total	1972 Television	1972 Press	1974 Total	1974 Television	1974 Press
Chrysler Imp	392.9	198.6	194.3	14.6	—	14.6	1.0	—	1.0	134.4	23.1	111.3
British Leyland Mini	55.9	—	55.9	165.9	—	165.9	149.0	—	149.0	267.4	—	267.4
Chrysler Avenger	n.a.	n.a.	n.a.	366.8	128.6	238.2	298.7	67.6	231.1	259.2	90.2	169.2
British Leyland 1100, 1300/Allegro[b]	54.2	—	54.2	292.3	—	292.3	145.8	—	145.8	555.9	—	555.9
Ford Escort	256.8	—	256.8	205.9	—	205.9	101.0	—	101.0	—	—	—
Vauxhall Viva	269.4	1.1	268.3	425.9	119.5	306.4	331.5	—	331.5	642.1	94.8	547.3
Chrysler Hunter	101.2	—	101.2	40.6	—	40.6	39.7	—	39.7	89.1	—	89.1
British Leyland Marina	n.a.	n.a.	n.a.	n.a.	n.a.	n.a.	250.6	—	250.6	252.2	28.2	224.0
British Leyland Maxi	n.a.	n.a.	n.a.	129.3	—	129.3	64.9	—	64.9	152.2	—	152.2
Ford Cortina	122.3	—	122.3	291.5	—	291.5	142.0	—	142.0	—	—	—
Ford Capri	n.a.	n.a.	n.a.	131.8	—	131.8	305.8	113.8	192.0	287.3	119.8	167.5

aIncludes expenditure on variants, for example, Imp includes Singer Chamois, Sunbeam Imp, and Stiletto.

bAllegro in 1974, 1100/1300 series earlier.

Note: n.a. = data not available (the vehicles concerned were not on the market).

Source: MEAL (London: Media Expenditure Analysis Ltd.), various issues.

The Avenger was launched at the beginning of 1970 backed by heavy press and television advertising expenditure. Ford and Leyland replied with advertising stressing the technology and price advantages of their Escort and 1100/1300 models, respectively, while Vauxhall responded in the autumn with an updated series of the Viva, complete with new body shell and styling and again promoted very vigorously. Indeed, of all the U.K. manufacturers, Vauxhall seems to have been most aggressive in its advertising policy. During 1970, the company spent £5 per car on press and television advertising for the Viva compared with £2 per unit sale by Leland and Ford and £7 by Chrysler. Expenditure by Chrysler on the Avenger dropped to £4 per car in 1974, whereas Vauxhall increased its advertising to match the spending of Leyland on the Allegro launch (£9 per unit sale). Given the overall importance of the Avenger to Chrysler, there must be considerable doubts as to whether the correct strategy would not have been to follow the approach of Vauxhall, particularly since the Avenger engines had been uprated at the end of 1973.

It seems clear that advertising has not been subject to implicit agreement among the car firms, but has been used, by some companies at least, as a fairly aggressive marketing weapon. Chrysler, however, does not seem to have used advertising as much as it might have to offset the inevitable erosion of its competitive position as other manufacturers launched new models at regular intervals. Inevitably, 1976 already has seen a change in this situation owing to the necessity of restoring public confidence in the company and to support the launch of the Chrysler Alpine.

DISTRIBUTION SYSTEMS

The Dealer Network under Rootes

There is no doubt that a strong dealer network is one of the key elements in the marketing of motor vehicles, and the Rootes dealer network was probably Chrysler's most valuable inheritance.[16] As noted earlier, Rootes' manufacturing activities emerged from its interests in motor vehicle distribution first in Kent and Sussex and later farther north in Manchester and Birmingham (and the significant stake that Chrysler, alone of the U.K. manufacturers, still has on the retail side is a relic of these early Rootes days). This fact more than any other probably explains the empathy of the Rootes family for their dealers and, conversely, the strong personal loyalty that the dealers, many themselves family owned businesses, felt for Lord Rootes. The claim that Rootes dealers considered themselves a class above other distributors is probably close to the truth.

The Rootes dealer netowrk was built up alongside its manufacturing acquisitions. By the 1930s, the company felt strong enough to include exclusivity clauses in its franchise agreements, meaning that company approval was required before any dealer could simultaneously handle another company's cars. The structure of the dealer network under Rootes can best be described as multitiered. A small number of large main distributors occupied a matriarchal position under this system, being responsible for retail dealers directly but also for smaller main distributors who might then have retail dealerships of their own. A main distributor with more than 30 retail dealers was not unknown. The main distributors had the responsibility of holding stocks of cars, parts, and spares and for supplying their retail dealers from these stocks, obtaining an extra 5 percent discount on such car sales to their retailers. Finally, only the main distributors had direct contact with the manufacturer, through either the sales director or Lord Rootes personally.

The Dealer Network under Chrysler

The Introduction of a Single-Tier Network

There is obviously some optimum in respect to the size of a manufacturer's dealer network, an optimum that will be principally dependent on the population density in a particular area or country. The Rootes system, with its large numbers of dealers, provided considerable geographic coverage, but meant that dealers themselves were too small to finance an efficient sales and service operation. Retail dealers, for example, might sell as few as 25 to 30 cars per year. Not only might sales volume mitigate against efficiency in these circumstances but also a lack of commitment of the dealers themselves to Rootes cars could have adverse effects on the customers' image of the company. The additional problem was the irrational duplication of networks for Hillman and Singer cars.

Chrysler's dissatisfaction with the existing setup was evidenced early on (for example, the margin on sales from main to retail dealers was reduced), but the major changes were initiated in 1969/70. In that year, the company began a "provisioning exercise" aimed at providing "a market for every dealer and a dealer for every market" and the replacement of the multitier by a single-tier network. The aim was, by 1975, to have a rationalized system in which, apart from exceptional circumstances, all dealers dealt directly with the manufacturer. As part of the plan, Chrysler set up five regional offices staffed with sales and service personnel to which all queries had to be directed. The old main dealer-factory links were being ended.

Before the system was finally introduced, however, some changes were instituted. First, the regional office structure was amended during 1975 in an attempt to produce economies and was then further pruned early in 1976 as part of the reorganization following the crisis. Second, the completion date for the implementation of the direct system was put back to the end of 1976. This seems to have been due partly to the difficulties in some isolated and rural areas of rationalizing the network, but also, perhaps, to some rethinking of the rationale behind the plan in such cases. For example, in areas with a low population density a termination of the system of retail dealerships could leave many customers short of service facilities and lead to a loss of goodwill. It has been suggested that the system used by Chrysler France could overcome some of these problems. In that system the dealer network contains equal numbers of main distributors and service dealers (agents); the latter have a commitment only for Chrysler service and parts sales, while getting a slightly more preferential discount on car sales than, say, the casual trader.

The effects of the rationalization program introduced by Chrysler and the other manufacturers is shown in Table 4.4. In 1970–75 the number of Chrysler dealers was reduced by 35 percent, in comparison with reductions of 18 percent and 33 percent, respectively, for Ford and Vauxhall. For the U.K. manufacturers as a whole, an important adverse effect of their rationalization programs has been to permit the importers to build up viable dealer networks. A Chrysler survey of 300 dealers that had lost a franchise from a U.K. manufacturer showed that 35 percent obtained import franchises, 15 percent gained another U.K. manufacturer's franchise, and 50 percent either obtained no replacement franchise or left the industry.[17]

The favorable impact of the rationalization programs on average dealer sales is shown in Table 4.5. Chrysler appears reasonably well placed, with average car sales in 1975 of 171 units. In fact, this represents some decline as compared with 1974, when the average car sales of Chrysler dealers were lower only than those of Datson.

Dealer Agreements and the Franchise System

Legislation in support of vehicle franchise holders has been established for many years in the United States and Belgium but not in the United Kingdom where the advantage in franchise agreements has been considered to be very strongly with the manufacturers. (It must be pointed out, of course, that, in general, motor dealers' returns on capital have been far in excess of those of the manufacturers.) In particular, the possibility of the manufacturer terminating dealers' agreements with only 90 days' notice is viewed by many as unfair in the light of the substantial financial commitment the dealer might have to

TABLE 4.4

Distribution Networks by Manufacturer

Franchise	1970 Number of Dealers			1971 Number of Dealers			1972 Number of Dealers			1973 Number of Dealers			1974^e Number of Dealers	1975^e Number of Dealers
	Main	Retail	Total	Main	Retail	Total	Main	Retail	Total	Main	Retail	Total		
Chrysler	182	884	1,066	210	668	878	299	523	822	299	523	822	737	692
Leyland Austin-Morris	370	3,475	3,845	338	3,000	3,338	348	2,894	3,170	344	2,698	3,042	2,565	2,943^d
Leyland Rover-Triumph^a	118	977	1,096	138	751	889	138	742	880	92	568	660	805	
										143	659	802		
Jaguar-Daimler	n.a.	n.a.	n.a.	n.a.	n.a.	n.a.	80	301	381	132	452	584		
Ford	386	1,076	1,462	386	1,000	1,386	380	913	1,293	380	900	1,280	1,258	1,203
Vauxhall	462	742	1,204	444	681	1,125	468	532	1,000	450	489	939	864	803
Citroen	33	67	100	—	105	105	—	131	131	—	158	158	168	184
Datsun	n.a.	n.a.	n.a.	—	135	135	—	187	187	—	200	200	230	290
Fiat	—	400	400	—	350	350	—	330	330	34	327	361	350	371
Peugeot	n.a.	n.a.	n.a.	—	115	115	—	137	137	—	158	158	180	174
Renault	—	391	391	—	389	389	—	379	379	64	301	365	360	390
Toyota	—	—	250^c	—	—	250^c	—	—	250^c	—	174	174	254	271
Volkswagen^b	—	270	270	—	240	240	—	230	230	—	231	231	355	350
										—	200	200		

[a] In 1973, Rover and Triumph dealerships are shown separately.
[b] In 1973, figures are given for Volkswagen and Audi/NSU separately. In 1974 and 1975 figures refer to both Volkswagen and Audi/NSU.
[c] Estimated.
[d] Total British Leyland.
[e] Split between main and retail dealer not available in general. But in 1974 Chrysler had 455 main and 282 retail dealers.

Note: n.a. = data not available.

Source: Motor Agents Association.

126

TABLE 4.5

New Car Sales[a] per Dealer, 1970 and 1975

Manufacturer or Importer	1970	1975
Ford	214	247
Datsun	n.a.	221
Vauxhall[b]	106	198
Chrysler[c]	115	171
Volkswagen/Audi	97[d]	152
Renault	80	149
British Leyland	91[e]	
	82[f]	142
Citroen	41	121
Fiat	60	108
Peugeot	n.a.	86
Toyota	5	84

[a]U.K. registrations, includes car-derived vans.
[b]Includes Opel sales.
[c]Includes Simca sales.
[d]Volkswagen only.
[e]Austin-Morris.
[f]Rover/Triumph.

Note: n.a. = data not available.

Sources: Motor Agents Association and the Society of Motor Manufacturers and Traders.

a particular manufacturer. In this context, the U.K. Motor Agents Association (MAA) and its Scottish branch, the Scottish Motor Trade Association (SMTA), the trade associations for garages and dealers, produced in 1972 a broad set of principles that they felt needed to be incorporated into franchise agreements in order to protect the dealers. As an example, the view was taken that main dealer agreements should be for five years instead of the usual one year. The right of both parties to terminate agreements with 90 days' notice under special circumstances was still accepted.

Subsequent to this report from the MAA, the Chrysler Dealer Agreement came up for renegotiation. It is a reflection of both the strength of the Chrysler Dealer Association (of which more will be said later) and of the importance that Chrysler attaches to its dealer network that many of the changes suggested by the MAA were incorporated into the new Chrysler agreement. This agreement, which became effective May 1975 onward, is accepted by most people in the trade as being the most liberal of any manufacturer. Termination by the manufacturer is only possible under very limited circumstances, and there is a requirement to buy back from the dealer all stocks of vehicles, parts, and so on at current prices.

From the dealers' viewpoint, the principal remaining grievance with respect to the agreement is the exlusivity clause. Exclusive dealer clauses are now standard in vehicle franchises in the United Kingdom, apparently imported by the U.S. manufacturers. Thus, Chrysler is not alone in its policy in this respect. The problem for Chrysler came up seriously during 1975 when fears began to be expressed about the possibility of the company pulling out of the United Kingdom. As public confidence and sales dropped, the market shares of many dealers declined to a level insufficient to cover their overheads. Dealers therefore were looking for a loophole in the exclusivity clause so that sales volume could be improved through additional franchises. Some dealers were able to keep their options open by taking out new franchises in different premises located outside the market area specified in their agreement with Chrysler; but in other cases this wan not possible. To some extent Chrysler could not afford to ignore the dealers, since the alternative to obtaining an additional franchise might be the resignation of many dealers' agreements with Chrysler (although the threat of many resignations never materialized). In general, it is very unlikely that Chrysler U.K. would ever allow a competitive franchise within the same showroom, and in normal circumstances the company seems to be fully justified in maintaining its stand on exclusivity. Whether or not Chrysler will be able to continue to do so in the current situation depends very much on the company's ability to rebuild its sales volume to a viable level.

The U.K. Chrysler Dealer Association

Dealer associations in the United Kingdom are very recent. Although Ford had had a dealer association in Scotland since World War I, the first national association was set up by Rootes early in the 1960s. Even today a company as large as British Leyland has no effective dealer organization, and as evidence of this the MAA acted on the dealers' behalf at the time of the U.K. government's rescue operation for the company in 1975. The Rootes, and subsequently the Chrysler Dealer Association, on the other hand, has gone from strength to strength.

The National Dealer Council meets with the top Chrysler management biannually. Additional meetings of the smaller policy committee are held with the company as and when the situation demands it In the negotiation of the dealer agreement, in the discussions over the payment of a wholesale commission and so on, the dealers' voice through their association has had a very important part to play. This is not to say that conflicts have not arisen in dealer-manufacturer relationships. Problems with the inconsistency and unreliability of the quality of new cars have been a constant bone of contention; and disputes over warranty claims, the failure to introduce new models, the role of factory-owned outlets, the introduction of the single-tier system, and, most recently, a lack of consultation over the pull-out threats have all caused serious dealer dissatisfaction. However, if Chrysler does survive the current crisis, this will be due in no small measure to the accumulated goodwill of the dealers, representing in turn Chrysler's investment in its dealer association.

Factory-Owned Outlets

Company-owned dealerships could be valuable for a number of reasons, but they generally have not been considered in the United Kingdom. Apart from Chrysler, none of the other manufacturers has a sizable stake on the retail side. Chrysler policy, moreover, seems to have been to rid itself of about half of such outlets (mainly the smaller ones) when suitable buyers could be found. According to Chrysler's 1974 annual report, a total of 24 factory-owned outlets existed, thus being of principal value only as a source of market information. Chrysler has been accused from time to time, through its dealer association, of using its dealerships to discount heavily cars to the public, thereby spoiling the market for other Chrysler dealers in the same locality. As far as can be ascertained, this seems to have been a problem only in parts of Scotland and not general to the United Kingdom. Although given the locations of these outlets, however, the factory-owned dealerships could have been used in a more aggressive marketing role in parts of the Midlands and south of England, where their greatest concentration exists.

RESULTS OF CHRYSLER MARKETING POLICY

This chapter has investigated the components of Chrysler marketing policy—the marketing mix—without taking an overall look at marketing strategy or at the results of the policy in terms of market share. Some concluding comments therefore are in order with respect to these aspects. The situation at the time of the company's entry into the U.K. market was undoubtedly grim. A proliferation of brands disguising a paucity of models could not be overcome by a first-class dealer network and a lot of goodwill. Two kinds of market-ing strategy might have suggested themselves in these circumstances: first, some kind of holding operation in the company's marketing ac-tivities while the firm was whipped into shape, with the emphasis on cost reduction, the reorganization of production facilities, and so on; and second, an aggressive marketing approach from the outset. The latter strategy would be singularly wasteful if not impossible without the first, and, in any event, the company had no new models at hand. The former approach would also seem more in keeping with the philos-ophy and strengths of the Chrysler Corporation in the United States.

It was not, therefore, until the very end of 1968 that Chrysler began to move aggressively on the marketing front. Over the 18 months or so from that date numerous changes, affecting both short- and long-term marketing policy, were introduced. However, given the product range that existed, a successful strategy could only be cen-tered on a series of new models. The successful launch of the Aven-ger was a hopeful sign in this direction, but the relative lack of suc-cess of the French Chrysler 180 must have proved a disappointment to the company; and the market momentum came to a standstill when no replacements appeared for the Hunter and Imp. It is perhaps a dubious argument to say that this was caused by a lack of finance in the United Kingdom, since models from other European subsidiaries might have been used in this role. If Chrysler had really pushed the integration of its European activities, the Simca range, for example, could have been marketed much earlier and much more forcefully in the United Kingdom without being too costly. As it was, less than 8,000 cars from Chrysler France were imported in 1970. Moreover, the president of Chrysler International stated in 1970 that the U.K. company would produce at least one new model a year.

Tables 4.6 and 4.7 show the end results of Chrysler's market-ing policy in terms of model sales and market shares in the United Kingdom. The Imp disaster emerges clearly from Table 4.6, sales falling for nine successive years until 1974. The total mini market was also declining during this period, and it was not until 1970 that falling demand for the Imp was reflected in a falling market share. Rootes' strength in the midrange market was on the wane by the time of the Chrysler takeover. The Avenger launch and the introduction of a smaller engine version of the Hillman Hunter came just in time. But, in fact, the two models did not pick up much additional market share for Chrysler, as the midrange market sector was expanding very rapidly at this time. As will be shown, however, supply difficul-ties played an important part in the Avenger situation.

Chrysler's marketing policy since the end of 1968 has been ad-venturous and aggressive in a number of respects, but limited editions, warranty plans, price cutting, and the whole panoply of marketing in-

TABLE 4.6

U.K. Registrations of Chrysler Cars[a]

Model	1965	1966	1967	1968	1969	1970	1971	1972	1973	1974	1975
Hillman Imp	29,389	27,601	22,536	18,725	18,600	14,081	15,574	14,645	15,207	16,558	10,463
Hillman Imp Californian	—	—	2,965	1,852	892	380	33	—			
Singer Chamois	13,274	10,621	9,504	7,008	3,526	1,126	29	11	15,207	16,558	10,463
Sunbeam Sports	—	648	2,756	1,582	861	593	591	452			
Sunbeam Stiletto	—	—	1,046	3,095	1,576	1,021	723	486			
Total Imp	42,663	38,870	38,807	32,262	25,455	17,201	16,950	15,594	15,207	16,558	10,463
Hillman Avenger	—	—	—	—	23	50,133	63,476	78,729	78,644	60,244	38,877
Hillman Hunter	—	3,361	17,553	11,199	8,906	9,533	41,996	50,342	55,934	33,048	28,966
Hillman Minx	24,829	24,950	39,903	36,999	36,094	14,023	572	—	—	—	—
Hillman GT–Super Minx	25,704	21,049	4,644		648	2,328	97	7	—	—	—
Singer Gazelle	9,807	10,415	10,712	7,063	3,246	934	13	43			
Singer Vogue	9,771	8,208	11,208	8,025	5,362	1,357	54				
Sunbeam Rapier	3,181	2,184	1,045	6,638	4,551	919	3,756	2,700			
Humber Sceptre	6,347	6,990	5,190	6,451	5,713	6,034	5,918	4,543	9,572	4,112	
Sunbeam Alpine	1,519	1,674	1,796	775	645	3,193	1,946	1,182			145
Hillman Husky	2,784	1,270	2,051	3,033	2,706	2,096	384	207			
Total Arrow[b]	83,942	80,101	94,102	80,183	67,871	43,417	54,736	59,094	65,506	37,160	29,111
Humber Hawk, Super Snipe–Imperial	4,063	4,003	2,038	40	28	2	—				
Other	356	199	89	21	1	1,837	67	348			
Total	131,024	123,173	135,036	112,506	93,378	112,590	135,229	153,765	159,357	113,962	78,451

[a] U.K.–manufactured cars only.

[b] Certain of these models were not strictly part of the Arrow range initially.

Source: Society of Motor Manufacturers and Traders, The Motor Industry of Great Britain, various editions.

TABLE 4.7

U.K. Registrations of Chrysler Cars by Cylinder Capacity[a]

Year	To 1,200 cc[b]	1,201– 1,800 cc[c]	1,801– 2,200 cc	Over 2,200 cc[d]
1965	42,663	84,298	—	4,063
	(6.4)	(23.3)	—	(5.0)
1966	38,870	80,300	—	4,003
	(6.6)	(21.2)	—	(5.8)
1967	38,807	94,191	—	2,038
	(7.3)	(20.1)	—	(3.3)
1968	32,262	80,204	—	40
	(6.5)	(16.3)	—	(0.1)
1969	25,455	67,895	—	28
	(7.1)	(13.2)	—	(<0.5)
1970	17,201	95,387	—	2
	(4.6)	(16.0)	—	(<0.5)
1971	16,950	118,279	—	—
	(4.2)	(16.3)	—	—
1972	15,594	138,171	—	—
	(4.0)	(13.9)	—	—
1973	15,207	144,150	—	—
	(4.2)	(14.6)	—	—
1974	16,558	97,404	—	—
	(5.2)	(13.9)	—	—
1975	10,463	67,988	—	—
	(3.0)	(10.4)	—	—

[a]U.K.-manufactured cars only.
[b]Chrysler U.K. represented by the Imp range.
[c]Chrysler U.K. represented by the Avenger and Arrow ranges; also includes "other" cars.
[d]Chrysler U.K. represented by Humber Hawk and Humber Super Snipe and Imperial.

Note: Numbers in parentheses are percent of U.K. total registrations.

Source: Society of Motor Manufacturers and Traders, The Motor Industry of Great Britain, various editions.

struments could not disguise the fundamental weaknesses in the product range. Such aggression, in any event, was misdirected in that it wasted Rootes' image and goodwill; and margin squeezing was hardly the policy to be operated by a small producer like Chrysler, which was probably unable to match the cost levels of much larger competitors.

EXPORT MARKETING POLICY

Nothing has been said about export marketing policy, although exporting offers the opportunity of breaking out of the constraints imposed by the size of the home market. In a multinational enterprise, however, export policy is likely to be much more of a parent company concern than domestic marketing policy. Thus, exporting and intraplant flows are strategic issues that may not be amenable to conventional explanation or analysis, as, for example, when the goals of an affiliate are overruled in the interests of the goals of the parent corporation. Export policy is closely related to the question of the integration of Chrysler's European activities, which will be a recurring theme throughout the remainder of this book, and export performance will be discussed in more detail in the next chapter. At this juncture, however, one or two points are worth noting.

Although Chrysler U.K. eliminated the interbrand competition (for example, Hillman versus Singer) that existed under Rootes, its parent company has not followed this policy when importing cars from overseas subsidiaries into the United States. For example, in January 1971, Chrysler Corporation began to import the Avenger (as the Plymouth Cricket) to compete in the subcompact market with the Ford Pinto and Chevrolet Vega. But supplies of the Avenger were limited and so Chrysler also imported the Colt from Mitsubishi, called it a Dodge, and ran it in competition with the British car. The situation in Canada is even more interesting. When the import of the Avenger was halted, the name Plymouth Cricket was applied to a Colt with a new grille designed to make it resemble the (Avenger) Cricket and look different from the Dodge model. [18]

The Avenger, in fact, has been reasonably successful in export markets, but the policy to concentrate imports of the Mitsubishi Colt into the United States and Canada has caused a severe setback. When imports of the Avenger into the United States were first suspended, this was dismissed by Don Lander, then deputy managing director of Chrysler U.K., as a question of stock levels. Later, however, it became clear that the greater variety of models available for the Colt, the fact that the Japanese company had spare manufacturing capacity available, and quality and supply problems with the Avenger had tipped the balance, and the decision was made to concentrate on imports of the Japanese line.

The 1976 deal between the Chrysler Corporation and Volkswagen of Germany for the supply of engines and transmission units for a new

small car for the North American market[19] has been another source
of gloom for the U.K. subsidiary. As will be shown, these decisions
leave Chrysler frighteningly dependent on a contract to supply CKD
(completely knockdown) units to Iran.

APPENDIX: RESEARCH AND DEVELOPMENT

It may seem incongrous to assess the research and development
activities of Chrysler U.K. when the only new model to be produced in
the United Kingdom during the years since Chrysler acquired its U.K.
company has been the Avenger. However, research and development
is an area where the European operations of the Chrysler Corporation
have been completely integrated, and the Whitley Technical Centre in
England, set up in 1969, handles product development on behalf of all
European subsidiaries. The basic styling units are in Whitley, and,
although there are engineering groups in each of the countries, they
operate under one director, with the respective companies paying for
work undertaken on their behalf. Thus, while the Avenger was the
only new model to be manufactured in Britain during the period 1967-
75, both the Chrysler 180/2 liter and the Alpine (the so-called C6
model) were also designed at Whitley.

It is difficult to establish performance criteria for development
departments. Since projects may abort at any stage from conception
to launch, a minimization of the rate of failure is obviously desirable.
But since the car market is a fashion market, projects abandoned at
one stage may later be revived. And from one viewpoint it is undoubtedly desirable to be in a position where projects can be taken off the
shelf when the situation demands it, since this goes some way to reduce the lead time in development. Against this, of course, must be
set the costs involved.

An inspection of the list of models designed at Whitley leads to
the perhaps superficial conclusion of a significant waste of resources.
Apart from the three cars that have reached the launch stage, an additional two designs were sent to the United States and scrapped, while
at least another dozen design studies were completed without any action being taken. Within the latter group, however, a number of the
projects now have been revived following agreement between the U.K.
government and Chrysler on future financing arrangements for the
company. In these cases, however, inaction was a result of lack of
funds for the production stage. Regarding the remaining shelved projects and those scrapped in the United States, the important question
from the point of view of Chrysler U.K. is "who pays?" It has been
alleged that one project canceled in 1970 had cost the U.K. company
£17 million, and, if correct, is obviously a cause for concern.

NOTES

1. Fourteenth Report from the Expenditure Committee, sess. 1974-75, The Motor Vehicle Industry, HC 617 (London: HMSO, August 1975), p. 29. This report noted the different strategies followed by Peugeot and Rootes from the 1950s when both were of a similar size and basically one-model firms. Peugeot began to create a quality image so as to enable higher prices to be charged. Rootes, conversely, tried to compete on price with larger firms in the mass market and ran into financial difficulties.

2. J. M. Loiseau, "The British Motor Car Industry and Europe" (D. Phil. thesis, Oxford University, 1969).

3. G. Foster, "Rough Road for Rootes," Management Today, July 1969.

4. Autocar, December 9, 1971. While only indirectly relevant to Chrysler policy on its product range it is worth noting that the concentration of British-manufactured cars in this market segment has been put forward as a major factor facilitating the sharp rise in imports that occurred from 1973 onward. See Central Policy Review Staff (CPRS), The Future of the British Car Industry (London: HMSO, 1975).

5. CPRS, The Future of the British Car Industry.

6. Autocar, July 19, 1973.

7. Foster, "Rough Road for Rootes."

8. CPRS, The Future of the British Car Industry.

9. Both examples are taken from D. G. Rhys, The Motor Industry: An Economic Survey (London: Butterworth, 1972), pp. 310-11.

10. Ibid., p. 311.

11. Ibid.

12. Motor, December 20, 1975. For the week ending December 20, 1975, the prices of the Avenger 1600 GL and its immediate competitors were as follows: Avenger 1600 GL, £1916; Austin Allegro 1500 S, £2055; Ford Cortina 1600 XL, £2084; Renault 12TS, £2018; Fiat 131 S 1600, £2126; Citroen GSX2, £2079.

13. G. Maxcy and A. Silberston, The Motor Industry (London: Allen & Unwin, 1959), chap. 5.

14. Autocar, April 28, 1971.

15. See, for example, T. McGuinness and K. Cowling, "Advertising and the Aggregate Demand for Cigarettes," European Economic Review 6 (1975): 311-28.

16. Sunday Times, November 30, 1975. It was estimated by W. B. Dewing, the 1975 chairman of the U.K. Chrysler Dealer Association that the approximately 800 dealers employed 30,000 people and had invested around £130 million—more than four times the value of Chrysler assets in the United Kingdom.

17. CPRS, The Future of the British Car Industry.

18. Autocar, April 6, 1972 and December 7, 1972.

19. The Guardian, February 13, 1976.

5

THE PERFORMANCE
OF CHRYSLER U.K.

Inevitably, the concept of performance can be deemed to cover a very wide range of issues, depending, for example, upon whether the viewpoint taken was that of the government, the motor industry, the consumer, or whatever. In addition, the criteria of successful performance might vary widely among individual firms in the vehicle industry, as the discussion in Chapter 2 on possible Chrysler strategies in Europe indicated. In order to try to narrow the problem, a number of key areas have been chosen for analysis in this chapter. Chrysler U.K.'s domestic sales and export performance have been included, as the outcome primarily of the marketing policies discussed in Chapter 4. To balance this assessment of the company's marketing record, three of the main factors determining production costs—scale, capacity utilization, and labor costs—are analyzed, while investment, both as a further cost determinant and as a major influence on growth, is also considered. The chapter ends with a discussion of financial performance—the end result of the interplay of these and all other factors affecting the firm and its operations.

To some extent, the comparative information presented in this chapter has been determined by the data available. Otherwise, in order to limit the scope of the problem, comparisons have been restricted in the main to other U.K. car firms, and Chrysler France, and in areas where a wider perspective is required, other U.S. subsidiaries in Europe.

U.K. SALES AND MARKET SHARE

The previous chapter emphasized the marketing problems that have faced Chrysler since its takeover of the Rootes Group, particularly those related to the product range. A first assessment of the effects on the company's sales performance on the U.K. market is given in Table 5.1. The company's declining market share from 1968 on is noticeable, although registrations of Chrysler cars were on an upward trend until 1973. The overall size of the U.K. market shrank by one quarter in 1974 and then by a further 6 percent in 1975 as gas price increased and a very rapid general inflation rate bit into consumer purchasing power. Chrysler registrations dropped slightly more rapidly than the overall market in 1974, but then fell catastrophically the following year as the effects of inflation were cumulated with the antiquity of the product range and very widespread speculation about the company's future. In June 1975, Chrysler U.K. penetration was as low as 4.7 percent. In December 1975 it was 5.1 percent.

Chrysler's loss of market share in the United Kingdom was not unique, and the other three volume manufacturers were adversely affected in a similar manner. Until the events of 1975, Vauxhall had been performing even worse than Chrysler U.K. and British Leyland's market share dropped by one-third in ten years. From this viewpoint alone, therefore, the Chrysler problem can be seen as a more general U.K. motor industry problem, as the share of imports in the U.K. domestic market rose from only 5 percent in 1965 to one-third in 1975.

While the various dimensions of Chrysler performance will be analyzed during the course of this chapter, it is of some interest to note the competitive weaknesses of the U.K. car industry as a whole as highlighted in the 1975 Report of the Central Policy Review Staff:[1]

1. The product ranges of U.K. manufacturers were unbalanced, provided less car for the money than those of the importers, and, since 1973, had lost their price competitiveness.

2. Quality, reliability, and delivery records were poor.

3. The distribution networks of the importers into the United Kingdom were not matched by the dealer networks of U.K. manufacturers abroad.

4. U.K. manufacturing costs were higher than those of foreign countries.

5. The industry had underinvested over a long period of time.

Although Chrysler's sales performance on the U.K. market has been very unsatisfactory in terms of output, its position is rather different. As Table 5.2 indicates, the company's share of total U.K. production rose from under 11 percent in 1966 to almost 18 percent in 1975. This is entirely due to export growth, with Chrysler's share of total export market allocations rising strikingly from 8 to 30 percent over the period. The reasons for the dramatic improvement are discussed in the next section.

TABLE 5.1

U.K. Market Penetration

Year	Total New Registrations	Chrysler U.K. Registrations	Chrysler France Registrations	Percent Penetration										
				British Leyland	Ford	Vaux-hall	Chrysler U.K.[a]	Chrysler France	Renault	Volkswagen and Audi-NSU	Opel	Fiat	Datsun	All Importers
1965	1,098,887	131,024	n.a.	44.5	26.3	11.8	11.9	n.a.	n.a.	n.a.	n.a.	n.a.	n.a.	5.1
1966	1,047,522	123,173	n.a.	45.2	25.1	11.2	11.8	n.a.	n.a.	n.a.	n.a.	n.a.	n.a.	6.4
1967	1,110,266	135,036	n.a.	40.7	25.3	13.2	12.2	n.a.	n.a.	n.a.	n.a.	n.a.	n.a.	8.3
1968	1,103,862	112,506	n.a.	40.6	27.3	13.1	10.2	n.a.	n.a.	n.a.	n.a.	n.a.	n.a.	8.3
1969	965,410	93,378	3,738	40.2	27.3	11.7	9.7	0.4	2.1	2.2[b]	n.a.	2.2	n.a.	10.4
1970	1,076,865	112,590	7,854	38.1	26.5	10.0	10.5	0.7	2.9	4.3	0.2	2.2	0.2	14.3
1971	1,285,661	135,229	24,243	40.2	18.7	10.7	10.5	1.9	3.2	4.7	0.7	2.8	0.5	19.3
1972	1,637,866	153,765	32,917	33.1	24.5	9.0	9.4	2.0	3.7	4.1	0.9	2.9	1.9	23.5
1973	1,661,639	159,357	30,725	31.9	22.6	8.0	9.6	1.9	4.0	3.8	0.9	3.1	3.6	27.4
1974	1,268,655	113,962	23,492	32.7	22.7	7.3	9.0	1.9	4.5	3.1	0.7	3.4	4.6	27.9
1975	1,194,088	78,451	16,985	30.9	21.7	7.3	6.6	1.4	4.8	4.0	0.9	3.2	5.4	33.2

[a]The name of the company, of course, was Rootes Motors Ltd. until 1970.
[b]Volkswagen only.

Note: n.a. = data not available.

Source: Society of Motor Manufacturers and Traders, The Motor Industry of Great Britain, various issues.

TABLE 5.2

U.K. Production of Cars and Allocations for Home and Export Markets

Manufacturer	1966	1967	1968	1969	1970	1971	1972	1973	1974	1975
Total U.K. production										
British Leyland	788,284	726,700	818,289	830,874	788,737	886,721	916,218	875,839	738,503	605,141
Ford	466,177	440,711	533,701	531,623	448,422	366,602	546,722	453,448	383,724	329,648
Vauxhall	172,777	196,877	244,819	171,674	178,089	199,092	183,957	138,353	136,903	98,621
Chrysler U.K.	173,706	181,046	187,300	212,820	216,995	281,538	263,893	265,413	261,801	226,612
Total*	1,603,679	1,552,013	1,815,936	1,717,073	1,640,966	1,741,940	1,921,311	1,747,316	1,534,119	1,267,695
Percent Chrysler U.K.	10.8	11.7	10.3	12.4	13.2	16.2	13.7	15.2	17.1	17.9
Home market allocation										
British Leyland	470,981	444,683	420,788	422,409	420,357	500,884	568,893	527,841	415,980	348,469
Ford	275,032	268,286	280,226	283,718	262,682	239,542	420,082	341,445	290,570	240,431
Vauxhall	109,239	140,460	163,822	98,822	112,426	143,881	146,770	112,033	108,310	77,316
Chrysler U.K.	123,154	132,037	121,352	82,395	117,276	138,267	165,321	153,470	117,752	65,651
Total*	978,684	988,273	1,013,163	892,758	918,109	1,027,461	1,307,881	1,142,211	937,920	735,531
Percent Chrysler U.K.	12.6	13.4	12.0	9.2	12.8	13.5	12.6	13.4	12.6	8.9
Export market allocation										
British Leyland	317,303	282,017	397,501	408,465	368,380	385,837	347,325	347,998	322,523	256,672
Ford	191,145	172,425	253,475	247,905	185,740	127,060	126,640	112,003	93,154	89,217
Vauxhall	63,538	56,417	80,997	72,852	65,663	55,211	37,187	26,320	28,593	21,305
Chrysler U.K.	50,552	49,009	65,948	91,468	99,719	143,271	98,572	111,943	144,049	160,961
Total*	642,995	563,740	802,773	824,315	722,857	714,479	613,430	605,105	596,199	532,164
Percent Chrysler U.K.	8.1	8.7	8.2	11.1	13.8	20.1	16.1	18.5	24.2	30.2

*Totals include other manufacturers.

Source: Society of Motor Manufacturers and Traders, The Motor Industry of Great Britain, various editions.

139

EXPORTS

To a company such as Chrysler U.K., with an unsatisfactory market share domestically, the export market, particularly within Europe, could offer considerable potential. Until 1975, Chrysler had taken only tentative steps to integrate its European operations. However, the company had expressed the view that "we . . . believe the EEC to be our metropolitan market,"[2] and certainly, given the production volumes widely believed necessary to obtain competitive cost levels, the implementation of such a policy would seem necessary for profitability.

The Profitability of Exports

Of course, the contribution of export sales to company profitability also depends on the returns available, an issue that has been the subject of considerable debate in the United Kingdom. The manufacturers have claimed that the return available from exports is lower than that on domestic sales, and on this basis they have argued consistently the case for a strong home market base. Undoubtedly, there are extra costs to be borne in export markets, including insurance, transport and administration charges, specification changes, and special tests and inspections to meet approval requirements of the countries of destination. The manufacturers also argue that overseas markets are more price competitive, often meaning that prices have to be set at a level that does not recover the full costs of production. It is considered, therefore, in the industry that there is for each firm a ratio of export to home sales (the suggested proportions are 40 to 60) that is the maximum compatible with the creation of adequate profits for future investment.[3]

On the other hand, an inspection of the home and export prices of manufacturers reveals that some firms are able to exploit a more inelastic demand in export markets by charging higher prices than at home.[4] But in the main this does not apply to exports of cars that compete in the volume market in which Chrysler is represented; and Chrysler, in its annual reports and elsewhere, consistently has expressed the view that profit margins are much tighter on export business.

In the context of pricing by multinational firms in export markets, allegations have been made that Chrysler has operated its transfer prices to the disadvantage of its U.K. subsidiary.[5] It was argued that the unit export prices charged by Chrysler U.K. were significantly lower than those charged by British Leyland, Ford, or Vauxhall, with the aim of transferring revenue from the United Kingdom to Switzerland via Chrysler International S.A. The accusations were fairly superficial, given the difficulties of obtaining substantive information, and the company vigorously denied their validity both in press releases and in evidence to the House of Commons Expenditure Committee in 1975. However, Chrysler was probably less forthcoming than it might have been in replying to the allegations, stating that transfer prices were determined "in order to put a profit in the price in the United Kingdom just as we would sell [the end product] to any other customer."[6]

The company was questioned again on the subject early in 1976, and once more denied adjusting prices anywhere in the world on the basis of prevailing rates of profit and taxation. The point was made that "we cannot operate companies in any country without them all having a fair share of the ultimate end profit of each vehicle" and "if we did . . . the best thing would be to put all the profits into Chrysler U.K. which pays no tax at all."[7] This specific issue remains unresolved, although undoubtedly transfer pricing does add a further dimension to export profitability in international firms such as Chrysler.

Export Performance

Rootes was in the forefront of the U.K. car industry's export drive in the early postwar years. However, as the export boom receded with the emergence of increased competition, Rootes' export-production ratio declined faster than the industry average to under one-third in the early 1960s. The financial difficulties of the company meant that it was in a weak position to develop overseas markets on a long-term basis through the establishment of assembly plants and investment in distribution networks.

Table 5.3 suggests, however, that under Chrysler the company has been extremely successful in export markets. From a position where Chrysler U.K. exported a lower proportion of its output than that of any of the volume manufacturers, the company's export ratio in 1975 was over 70 percent compared with 42 percent for the industry as a whole. In different terms, Chrysler accounted for 30 percent of car exports from the United Kingdom in 1975. As will be seen, virtually all of the increase in Chrysler's unit exports is represented by sales to a single country—Iran. (Chrysler's contract with Iran will be discussed in a later section.) It is noteworthy that the export ratios of the other two U.S. subsidiaries manufacturing in the United Kingdom have shown the reverse trend, a reflection of parent company strategy and of the poorer performance of these companies in comparison with the respective German subsidiaries of Ford and GM.

TABLE 5.3

Percentage of Car Output Exported by U.K. Manufacturers

	British Leyland	Ford	Vaux-hall	Chrysler U.K.	All Manufacturers
1966	40.3	41.0	36.8	29.1	39.0
1967	38.8	39.1	28.7	27.1	36.3
1968	48.6	47.5	33.1	35.2	44.2
1969	49.2	46.6	42.4	43.0	48.0
1970	46.7	41.4	36.9	46.0	44.1
1971	43.5	34.7	27.7	50.9	41.0
1972	37.9	23.2	20.2	37.4	31.9
1973	39.7	24.7	19.0	42.2	34.6
1974	43.7	24.3	20.9	55.0	38.9
1975	42.4	27.1	21.6	71.0	42.0

Sources: Society of Motor Manufacturers and Traders, The Motor Industry of Great Britain, various editions.

As a member of a corporation operating worldwide, and with other subsidiaries of that corporation also existing in Europe, the export performance of Chrysler U.K. cannot be assessed without reference to the wider issues accruing from membership of such a multinational enterprise. In general terms, exports from the subsidiaries of international firms may benefit from access to wider markets but, against this, market-sharing agreements may be operated that inhibit export sales. With regard to Chrysler U.K. and Chrysler France, for example, some overlaps in the ranges produced by the two companies could mean that gains in sales by one company in a particular market were partly at the expense of the market share of the other.

There has been some integration between the two subsidiaries in a number of ways. Product development has been completely integrated with the centralization of design and development at Whitley in England; and the dealer networks of the two companies handle each other's vehicles to some extent (subject to the comments made in a later paragraph). But a fully developed integration strategy would also require a common product range, and very limited progress has been made in this direction. The company says that "the primary reason is the tremendous cost involved: and that while, for example, it was interested in getting the Simca 1100 built in the United Kingdom,

"the costs were something we could not stomach out of our own resources in the United Kingdom."[8]

Given this lack of integration, together with the more acceptable
Simca range, as well as other factors, Chrysler France had a much
higher export ratio than its fellow subsidiary in the United Kingdom until the benefits of the Iranian contract began to be felt. Simca's export
ratio doubled during the 1960s from 29 percent in 1961 to 58 percent
in 1969 and increased further to represent about two-thirds of output
in the early 1970s.[9] The French subsidiary's exports are concentrated
on the European market, where its penetration is much more satisfactory than that of Chrysler U.K. In 1975, 52 percent of Chrysler France
output was sold outside its home country but within the EEC, in comparison with 4 percent for Chrysler U.K. A large part of this clearly
reflects an "EEC effect" brought about by the abolition of tariffs, but
in addition, the continental European manufacturers have always been
more closely tied to Europe as a market base than U.K. manufacturers. Having said this, Chrysler France also outsells Chrysler U.K.
in all of the former EFTA countries.

It is possible to argue that Chrysler U.K.'s performance in Europe has been adversely affected by uncertainty over U.K. membership
in the EEC, but, on the other hand, as the chairman of Chrysler U.K.
stated in 1975, "We have believed . . . for the best part of ten years
that this country would eventually join the EEC."[10] Chrysler U.K.
also has been in a better position than, say, Ford U.K. or Vauxhall to
launch a sustained export drive in Europe in that, ostensibly at least,
it has not been inhibited by the market-sharing agreements that have
affected these other two companies. Table 5.4 shows that Ford U.K.
sold no cars in West Germany or the Netherlands and only token numbers in France, Belgium, and Italy, whereas Ford Germany was only
restricted from selling to the British market. Vauxhall, too, has effectively been prevented from competing in the two of the largest continental European markets, France and Italy. While no such restrictions apparently apply to Chrysler U.K., the small numbers of cars
that the company sold in all the EEC countries suggests a complete
lack of commitment. With an acceptable car such as the Avenger,
the sales potential foregone in the Community is undoubtedly very substantial. In 1975, indeed, registrations of Chrysler U.K. cars in the
main markets of France and West Germany were so low (663 and 698,
respectively) as to suggest mere window dressing.

Of course, increased exports by Chrysler U.K. to the EEC
would be likely to affect Simca sales adversely (for example, Avenger
versus Simca 1301/1501). In this context, there were suggestions
during 1975 that the corporation's marketing policy (as implemented
by Chrysler International S.A.) in Belgium, in particular, but also
elsewhere in Europe, discriminated against Chrysler U.K. cars while

TABLE 5.4

Intra-EEC Sales of Cars by U.S. Subsidiaries in Europe, 1975

From	To Belgium Luxembourg	Denmark	France	Germany	Italy	Netherlands	Ireland	Total EEC Sales	EEC Sales as Percent of Production	EEC Sales Outside Home Country as Percent of Production
Ford Germany	37,940	9,458	49,554	283,697	25,550	36,370	—	442,569	107.1[a]	38.5
Ford U.K.	5	3,019	71	—	5	—	258,496	261,596	79.4	0.9
Total Ford (Europe)	37,945	12,477	49,625	283,697	25,555	36,370	258,496	704,165	94.8	21.8
Opel	23,891	8,917	26,734	381,397	28,950	48,773	10,306	528,968	80.7	22.5
Vauxhall	4,304	1,107	1	1,211	130	3,732	87,570	98,055	99.4	10.6
Total GM (Europe)	28,195	10,024	26,735	382,608	29,080	52,505	97,876	627,023	83.1	20.9
Chrysler France	22,896	6,968	132,396	55,903	58,250	36,528	16,985	329,926	86.1	51.5
Chrysler U.K.	2,424	1,844	663	699	700	2,513	78,451	87,294	38.5	3.9
Total Chrysler (Europe)[b]	25,320	8,812	133,059	56,602	58,950	39,041	95,436	417,220	68.4	33.8
Model Breakdown of Sales										
Chrysler France										
Simca 1000	4,051	186	19,171	8,955	29,440	6,351	3,163	71,277		
Simca 1100	11,062	5,162	77,755	20,125	17,700	22,668	8,613	162,485		
Simca 1301/1501	5,018	1,013	16,146	18,171	10,300	5,986	3,449	60,083		
Simca 160/180/2 litre	2,196	334	4,447	3,735	800	2,123	1,714	15,349		
Simca 1307/1308	569	273	14,874	4,497	—	—	—	20,213		
Chrysler U.K.										
Imp	—	—	—	—	3	—	10,463	10,466		
Avenger	2,104	1,844	592	—	—	2,200	38,877	45,617		
Hunter	187	—	71	—	690	190	28,966	30,104		

[a]Represents stock rundown.
[b]Excluding Chrysler Spain.
Source: L'Argus de L'Automobile (Paris), June 1976.

conferring artificial advantage to Simca cars.[11] The specific allegation was that dealers in Belgium had sales quotas fixed for Chrysler
U.K. and Simca cars in the ratio 1:7. While the particular issue may
not have too much substance, explanations of the situation brought up
facts that go some way in explaining Chrysler U.K.'s poor performance in Europe. For example, it was revealed that it was not until
1974 that the corporation began to create a unified British-French
dealer network in Belgium, and in so doing increased the number of
dealers selling Chrysler U.K. cars from 104 in 1974 to 187 in 1975.
On the principle (which the Japanese have exploited so brilliantly) that
a strong dealer network is a prerequisite for successful exporting, the
Belgian data may provide one of the main reasons for Chrysler U.K.'s
inadequate export performance in Europe.

Chrysler U.K.'s emphasis on non-European markets is partly a
question of traditional links. Before the Chrysler takeover, Rootes
had assembly facilities in Australia, South Africa, the Philippines,
Turkey, Venezuela, and elsewhere. The company's annual report for
1967 showed the following breakdown of exports by destination: Europe, 23.6 percent; North and South America, 26 percent; Africa and
the Middle East, 24.8 percent; the Far East, 12.8 percent; and Australasia, 12.8 percent. Since then, the two major changes affecting
the level and destination of Chrysler U.K. exports have been the development of the market in Iran and the rapid expansion, for a short
period of time, in sales of the Avenger to the United States (until its
replacement by the Mitsubishi Colt). The decision to import the
Avenger to compete in the subcompact market had a striking effect
on Chrysler U.K.'s sales to the United States, which rose from 3,200
units in 1970 to 28,000 in 1971 (Table 5.5). The subsequent move to
import the Mitsubishi model alone, more than any other perhaps,
forced the U.K. subsidiary to try to cultivate Europe. But with success in this highly competitive market a long-term prospect, Chrysler U.K. has become virtually a single-market exporter.

The Iranian Contract

Links between Chrysler U.K. (or Rootes as it then was) and
Iran go back a number of years. As early as 1967, a plant designed
by Rootes engineers for the assembly and progressive manufacture
of Hillman Hunter and Minx cars was opened in Teheran. It was not,
however, until May 1970 that the present manufacturing and license
agreement between Chrysler U.K. and the Iran National Industrial
Manufacturing Company (INIM) for the supply of passenger cars was
signed, and followed up with a sales and distribution agreement in
January 1972. The contracts run until 1980, short of default, and

TABLE 5.5

U.S. Motor Vehicle Imports[a]

	1966	1967	1968	1969	1970	1971	1972	1973	1974	1975
Captive imports[b]										
Opel	32,044	51,693	84,680	93,520	86,630	88,535	69,407	68,400	59,279	36,893
Vauxhall	—	—	—	—	—	—	—	—	—	—
Total GM (Europe)	32,044	51,693	84,680	93,520	86,630	88,535	69,407	68,400	59,279	36,893
Ford U.K.	—	4,810	24,402	21,675	10,216	757	—	—	—	—
Ford Germany	—	—	—	—	17,258	56,118	91,995	113,069	75,260	54,585
Total Ford (Europe)	—	4,810	24,402	21,675	27,474	56,875	91,995	113,069	75,260	54,585
Chrysler U.K.	—	7,764	3,477	2,994	3,160	29,038	13,882	4,819	—	—
Chrysler France	13,205	5,955	5,531	8,120	6,035	4,877	1,026	—	—	—
Total Chrysler (Europe)	13,205	13,719	9,008	11,114	9,195	32,915	14,908	—	—	—
Total captive imports from Europe	45,249	70,222	118,090	126,039	123,299	178,325	176,310	186,288	134,529	91,478
Other										
Volkswagen and Audi	427,694	454,801	582,009	566,356	590,280	554,151	521,012	526,738	387,008	321,513
Toyota	20,908	38,073	71,463	13,044	208,315	309,363	311,770	326,844	269,376	322,553
Datsun	29,131	45,491	56,233	86,883	151,509	251,925	268,666	319,007	254,273	331,203
Mazda	—	—	—	—	2,098	20,474	62,818	119,004	75,079	69,384
Fiat	—	15,933	30,521	21,496	36,096	46,819	58,375	58,447	72,129	101,820
Mitsubishi	—	—	—	—	—	28,381	34,057	35,523	42,925	60,356
British Leyland	56,685	57,691	58,616	69,026	68,852	65,924	68,641	65,948	54,870	70,839
Volvo	25,155	34,396	38,826	36,146	44,513	48,222	57,772	60,761	53,043	60,338
Mercedes-Benz	16,465	20,691	24,533	26,193	29,108	35,156	41,998	42,405	38,826	42,232
All imports[c]	706,495	837,857	1,084,350	1,173,499	1,400,823	1,703,709	1,785,079	19,453,631	1,558,729	1,762,004

[a]Import sales of cars, tourist deliveries, and trucks.

[b]Imports by the Big Three from their European subsidiaries.

[c]Includes manufacturers, such as Honda, Renault, Saab, and so on, which are not shown separately.

Source: Ward's Automotive Yearbook (Detroit: Wards), 1975 and 1976.

146

thereafter may be continued with the agreement of both parties. The arrangements conducted with Iran are of major importance for two reasons: first, there is considerable political significance and second, the size of the contract means that it has a very important bearing on the future viability of Chrysler U.K.

At the time of the Chrysler crisis in December 1975, the press was speculating that one of the major factors that swung the cabinet toward a policy of supporting Chrysler was the reaction of the Iranian government.[12] Whether or not the events were actually as dramatic as reported is doubtful, but certainly the secretary of state for industry confirmed later that: "The Iranian Government made it clear that the loss of the Iranian contract could seriously affect U.K. business dealings with Iran. It would also have been very bad for our competitive position as exporters throughout the valuable Middle East market."[13]

The Iranian contract is essentially for the supply of knockdown (KD) Hillman Hunter cars, assembled and sold in Iran as the Peykan, although in 1975 Avengers were also exported in both built-up and KD forms to meet the shortfall in local assembly production. Sales of the Peykan are promoted through protective import tariffs in Iran that make imported cars 30 percent more expensive than the locally assembled vehicle. In 1974, about 80,000 vehicles were supplied, representing 55 percent of Chrysler's export market allocations for that year and 30 percent of the company's total U.K. output. In 1975, approximately 150,000 cars were to be exported to Iran, with an estimated 3,000 jobs associated with the contract. A target of 200,000 cars was set for 1976, and increases thereafter would bring sales to an annual maximum of between 500,000 and 1 million cars. These targets, however, and particularly those for 1976 and 1977, will not be achieved because of a shortage of assembly capacity in Iran. Under the terms of a Technical Assistance Program between Chrysler U.K. and INIM at the end of 1974, 12 personnel from Chrysler Corporation were assigned to Iran to provide technical expertise in building a new press shop. But the program was delayed, and only about half of the kits shipped to Iran were assembled during 1975. The implication is that Chrysler exports in 1976 will be only about 80,000 units, rising to 125,000 units in 1977.

At present, all of the cars exported are in completely knockdown form (CKD) with assembly in Iran, but the intention is that local manufacture should progressively take the place of imports. A new iron casting foundry was opened in Iran at the end of 1974, and inevitably domestic production will reduce the need for imports from Chrysler U.K. to some extent in terms of the percentage of each car, if not in terms of the total number of cars. Nevertheless, during the rest of the contract period at least, Chrysler U.K.'s sales to Iran are

certain to remain highly significant to the company. After that, the
position is more doubtful, not only because of the increased work undertaken locally but also because Renault, Peugeot, Toyota, and Volkswagen are all believed to be planning to build assembly plants in Iran.

The crucial, but regrettably unanswerable, question is how
profitable the contract is to Chrysler U.K. The Trade and Industry
Sub-Committee investigating the Public Expenditure on Chrysler U.K.
Ltd. raised a number of issues relevant to the profitability of the contract with Gwain Gillespie, the Chrysler Corporation's executive vice-
president—Europe.[14] The allegation that a company called Exporters
Forwarding Company, Inc. in Germany derived commission at the rate
of 5 percent on sales of CKD units to Iran (implicitly therefore to the
detriment of Chrysler U.K.) was investigated inconclusively. On another issue, the vice-president agreed that Chrysler U.K. gives INIM
a credit facility of £20 million with interest payable at 1.5 percent
above Chrysler's clearing bank base rate. However, he denied that
this had any effect upon the borrowing power of the company in the
United Kingdom since the credit facility was a loan arranged quite
separately through the Export Credits Guarantee Department (ECGD).

The managing director of the U.K. subsidiary is reported to
have stated that with regard to CKD activities, of which the Iranian
contract is by far the largest, the company always covers its fixed
costs but not necessarily its variable costs because of the tight margin. However, such operations were considered to be important in
that they assisted in meeting fixed overheads and so on for home market production.[15] Bearing out this point, estimates indicate unit
revenue on sales to Iran to be about 17 percent lower than equivalent
sales made in the United Kingdom.[16] But this in itself is not particularly meaningful since the effects of the extra output on unit costs
also need to be considered.

COST PERFORMANCE

In assessing Chrysler's performance record in the past ten
years or so, so far the emphasis has been almost entirely on the demand side, with attention being drawn to the company's marketing
problems both at home and abroad. In this section, the focus is redirected to examine the impact of production and cost factors. Two
key issues of relevance to cost performance, industrial relations
and government policy, will be pursued further in Chapters 7 and 8.

Apart from requiring a competitive product range that is marketed efficiently, a successful profit performance will also necessitate
a competitive level of costs. The costs of production will be a function
of a number of factors: the scale of operations, the degree of utiliza-

tion of the capacity installed, the level of capital and labor costs, and so on. These will be considered in turn.

Scale of Operations

Returns to scale (economies and diseconomies) refer to the effects on average costs of production in a certain time period of different rates of output, assuming that at each scale production is as efficient as possible. (This is the long-run average cost, or scale curve, of the firm.) Studies have shown that in the motor industry the potential economies of scale are significant, although varying among the main manufacturing operations. The annual production volumes required for the use of the most efficient techniques are suggested to be final assembly, 250,000 to 300,000 units; casting of the engine block, 100,000 units; and engine and transmission machining and assembly, 500,000 units.[17] The important question is, however, the size of the cost disadvantage facing any firm with plants of less than optimum size. It is estimated that for a plant of only half the minimum efficient size, average total costs rise by about 6 percent.[18] While this may not seem large in terms of costs, its significance lies in the effect it has on profit margins per unit, particularly, as will be seen, when taken together with the possibility of underutilization of plants.

Given these optima, only British Leyland and Ford in the United Kingdom have present production volumes large enough to achieve the minimum optimum scale in casting, forging, and final assembly operations. In engine production, these companies could approach the optimum by limiting the number of basic engine and transmission ranges. In the case of Chrysler U.K., with the combined capacity of the two assembly plants at Ryton and Linwood being only 365,000 units, neither is sufficiently large to achieve optimum costings, and the Stoke engine plant is also well below minimum efficient size in relation to the figures quoted. The same problem does not exist with Chrysler France. Here the Poissy assembly plant has a capacity more than 50 percent greater than the combined capacity of the U.K. subsidiary's two plants.

Comments on economies of scale must always be heavily qualified. For example, smaller firms may offset the advantages of their larger competitors by keeping particular models in production over a longer period of years and by having a smaller product range and a small range of derivatives. These are, indeed, some of the types of policies followed by Chrysler since its takeover of Rootes, although such policies create their own problems on the marketing side. At the same time, smaller companies are able to obtain economies of scale secondhand by purchasing standardized components from outside

TABLE 5.6

Sample Percentages of Material Cost of Cars Accounted for by
Bought-Out Components

GM U.S.	46
Ford U.S.	61
Chrysler U.S.	60
Mazda Japan	54
Toyota Japan	59
Datsun Japan	65
Ford U.K.	65–70
British Leyland U.K.	
Chrysler U.K.	71
Vauxhall U.K.	85

Source: Fourteenth Report from the Expenditure Committee,
sess. 1974-75, The Motor Vehicle Industry, HC 617 (London: HMSO,
August 1975), p. 19.

suppliers; and, as Table 5.6 indicates, Chrysler U.K. and Vauxhall
cars contain a higher proportion of purchased components than those
of many other manufacturers.

These were the types of arguments that Vauxhall used when it
stated before the Expenditure Committee that "an operation of the
size of Vauxhall . . . could be quite viable."[19] The chairman of
Chrysler also thought that his company could compete with the major
Japanese manufacturers, provided its cost structures were right.
Against this must be set the reasoning of Ford U.K. that "we need
in this business to get economies of scale to remain profitable, [and]
these are real problems for small-volume producers."[20] The company also argued strongly that the integration of its U.K. and German
operations and the commensurate increase in volumes thereby obtained
were of great importance in achieving maximum economies of scale.

There are other dimensions to economies of scale in car production than the strictly technical economies that have been discussed
here, including economies and diseconomies in research and development, marketing, management, and finance. In addition, external
economies are likely to develop with the location of a number of car
firms in the same area; diseconomies may arise in situations where
government regional policy instruments have been used to channel ex-

pansion away from traditional areas. This is particularly relevant to
Chrysler U.K. with its Linwood plant, and the effects on the company
of operating in Scotland are considered fully in Chapter 8. Overall,
therefore, while impossible to quantify, there do appear to be significant cost penalties in operating as a volume producer at the scale of
Chrysler U.K. or Vauxhall. This assumes, however, that all firms
are utilizing their plants as fully as possible. To the extent that this
is not done, a further element is introduced into cost comparisons between manufacturers.

Utilization of Capacity

It is generally agreed that car manufacture, as a capital-intensive industry, requires high capacity utilization for profitable operation. Chrysler U.K., for example, has suggested that if one of its
plants producing approximately 100,000 units annually was to increase
output to its capacity of 160,000 units, the cost per unit would decrease
by approximately £60.[21] While this is only perhaps 5 or 6 percent of
total costs, it is very important to a firm such as Chrysler since profit
margins may be tight to begin with because of the company's disadvantages of scale.

High capacity utilization requires, first, stability in the growth
of demand and, second, the avoidance of interruptions in supply.
Stable growth is partly a function of a company's own marketing poli -
cies, but in addition, in the United Kingdom it has been influenced very
markedly by successive governments' use of the motor industry as an
economic regulator. This important issue will be discussed more fully
in Chapter 7, but the general view of the U.K. manufacturers has been
summed up by the chairman of Chrysler U.K. as: "The many changes
in fiscal policies and in their execution during the period and the artificial depression on the home market . . . have been very significant
factors in making the United Kingdom position, not only of Chrysler,
much worse than that of the rest of the European automobile manufacturers." He added that this had affected investment decisions in the
United Kingdom "because the shortage of volume [volume being one
function of profit making] has meant relatively poor performance in
cash flow and therefore inadequate monies for the investments which
would otherwise have been made."[22]

Continuity of production is equally important, and Chrysler's
record in this direction is indicated in Figure 5.1. It has been estimated that a stoppage resulting in the loss of a single hour's production in an eight-hour shift would reduce profitability for the day by at
least 40 percent.[23] The integrated nature of car manufacturing operations makes the industry very vulnerable to production interruptions.

FIGURE 5.1

Chrysler U.K.: Quarterly Car Production
(seasonally adjusted)

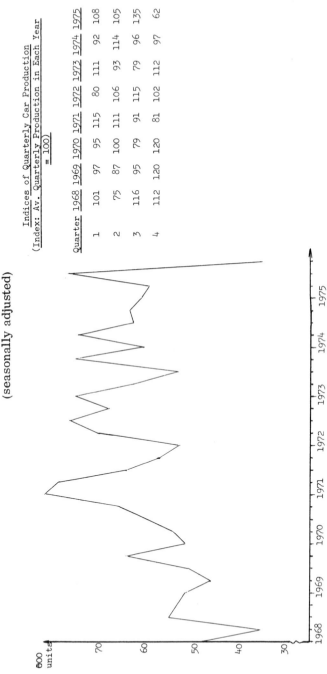

	Indices of Quarterly Car Production							
	(Index: Av. Quarterly Production in Each Year = 100)							
Quarter	1968	1969	1970	1971	1972	1973	1974	1975
1	101	97	95	115	80	111	92	108
2	75	87	100	111	106	93	114	105
3	116	95	79	91	115	79	96	135
4	112	120	120	81	102	112	97	62

Source: Derived from data in Society of Motor Manufacturers and Traders, Monthly Statistical Bulletins, various issues.

Such stoppages are not merely related to labor disputes, for with several thousand parts being supplied by at least 70 companies to any one vehicle assembly point, the possibilities of interruptions are endless. Nevertheless, as Chapter 8 will show, industrial disputes have posed very major problems for Chrysler U.K., as well as for the entire U.K. car industry. Apart from the short-run impact on costs and profits, these persistent stoppages, which have been the hallmark of the U.K. motor industry, may have serious long-term repercussions through their effects on consumers and dealers and on investment decisions.

In attempting to assess the degree to which the U.K. car industry and Chrysler U.K. have suffered from underutilization of capacity, severe difficulties are posed by definitional problems. "Capacity" can mean many things, depending upon the manufacturing operation considered, the number of shifts worked, assumptions on overtime, the size of the labor force, the product mix, and so on. In one definition, the four volume manufacturers in the United Kingdom have a two-shift capacity of just over 2.5 million cars; by comparison, 1975 output was almost exactly half this figure (Table 5.7). The performance of Chrysler U.K. was the best of the major manufacturers, assisted by the relatively recession-proof contract with Iran, but even here about two-fifths of capacity was unused. In spite of the Chrysler crisis, Vauxhall, with a similar capacity on paper to Chrysler, produced less than half as many cars.

Given the considerable spare capacity existing in the industry, the important issue is the level of utilization required to break even within different firms. With a rise in the proportion of fixed costs in total costs and increasing international competition squeezing profit margins, there has been a rise in break-even levels overall. It is estimated that 1.8 million units are now required for break-even in the U.K. car industry, approximately 70 percent of present capacity.[24] While it would be misleading to try to derive break-even levels for individual manufacturers from profit performance directly, given the wide variety of additional factors that affect the latter, a comparison between utilization levels and profitability is of interest.

Ford recorded substantial losses in 1971 when only half the company's capacity was being utilized; and British Leyland was only marginally profitable at between 65 and 70 percent of capacity. Chrysler U.K. made small profits in the three years from 1971 on a throughput of about 75 percent of capacity. Although Chrysler's utilization was maintained in 1974, the heavy losses can be attributed to the fact that sales did not match output levels and a significant stock buildup occurred, while additionally, high wage settlements affected costs adversely.

On the basis of this tenuous evidence, Chrysler seems to require a much higher throughput than Vauxhall to achieve profitability and per-

TABLE 5.7

U.K. Motor Industry: Capacity Utilization

Manufacturer	Maximum Planned Capacity on a Two-Shift Basis	Record Output	1975 Output	1975 Percent Utilization
Autin-Morris	850,000	720,000 (1964)	450,000	53
Jaguar	45,000	31,500 (1971)		
Triumph	190,000	144,000 (1968)	155,200	53
Rover	60,000	55,800 (1972)		
British Leyland	1,145,000		605,200	
Ford	650,000	533,700 (1968)	329,600	51
Vauxhall	365,000	245,000 (1968)	98,600	27
Chrysler U.K.	365,000	281,500 (1971)	226,600	62
	2,525,000	2,030,800	1,260,000	50

Sources: Society of Motor Manufacturers and Traders, The Motor Industry of Great Britain, 1976, Fourteenth Report from the Expenditure Committee, sess. 1974-75, The Motor Vehicle Industry, HC 617 (London: HMSO, August 1975), p. 22.

haps also a somewhat higher level of utilization than either Ford or British Leyland. If this interpretation is correct, then it marks a profound change, for in the years immediately after Chrysler took control of Rootes, it was suggested that the company's break-even point between total costs per unit and total revenue per unit was reached at just under 60 percent of maximum capacity.[25] The implications of this become apparent when consideration is given to the prospects for the industry as a whole, both in the United Kingdom and in the rest of Europe over the next few years, as discussed in Chapter 1. With substantial excess capacity likely to exist on a long-term basis in Europe, clearly Chrysler's ability to attain the utilization levels required for profitability becomes much more difficult.

Labor Costs

Labor costs per hour are basically a function of two elements: hourly wage costs and productivity (output per worker). Within the United Kingdom, differences in labor costs among manufacturers are perhaps less important in an efficiency than in an industrial relations context, and some reference to this will be made in Chapter 7. As among countries in Europe, on the other hand, very large differences exist in labor costs per hour. For example, in the middle of 1975 labor costs for assembly workers in Belgium and West Germany were about 80 percent higher than in the United Kingdom (see Table 5.8).

The important factor is, however, the efficiency wage that takes account not only of labor costs but also relative productivities. Labor productivity is determined by a number of factors—manning levels, number of stoppages, level of investment, and so on—and thus is closely related to issues discussed in previous sections. The instability of demand, which has been a feature of the U.K. car market, represents an obstacle to productivity improvement because it creates conditions that discourage cost-saving investment. A more intensive utilization of plant would increase productivity, as would a greater overall level of output, since advantage could then be taken of economies of scale. But, in addition, in the U.K. industry there is evidence of substantial overmanning, reflecting partly at least the impact of trade demarcations on the mobility and interchangeability of labor. The combined effect of these and other factors has been to produce a rate of productivity growth in the U.K. motor industry that has only been about half that of U.K. manufacturing industry as a whole since the early 1960s.[26]

TABLE 5.8

Index of Cost per Hour to Employers for Assembly Line Workers,
August 1975
(U.K. cost = 100)

France	120
Italy	130
West Germany	180
Belgium	180

Source: Central Policy Review Staff Report, The Future of the British Car Industry (London: HMSO, 1975).

In a crude comparison of vehicles produced per employee, U.K. manufacturers compare very unfavorably with their continental counterparts, as Table 5.9 indicates. When adjustment is made for the greater importance of commercial vehicle output to the U.K. manufacturers (where labor content is higher), the position is changed somewhat. Productivity in Ford U.K., for example, was probably about equal to that of Ford Germany in 1974, although output per worker was admittedly very depressed in the German subsidiary in that year. Because of the fact that commercial vehicle manufacture is of less importance to Chrysler U.K. than to either Ford U.K. or Vauxhall, however, the adjusted output per worker was still markedly below that of Chrysler France—a productivity difference of at least 50 percent. In the peak output year of 1971, the adjusted production per year in Chrysler U.K. was still just over 11 vehicles.

These comparisons still fail to take account of differences in the degrees of integration among individual manufacturers, and the extent to which manufacturers rely on purchase components. As a result, it has been suggested that a more reliable indicator of productivity performance is value added per worker. In fact, definitional difficulties still loom large, and there are additional complications created by exchange rate movements. However, the same kinds of conclusions are borne out in the data (see Table 5.10). In 1974, value added per worker in Chrysler France was 50 percent higher than in Chrysler U.K. Even in the case of Chrysler France, however, value added per worker was low by international standards.

Clearly, the important factor is how far these differences can be explained, and in particular how far they can be attributed to differences in the level of investment among manufacturers as opposed to overmanning, underutilization of capacity, industrial stoppages, and so forth. In Table 5.10 figures of value added per worker are shown alongside data on gross output and fixed assets per employee. A fairly close relationship exists between value added and the level of fixed assets, tempting a conclusion that underinvestment is the major source of productivity differences. That it is one factor, there can be no doubt. As a Ford U.K. union official put it: "If a Ford worker in Germany can feed in 60 sheets of metal into a press and in Dagenham he can only feed in 45 due to the age and speed of the press, who is the more productive?"[27] However, other evidence has shown that even where facilities are similar between U.K. and continental European plants, it still takes substantially more man-hours to manufacture a car in Britain.

When labor costs per hour are taken together with labor productivity, some indication can be given of relative labor costs per unit among manufacturers. Assuming that wage costs per hour for assembly workers in Simca are about 20 percent higher than in Chrysler

TABLE 5.9

Estimated Number of Vehicles Produced per Employee

	1965[a]	1973	1974
British Leyland[b]	6.5	5.9	5.0
Ford U.K.[b]	10.9	9.7 (10.8–11.7)[c]	8.5 (9.5–10.5)[c]
Vauxhall	10.1	7.1 (8.6–10.3)[c]	7.4 (8.9–10.8)[c]
Chrysler U.K.	7.0	9.4 (9.7)[c]	9.3 (9.5)[c]
Ford Germany	13.8	13.9	9.5
Opel	12.0	n.a.	10.0
Chrysler France	n.a.	n.a.	14.9
Volkswagen	13.8	n.a.	18.5
Renault	9.8	n.a.	15.4

[a]1965 figures from Pratten and Silberston. Note their cautionary remarks.

[b]Based on U.K. employees only. Ford U.K. includes tractor output.

[c]Estimates of vehicles produced per employee adjusted to take product mix into account. Range reflects differing assumptions about proportions of commercial vehicle output in gross vehicle weight groups. Basic methodology follows Pratten and Silberston.

Note: n.a. = data not available.

Sources: Company accounts; Society of Motor Manufacturers and Traders, The Motor Industry of Great Britain, various editions; C. Pratton and A. Silberston, "International Comparisons of Labour Productivity in the Automobile Industry 1950–1965," Bulletin of the Oxford Institute of Economics and Statistics 29 (1967).

U.K., but productivity is 50 percent greater, in Simca labor costs per unit will be about one-fifth less than in the U.K. subsidiary. While this is only a hypothetical calculation based on aggregate figures presented earlier, it does at least provide some indication of the magnitude of the cost penalties of operating in the United Kingdom.

INVESTMENT

The discussion on the impact of investment on productivity (Table 5.10) showed that fixed assets per employee in Chrysler U.K. were very low in international terms. The U.K. company admitted this

158   CHRYSLER U.K.: A CORPORATION IN TRANSITION

TABLE 5.10

Comparisons of Labor Productivity, 1974
(in pounds)

Manufacturer	Value Added per Employee	Gross Output per Employee	Fixed Assets per Employee
GM U.S.	8,600	17,495	4,346
Ford U.S.	7,966	19,905	5,602
Opel	5,875	14,747	3,612
Daimler-Benz	5,207	12,672	2,694
Volvo	4,886	14,790	4,662
Ford Germany	4,883	14,186	3,608
Volkswagen	4,767	11,087	3,632
Saab	4,637	19,972	3,141
Renault	4,133	12,928	2,396
Chrysler France[a]	4,123	13,614	2,469
Ford U.K.	3,901	11,397	2,657
Chrysler U.K.[b]	2,765	9,968	1,456
Vauxhall	2,560	7,975	1,356
Fiat	2,259	8,142	3,160
British Leyland	2,129	6,539	920

[a]Based on number of employees and fixed assets at 1974 year-end. Converted at midyear exchange rates.

[b]Based on data in Chrysler's 1973 annual report. In 1974, gross output per employee was £10,067 and fixed assets per employee £1,330.

Sources: Fourteenth Report from the Expenditure Committee, sess. 1974-75, The Motor Vehicle Industry, HC 617 (London: HMSO, August 1975), p. 36; and Chrysler France and Chrysler U.K. annual reports, 1973 and 1974.

when it released figures for fixed assets per employee in the Chrysler Corporation and European subsidiaries in 1973: Chrysler Corporation, £3,377; Chrysler Espana, £2,836; Chrysler France, £2,274; and Chrysler U.K., £1,550.[28] Although the U.K. subsidiary argued that the U.K. figure should be raised to £2,146, the relative position is still unchanged. Given the undoubted importance of the level of investment for company performance, the aim of the present section is to assess how this disturbing position came about.

Soon after the takeover of Rootes, Chrysler set in motion a
big investment program in the United Kingdom to reequip and restructure the production facilities of its subsidiary. Capital expenditure
reached a peak of £21 million in 1968/69 with the introduction of new
paint and body manufacturing shops at Ryton and the expansion of
capacity in the pressing plant and the machine shop at Linwood (Table
5.11). Until 1970, therefore, the majority of the corporation's European investment was allocated to the United Kingdom, with Chrysler
U.K.'s net capital employed rising in money terms from £59 to £69.5
million (see Table 5.14). This emphasis on Chrysler U.K. was not
particularly surprising, of course, since the initial posttakeover investment program in Simca was substantially completed by the end of
1967. In that year, capital expenditure peaked at 295 million francs,
15 percent of turnover.

In viewing the investment situation in the 1970s, an understanding of the Chrysler Corporation's overall policy toward its subsidiaries is of importance. The chairman of Chrysler U.K. gave a clear
indication of this policy when he declared:

> After initial injection of capital into its daughter companies,
> assuming they are capably run and the economic climate is
> right, it expects them to generate their own funds for their

TABLE 5.11

Gross Fixed Capital Expenditure in Chrysler U.K.
(millions of pounds)

	1968	1969	1970	1971	1972	1973	1974	1975
Property	2.1	4.6	5.3	0.5	0.6	1.1	0.6	0.3
Plant and equipment	3.8	8.5	6.6	3.0	1.9	3.3	0.5	0.2
Special tools[a]	1.8	8.6	4.6	n.a.	n.a.	n.a.	n.a.	n.a.
Total[b]	9.3	20.9	18.4	3.2	2.7	4.4	1.2	0.5
Percent of sales	5.3	12.7	10.3	1.0	1.0	1.4	0.4	0.1

[a]Expenditure on special tools not shown in accounts from 1971.
[b]Totals include investment grants, which are not allocated separately between property and plant and equipment. From 1971 onward,
totals exclude expenditure on special tools.

Note: n.a. = data not available.

Source: Company accounts.

> future self-sustenance—as it has in France, for example.
> Apart from its first injection of capital into that company,
> it has put no money into Chrysler France who have had no
> industrial problems for 22 years and who have been totally
> capable of generating their own cash for their new model
> policies and for all their programmes.

And again: "We are distinct, an entity on our own, supposedly capable
of self-sustainment" with the parent company only "the last resort of
assistance. "[29]

The belief appears to have been that the investment undertaken
in Chrysler U.K. in these early years, when taken together with tighter
financial controls and a complete reorganization of management, would
be sufficient to permit viability. This would mean that the company
would be able to provide adequate funds in the form of retained profits
plus depreciation and other reserves to finance capital expenditures—
or at least that profitability would be adequate to facilitate the raising
of such funds locally. The converse, of course, would be that Chrysler Corporation would not hinder this by requiring substantial dividend
repatriation (and certainly until 1973 no dividends were paid by Chrysler France to the parent corporation).

Given these facts and Chrysler U.K.'s profit record in the 1970s,
the possibility of a continuing heavy program of investment to update
plant facilities, expand capacity, and finance new models was fairly
remote. As Table 5.14 shows, the substantial investment in Chrysler U.K. up to 1970 was more than lost in real terms by 1973. Then,
with a sharp fall in the value of the capital employed in 1973 and 1974,
the money value of the investment by the end of the period was only
about equal to what it had been ten years earlier. The effects of the
lack of investment began to show up in an escalation of machine
breakdowns, particularly at the Stoke engine plant. With most machinery in the automotive industry requiring replacement after 8 to
12 years, the Stoke plant has been described as a "museum for vin-
tage equipment, "[30] with annual breakdown costs running at about £1.35
million. The machine tools used in the Arrow power train are particularly antiquated, as Table 5.12 reveals.

The Ryton assembly plant utilizes equipment that is relatively
new, much having been commissioned for the Avenger, but there have
been problems in certain areas within the Linwood operation. Lack
of investment in the press shop has created major problems in maintenance and shortage of capacity in the paint shop has caused serious
bottlenecks. In fact, a major portion of the funds allocated to Linwood
under the government's rescue operation are to be used for a new paint
shop. There have been accusations that Chrysler U.K. has worsened
the situation by transferring machine tools from the United Kingdom to

TABLE 5.12

Age of Machine Tools Used in the Arrow and Avenger Power Trains,
1975

	Arrow		Avenger	
	Number of		Number of	
Age (Years)	Machines	Percent	Machines	Percent
Under 8	52	2.9	196	66.6
8–13	287	16.0	9	3.1
14–23	1,150	63.9	72	24.5
24–33	259	14.4	17	5.8
Over 33	51	2.8	0	—
Total	1,799	100.0	294	100.0

Source: Joint Union Delegation of Shop Stewards and Staff Representatives, Chrysler's Crisis: The Workers Answer (mimeo.,
1975).

other Chrysler subsidiaries.[31] The machinery involved was apparently
valued at about £0.87 million, but how far this machinery was surplus
to the requirements of the U.K. company and what finance changed
hands as part of the deal are not known.

Of course, Chrysler France did not have a heavy investment program in those years either. The capital expenditure at Simca during
1970-73 was about 17 percent greater than that for Chrysler U.K. (see
Figure 1.3). This level of investment spending represented a smaller
proportion of sales (4.5 percent) than for any of the other major European car manufacturers, and a smaller percent of value added than
for any firm except British Leyland. But with up to two-thirds of capital expenditure being related to the introduction of new models, the
figures merely reflect the fact that the only new car to come out of
Simca in the period was the Chrysler 180. Given that the Chrysler
France model range was generally younger than that of Chrysler U.K.,
the lack of capital expenditure was much more serious in the latter
case, particularly when the decision was taken to produce the Alpine
in France starting in 1975.

When comparisons are made between the investment programs
of Chrysler's U.K. and French subsidiaries, it is instructive to look
also at the relative positions of the U.K. and German subsidiaries
of Ford and GM. The changes in net fixed assets in the companies over

time are shown in Table 5.13. Until the late 1960s, both of the two major U.S. manufacturers concentrated their European expansion and investment in Germany. At Ford, for example, it was not until the profit performance of Ford U.K. took a sharp turn for the better in 1968 that its relative investment position began to improve. Similarly, therefore, with a clear distinction between the profit performances of the U.K. and French Chrysler subsidiaries, the decision to concentrate investment in the latter was undoubtedly the correct one. However, whether or not the failure of the U.K. subsidiary to perform up to Chrysler Corporation's expectations, after the initial injection of capital, was a reflection of overoptimism on the part of Detroit management, or owing merely to weaknesses within the U.K. company (or the U.K. economy), represents the key to the whole Chrysler U.K. problem.

FINANCIAL PERFORMANCE

As has been shown, Rootes was experiencing serious financial difficulties in the years immediately preceding Chrysler's acquisition of the company, recording losses in four of the five years up to 1966. The transition from profits to losses began in the early 1960s, sparked off essentially by labor problems. Thereafter the company's losses coincided with the problems of the Hillman Imp and the Linwood factory.

The initial rationalization and reorganization undertaken by Chrysler, and improved market conditions, brought the company back to brief profitability before a further heavy loss was incurred in 1970 (Table 5.14). A second revival ended abruptly in 1974, with the largest loss in the company's history, a loss that then doubled in the next financial year as the overall level of demand dropped dramatically. The company's explanations for its performance, as reflected in the statements by Chrysler U.K. Chairman, Lord Roots and Gilbert A. Hunt, in the company accounts, are presented in the Appendix. In virtually every case, government policy—influencing the level of demand, the general level of wage settlements, and/or internal and external labor disputes—is blamed for the results recorded. Few comments were made, for example, about the inadequacy of the product range, which has been shown to be a major factor in the company's performance, or about Chrysler's lack of scale. Although Gwain Gillespie, the executive vice-president (Europe) stated early in 1976 that: "We have proven that in particular years, Chrysler U.K. can be a profitable company,"[32] in fact, profits have been marginal. For 1968, the best year since the takeover, the £3.1 million after-tax profits represented a return on capital of 5 percent, a return on sales of 1.7 percent and a profit per unit sale of £14.

TABLE 5.13

Net Fixed Assets of U.S. Subsidiaries in Europe

	1967	1969	1971	1973	1974	1975	Percent Change, 1967–74
Ford Germany[a] (millions of marks)	1,394.8	1,352.8	1,511.0	1,332.7	1,234.9	n.a.	-11.5
Ford U.K. [a] (millions of pounds)	187.6	175.9	213.1	211.2	225.1	231.9	+20.0
Opel[a] (millions of marks)	1,394.8[b]	n.a.	1,569.3	1,607.1	1,657.5	n.a.	+18.8
Vauxhall[a] (millions of pounds)	79.1	72.4	79.6	69.5	79.3	77.8	+0.3
Chrysler France (millions of francs)	854.2	872.1	1,010.8	887.2	905.9	n.a.	+6.1
Chrysler U.K. (millions of pounds)	41.1	46.0	47.9	44.4	39.9	36.5	-2.9

[a]In 1959, the net fixed assets were Ford Germany, 268.0; Ford U.K., 40.2; Opel, 416.6; Vauxhall, 38.4.
[b]1968.

Note: n.a. = data not available.

Sources; Y. S. Hu, The Impact of U.S. Investment in Europe: A Case Study of the Computer and Automotive Industries (New York: Praeger, 1973), p. 179; and company accounts.

TABLE 5.14

Chrysler U.K. Profits and Return on Investment
(thousands of pounds)

Financial Period[a]	Pretax Profit/(loss)	Posttax Profit/(loss)	Investment (shareholders' interest, long-term debt, and deferred liabilities)	Percent Return on Investment	
				Pretax	Posttax
1960	6,860	4,745	26,935	25.5	17.6
1961	887	1,006	27,634	3.2	3.6
1962	(2,054)	(772)	29,133	(7.1)	(2.6)
1963	(224)	(203)	35,921	(0.6)	(0.6)
1964	1,554	1,746	39,682	3.9	4.4
1965	(2,476)	(2,092)	52,316	(4.7)	(4.0)
1966	(3,411)	(3,587)	59,090	(5.8)	(6.1)
1967	(10,832)	(10,515)	58,801	(18.4)	(17.9)
1968	3,678	3,058	59,248	6.2	5.2
1969	724	607	66,496	1.1	0.9
1970	(10,656)	(10,884)	69,496	(15.3)	(15.7)
1971	405	514	66,549	0.6	0.8
1972	1,641	1,600	66,445	2.5	2.4
1973	3,724	3,750	59,514	6.3	6.3
1974	(17,734)	(17,734)	51,766	(34.3)	(34.3)
1975	(35,453)	(35,519)	22,940	—[b]	—[b]

[a]Years ended July 31 until 1970. The 1971 period covers 16 months to November 1971; and 1973 covers 13 months to December 1973. Thereafter, financial period is the calendar year.
[b]No figure included because losses were greater than the capital employed in the company.

Source: Company accounts.

164

TABLE 5.15

Financial Performance of Chrysler France, 1967-75
(millions of francs)

	Net Profit after Tax	Sales	Net Profit as Percent of Sales
1967	11.9	2169.4	0.54
1968	31.8	2650.7	1.12
1969	36.6	2845.2	1.29
1970	10.8	3327.0	0.32
1971	91.1	3989.4	2.34
1972	98.3	4897.3	2.01
1973	154.0	5383.6	2.86
1974	(71.8)	4533.2	(1.58)
1975	(110.6)	5568.8	(1.99)

Source: Company accounts.

A comparison with Chrysler France is instructive. Note its financial performance as presented in Table 5.15. Until the recent recession, the company was consistently profitable and the 1974 and 1975 reversals were not unusual in European car industry terms. Again, its return, while low, had been improving fairly steadily. By any criteria, the French company looked much healthier than its fellow subsidiary in the United Kingdom.

The problems produced by Chrysler U.K.'s slide into a serious loss-making position are indicated clearly in Table 5.16. The losses* of the U.K. company, reflected in the movements in the reserves, undoubtedly have introduced very severe financing difficulties. The large increases in the net amounts due to creditors and in bank bor-

---

*These data relate to Chrysler U.K.'s total activities, including nonautomotive interests. In fact, while other vehicle manufacturers have been pursuing an active diversification policy, Chrysler has rid itself of its interests in tooling and plastics. Until the end of 1975, the firm's sole remaining nonvehicle interest was in the manufacture of air-conditioning equipment through Chrysler Airtemp Ltd. and Tempair Ltd. These companies produced £370,000 profit in 1975, but the 1975 annual report indicated that the company had entered into negotiations to dispose of them.

TABLE 5.16

Chrysler U.K.: Year-End Balance Sheets
(millions of pounds)

	1967	1968	1969	1970	1971[a]	1972	1973[b]	1974	1975
Capital employed									
Property, plant, and equipment	35.7	33.4	42.1	46.0	42.5	38.7	37.3	33.1	29.7
Special tools	5.4	3.5	3.9	5.7	5.4	6.7	7.1	6.8	6.8
Investments	2.8	0.8	0.8	0.8	0.4	0.4	0.5	1.3	1.6
Inventories	34.5	32.2	43.9	47.6	54.1	56.9	77.7	93.6	90.8
Net debtors (creditors)	(17.2)	(16.5)	(14.2)	(18.8)	(29.5)	(36.9)	(33.3)	(39.1)	(36.4)
Net liquid funds[c]	(0.9)	5.9	(12.6)	(10.1)	(5.7)	(2.7)	(16.8)	(40.0)	(48.4)
Net amounts due by Chrysler Corporation and subsidiaries	0.9	3.1	6.2	1.4	2.5	5.4	(1.8)	3.2	(18.3)[f]
Current portion of long-term debt	–	–	(1.9)	(2.0)	(2.5)	(1.5)	(10.5)	(6.6)	(2.8)
Dividends	(0.3)	–	–	–	–	–	–	–	–
Other current liabilities[d]	(0.8)	(1.0)	(1.2)	(1.1)	(0.6)	(0.6)	(0.8)	(0.6)	(0.1)
Total	60.0	61.3	66.9	69.6	66.5	66.4	59.5	51.8	22.9
Financed by									
Share capital	22.9	22.9	22.9	33.7[e]	33.7	33.7	33.7	33.7	33.7
Share premium account	13.3	13.3	13.3	13.3	13.3	13.3	13.3	13.3	13.3
Reserves	(2.8)	0.6	0.7	(10.2)	(9.6)	(8.1)	(4.4)	(21.7)	(57.2)
Total	33.4	36.8	36.9	36.8	37.4	38.9	42.7	25.3	(10.2)
Long-term debt									
Chrysler Corporation	0.9	0.9	0.9	0.9	1.0	1.0	1.0	6.1	13.4
Other	24.5	23.1	28.7	31.7	28.1	26.5	15.8	20.0	19.4
Minority interests	1.2	0.5	0.4	0.1	–	–	–	0.3	0.4
Total	60.0	61.3	66.9	69.6	66.5	66.4	59.5	51.8	22.9

[a] Sixteen-month period.
[b] Thirteen-month period.
[c] Balances at bank and cash minus bank loans, overdrafts, and short-term notes payable.
[d] Accrued interest on long-term debt, taxation payable, provision for foreign exchange adjustments, and in 1967 only provision for dilapidations.
[e] Share capital.
[f] Of which £8.5 million owed by, and £26.8 million owed to, Chrysler Corporation and subsidiaries.

Source: Company accounts.

rowing, and particularly the increased reliance being placed upon parent corporation finance, are all evidence of this. The Chrysler Corporation first began to be heavily involved during 1974 when a £5.1 million long-term loan was made available to Chrysler U.K. The 1974 annual accounts then reported that since the end of that year, Chrysler U.K. had received a further £11 million from its parent, and that the latter had agreed to provide such additional sums as necessary to finance operations during 1975. By the end of 1975, £40 million had been provided by the Chrysler Corporation, and the potential involvement was even greater through the guarantees given on bank borrowing—all at a time when the corporation was under severe financial pressure at home. Approximately one-half of these parent company loans have not been written off, having been incorporated into the reserves of Chrysler U.K. as part of the agreement reached with the U.K. government.

In addition to financial assistance from within the group, Chrysler U.K. also was being supported by a variety of banks to the tune of £64 million at the end of 1975. The very big increase in borrowing from this source came during 1974 when bank loans and overdrafts (before deducting cash and bank balances) increased from £19 to £54 million. Of this total, £11 million in 1974 and £13 million in 1975 represented loans repayable over a period up to four years. It is noteworthy that the chairman of Chrysler U.K. has on occasion criticized the U.K. banking system for its inflexibility in comparison with the U.S. Federal Reserve.

That Chrysler has not been alone in its inability to make profits in the United Kingdom is evident from Table 5.17. The profits earned by all the major motor manufacturers have fluctuated widely from year to year, and much more markedly than the profits of the manufacturing industry as a whole. Aside from the fluctuations, rates of return on capital usually have been lower than for the entire manufacturing industry, although, arguably, higher rates are necessary because of the need to amortize equipment more rapidly. Average rates of return also were significantly lower than in the other major vehicle manufacturing countries in Europe.

Among the individual companies, the performance of Vauxhall was worse than that of Chrysler during the early 1970s, although the company's 1975 loss was nowhere near as bad as that of Chrysler. However, GM has reacted differently from the Chrysler Corporation in trying to deal with the situation. The suggestion was made in Chapter 1 that perhaps GM's long-term aim is to use Vauxhall merely as an assembly point for Opel cars, unless the situation in the United Kingdom improves dramatically, and is prepared to write off the recurring losses of its U.K. subsidiary until this can be achieved. While the financial position of GM in the United States is much stronger than that of Chrysler, Vauxhall remains another potential time bomb for the U.K. government.

The profitability of British Leyland also has been very low, and that company's difficulties have been exacerbated by its high level of dividend distribution (£70 million out of total net profits of £74 million between 1968 and 1974). The position of British Leyland deteriorated rapidly from the autumn of 1973, as the general economic situation worsened, until the company reached the limit of its existing U.K. overdraft facilities toward the end of the following year. Early in December 1974, a team of inquiry was set up under Sir Don Ryder, which subsequently recommended a government takeover of the company and financial support to the tune of £1,264 million in constant price terms between 1975 and 1982.

The performance of Ford has been very satisfactory in comparison with that of other motor manufacturers in the United Kingdom. It is the only company able to finance capital expenditures from retained profits plus depreciation. In broader European terms and in comparison with Ford of Germany (at least until the recession), the performance of its U.K. operation has been fairly mediocre (see Chapter 1). On the other hand, the company's achievements in operating profitably in both 1974 and 1975 must not be overlooked. As have the other U.K. companies, the management of Ford U.K. has stated on numerous occasions that the basic problem lies in its inability to make adequate use of installed capacity.

CONCLUSIONS

On the basis of the evidence presented in this chapter, it is clear that in some respects Chrysler's performance merely mirrors that of the U.K. motor industry as a whole. In its loss of market share at home, Chrysler has not been too different from other U.K. manufacturers; indeed, on the export side, for various reasons, the company has been more successful than the other domestic producers. Chrysler utilization of capacity has been somewhat better than the industry as a whole in recent years, although this is offset by the suggestion that perhaps the company requires a higher level of throughput to break even. In common with some other U.K. manufacturers, investment and productivity are low, and the company shares with Vauxhall its lack of scale.

It would be unwise to take this interim assessment too far. In the end result, the net losses of Chrysler U.K. since 1967 have been greater than those of any other company. Investment and value added per year were close to the bottom of the international table, and at the end of 1975, the company was responsible for only 5 out of every 100

TABLE 5.17

U.K. Manufacturers' Pretax Profits and Returns on Sales and Capital Employed[a]
(millions of pounds)

	British Leyland	Ford	Vauxhall	Chrysler U.K.
Pretax profits (losses)				
1966	n. a.	7.4	3.7	(3.4)
1967	n. a.	2.6	5.8	(10.8)
1968	38	43.0	9.0	3.7
1969	40.4	38.1	(1.9)	0.7
1970	3.9	25.2	(9.7)	(10.7)
1971	32.4	(30.7)	1.8	0.4
1972	31.9	46.8	(4.3)	1.6
1973	51.3	65.4	(4.1)	3.7
1974	2.3	8.7	(18.1)	(17.7)
1975	(76.1)	14.1	(13.1)	(35.5)
Pretax profits (losses)/sales (percent)				
1966	n. a.	1.8	2.1	(1.9)
1967	n. a.	0.6	3.0	(6.3)
1968	3.9	8.8	4.2	2.1
1969	4.2	7.1	(1.0)	0.4
1970	0.4	4.3	(4.6)	(6.0)
1971	2.8	(5.2)	0.6	0.1
1972	2.5	5.9	(1.6)	0.6
1973	3.3	7.3	(1.5)	1.2
1974	0.1	0.9	(5.6)	(5.7)
1975	(4.1)	1.2	(3.4)	(10.1)
Pretax profits (losses)/capital employed (percent)				
1966	n. a.	4.3	4.5	(5.8)
1967	n. a.	1.6	6.0	(18.4)
1968	11.9	23.6	9.3	6.2
1969	12.0	19.7	(2.4)	1.1
1970	1.2	11.6	(14.0)	(15.3)
1971	9.5	(12.8)	2.0	0.6
1972	8.4	18.4	(4.9)	2.5
1973	12.2	23.6	(4.7)	6.3
1974	0.6	3.0	(25.1)	(34.3)
1975	(30.2)	4.4	(22.1)	—[b]

[a]There are inevitably problems in comparisons based on capital employed because of different accounting procedures. The figures quoted basically take capital employed as total assets minus current liabilities.

[b]No figure included because losses were greater than the capital employed in the company.

Note: n. a. = data not available.

Source: Company accounts.

cars sold in Britain. The investigation of the causes of this situation is therefore pursued in the following two chapters, particularly in light of the assertion that Chrysler has been affected more adversely than other U.K. firms by industrial disputes and in the context of the geographic isolation of nearly half of Chrysler's assembly capacity.

Even if the U.K. motor industry is taken as the base for comparison, Ford U.K. has shown that it is possible to operate profitably in the United Kingdom. The Ford experience may indeed provide a valid benchmark for assessing Chrysler's position. It is not coincidental that the fortunes of Ford U.K. revived with the creation of Ford of Europe. The discussion on strategy in Chapter 2 suggested that for Chrysler, too, the development of an integrated car and commercial vehicle facility should have received overriding priority. The evidence provided, however, indicates that, on the whole, Chrysler's European subsidiaries "still seemingly behave as individual firms rather than as parts of a company with a coherent European plan."[33] In insisting that subsidiaries stand on their own feet after initial reorganization, the corporation was placing great faith in U.S. management advantage, when all the indications were that this management gap was being narrowed. This strategy is not too surprising given the corporation's reputation in the United States for lack of market judgment and its "me-too" policy. And it certainly proved inadequate in Europe where a coherent integrative strategy is an urgent necessity.

APPENDIX: SUMMARY OF STATEMENTS BY CHRYSLER U.K. CHAIRMAN, LORD ROOTES (1967 TO 1972) AND GILBERT A. HUNT (1973 TO 1975)

1967   The continuation of difficult trading conditions and low volume, at a time when Rootes had taken on additional commitments in the interests of future manufacturing rationalization and long-term profitability, resulted in the heavy loss for the year.

The injection of additional capital has enabled the directors to proceed with essential plans for the future. Progress has resulted from measures taken by management to economize and to reduce costs. There is an improved product range and market penetration has increased.

1968   During the year a massive attack has been mounted on the main problems that stood in the way of achieving an economic return on funds invested in the business. These consisted of underutilization of capacity at certain manufacturing locations while others had reached the limit of their capacity, insufficient "made in" content of vehicles to allow adequate profitability, and low labor productivity, partly due to the physical limitations of existing facilities and partly to outmoded wage structures.

1969 Although the highly adverse economic environment inevitably prevented, in the short term, improvements in profitability, sound and substantial progress was made.

Increases in purchase tax and additional hire purchase restrictions, together with a credit squeeze of unparalleled severity, resulted in a decline in total registrations. Moreover, in this depressed market the pattern of demand continued to change in favor of a segment in which the company does not at present offer a product.

1970 The trend in trading profits suffered a reverse in June and July owing to loss of production and sales resulting from strikes at major suppliers and at our own plants and the national dock strike. These setbacks had a significant adverse effect on the results and served to emphasize the paramount importance of industrial relations.

1971 In the first six months of the period, production was badly affected by strikes occurring mainly at suppliers' plants; during the last three months, production was curtailed due to the Coventry toolroom dispute. More recently, production and sales again have been set back by a four-week strike over a wage claim at Linwood. In common with industry as a whole, the company is now severely affected by the power cuts caused by the miners' strike.

The labor situation was only one of a number of general economic problems that the company had to face. The domestic car market was affected by the severe restrictions in existence until the government's July 1971 measures, which immediately improved demand.

1972 The losses of the first half year were redressed by improved output during the second six months when the plants were less affected by interruptions in production.

1973 The company's ability to take advantage of the high demand for its products was seriously impaired by two major strikes that affected production for a total of 18 weeks. In total, the production of 91,129 vehicles was lost owing to internal and external industrial disruptions, thereby eroding a net profit of £6.8 million for the first six months.

Trading conditions in the motor industry suffered a major setback at the end of 1973 with the onset of the oil crisis and the miners' dispute. The introduction of a restricted working pattern for industry resulted in the loss of 28,851 units between January 1 and March 31, 1974.

Chrysler U.K. was the only major British manufacturer to improve its share of the British car market during 1973.

1974 The losses were due to four main factors: the worldwide de-
      cline in the car market, the high level of inflation that increased
      the costs of components and materials, the cost of the annual
      wage settlements that were significantly increased because of
      the repeal of legislation on pay, and the high cost of financing
      stocks of unsold cars that accumulated as a result of the drop in
      sales.
1975 The problems that the industry worldwide encountered following
      the energy crisis were very much in evidence. The company's
      problems were given a great deal of publicity, much speculative
      and harmful. Early in 1975, the company agreed that it would
      need funds to refinance short-term debt and to meet the need for
      increased working capital brought about by inflation. In the
      second half of the year, it became clear that with the continuing
      deterioration in world vehicle markets, the company faced sig-
      nificant losses and that very large additional funds would be re-
      quired.

NOTES

1. Central Policy Review Staff (CPRS), The Future of the
British Car Industry (London: HMSO, 1975), chap. 3.
2. Fourteenth Report from the Expenditure Committee,
sess. 1974-75, The Motor Vehicle Industry, HC 67(I) (London: HMSO,
August 1975), p. 212.
3. Ibid., memorandum from Society of Motor Manufacturers
and Traders, pp. 373 ff.
4. D. G. Rhys, "Barking up the Wrong Carriageway," Guardian,
October 22, 1974.
5. Fourteenth Report from the Expenditure Committee, The
Motor Vehicle Industry, pp. 214, 215.
6. Ibid.
7. Expenditure Committee, sess. 1975-76, Public Expenditure
on Chrysler U.K. Ltd., Minutes of Evidence, HC 104 (iii) (London:
HMSO, January 28, 1976), p. 139. The comments quoted were those
of Gwain Gillespie.
8. Ibid., pp. 142, 143.
9. Chrysler France accounts. In 1974, production was 409,685
units, of which 263,633 units (64.9 percent) were exported. In 1975,
out of total production of 473,796 units, exports were 342,691 (72.3
percent).
10. Fourteenth Report from the Expenditure Committee, The
Motor Vehicle Industry, p. 211.
11. Chrysler's Crisis: The Workers Answer, Joint Union Delegation of Shop Stewards and Staff Representatives.

12. Sunday Times (London), December 14, 1975.

13. Expenditure Committee, sess. 1975-76, Public Expenditure on Chrysler U.K. Ltd., Minutes of Evidence, HC 104 (i) (London: HMSO, January 15, 1976), p. 2.

14. Expenditure Committee, Public Expenditure on Chrysler U.K. Ltd., HC 104 (iii), p. 141.

15. Quoted in Chrysler's Crisis.

16. Ibid.

17. CPRS, The Future of the British Car Industry, p. 16.

18. A. Silberston, "Economies of Scale in Theory and Practice," Economic Journal, March 1972, pp. 369-91.

19. Fourteenth Report from the Expenditure Committee, The Motor Vehicle Industry, p. 325.

20. Ibid., pp. 237 ff.

21. Ibid., p. 201.

22. Ibid., p. 209.

23. CPRS, The Future of the British Car Industry, p. 24.

24. Ibid., p. 134.

25. D. G. Rhys, The Motor Industry: An Economic Survey (London: Butterworth, 1972), p. 277.

26. National Economic Development Office, Motors: Industrial Review to 1977 (London, 1973), p. 36.

27. Fourteenth Report from the Expenditure Committee, sess. 1974-75, The Motor Vehicle Industry, HC 617 (II) (London: HMSO, August 1975), p. 191.

28. Fourteenth Report from the Expenditure Committee, The Motor Vehicle Industry, HC 617 (I), p. 224.

29. Fourteenth Report from the Expenditure Committee, The Motor Vehicle Industry, HC 617 (II), p. 120.

30. Chrysler's Crisis.

31. Ibid.

32. Expenditure Committee, Public Expenditure in Chrysler U.K. Ltd., HC 104 (III), p. 151.

33. "Why Chrysler Turned the Heat on Britain," Sunday Times (London), November 9, 1975.

CHAPTER

6

THE COMMERCIAL
VEHICLE OPERATIONS
OF CHRYSLER U.K.

Beginning with a review of the early activities of Dodge and Rootes in the commercial vehicle market, this chapter assesses the process of integration in the two companies since Chrysler's take-over. An attempt is then made to analyze Chrysler's performance within the wider framework of the European truck industry.

DODGE AND ROOTES IN THE U.K.
COMMERCIAL VEHICLE MARKET

The Position of Dodge, Commer, and
Karrier, Pre-1945

As on the car side, the period up to World War II saw considerable progress in the commercial vehicle sector from humble beginnings. The two largest U.S. manufacturers, Ford and General Motors, saw the potential of the U.K. market early, and progressed steadily from exporting to U.K. assembly and, by increasing the proportion of local content, to manufacture and the establishment of strong market positions. Ford, for example, either imported commercial vehicles into the United Kingdom or assembled them from imported parts for 17 years after 1911. U.K. manufacture was increased until, in 1928, the first all-U.K. vehicle appeared. Similarly, a U.K.-designed and -built GM truck made its appearance in 1931, six years after GM

had purchased Vauxhall. By 1938, Ford and GM (Bedford) accounted
for 45 percent of U.K. commercial vehicle production, concentrating
on the mass truck market, namely, that for vehicles up to 2 tons payload in the 1920s and up to 3 tons payload in the 1930s.

The main U.K. contender at this time was Nuffield (later combined with Austin to form BMC), which benefited from the imposition
of a 33.3 percent tariff on commercial vehicles and vehicle parts in
1926 to build up its market position. The company was market leader
in the car derivative sector, but, facing strong competition from Ford
and GM in the light truck field, it moved up the weight scale in the
1930s to manufacture a range of vehicles up to 7 tons.

While a considerable reduction in the numbers of domestic commercial vehicle producers took place in this period, the process was
less rapid than in the car industry. Even in these early years, the
commercial vehicle market was composed of numerous submarkets,
enabling small independent manufacturers, such as AEC, Albion,
Dennis, Guy, and Leyland, to exist profitably by concentrating on
particular market segments or on the manufacture of custom-built
vehicles. In particular, these producers were strongest in the 2- to
4-ton market during the 1920s and in the over-4-ton market in the
following decade.

Among these specialist producers, the only nondomestic company was Dodge Brothers (Britain) Ltd., which was established in
Northwest London in 1921 for the small-scale assembly and distribution of Dodge trucks. In these early years, the company's range comprised vehicles of 1, 1.5, 2, and 3 tons to which a 15 hundredweight
(cwt) van was added in 1929. Initially, Chrysler Corporation operated
as a separate entity in Kew in Surrey, but the two organizations were
combined at the end of 1929, following Chrysler's acquisition of Dodge.
As with the other U.S. manufacturers, the U.K. content of Dodge
trucks was gradually increased. For example, it was announced in
1932 that the headlights and batteries of Dodge vehicles would hence-
forth be sourced in the United Kingdom, and a year later, the Surrey
Dodge 30-cwt. and 2-ton chassis was launched as an all-U.K. product,
except for the engine and transmission. In 1935, a 4-ton model designed in the United Kingdom for use under U.K. conditions and with
no U.S. counterpart was announced. It proved so successful that
U.K. design features, evolved from a newly established drawing and
design section at the Kew works of the company, were incorporated
into virtually the entire range for 1938. By this time the company
was marketing vehicles of 15 cwt. to 5 tons payload, as well as a 26-
seater passenger chassis and ambulances, tankers, and other special-
purpose vehicles. As part of the more aggressive marketing policy
being pursued by the company immediately before World War II,
numerous new dealerships were established, and advertising, in the

form of touring convoys of Dodge trucks, was stepped up. While a small operation in the United Kingdom, the company was profitable and had built up a "reputation for providing vehicles of utility and reli-ability,"[1] the same qualities that were the hallmark of Dodge vehicles in the United States.

As in the car market, Rootes had its sights set on the mass mar-ket for commercial vehicles. Its entry into the market was facilitated, first, by the acquisition of Commer Cars Ltd., as part of the Humber Group, in 1932, and second, by the purchase of Karrier Motors Ltd., a producer of commercial vehicles at a factory in Huddersfield since 1907. The Commer acquisition brought Rootes a range that included 6- to 8-cwt. vans, goods chassis up to 4-ton capacity, and passenger vehicles from 24/26 to 32 seaters. The Karrier range emanated from the company's pioneering work in the commercial vehicle field, which had produced highly specialized mechanical street sweepers and refuse collectors and the first "mechanical horse,"[2] but which had also pro-duced losses of £37,000 in 1931 and £43,000 in 1932. The range was continued with only minor changes immediately after the takeover, although the group's production facilities were significantly reorganized as Rootes closed the factory in the north of England and centralized manufacture, with the further extension and reequipment of the Com-mer Luton plant.[3]

The dominance of Ford, Bedford, and Nuffield posed a severe barrier to Rootes' efforts in the mass commercial vehicle market, forcing the company to seek out less competitive market segments within the higher payload groups. This it attempted to do, preceding similar efforts by Nuffield, first with the launch of a 5-ton truck in 1936 and then of a 6-ton vehicle in 1939 as part of a new Superpoise range. The latter went some way to improve Rootes' highly unsatis-factory 5.5 percent market share of 1938,[4] but at the outbreak of war, the company was facing disquietingly similar problems to those in the car market.

Postwar Changes

U.K. commercial vehicle production recovered quickly after the end of the war and by 1947 was already 50 percent greater than it had been in 1938. The market shares of the main producers in 1947 and in 1954 are shown in Table 6.1. These early postwar years saw a continuation of the events that had begun to develop in the late 1930s. Thus, a number of the specialist manufacturers were facing severe competition as the mass producers, led by Rootes, began to encroach on their markets by extending their vehicle ranges into the higher pay-load categories. By the late 1940s, all produced 5-ton vehicles and moved upward to the 7-ton category in the 1950s and into the 8/16-ton group during the early 1960s.

The specialist manufacturers of light- and medium-weight trucks were most adversely affected by this trend. Tilling Stevens-Vulcan of Maidstone was acquired by Rootes in 1950 and "only Dodge prospered in the specialist sector left outside that held by the heavy vehicle builders."[5] The company produced a relatively standardized truck range that, in 1949, was composed of models with nominal payload ranging from 2 to 6 tons. Dodge entered the 7-ton class in 1952, although as was evidenced each time larger vehicles were produced, initial production was for export only. The company's success seemed to be in its ability to maintain tight control of costs by buying-in competitively priced components but then utilizing more labor-intensive assembly methods to produce a quality premium vehicle. The profitable nature of the enterprise was reflected in the decision in 1955 to build a £1 million extension to the Kew factory to produce a Dodge six-cylinder gasoline engine, previously imported from Canada, while in 1959 the factory's activities were expanded further to incorporate U.K. distribution of the French Simca car.

Throughout the period, of course, Dodge was a small-scale venture in the United Kingdom, accounting for only about 1 percent of total U.K. output. The Chrysler subsidiary was, however, a significant exporter of Dodge, Fargo, and De Soto trucks (the latter two names being used in export markets exclusively) in built-up and knockdown forms and of vehicle components. By value, exports in 1960 totaled almost £6 million, representing nearly half its total output. Dodge returned to the U.K. passenger vehicle market in 1962 for the first time since 1939, although export passenger models had been built more or less continuously, and by that year produced a range of vehicles from 3.5 to 9.5 tons payload. As Table 6.2 shows, however, 95 percent of trucks produced by the U.S. subsidiary were of over 6 tons payload and, in fact, two years later Dodge was claiming market leadership in the 8-ton sector. Pretax profits of Dodge Brothers (Britain) Ltd. amounted to £580,000 in 1962/63 and £745,000 in 1963/64

In the Commer Superpoise range, which had been launched just before the war in 1939, Rootes was more than adequately placed to take advantage of the demand boom after 1945. The problem of lack of scale, however, as in the car market, restricted the company's ability to make significant inroads into the overwhelmingly dominant position held by Ford, Bedford, and BMC. In the specialist market, reorganization of Karrier Motors after its takeover by Rootes quickly restored the company to a profitable position.[6] However, as Rootes seemed content to maintain the basic product range, the potential for large-scale expansion was necessarily precluded. Karrier after the war was not just a producer of municipal vehicles, but these vehicles

TABLE 6.1

Market Shares in the Commercial Vehicle Industry in the United
Kingdom, 1947 and 1954
(percent)

Mass Producers	1947		1954	
	Production	Market Share	Production	Market Share
Mass producers				
Nuffield*	21,200	13.6	94,000	34.8
Austin*	22,300	14.3		
Ford	36,000	22.9	42,000	15.5
Bedford	32,000	20.3	58,000	21.5
Rootes	12,500	7.9	24,000	8.9
Other	5,000	4.3	25,000	9.3
Subtotal	129,000	83.3	243,000	90.0
Specialist producers				
AEC	4,500	2.9	5,000	1.9
Dodge	n.a.	n.a.	n.a.	n.a.
Leyland	3,400	2.2	10,000	3.7
Other	18,050	11.6	12,000	4.4
Subtotal	25,950	16.7	27,000	10.0
Overall total	154,950	100.0	270,000	100.0

*BMC in 1954.

Note: Production figures are approximate; n.a. = data not available.

Sources: Political Economic Planning, Motor Vehicles (London), 1950, p. 34; G. Maxcy and A. Silberston, The Motor Industry (London: Allen & Unwin, 1959), p. 25.

remained the company's specialty, as the copy of a 1947 advertisement for the firm reveals: "Supreme in the highly specialised 'Municipal' and 'Inner Zone' transport fields, Karrier vehicles are the choice of over 600 leading Municipalities, and a host of progressive firms both at home and abroad."[7]

Mention already has been made of the fact that in these years Rootes, through Commer, played an innovative role in being succes-

TABLE 6.2

U.K. Commercial Vehicle Production by Payload, 1962

Make	Under 15 Cwt.	15 Cwt. to 3 Tons	3 to 6 Tons	Over 6 Tons	Public Service Vehicles	Total
Austin-Morris						
Morris	122,430	24,540	11,030	5,040	1,590	164,610
Ford	42,970	22,900	10,970	9,030	2,830	88,690
Commer-						
Karrier	6,900	12,910	3,080	4,330	2,030	29,250
Rover	15,850	13,380	180	—	—	29,400
Standard	6,820	210	—	—	—	7,830
Bedford	19,690	9,360	23,260	21,890	2,100	76,300
Leyland-						
Albion	—	—	200	7,440	3,570	11,210
Scammell	—	100	310	400	—	810
Dodge	—	—	200	3,990	120	4,310
Other	1,020	390	1,540	6,180	4,360	13,490
Total	215,680	83,790	50,760	58,290	16,590	425,100
Commer-Karrier share (percent)	3.2	15.4	6.1	7.4	12.2	6.9
Dodge share	—	—	0.4	6.8	0.7	1.0

Source: Commercial Motor, February 14, 1964.

sively the first of the mass producers to introduce higher capacity vehicles. Conversely, Commer was a late entrant for the emerging van market and a 15-cwt. model did not appear until 1960. In order to tap as many market segments as possible, however, the model was made available in 16 bodywork versions through an arrangement with four body builders and the company's own associates Rootes Ltd. of Maidstone, and was known as the 1500 series. The 2500 series, a larger engine version of the van, emerged for the first time at the Paris Show two years later, while a new range of 1.5- to 3-ton vans, the Walk-Thru range, had been announced in 1961. Although both of these ranges have been subject to subsequent changes, particularly in the engines used (which initially in the 1500 series, for example, were the same gasoline engines as in the Hillman Minx car), but also in some facets of body design, both still form the backbone of the Chrysler van range as marketed at the present time.

Overseas markets offered Rootes an escape from the intense competition it faced domestically, and strenuous efforts were made in this direction in the late 1950s and early 1960s with particular emphasis on Europe. After the possibility of links with BMW, rumored strongly in the press, apparently had been rejected, Rootes turned to another German manufacturer, Henschel. A joint sales and service organization was set up between the two companies to market a combined range of commercial vehicles in seven European countries, based essentially on existing Henschel distributorships. Only a few months later a joint manufacturing and marketing agreement was reached between Rootes and Metalurgica de Santa Ana (MSA) of Spain, under the terms of which a 2-ton van, based on the Commer Walk-Thru, was to be built at the MSA factory. Finally, agreement was reached two years later for Commer vehicles to be built in Portugal by Sociedade Tassa de Sousa.

Perhaps these efforts came too late, for after achieving an 8.9 percent market share in 1954, Rootes accounted for a declining proportion of U.K. commercial vehicle production up to 1960. By that date, the company's market penetration (5.6 percent) had almost dropped to its prewar level. The developments noted above, therefore, did no more than permit partial recovery. Except in the first year after the Rootes-Dodge merger, the company's market share never again reached its 1954 peak.

Without these developments, of course, the situation might well have been disastrous, for, as Table 6.2 reveals, together the 1500 and 2500 series and the Walk-Thru range were largely instrumental in giving Rootes, in 1962, a 15.5 percent market penetration in the 15-cwt. to 3-ton weight range.

CHRYSLER'S TAKEOVER OF ROOTES AND
SUBSEQUENT DEVELOPMENTS

When the first links were announced between Chrysler and Rootes at the beginning of June 1964, a statement was issued declaring that the Dodge commercial vehicle operation would be combined with the Rootes Group as soon as possible. This part of the package was not completed until February 1965, when Rootes Motors Ltd. acquired Dodge Brothers (Britain) Ltd., the consideration being over 5 million Rootes ordinary shares priced at 21 shillings; the net tangible assets acquired in the transaction amounted to £3.6 million. Rootes stated that Dodge would continue to trade as a separate entity under its present management and that plant rearrangements were already under way at Kew for the appearance of a new range of Dodge models later in 1965. The statement pointed out that the Dodge range was largely complementary to the Commer and Karrier ranges and that "the result of these well-established companies jointly pursuing their development plans will be to offer their customers the most comprehensive range of vehicles of any manufacturer."[8] The data in Table 6.2 do indicate that the ranges of the two firms were reasonably complementary in 1962, although, in fact, they had become less so with Dodge's reentry into the light van market in the spring of 1964.

Production and Marketing Changes Post-1964

Marketing: Product Policy

Soon after the Rootes statement on the terms of the deal, and as forecast in that statement, the new Dodge 500 series of trucks was announced to replace all Dodge forward control models.[9] In November 1965, the Dodge range was extended into the medium-weight class by the inclusion of the Commer Walk-Thru vans and Commer medium-weight trucks, to which Dodge model designations were attached. At the same time, Rootes launched a car derivative version of the Hillman Imp as the Commer Imp van; Rootes had been very weak in this market, which was large in volume terms, having been represented only by the Commer Cob (a van version of the Hillman Husky car).

The major changes on the marketing side, however, did not occur until 1968 and 1969, by which time Chrysler had full control of Rootes. In a press statement announcing the proposed changes in May 1968, the company claimed that they were the "fruits of considerable reorganisation in structure, staff and product planning."[10] The changes affected both the dealer organization and product policy. In the latter context, it was decided that car-based vans, light-medium vans, and the lighter trucks would all bear the Commer name. The name Dodge was to be used for the heavy end of Chrysler's range. Except that there were also Commer models for 13- and 16-ton gross vehicle weight (gvw), the ranges thus were to complement each other. * Karrier was to change from being a brand name to a model name, for example, Dodge Karrier municipal and specialized vehicles. In these ways, it was planned to eliminate more or less the overlap in the ranges that had been instituted soon after Chrysler had taken a share-

----

*With legislative changes, "gross vehicle weight" replaced "payload" for the purpose of categorizing commercial vehicles.

holding in Rootes. Thus marketing efforts could be directed to ex-
ploiting the products and qualities upon which Commer and Dodge had
built their separate businesses, namely, the heavy, tough, and reliable attributes of Dodge trucks and the space and economy of Commer
vehicles. This remained the position until late in 1976 when the
Commer name (the last links with Rootes) was dropped completely.

At the time these changes were taking place, the Commer product range comprised the Imp van, the PB van (1500/2500 series), the
Commer Walk-Thrus, and a medium-weight truck range, the VC/CE
Maxiload series. The 500 series was being marketed under the Dodge
name, while the two basic Karrier models were the Bantam and Gamecock. Chrysler's strengths thus lay in the medium sector of the market. The company's basic marketing philosophy was summed up by
its marketing director at the beginning of 1971: "We believe that
truck quality and technical excellence are a better marketing platform
than price. Our products have a reputation based on quality—it has
never been our policy to build down to a price."[11]

As with the Imp car, the van failed to make much market impact
and it was eventually phased out, replaced by the much more suitable
and successful van version of the Simca 1100, imported from Chrysler
France. This left a particular problem in the early 1970s with the
Commer VC/CE series, for the 500 was a relatively recent introduction and the PB and Walk-Thru vans were still selling satisfactorily
in spite of having been in the market for around ten years. A replacement for the former range was intended for the end of 1971, but by
this time financing was becoming a problem and the commercial vehicle division was perhaps suffering from some lack of interest on the
part of top management. Fears began to be expressed that the
phase-out of the medium truck range would be instituted before a replacement became available, and, as tends to happen in such circumstances, the myth became the reality as fleet buyers postponed replacement purchases until the situation was clarified. The problems that
Chrysler was facing in the car market were being repeated in the commercial vehicle sector, as the company was having to deny speculation
that it was about to pull out of the truck market and that its Donstable
plant was to be sold to Vauxhall.

Difficulties were compounded by an extremely tight supply situation during 1973 and 1974 consequent to a series of labor disputes
and the widespread material shortages that developed in the wake of
the oil crisis. But the problems were more deep-rooted than this as
the following quote reveals:

> Some British manufacturers' factories produce far fewer
> vehicles than operators require and for many reasons.
> The obvious immediate answer is the current cutback on

fuel and power but the trouble goes much deeper. Industrial problems, unnecessary duplication of models, inadequate development of units to meet the current situation,
misreading of market trends, retention of too many old
school engineers, outmoded and inflexible production
methods, inadequate parts back-up are just some of the
root causes of an unhealthy industry. . . . Faced with a
shortage of new trucks, and lack of reliability or spares
or both, for existing ones, many [operators] have turned
to the Continental makes.[12]

It was within this situation that Chrysler's replacement for its
medium truck range was eventually launched in the spring of 1974.
The Commando range, backed by a £15 million investment, was aimed
principally at the U.K. and European markets, although it was also
to be sold elsewhere; export versions were to be marketed as the 100
series under Commer, Dodge, or Fargo. The range, which extended
from 7- to 16-ton gvw, was to replace the Commer VC/CE series,
part of the Dodge 500 series, and the Karrier Gamecock. Muncipal
versions were to be called Karriers.[13]
    Fortunately, reaction to the vehicle was very favorable, as
this was the first new vehicle range to be produced by the company for
ten years. However, Chrysler's ability to capitalize on this situation
was hampered by supply difficulties from the start. As mentioned
elsewhere, it was about a year before the truck became readily available, by which time the economic recession was hitting the level of
demand significantly. Nevertheless, given the fairly long life cycle
of commercial vehicles, Chrysler will be able to look forward to marketing the Commando successfully for a number of years to come.
Since the Commando is also the first commercial vehicle range from
Chrysler to be conceived as a European vehicle, and the Dunstable
plant is the only Chrysler factory in Europe to be producing medium-
weight trucks, Chrysler's aspirations as a European commercial
vehicle producer heavily depend on this truck.
    Following the United Kingdom's entry into the EEC, the major
U.K. manufacturers found themselves noticeably weak in the heavy
sector of the commercial vehicle market, particularly in the expanding market for the over-32-ton articulated tractor. The U.K. maximum truck weight was (and is) 32 tons as compared with the average
38-ton gvw throughout the EEC and Scandinavia. In May 1972, the
EEC transport ministers, after ten years' debate, agreed on 40-ton
gvw, but the United Kingdom refused to accept this, following a successful campaign by the antijuggernaut lobby. Nevertheless, operators in the United Kingdom, believing that the gvw limit would inevitably be raised, began increasingly to purchase 38- to 40-ton vehicles

and operate them with a payload that kept the gvw below 32 tons. Importers, such as the Swedish firms Volvo and Scania, were ideally placed to take advantage of this trend and quickly captured a significant share of the market.

At the same time, the Chrysler Corporation was beginning to take the first steps to integrate its European commercial vehicle operations. The Spanish Barreiros plant of Chrysler Espana was chosen as the company's base for the European manufacture of heavy commercial vehicles, and it was from here that Chrysler's 38-ton truck appeared in November 1973. Known in the United Kingdom as the K3820P and abroad as the 200 series, the vehicle was to be exported exlusively to the United Kingdom, with target sales 5 percent of the heavy vehicle market in 1974, representing 700 to 750 trucks.

In launching this heavy vehicle, Chrysler had gained a head start over both Ford and Bedford. The Bedford heavy range appeared in September 1974, while the Ford challenger was delayed even longer because of the economic climate. From the viewpoint of its competitive position at least, Chrysler had chosen an opportune moment to launch the Barreiros truck. After an encouraging start, however, complaints began to be heard of defects in the vehicle and questions were raised over its reliability. But more than anything, the economic situation was unfavorable. As a commercial vehicle correspondent observed in 1975:

> Most transport industry men are, with hindsight, now
> agreeing that the three big American-owned vehicle manu-
> facturers could not have chosen a worse time to launch
> their mass produced heavy vehicles on the British mar-
> ket. The demand for 32/38 tonners has fallen right away
> and . . . [the companies] are having to apply their re-
> spective American-inspired marketing wiles, using every
> trick in the book. [14]

By the time the U.K. government's rescue operation for Chrysler U.K. was announced, the problems the company faced in the truck business were not dissimilar to those of the more widely publicized car division. [15] With the exception of the Commando, all of the designs were long in the tooth and were meeting strong competition from newer models of U.K. manufacturers and importers, as well as a falling market. The net effect on Chrysler's share of U.K. production is shown in Table 6.3. At the bottom end of the light range, the PB series, while still comfortable, reliable, very competitively priced, and selling satisfactory, is at least in need of modernization after one and a half decades. Quality problems were experienced with this vehicle in the early 1970s, but these were overcome when a major ma-

TABLE 6.3

Percentage Shares of Commercial Vehicle Production in the
United Kingdom

Year	British Leyland	Ford	Bedford	Chrysler	Other
1938	30.7	20.0	24.6	5.5	19.2
1947	27.9	22.9	20.3	7.9	21.0
1954	31.8	15.4	20.8	8.9	23.1
1957	33.7	18.7	20.4	7.6	19.6
1960	28.4	21.8	22.9	5.6	21.3
1961	40.2	19.6	20.7	6.5	13.0
1962	40.0	20.7	17.6	7.0	14.7
1963	35.2	20.6	21.1	7.4	15.7
1964	35.5	19.7	23.0	6.5	15.3
1965	30.7	18.7	24.6	6.6	19.4
1966	25.0	25.9	23.2	9.3[b]	16.6
1967	27.8	24.3	23.2	7.6	17.1
1968	25.7	26.4	23.8	6.6	17.5
1969	39.8[a]	29.4	22.0	6.9	1.9
1970	37.8	30.8	22.2	7.0	2.2
1971	38.2	26.4	27.7	5.7	1.9
1972	34.3	35.2	23.2	6.0	2.2
1973	32.8	32.9	25.7	6.3	2.3
1974	31.0	32.6	27.9	6.2	2.4
1975	35.0	33.9	24.0	5.0	2.1

[a]British Leyland from 1969 onward; BMC in earlier years.
[b]Rootes and Dodge from 1966 onward; Rootes only in earlier
years.

Sources: Society of Motor Manufacturers and Traders, The
Motor Industry of Great Britain, various editions; Political and Economic Planning, Motor Vehicles (London, 1950), p. 34; G. Maxcy
and A. Silberston, The Motor Industry (London: Allen & Unwin, 1959),
p. 25.

chine tool replacement program was instituted. The Walk-Thrus,
with their largest market in the urban delivery field, again have continued to sell. However, the design characteristics of competitive
models in this range have altered more significantly than in the lighter
van market and the model is nearing the end of its useful life. A re-

placement for the Walk-Thru was rumored in fact as long ago as 1969. The Karrier Bantam is in a similar position.

This leaves only the Dodge 500 (K) series and derivatives and the Commando range. The former continues to sell in the domestic market, particularly overseas, and may do so for some time yet. As at 1976, however, Chrysler U.K's truck division depends very crucially on the success of the Commando, assuming that the Chrysler Corporation will continue the policy of supplying the U.K. car derivative and heavy vehicle markets from the company's subsidiaries in France and Spain.

Marketing: Dealer Network

The marketing reorganization on the commercial vehicle side announced a year after Chrysler had taken a controlling interest in the Rootes Group also affected the dealer network for commercial vehicles. It was decided that the car-based vans would be sold and serviced through car franchise holders; other light-medium vans and trucks up to just over 12 tons gross, now named Commer, would be handled exclusively through Commer main and retail dealers, for which Rootes car dealers were to be favored candidates provided they met financial and equipment standards. The heavy Dodge range was then to be sold and serviced through 30 to 40 Dodge truck centers in the United Kingdom. These centers would support a network of retail dealers for which Commer dealers would be prime candidates. Thus, with the elimination of the range overlap between Commer and Dodge came the establishment of a new level of organization to handle the heavy truck business.

The possible alternative system of having manufacturer-operated depots throughout the country was not considered because of the investment requirements. Although other manufacturers have tended to rely on direct selling, particularly for top-weight trucks and buses, the trend has been toward the development of specialist dealer chains. Thus Leyland established a strong dealer network to sell its lighter and more standardized vehicles and backed this up with the company's own chain of depots. Chrysler itself justified its setup in terms of protecting "the product reputation" and maximizing dealer profitability. Except in very exceptional circumstances, it was planned that operators would never be more than 35 miles away from a Chrysler heavy truck outlet. With the medium range of vehicles being handled through the much larger Commer dealer network, spares and service facilities were commensurately easier to obtain.

Of course the borderline between medium and heavy trucks is necessarily arbitrary, since the uses to which the vehicles would be put would be similar in the majority of instances. As a consequence, presumably, Chrysler altered the commercial vehicle franchise system again in the autumn of 1972. Franchises for compact vans (PB series and Walk-Thrus) were to be available to all direct dealers, whether car or truck dealers, and the Commer and Dodge franchises were combined into one Chrysler U.K. truck franchise. While this seemed sensible in the light of the comment made earlier, it does begin to throw some doubts on the efficacy of continuing to maintain the separate Commer and Dodge brand names.

Marketing: Advertising

Press and television advertising expenditure data for Chrysler commercial vehicles are given in Table 6.4. As with its advertising policy for cars, the first two years after Chrysler took control of Rootes were marked by heavy promotional expenditures. Thereafter, expenditure was reduced, and in 1971 the company's share of total advertising spending about matched its market share. Another similarity between car and commercial vehicle advertising was in the tendency for a significant proportion of advertising support to be directed to the overall commercial vehicle range and the Chrysler name from 1972 onward.

In 1973 and 1974, advertising spending by commercial vehicle producers in the United Kingdom as a whole was reduced sharply (in 1973, expenditure was little more than half that a year earlier) since a seller's market existed and manufacturers were unable to produce the vehicles to meet demand. Chrysler, on the other hand, maintained its advertising expenditure in 1973 and increased spending sharply in the following year for the launch of the Commer Commando. As a consequence the U.S. subsidiary's share of advertising rose to 17 and 18.5 percent, respectively, in the two years. Conversely, when a buyer's market returned in 1975, total advertising expenditure increased by 70 percent over its 1974 level, whereas Chrysler spending was pruned significantly. While this action seems somewhat irrational, it is impossible to pass judgment on Chrysler's policy in these circumstances without a knowledge of the operation of the other marketing instruments.

Reflecting the importance of the commercial vehicle press, the television component in the expenditure data given was almost nonexistent. Virtually all the expenditure has been directed to the specialist publications, although a very recent trend seems to have been toward the use of the national dailies as an advertising medium. For Chrysler this may only be a confidence-boosting exercise following the U.K. government's rescue operation. However, the tone of the advertisements—"they all make money—these are the trucks that you don't read about in the newspapers. The trucks that are making money for people all along the line"[16]—seems to suggest a drive to make the general

TABLE 6.4

Press and Television Advertising Expenditure for Commercial
Vehicles in the United Kingdom
(thousands of pounds)

Year	Commer	Dodge	Kar- rier	Other*	Total Chrys- ler	Total (all manu- facturers)	Chrysler Share (percent)
1968	50.6	31.3	2.7	—	84.6	391.7	21.6
1969	83.3	33.5	—	5.4	122.2	310.5	39.4
1970	45.4	5.4	2.4	—	53.2	430.6	12.4
1971	22.7	29.5	—	—	52.2	585.4	8.9
1972	16.5	23.7	4.4	19.6	64.2	717.0	9.0
1973	27.3	8.0	4.1	22.6	62.0	369.1	16.8
1974	89.7	—	—	11.7	101.4	547.5	18.5
1975	42.5	18.5	—	22.6	83.6	926.8	9.0

*Rootes trucks in 1969, Chrysler commercial vehicles in 1972-75.

Source: MEAL (London: Media Expenditure Analysis Ltd.), various issues.

public aware of the fact that there is at least one profitable division in the Chrysler U.K. organization.

Other Marketing Aspects

To a much greater extent than in the car market, prices of commercial vehicles, per se, can be taken as only one of a number of factors to be assessed when firms are contemplating purchasing. Overall operating costs, reliability, spares and service availability, delivery dates, and so on are likely to be closely compared. In addition, because the fleet buyer is proportionately more important in the commercial vehicle market, manufacturers' list prices take on little significance. Price probably assumes most importance lower down the scale, but even here the range of options included in the price would need to be considered carefully. In a comparative test of four U.K. panel vans undertaken at the end of 1974, prices for the basic models ranged from £1,120 (Commer PB2500) to £1,386 (Leyland 240),[17] a spread not too different from that in the car market. On the other hand, the prices of the models as tested ranged from £1,224 for

the Commer to £1,672 for the Ford Transit 90. While only one example, an inspection of comparative prices for other ranges does indicate that Chrysler has pursued a highly competitive pricing policy for
commercial vehicles as well as for cars, particularly in the light-
medium commercial vehicle market. Indeed, in spite of the marketing
director's claims to the contrary, Chrysler has used price competitiveness as a selling point in its advertising: "In fact there are cases where
our prices are lower than anybody's bar none!"[18]

Again the policies pursued by the three U.S. subsidiaries in the
United Kingdom during the desperate search for business in the middle
of 1975 is instructive in this regard. While Ford was pushing vehicle
finance plans as a selling point (although Chrysler was the first company to introduce a low cost credit plan for vehicle purchase a few
months earlier) and Vauxhall was effectively trying to sell from the
factory direct, with the dealer playing only a token role, with Chrysler
the key phrase was "value for money"; the price was being held down
to an attractive level.[19]

Chrysler dealers themselves, however, have expressed the view
that, for heavy vehicles at least, inexpensive and reliable service was
a better marketing platform than price, and thus the Truck Care and
Certified Truck Care programs that Chrysler introduced in 1974 were
welcomed as a move in this direction. Through these plans, the company guaranteed the dispatch of 95 percent of all spares with 24 hours,
and operator administration was reduced by the provision of a planned
maintenance schedule.

Warranty provisions are also important in the commercial vehicle market, as in the car fleet market, given the mileages accrued by
commercial operators. Once again, extensions of warranty plans have
been introduced by various companies, including Chrysler, from time
to time as short-term competitive strategies. As an example, Chrysler extended commercial vehicle warranties in the spring of 1968 at
the time of the company's marketing reorganization. All new Commer
and Dodge vehicles over 2.5 tons gross weight were covered for 12
months or 25,000 miles for both labor and materials and their engines
for 12 months or 50,000 miles. Models below 2.5 tons were covered
for 12 months or 12,000 miles (including labor). Again, in the autumn
of the following year, the 12-month unlimited mileage warranty that
Chrysler had introduced for passenger cars was extended to all Hillman and Commer vans up to 22 cwt. payload.

A significant feature of the commercial vehicle market is its
diversity, emanating from widely varying customer requirements.
This diversity is reflected both in the ability of small specialist manufacturers to exist side by side with the mass producers and in the
wide choice of optional extras or alternatives that the mass producers
themselves offer within their fairly standard ranges of goods vehicles.

Even with this degree of choice, the mass producers have found that many customers require vehicles that are not available as standard production units. It was to cater to this market that Ford, for example, in 1964 established a Special Vehicles Division aimed at matching the product to customer needs.

In 1969, Chrysler followed suit and set up a Special Equipment Operation (SEO) at its Dunbstable plant to cater to this nonstandard vehicle market. The function of the department is to give detailed assistance to Chrysler dealers through technical advice, consultations on customer requirements, the fitting of equipment to meet special orders, and the approval for warranty purposes of bodywork and chassis conversions carried out by other manufacturers. The success of Chrysler's SEO can be judged by the fact that only a year after the department had been set up, it was reported to be handling nearly 25 percent of production from the Dunstable plant. [20]

Production: Facilities

Early in 1966, a £3 million expansion and reorganization program for the commercial vehicle factories in Luton and Dunstable was unveiled. The overall aim was, according to the managing director of the commercial vehicle division, to permit the company to "build trucks as heavy as they can go." [21] The program included a 172,000 square foot extension to the assembly plant at Dunstable to increase building capacity for medium and heavy trucks by 80 percent. In this program, production of some of the Dodge models was transferred from Kew to Dunstable, anticipating the sale of the Kew factory a year later. Similarly, the body shop was transferred from Luton to Dunstable to allow reorganization of the Luton factory. This enabled the production of chassis components to keep pace with the increased assembly capacity at Dunstable.

With the disposal of the Kew factory and the phase-out of U.K. manufacture of car-derived vans, affecting Ryton and Linwood, Dunstable became the hub of Chrysler's operations. Situated literally across the road from a fellow U.S. subsidiary, Vauxhall, the Chrysler factory is located on a site of 51.5 acres and includes a covered area of 714,000 square feet. It is primarily an assembly plant, undertaking no machining, but sales, the special equipment operation, and costing are all located at the factory. In the early 1970s, the plant had a double-shift capacity of around 50,000 trucks and vans a year. Three assembly lines were operated, one for light vehicles (PB series), one for mediums (from the 2-ton Walk-Thru upward), and the third for trucks from 7-ton gvw. Although plans were formulated in 1974 to increase capacity for the heavier vehicles, Table 6.5 shows that the plant consistently has been operating at only between 50 and 60 percent of its optimum.

TABLE 6.5

Chrysler Annual Production of Built-Up and Knockdown Commercial
Vehicles by Plant

Year	Linwood-Ryton*	Kew	Dunstable	Total
1960	8,150	5,318	34,226	47,694
1961	7,174	4,320	22,845	34,339
1962	1,680	4,567	22,868	29,115
1963	3,477	6,109	23,899	33,485
1964	3,356	8,483	26,150	37,989
1965	5,246	6,419	25,975	37,640
1966	4,208	9,630	26,967	40,805
1967	3,153	4,737	21,028	28,918
1968	3,575	—	24,124	27,699
1969	3,145	—	28,277	31,422
1970	2,323	—	29,702	32,025
1971	—	—	26,027	26,027
1972	—	—	24,145	24,145
1973	—	—	26,100	26,100
1974	—	—	25,004	25,004
1975	—	—	19,211	19,211

*Car-derived vans.

Source: Fourteenth Report from the Expenditure Committee,
sess. 1974–75, The Motor Vehicle Industry, HC 617 (I) (London:
HMSO, August 1975), p. 195.

A stone's throw from Dunstable is Chrysler's Luton works,
which machines transmissions, axles, and other parts in the vehicle
power train. The Luton plant is located on a 9.1-acre site including
a covered area of 345,000 square feet. The other main section of the
company's truck manufacturing operation is at Maidstone in Kent.
This is a machining plant that supports the Luton factory and the Stoke
car-engine factory and also prepares some engines for Dunstable. It
is located on a site of 7.2 acres with a covered area of 278,000 square
feet.

Clearly, Chrysler's commercial vehicle division, centered in
Dunstable, is much more integrated and compact than is its operation
for cars. The advantages in terms of reduced transport and communication costs are undoubtedly significant. However, a disadvantage is

that the commercial vehicle division is more reliant on purchased
components and is therefore more vulnerable to production stoppages
in supplying firms.

Chrysler's Problems with Diesel Engines

Purchased components are estimated to account for 90 percent
of the material cost of Chrysler-manufactured commercial vehicles
(the comparable figure for cars is 71 percent). [22] Perhaps most significance attaches to diesel engine supplies to the commercial vehicle
industry because on the only two occasions since 1964 that Chrysler
has launched completely new ranges, problems have arisen immediately with supplies of engines. In the first instance, the range to be
adversely affected was the Dodge 500 series and more recently the
Commer Commando experienced problems for about a year after the
date of its launch.

In 1964, U.K. legislation was changed, via an amendment to the
Construction and Use regulations, to permit heavier vehicles, up to
32-ton gvw, on U.K. roads. Because of the dramatic impact that such
increases in permitted size can have on operating costs, a new market
immediately opened up to commercial vehicle producers, and it was to
exploit this that the Dodge 500 series was launched in September 1965.

As with a number of other manufacturers, Dodge relied heavily
on Perkins Diesel Engines (a subsidiary of Massey-Ferguson) for the
supply of truck engines, but until late 1965 Perkins did not have a unit
large enough to power the Dodge 500 series. The Cummins Engine
Company Ltd. had been manufacturing in the United Kingdom since
1957; its Scottish factory was set up to gain access to the European
market, which, at the time, was larger than the U.S. market for
diesel engines, and to take advantage of lower labor costs. However,
the operation was unprofitable prior to 1964. [23] Cummins, however,
was able to offer a diesel engine of sufficient power to satisfy the
newly emergent market.

Dodge, meanwhile, was anxious to reduce its dependence on
Perkins and to increase its in-sourcing, and entered into a joint venture with Cummins in 1964 to build a factory in the north of England
for the manufacture of diesel engines. Chrysler-Cummins was to
market the 140 to 185 brake horse power V6 and V8 engines in two
ways: direct to Dodge, which it was assumed would take one-third of
the plant's 30,000-unit capacity, and through Cummins' outlets.
Apart from this jointly owned factory, Cummins established another
plant in the same location (Darlington) for the production of components,
and in 1965, as part of its big expansion program, entered into a joint
venture with Jaguar (although this was never operational). In a rela-

tively short time, six manufacturers announced their intention of using Cummins' engines. This evoked a considerable anti-American response in the commercial vehicle press, of which the following quote is an example: "Performance apart, the eventual large scale use of these machines will be seen to have a strong political flavour, bearing in mind the large U.S. stake in our vehicle industry. American-controlled firms strongly favour the use of U.S. originated units."[24]

In the Dodge 500 series, therefore, Cummins' engines came as standard, although a Perkins unit was optional, since the company had announced a new 170 bhp V8 diesel only days before. As Perkins' advertising at the launch emphasized: "New Dodge 500 series owners can make sure its a Perkins in 15 seconds flat."[25]

It was soon apparent that Rootes-Dodge had made the wrong choice. As road tests emphasized, the lightness of the Cummins product did not outweigh its slightly additional noise and cost and reduced fuel efficiency, but the major adverse reaction came from drivers unaccustomed to the different technique of driving high-revving engines. Within a year, Rootes-Dodge was forced to backtrack; with the announcement of an additional model in the 500 series in September 1966, came the decision to offer a Perkins diesel engine as the only power unit available. With the greatest majority of operators also choosing the optional Perkins engines on other trucks in the range, the joint venture agreement collapsed. At the end of April 1968, Cummins bought out Chrysler from Chrysler-Cummins Ltd.

Chrysler was still concerned about the adverse impact of the fiasco on its position in the United Kingdom. Advertising stressed "the proven Dodge-Perkins V8 partnership,"[26] and the relaunch of the 500 series with the Perkins diesel as standard in 1969 was accompanied by a confidence-boosting avalanche of displays and demonstrations throughout the country.

Cummins Engine Company, meanwhile, was forced to retrench in the United Kingdom. Apart from Chrysler, other manufacturers chose to reverse their decisions to offer Cummins diesels as standard; the Ford decision was a particularly severe blow in this respect. The European marketing headquarters of Cummins in London was abandoned (although the company claimed that this was a consequence of the United Kingdom's failure to join the EEC) and some redundancies occurred in Darlington and Shotts. The export orientation of the firm did, in fact, prevent the situation becoming too serious. Although Cummins admitted fewer than expected sales of its V engines in the United Kingdom, it stated that its two Darlington factories were meeting their expected production target of 60 percent of capacity. Lower sales in the United Kingdom were cushioned by the fact that between 70 and 80 percent of output was exported.

For the 1974 launch of the Commer Commando, a series encompassing the 7.38- to 16-ton gvw rigid categories, Chrysler chose versions of the Perkins 6.354 diesel engine as the standard unit for all vehicles in the range, except the top weight version. For the latter a Mercedes-Benz diesel engine was standard; this was the first time that an engine from the German company had been used in a competitor's vehicle. The Mercedes-Benz diesel was also included in the list of options for versions of the Commando down to 11.2-ton gvw. Chrysler's decision on the Mercedes-Benz was made with a view to increasing the selling potential of the truck in Europe, although some questions were raised regarding its lack of power in comparison with the Perkins diesel.

Such comparisons in any event proved academic, given the supply situation that existed at the time. Chrysler had been given an early indication of the problems that could arise with components suppliers, first, when labor disputes at Rubery Owen affected supplies of chassis frames, axle casings, gasoline tanks, and so on during 1972, and second, when the Perkins Peterborough plant was closed for a month in the middle of 1973 by industrial action. The difficulties caused by this strike were exacerbated by the fact that Chrysler's truck division at Dunstable was affected by a shortage of its own engines, since the engine manufacturing plant at Stoke was being heavily picketed as a result of the company's own industrial problems.

The situation had hardly recovered by the time the Commando was unveiled at the Amsterdam Show in February 1974. Shortages, particularly of Perkins engines, were apparent immediately at the date of launch. Labor problems, compounded by the worldwide fuel, power, and steel shortages, which had adverse effects on Perkins' own components suppliers, caused overall registrations of Chrysler commercial vehicles to drop by a quarter in the first eight months of 1974. The Commando, whose demand has been boosted, ironically, by excellent press reports, was largely unavailable with Perkins engines. In desperation, Chrysler turned to Mercedes-Benz as an alternative source of supply. Dealer's orders for the Commando could then be met provided they were prepared to accept Mercedes-Benz engines; conversely, no delivery dates could be quoted if the dealers insisted on Perkins engines.

Chrysler's problems at this time were not unique, with most manufacturers in a similarly unhappy situation. In the middle of 1974, the press was reporting that "the sad tale of shortages of engines and spares continue. Engine makers and others report serious material shortages."[27] The supply situation did not begin to ease until the spring of 1975. By this time Chrysler, answering press queries, stated that "the ease with which it could supply vehicles depended on the specification and model chosen, but light vans and Walk-Thrus were generally available ex-stock. Commando models were on longer delivery, and Dodge models were in reasonable availability."[28] By this time, unfortunately, demand had slumped, since operators, hampered by the poor supply situation during 1974, had been ordering farther ahead than necessary; in addition, the level of economic activity had dropped off sharply as the world recession deepened.

It is often argued that Chrysler U.K.'s dependence on purchased components has enabled the company to take advantage of external econ-omies of scale, thereby partially offsetting the disadvantages occurring from the firm's size. This advantage, however, is obtained at the cost of greater insecurity of supplies, and it has led Chrysler, and other manufacturers, both to expand their own manufacturing capabilities and to develop dual sources of supply. Indeed, British Leyland was reported in the spring of 1976 to be insisting on three suppliers for every major contract. Such deals, even if successful, may have an inhibiting effect on the investment plans of the components manufactur-ers and thereby exacerbate supply problems in the long term. In any event, the relationship between the assemblers and the powerful com-ponents manufacturers seems guaranteed to remain a distinctly uneasy one. As recently as February 1976, the member of Parliament for Dunstable was asking the undersecretary of state in Parliament to negotiate with Perkins to see whether supplies could be increased so that a three-day bank of engines was in reserve.[29]

THE STRUCTURE AND GROWTH OF THE EUROPEAN COMMERCIAL VEHICLE INDUSTRY

The aim of this section is to assess the performance of Chrys-ler's U.K. commercial vehicle operations within the general frame-work of the commercial vehicle industry in Europe and in relation to the performance of the other U.S. subsidiaries in this market.

Growth

The development of output in the leading producing countries in Europe is shown in Table 6.6. In order to permit a comparison to be made with the size and growth of the industry elsewhere, production figures for the United States, Canada, and Japan are also included. Such a comparison is necessary in order to record the explosive growth of output in Japan, whose 1959 production was only half that of the United Kingdom and, by 1975, was six times as great. To some extent, volume comparisons are misleading, because a large part of Japanese production is accounted for by minitrucks of a kind that are not manufactured in significant quantities in other countries. Even so, the implications for the European industry are clear.

In the principal European producing countries, output has grown by less than one-third since 1960, and with production stagnant in the United Kingdom and Germany, virtually all of the increase has come from France and Italy. The poor performance of the European industry is reflected in the decline in the leading European countries' share of output, which had fallen from over one-third to about one-sixth during the period. The United Kingdom until recently had occupied a dominant position in the European commercial vehicle industry, but, depending on the statistical classifications used, French production may have exceeded that in the United Kingdom in 1974 for the first time.[30] The product mix is again important in any such comparisons, since output in France is concentrated on smaller vehicles: 70 percent of production was of vehicles under 2.5-ton gvw in 1974.

The production shares of the leading countries are shown in the export data given in Table 6.7. Movements in world exports were more erratic for commercial vehicles than for the cars during most of the 1960s, although the change in the classification of U.S. exports during the period exaggerates this. A fairly strong upward growth trend has emerged since the end of the decade. Within the major producing countries, the decline in the U.K. share of exports, from its position as the major world commercial vehicle exporter, is apparent. This is less striking, once again, however, than the rise of Japan, which displaced the United Kingdom as export market leader in 1968 and presently accounts for three-fifths of total exports from the major producing countries. West Germany took over second place from the United Kingdom in 1970, and although its market share has also dropped sharply in the 1970s, it has retained this position in most years. In 1975, in spite of the recession, truck exports from Germany were maintained largely through overseas deals with the oil-producing countries (the acquisition by Kuwait of a 15 percent stake in Daimler-Benz must be a help in this area). The strength of the French commercial vehicle industry in recent years has rested on buoyant exports, particularly in the light commercial vehicle and heavy truck categories. As Table 6.7 shows, unlike the other principal producing countries in Europe, France's share of total exports has shown some increase.

When considering the aggregate position, an equally important consideration is the destination of exports. For Japan, the U.S. market is about as important for commercial vehicles as for cars, accounting for between 35 and 40 percent of total exports in both cases. Japanese commercial vehicles exports to Europe, however, represent only 8.5 percent of the total in contrast to 20 percent for cars. The European market thus can expect to face an onslaught from Japanese commercial vehicle producers, on the model already established in the

TABLE 6.6

Percentage Shares of Commercial Vehicle Production by Principal Producing Countries

Country	1960	1962	1964	1966	1968	1970	1971	1972	1973	1974	1975
United Kingdom	18.0	14.2	12.2	10.1	7.7	8.6	8.1	6.5	5.7	5.8	6.2
France	7.6	6.5	5.9	5.5	4.6	5.5	5.6	5.4	5.4	6.0	5.1*
West Germany	9.4	8.2	6.8	5.1	4.6	5.9	5.0	4.6	4.1	3.7	4.5
Italy	1.9	2.3	1.6	1.9	2.2	2.5	2.0	1.7	1.9	2.0	1.8
Sweden	0.8	0.7	0.6	0.6	0.4	0.6	0.5	0.5	0.5	0.6	0.8
Japan	12.4	24.0	29.5	32.4	38.2	39.7	36.9	36.3	36.0	37.5	38.5
United States	47.0	41.3	40.4	39.8	37.1	32.6	36.9	39.7	41.5	39.3	36.8
Canada	2.8	2.7	2.9	4.6	5.2	4.6	4.9	5.1	4.8	5.1	6.3
Number of vehicles (000s)	2,540	3,001	3,806	4,348	5,318	5,321	5,665	6,253	7,255	6,990	6,168
Number of U.K. vehicles (000s)	458	425	465	439	409	458	456	408	416	403	381

*French share not comparable with that for previous years. Comparable output figures for France for 1972-75 as follows:

1972	1973	1974	1975
298,054	351,121	376,288	315,152

Sources: Society of Motor Manufacturers and Traders, The Motor Industry of Great Britain, 1975 and 1976; NEDO, Motor Industry Statistics, 1959-68 (London: HMSO, 1969).

TABLE 6.7

Percentage Shares of Commercial Vehicle Exports by Principal Producing Countries

Country	1960	1962	1964	1966	1968	1970	1971	1972	1973	1974	1975
United Kingdom	25.9	31.5	28.4	31.6	21.8	18.9	18.9	13.3	14.0	10.6	11.7
France	11.4	8.8	6.9	8.0	7.4	7.2	6.4	6.6	6.5	8.2	7.8
West Germany	20.6	25.0	19.5	20.2	22.5	19.5	15.9	15.9	15.6	11.7	11.0
Italy	1.1	2.9	3.0	4.2	4.5	4.3	3.9	3.9	4.2	3.1	3.2
Sweden	2.0	2.7	2.5	3.2	2.3	2.6	2.3	2.3	2.2	2.0	2.2
Japan	2.7	7.0	13.8	19.6	31.7	39.6	46.7	53.1	52.9	58.9	55.3
United States-Canada*	36.3	22.1	25.9	13.2	9.8	8.0	5.9	4.9	4.6	5.3	8.9
Number of vehicles (000s)	562	476	595	525	650	913	1,028	1,051	1,166	1,512	1,539
Number of vehicles (000s)	146	150	169	166	142	172	195	140	163	161	180

*Trade between the United States and Canada is excluded.

Sources: Society of Motor Manufacturers and Traders, The Motor Industry of Great Britain, various editions; NEDO, Motor Industry Statistics 1959-68 (London: HMSO, 1969).

car sector, particularly in the markets for light-to-medium heavy trucks and large buses. Already Hino has begun to use the Republic of Ireland as a base for the assembly of trucks for sale to the United Kingdom and perhaps other EEC markets.

For the European countries, the pattern of commercial vehicle exports differs markedly from that for cars and, except in Germany, Canada, and the United States, are of negligible importance as markets for goods vehicles. Only the German manufacturer Daimler-Benz is making a serious effort in the U.S. market through supplies from its Brazilian plant. European sales to Japan are also virtually nonexistent, thus producing overall a difficult situation for the industry, since competition is necessarily intensified within the remaining markets—Europe itself, Africa, Asia, and Latin America.

Structure and Ownership

France

As Figure 6.1 indicates, most commercial vehicles in France are made by firms associated with car production, but the degree of concentration of output is greater than is suggested because of the ownership pattern. For example, Saviem has been owned by Renault since the 1950s, and although it operates separately it can be regarded as the medium and heavy truck division of Renault. In addition, Berliet had been acquired by Citroen in 1967, and, as part of the 1974 deal in which Peugeot took a holding in Citroen, Renault-Saviem and Berliet were merged, assisted by a government loan of over £40 million. Berliet and Saviem are both volume manufacturers of medium and heavy trucks and buses, and in 1974 manufactured over four-fifths of all trucks of 4-ton gvw and over. Together with Renault they form a group accounting for 47 percent of French output and produce a full range of vehicles. The ultimate success of the combine will require considerable rationalization, but the group is potentially a powerful force in the European truck industry. The other major indigenous group, Peugeot-Citroen, is very strong in the light commercial vehicle sector, but does not produce any vehicles above 6-ton gvw; the two companies were responsible for over 40 percent of French production in 1975.

As in the car industry, the intercompany links forged in the commercial vehicle market, with active government support, have left the foreign manufacturers in France very isolated. This is particularly true for Chrysler France, which produces only car-derived vans. Unic, the third largest French medium-heavy commercial vehicle manufacturer, was taken over by Fiat in 1963. With Fiat's sale of its

FIGURE 6.1

Production of Commercial Vehicles by Principal Producing Countries
in Western Europe, 1975

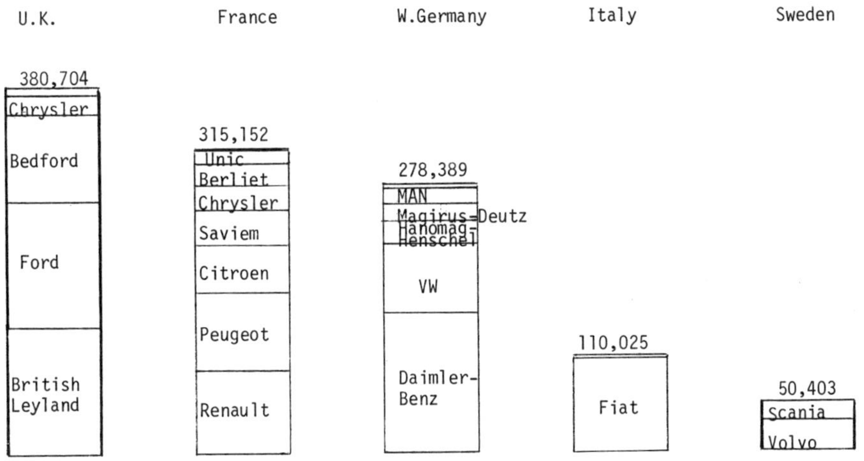

U.K.	France	W.Germany	Italy	Sweden

380,704
Chrysler
Bedford
Ford
British
Leyland

315,152
Unic
Berliet
Chrysler
Saviem
Citroen
Peugeot
Renault

278,389
MAN
Magirus-Deutz
Hanomag-Henschel
VW
Daimler-Benz

110,025
Fiat

50,403
Scania
Volvo

Source: Society of Motor Manufacturers and Traders, The
Motor Industry of Great Britain, 1976.

interest in Simca cars to Chrysler in that year, Fiat obtained in exchange Simca Industries, which included Unic.

Interrelationships in the European commercial vehicle industry
in which French producers are involved go much farther, as Figure
6.2 reveals. Saviem and Maschinenfabrik Augsburg-Nürnberg A.G.
(MAN) of Germany have close marketing and technical links, involving,
for example, the use of MAN engines in heavy Saviem vehicles and

FIGURE 6.2

Financial Holdings and Technical Collaboration in the European Commercial Vehicle Industry

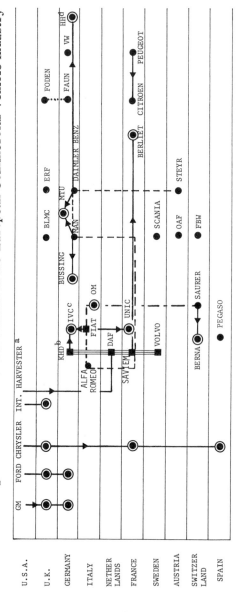

Note: Excludes licensing or manufacturing agreements involving East European countries.

a The U.K. subsidiary of International Harvester is Seddon-Atkinson.

b KHD – Klockner Humboldt-Deutz (Magirus-Deutz).

c IVC is the Industrial Vehicles Corporation (IVECO).

d HH – Hanomag-Henschel.

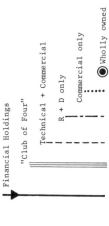

Source: Adapted from Motor Transport, November 8, 1974.

Saviem engines for some of the lighter MAN range, as well as the sale of Saviem trucks through MAN distributors. More important, DAF, Volvo, Saviem, and Magirus-Deutz formed the Club of Four in 1970 to launch a common range of medium trucks to compete in the market dominated by British Leyland, Daimler-Benz, and Fiat. Saviem was the leader in this arrangement and acted as the main purchasing agent; and the French company also has technical and commercial links with Alfa Romeo.

Although too early to make firm judgments, these recent moves in the French industry seem likely to improve the competitive position of the indigenous manufacturers quite significantly, particularly in the fastest growing medium-heavy sector of the market, where French producers traditionally have been weak. The moves are also evidence of the French government's fierce determination to resist foreign domination of the industry. From a situation less than a decade ago when only Peugeot-Renault was entirely French owned, presently only one true truck manufacturer (Unic) is foreign owned. To date, Chrysler France produces only van versions of the Simca 1100 car, and while this is a successful operation, no moves are afoot to produce any trucks in France. Indeed, at the time of the Chrysler U.K. crisis in 1975, the alternative to the U.K. government rescue operation was to transfer the car business to Simca but to allow the truck operation to disappear altogether.

West Germany

The German commercial vehicle industry is unlike that of the other major producing countries in Western Europe. Two of the major car firms, Volkswagen and GM, do not have true truck-making divisions and are represented in the commercial vehicle industry only through the manufacture of light- or medium-weight vans or pickups, relying upon car components principally. Ford, the other major car manufacturer, assembled light trucks from U.K. parts in the 1960s, but the operation was phased out, and a further attempt in the market with medium-sized vans was also unsuccessful and was dropped. The most important manufacturer of commercial vehicles in Germany and of vehicles over 3-ton gvw in the whole of Europe is Daimler-Benz. The company itself produces a complete range of vehicles and it has owned Hanomag-Henschel, a strong competitor to Volkswagen in the light goods sector, since 1969; together they accounted for nearly 60 percent of output in 1974. Daimler-Benz also has joint manufacturing links with MAN on engines and axles, as well as important international manufacturing facilities that produced 47,000 trucks in 1974.

The other significant producers are MAN, which concentrates on the manufacture of heavy trucks and buses, and Magirus-Deutz, which produces medium and heavy trucks. The structure of the West German commercial vehicle industry is still very fluid, and the position of these two manufacturers is in some doubt. Magirus-Deutz is a member of the Club of Four, but it also has formed a joint company with Fiat for the development of trucks using Deutz air-cooled engines in some models. This has ended speculation, at least for the time being, of a takeover by Daimler-Benz. MAN has links both with Daimler-Benz and with Saviem in France. Other manufacturers have found competition too keen in the German market. In 1968, MAN acquired Bussing, while both Krupp and International Harvester ceased production, strongly increasing the level of concentration in the German industry.

For the U.S. car manufacturers in Germany, Ford and GM (Opel), the heavy investment requirements and the powerful position of Daimler-Benz appear to preclude moves into the commercial vehicle market with vehicles larger than light- and medium-weight vans. This inevitably puts pressure on the U.S. companies to make full use of their U.K. truck operations as a means of improving their market share. To date, this has not been done. Nor is there any indication that the U.S. firms will enter the acquisition field in order to redeem their position, although both Ford and GM considered this a strong possibility in the 1960s.

Italy

To an even greater extent than in the car industry, Fiat and its subsidiary Officine Meccaniche (OM), dominate the commercial vehicle scene in Italy, with only one other manufacturer, Alfa Romeo, represented. However, OM, which was purchased by Fiat before World War II, operates fairly independently of its parent, having a separate dealer network and independent links in engine research with the Swiss Sauer concern.

Fiat began to think European from 1963 when it took over the French firm Unic, but its major move to establish itself as a force in the European commercial vehicle industry came at the beginning of 1975 when it merged with Magirus-Deutz. A holding company, Industrial Vehicles Corporation (IVECO), was established in which Fiat has an 80 percent interest and Klockner-Humboldt-Deutz (the present group of which Magirus-Deutz is the commercial vehicle component) the remaining 20 percent. Now with the widest range of commercial vehicles of any European manufacturer except British Leyland, Fiat's move can be seen as a direct challenge for leadership in the European goods vehicle industry.

While growth prospects have been extremely limited in the past few years because of general economic problems, particularly the difficulties of the Italian economy, Fiat undoubtedly is in an extremely strong position to take advantage of the expected upturn in trade in the late 1970s.

Other European Producers

While much smaller in terms of output than the other four major producing countries in Europe, the Swedish industry is nevertheless highly significant because of its concentration in the heavy truck and bus markets. Volvo and Scania are important for another reason. Because of the limited size of their domestic market, they have been forced to compete vigorously internationally. Besides production in Sweden, they have assembly operations in Benelux and Volvo is also represented in the United Kingdom. Output is expected to continue to rise, particularly since Volvo will be broadening its range with the production of the Club of Four trucks.

The commercial vehicle industry in the Netherlands is again highly concentrated, with one company, DAF, accounting for 97 percent of the 16,000 units produced in 1974. The Dutch situation is of interest because the U.S. producer International Harvester has a 33.3 percent interest in DAF, as well as owning the U.K. heavy truck producer Seddon-Atkinson. The future strategy of International Harvester is of some interest given that the company had its fingers burned in previous attempts in the mid-1960s to enter the European market with operations in the United Kingdom and Germany. The potential importance of the Netherlands is further increased by the fact that Ford's first European top-weight truck range, the H series, is being assembled in Amsterdam.

Mention should also be made of the goods vehicle industry in Spain, which is now about as large as that in Italy. Chrysler Espana accounts for about 6 percent of total output, much smaller than the Spanish operations of, for example, Renault and Citroen, which, between them, produce about 30 percent of annual production.

Conclusions

As was noted earlier with respect to the car industry, the structure of the European commercial vehicle industry has polarized rapidly in the last few years. Several of the continental European firms were medium sized, but with heavy capital commitments, were at a competitive disadvantage both against small labor-intensive firms and the large capital-intensive mass producers. Presently, through defensive mergers, one or at most two producers dominate the market in each of the mainland European countries, and through marketing, financial, or technical links extend their influence across national boundaries. In these ways, too, the former weaknesses of continental manufacturers in particular market segments essentially have been remedied and the emerging groups generally produce full model ranges.

The net result of these moves has been substantially increased capacity (the Club of Four manufacturers alone, for example, created 50,000 units extra capacity). With the growth of the European market likely to be slow for the rest of the decade and subject to increased Japanese penetration, and developing countries seeking to establish their own industries, oversupply and an intensely competitive market situation are in prospect. Further integration and rationalization are inevitable, therefore, and once again the likelihood of increased government support for indigenous industries looms large.

While the U.K. commercial vehicle industry will be operating in this same highly competitive environment, the structure of the industry is substantially different, particularly in the sense of being less concentrated. From its position in the early 1960s (see Table 6.2), the major changes in the structure of the commercial vehicle industry came with the formation of British Leyland Motor Corporation (BLMC), the outcome of a merger between Leyland and BMC in 1968. By the mid-1970s, British Leyland, Ford, and Bedford each accounted for between 28 and 33 percent of production, leaving Chrysler U.K. with 6 percent and a number of specialist producers of heavy vehicles with just over 2 percent of output. British Leyland is in the throes of rationalization following the U.K. government's rescue operation, and its future position remains very uncertain. Thus, the remaining three mass producers of commercial vehicles in the United Kingdom are U.S. owned. Since the U.K. subsidiaries of the Big Three have become the base for the companies' European truck-producing operations, an assessment of their position within the European commercial vehicle industry follows.

U.S. MANUFACTURERS IN THE EUROPEAN COMMERCIAL VEHICLE INDUSTRY

Development Strategies

As already shown, the major U.S. manufacturers had established commercial vehicle operations in the United Kingdom from early in the present century, and with Nuffield dominated the domestic market. Unlike the situation in the car industry, however, Ford and GM did not use the United Kingdom as a base from which to develop further commercial vehicle manufacturing operations on the European mainland.

A number of reasons would seem to explain this. In the first place, the U.K. market, particularly for medium-weight vehicles, developed early in the United Kingdom, with traffic being much less rigidly tied to the railways than in, say, France. In association with this, an important components manufacturing industry grew up, both factors permitting the use of mass production methods and low cost output. The U.K. industry was stronger than that on the Continent not only because of its size but also its range, for until the spate of takeovers in the late 1960s and early 1970s all the continental producing countries were inadequately represented in particular market segments. Moreover, a U.K. manufacturing base offered important entrees to certain overseas, particularly Commonwealth, markets.

By the early 1960s, however, the problem of possible exlusion from the rapidly expanding EEC market began to emerge. While GM had made some progress in the Netherlands, neither GM nor Ford was well represented in the main Community markets, as evidenced by the fact that in these years well over half of Ford's exports went to EFTA, Australia, South Africa, and New Zealand. The companies had a number of options: they could tailor the ranges of their successful U.K. operations to fit the European market, they could use their car manufacturing subsidiaries in the EEC to produce trucks, they could seek to gain control of existing EEC manufacturers, or they could establish new production facilities. The last option was perhaps the least likely for Ford or GM, given the failure of International Harvester to establish itself in West Germany. GM, furthermore, seemed to reject the possibility of using Opel as a truck-manufacturing base.

In 1966, GM made the bold move of attempting to purchase Daimler-Benz, but was thwarted by a consortium of West German banks possibly backed by the West German government. With this failure, the decision on future marketing strategy in Europe was postponed until the position with respect to possible U.K. membership in the EEC was clarified. Therefore, it was probably not until the early 1970s that the decision was taken to concentrate production efforts on Bedford in the United Kingdom. Since then, Vauxhall has assumed an extremely important position in the GM empire, being the only subsidiary outside North America that designs and manufactures commercial vehicles, except for the light commercials (currently car derivatives and 15- to 30-cwt. vans) produced by Opel. GM's determination to provide Bedford with the necessary tools to fulfill this role was shown most recently in the allocation of £25 million for production facilities and tooling for the launch of the TM series of trucks in the autumn of 1974.

With regard to Ford, the decision was taken in 1962/63 that the United Kingdom should become the manufacturing home for all heavy commercials produced by the company outside the United States. With the situation clarified, Ford's subsequent progress in the United Kingdom was little short of phenomenal. In the three years from 1965, the company's entire commercial vehicle range was replaced and extended. Following its U.S. pattern, where Ford had come from behind to take market leadership, so in the United Kingdom the company became the biggest manufacturer of commercial vehicles. The aim was, as in the car market, to design and build European models, but the company's moves in this direction were very tentative and not altogether successful. The Ford Transit van was launched in the United Kingdom in 1965 and a year later in Germany, but few of the components were common; while the vehicle was highly successful in the United Kingdom, it failed to make much impact in Germany.

In spite of the declared aim of using the United Kingdom as its non-U.S. truck center, there were rumors of joint-venture talks in 1966-67 with Krupp, a German commercial vehicle manufacturer, but nothing materialized from them. Nevertheless, for the launch of its heavyweight H series truck in 1975, Ford chose Amsterdam as the location for the final assembly of the vehicle, although mainly using U.K. components. For this purpose the old Cortina assembly plant was converted into a truck factory. The company is watching the emerging situation carefully.

Chrysler was in a similar position to both Ford and GM in having an established commercial vehicle operation in the United Kingdom (Dodge and Rootes) plus a major continental subsidiary with no tradition of truck manufacture (Simca). Unlike the other two, however, Chrysler also acquired an established bus and truck manufacturer on the European mainland when it completed the takeover of Barreiros in 1967. This was an astute move. The Spanish domestic market was expanding rapidly, but import tariffs were prohibitive ranging in the 1970s from 40 percent on heavy vehicles to 70 percent on small vans. On the other hand, the EEC adopted a very liberal policy toward Spanish exports, and in addition the company was able to take advantage of the lower labor costs in Spain in comparison with the EEC itself. Arguably, also, Chrysler could benefit from the fact that Barreiros had had an earlier experience with a foreign company, through its links with the U.K. specialist manufacturer AEC from 1961.

As with its larger car subsidiaries, Chrysler moved hesitatingly toward defining a role for its Spanish and U.K. truck operations. Vehicle output from the Spanish plant dropped from just over 10,000 units in 1967 to 3,600 in 1971, and it was not until the United Kingdom's entry into the EEC that production began to pick up with the emergence of a joint strategy. Chrysler U.K. was to concentrate on the production of light vehicles and trucks up to medium weight, while Chrysler Espana was to become the center of heavy vehicle production. The split was logical in that the Barreiros plant was already building heavy vehicles. Design, styling, and production planning for the whole of Chrysler in Europe are undertaken at Whitley, near the company's Ryton plant in England, and it was from here that the plans for the top weight 32/38 ton vehicle (the K 3820 P) emerged, to be built in Spain for export to the United Kingdom. Together with the Commer Commando, built in the United Kingdom, and the van derivative of the Simca 1100 from France, these vehicles represent Chrysler's first response to the pan-European concept. How far the company has still to go in this direction will be explored in the following sections.

It is clear that all U.S. manufacturers are still searching for a European strategy. To a large extent, this was inevitable, as the United Kingdom did not enter the EEC until 1973, and the long-term position was not finally clarified until after the referendum in the United Kingdom in the middle of 1975. Moreover, all U.K. manufacturers have been adversely affected in their planning by the U.K. legislative position and delays in decisions on axle loads and maximum vehicle weights. All U.S. manufacturers finally had trucks to compete in the 32-ton-and-over market by 1975, but the economic climate for the launches was hardly ideal. The U.K. companies' position is made that much more difficult by the fact that they are outside the network of increasingly tightly woven interlocking agreements among the indigenous European manufacturers.

It may be, of course, that the U.S. companies are thinking much wider than a mere European strategy. Europe's declining importance in world terms in both car and commercial vehicle output has already been indicated, and this may point toward the integration of production operations on a world scale. Chrysler appears to be making tentative moves in this direction, and the possibility of cooperation between the truck divisions of the U.S. and U.K. companies in the development of a replacement for Chrysler U.K.'s Walk-Thru range reportedly is being considered.[31] Given the importance of the European market, now and in the foreseeable future, in terms of its size, nevertheless, it is the performance of Chrysler U.K. in Europe that will make or break the company.

Performance

In 1975, the three U.S. subsidiaries accounted for 56 percent of commercial vehicle registrations in the United Kingdom (Table 6.8). Imports from France and Spain boosted Chrysler's market share to over 9 percent, but it was still less than half that of its nearest rival, Bedford. Over time, the aggregate share of the Big Three has fluctuated, depending on dates of new model launches, the supply situation, and so on, but the progress of Ford is clear (see Table 6.8). That company's improved market share has been obtained mainly at the expense of domestic competitors, principally British Leyland but also Vauxhall. Setbacks have occurred, however, such as in 1971 when production was severely curtailed by a labor dispute.

Regarding Chrysler, there is no evidence that the company has performed better in terms of market share after its takeover of Rootes than beforehand, in spite of the opportunities provided by the complementarity between the Dodge and Rootes ranges. Indeed, after the initial boost given to the company by the introduction of a new Dodge range in 1965, Chrysler's domestic market share dropped by a third up to 1971. Consideration needs to be given, of course, to performance within particular market segments. As Table 6.9 shows, Chrysler's declining market penetration overall is due to a combination of factors: the lack of success of the Hillman Imp van in the car derivative sector and a steady decline in penetration in the truck market, although the launch of the Commando was begun to be reflected in the company's market share in 1975 after the initial supply problems with the vehicle had been overcome. Conversely, the only improvements in market share were obtained in the light-medium van market where the PB and Walk-Thru vans had 11 percent of the market in 1974 in comparison with 6.5 percent in 1968. Data for 1975 and the early part of 1976, however, indicate that sales of these vehicles are now past their peak, which may leave an uncomfortable period for the next two or three years until planned replacements appear.

The competitive position of all U.K.-based manufacturers deteriorated in the 1970s, with import penetration rising from 2 percent in 1968 to a maximum of 11.5 percent in 1973. Some of the factors producing the sharp rise were only temporary, such as the supply difficulties in components firms and the absence of models at the heavy end of the market. The problem is much less acute than in the car industry, but it nevertheless poses problems because of its concentration in some market segments, particularly those for vans and for heavy trucks.

In the car derivative sector the main importer is Chrysler France; in the medium-weight van market, Volkswagen, Fiat, Mercedes-Benz, and the Japanese manufacturers Toytoa and Mazda are strong; and in the heavy truck segment, Volvo, Scania, DAF, and Mercedes-Benz are all prominent. The van imports are significant in that the longer Chrysler delays in replacing existing models within this market sector, the more difficult it is likely to be, on past experience, to recapture market share. The expansion of heavy truck imports is also interesting because it is here that the main growth market exists, with sales containing a greater element of new as opposed to replacement business,

TABLE 6.8

Manufacturers' Shares of U.K. Registrations of Commercial Vehicles

Manufacturer	1966	1967	1968	1969	1970	1971	1972	1973	1974	1975
Percent										
British Leyland	39.4	37.1	38.4	37.6	35.3	35.5	n.a.	26.4	27.7	30.1
Ford	23.9	27.0	26.6	27.5	31.2	25.4	n.a.	29.6	29.6	30.4
Vauxhall	21.5	21.5	21.4	21.3	18.1	22.2	n.a.	20.3	18.8	18.8
Chrysler U.K.	9.8	8.5	8.0	7.5	7.7	6.8	n.a.	7.1	7.0	6.8
Other U.K. manufacturers	{5.4	5.9}	3.6	3.6	3.7	3.8	n.a.	2.7	3.1	2.7
Chrysler France			—	*	0.2	0.8	n.a.	2.4	3.2	2.3
Other importers			2.0	2.6	3.8	5.5	n.a.	11.5	10.6	8.9
Units										
British Leyland	94,518	83,557	93,725	96,656	90,733	91,152	n.a.	79,354	65,655	66,254
Ford	57,359	60,879	64,797	70,713	80,124	65,207	n.a.	88,900	70,038	66,899
Vauxhall	51,651	48,477	52,205	54,824	46,549	57,094	n.a.	61,096	44,610	41,276
Chrysler U.K.	23,490	19,290	19,433	19,231	19,684	17,388	n.a.	21,380	16,537	15,044
Other U.K. manufacturers	{12,995	13,294}	8,872	9,164	9,514	9,659	n.a.	8,217	7,348	6,025
Chrysler France			—	49	404	2,004	n.a.	7,085	7,575	5,088
Other importers			4,767	6,672	9,774	14,433	n.a.	34,316	25,019	19,501
Total	240,013	225,497	243,799	257,309	256,781	256,937		300,348	236,782	220,087

*Less than 0.05 percent.

Note: n.a. = data not available.

Source: Society of Motor Manufacturers and Traders, The Motor Industry of Great Britain, various editions.

TABLE 6.9

Manufacturers' Shares of U.K. Registrations of Commercial Vehicles by Category
(percent)

	1966	1967	1968	1969	1970	1971	1972	1973	1974	1975
Car derived vans										
British Leyland	48.8	49.6	52.1	47.6	44.9	48.5	n.a.	34.0	39.1	44.4
Ford	24.6	25.1	21.7	25.1	30.1	21.3	n.a.	31.0	27.5	24.7
Vauxhall	19.7	20.5	21.2	22.0	19.1	22.7	n.a.	20.9	39.2	20.8
Chrysler U.K.	5.8	4.2	3.8	3.3	2.3	0.1	n.a.	—	—	*
Other U.K. manufacturers	1.0	0.6	0.6	0.6	0.7	0.9	n.a.	0.2	*	
Importers			0.5	1.3	2.9	6.4	n.a.	13.9	14.2	10.1
Total units	77,301	75,319	78,702	82,387	88,532	93,098	n.a.	99,459	76,546	71,674
Other vans										
British Leyland	39.0	33.1	33.6	34.2	28.5	26.0	n.a.	19.0	19.5	22.4
Ford	27.1	32.7	33.9	33.9	40.1	32.5	n.a.	33.3	36.2	38.2
Vauxhall	20.8	20.6	19.4	17.7	15.1	21.8	n.a.	19.2	18.3	16.0
Chrysler U.K.	7.0	6.7	6.5	6.9	8.3	9.4	n.a.	11.1	11.1	10.3
Other U.K. manufacturers			2.4	2.3	1.7	1.9	n.a.	0.1	0.1	0.1
Importers	6.1	6.9	4.1	5.0	6.3	8.4	n.a.	17.3	14.9	13.0
Total units	83,459	78,025	88,573	91,668	92,151	98,185	n.a.	125,947	101,663	91,166
Other goods vehicles										
British Leyland	30.6	28.2	29.9	31.3	32.6	31.2	n.a.	28.1	27.2	24.4
Ford	19.8	22.8	23.2	22.7	21.7	20.5	n.a.	20.8	20.8	25.2
Vauxhall	24.1	23.5	23.8	24.6	20.6	22.1	n.a.	20.9	19.3	20.6
Chrysler U.K.	16.6	15.1	13.9	12.2	13.1	12.2	n.a.	9.7	9.0	9.8
Other U.K. manufacturers	9.0	10.4	8.3	7.9	9.6	10.6	n.a.	13.0	12.4	10.4
Importers			0.9	1.3	2.4	3.4	n.a.	7.5	11.3	9.6
Total units	79,253	72,153	76,524	83,254	76,098	65,654	n.a.	77,024	58,573	57,247

*Less than 0.05 percent.

Note: n.a. = data not available.

Source: Society of Motor Manufacturers and Traders, The Motor Industry of Great Britain, various editions.

and where, though the volume of business may be lower, unit profitability has tended to be higher. Chrysler is represented in this market by the Spanish Barreiros model but is facing intense competition not only from the growth in imports from more established continental heavy vehicle manufacturers, such as Volvo and Scania, but also from the new models available from Ford, Bedford, and British Leyland.

Chrysler has one advantage over some of its rivals in that it can sell in low volume on the strength of a dealer network also handling other Dodge and Commer vehicles. Registration statistics for Chrysler Espana are not broken down separately, but in 1974 and 1975 registrations of "other" importers totaled 588 and 186 units, respectively. Even if the largest proportion of these was the Barreiros truck, the registrations are much lower than Chrysler's planned sales of 700 to 750 units in 1974. The success of this vehicle is by no means assured, which, in turn, raises some doubts about Chrysler's European production and marketing strategy for commercial vehicles in general.

To consider performance on the U.K. market alone, of course, is inadequate. The demand for commercial vehicles in Western Europe as a whole has been growing twice as fast as in the United Kingdom, and the major continental producing countries, at least, have not been subject to the same degree of import penetration. This, together with the enlargement of the EEC, requires performance to be assessed in relation to a European, if not a worldwide, market.

Table 6.10 shows the proportion of output exported by U.K. manufacturers from 1963 onward. For the industry as a whole during the years covered, no clear trend can be identified, but from 1972 onward, the export ratio has risen strongly. In 1972, tax reductions and the removel of hire purchase restrictions led to a boom in home demand and caused all manufacturers to switch allocations to the home market. Thereafter, with the sharp depreciation in the value of the pound and price controls in operation in the domestic market, the profitability of exporting was substantially improved, and manufacturers responded by switching output to foreign markets.

Among the U.S. manufacturers in the United Kingdom, a significant increase was apparent in Ford's export-production ratio over the period, but the most noteworthy feature was Chrysler's declining export performance. From a position where the company exported the same proportion of its output as the industry as a whole in 1963, Chrysler sold just under one-third of its production abroad in 1975, in contrast with almost one-half for all manufacturers as a group. Chrysler's weakness in export markets stems from its model range, for the best-selling PB and Walk-Thru vans were designed to meet the requirements of the U.K. domestic market. It was not until the Commando series of trucks was launched that Chrysler possessed a model that was planned and designed for both home and export markets.

The more detailed data on which Table 6.10 is based are presented in Table 6.11. This shows even more clearly Chrysler's inadequate export performance in comparison with other U.K. manufacturers. Chrysler's share of export market allocations dropped from 7.7 percent in 1966/67 (average of two years) to 3.5 percent in 1975, whereas its production share dropped less dramatically from 8.5 to 5 percent, as output was switched to the home market.

All of the U.K. truck manufacturers are strongest in non-European markets, reflecting in the main old colonial links. U.K. goods vehicle exports to the EEC and EFTA in 1974, for example, accounted for 29 percent of total commercial vehicle exports. In the other major European producing countries, the proportion sold in these same markets ranged from 39 percent for France to 48 to 49 percent for Italy and Germany to 70 percent for Sweden. The inevitable effect of U.K. membership in the EEC will be to alter the export strategy of U.K. manufacturers to produce a greater European orientation. An inter-

TABLE 6.10

Percentage of Commercial Vehicle Output Exported by U.K. Manufacturers

	British Leyland	Ford	Vauxhall	Chrysler U.K.	All Manufacturers
1963*	n.a.	37.5	52.5	40.0	40.0
1964*	n.a.	32.5	47.5	32.5	37.5
1966	38.6	41.3	44.6	39.7	40.6
1967	34.9	34.4	45.2	27.9	36.2
1968	38.4	36.2	38.2	28.2	36.6
1969	40.5	42.8	45.9	34.2	41.4
1970	41.8	41.0	47.1	33.6	41.6
1971	41.8	39.3	46.8	28.9	41.2
1972	36.5	34.8	32.3	17.2	32.2
1973	36.8	39.5	45.0	21.7	38.2
1974	39.5	43.9	49.5	27.1	42.3
1975	44.6	52.5	56.5	32.9	49.0

*Estimated.

Source: For 1963-64 figures, Economist Intelligence Unit, Motor Business, no. 45 (January 1966); other figures were derived from Table 6.11.

TABLE 6.11

U.K. Production of Commercial Vehicles and Allocations for Home and Export Markets

	1966	1967	1968	1969	1970	1971	1972	1973	1974	1975
Total U.K. production										
Leyland	172,818	164,976	168,364	185,406	172,968	174,235	140,099	136,649	124,658	133,099
Ford	113,623	93,861	108,017	137,029	140,848	120,661	143,519	137,217	131,268	129,111
Vauxhall	101,897	89,296	97,222	102,524	101,660	126,394	90,813	107,257	112,151	91,421
Chrysler U.K.	40,998	29,212	27,066	31,909	31,972	26,027	24,419	26,100	25,004	19,211
Total*	438,675	385,106	409,186	465,720	457,532	456,206	408,019	416,626	402,566	380,704
Percent Chrysler	9.3	7.6	6.6	6.9	7.0	5.7	6.0	6.3	6.2	5.0
Home market allocation										
Leyland	105,966	107,429	103,636	110,284	100,736	101,367	88,923	86,334	75,367	73,679
Ford	66,707	61,549	68,966	78,444	83,041	73,273	93,599	83,271	73,650	61,368
Vauxhall	56,420	48,974	60,076	55,472	53,743	67,216	61,514	58,932	56,629	39,758
Chrysler U.K.	24,730	21,060	19,435	20,981	21,225	18,507	20,212	20,429	18,225	12,881
Total*	260,614	245,692	259,331	272,942	267,407	268,279	272,549	257,577	232,272	194,318
Percent Chrysler	9.5	8.6	7.5	7.7	7.9	6.9	7.4	7.9	7.8	6.6
Export market allocation										
Leyland	66,852	57,547	64,728	75,122	72,232	72,868	51,176	50,315	49,291	59,420
Ford	46,916	32,312	39,051	58,585	57,807	47,388	49,920	53,946	57,618	67,743
Vauxhall	45,477	40,322	37,146	47,052	47,917	59,178	29,299	48,325	55,522	51,663
Chrysler U.K.	16,268	8,152	7,631	10,928	10,747	7,520	4,207	5,671	6,779	6,330
Total*	178,061	139,414	149,855	192,778	190,125	187,927	135,470	159,949	170,194	186,386
Percent Chrysler	9.1	5.8	5.1	5.7	5.7	4.0	3.1	3.6	4.0	3.4

*Totals include other manufacturers.

Source: Society of Motor Manufacturers and Traders, The Motor Industry of Great Britain, various editions.

TABLE 6.12

U.S. Subsidiaries' Shares[a] of Registrations in Some European Countries, 1975
(percent)

	France	West Germany[b]	Italy[c]	Nether- lands[c]	Bel- gium	Den- mark	Swe- den	Switzer- land	Aus- tria	Nor- way
Ford										
Ford U.K.	0.3	n.a.	—	9.8	0.9	12.9	14.3	1.2	8.4	8.6
Ford Germany	1.8	n.a.	9.4	1.3	10.0	1.0	0.7	9.3	4.7	0.3
Total	2.1	n.a.	9.4	11.1	10.9	13.9	15.0	10.5	13.1	8.9
GM										
Bedford	0.5	n.a.	1.3	3.1	6.8	3.5	2.7	4.2	5.5	2.6
Opel	0.3	n.a.	0.7	2.5	0.4	2.8	0.3	4.4	0.6	0.7
Total	0.8	n.a.	2.0	5.6	7.2	6.3	3.0	8.6	6.1	3.3
Chrysler										
Chrysler U.K.	—	n.a.	—	0.5	e	0.7	—	0.3	0.3	0.1
Chrysler France	n.a.	n.a.	1.3	6.1	2.9	2.0	0.9	1.6	0.8	0.9
Total	n.a.	n.a.	1.3	6.6	2.9	2.7	0.9	1.9	1.1	1.0
Chrysler U.S.[d]	e	n.a.	—	—	1.4	0.4	0.4	0.4	—	2.0

[a]Excludes shares in country of manufacture.
[b]No commercial vehicle statistics available at time of writing.
[c]1974 data.
[d]Chrysler U.S. data included for comparison purposes.
[e]Less than 0.05 percent.

Source: Society of Motor Manufacturers and Traders.

214

esting measure of performance, therefore, relates to individual U.K. manufacturers' sales within Europe, since this will reflect companies' speed of reaction to the opportunities offered by the EEC's enlargement.

In the absence of export data for individual manufactuers, registration figures for European countries can be used to assess manufacturers' penetration. The data given in Table 6.12 are incomplete, particularly since West German figures are unavailable, but also because some of the statistics are out of date. Table 6.12 is revealing nonetheless. Ford, through its U.K. and German operations, has made by far the most impact in Europe, both in terms of overall penetration and in respect to geographic coverage. The only country in which the company has failed to make an impact is France, but neither GM nor Chrysler has been successful in that market either. Even for Ford, however, integration of the company's activities still has some way to go. This is evidenced by the fact that Ford U.K. is most successful in former EFTA countries and has not yet made much progress in the original EEC apart from the Netherlands.

GM is also weakest in the EEC, but overall its penetration is less than half that of Ford. Chrysler Corporation has made even less progress, and 92.5 percent of the company's sales in unit terms from its European subsidiaries are made by Chrysler France. Furthermore, exports from Chrysler U.S. were 70 percent greater than the sales of Chrysler U.K. in continental Europe. It is arguable that if Chrysler U.K. has a comparative advantage in sales to Asia, Africa, and Australia, then this should be exploited to the fullest. But the aggregate export data do not suggest that this is the case. Ultimately, unless a company can compete with the major manufacturers in Europe, it is unlikely to be competitive outside Europe, given the end of Commonwealth preference.

NOTES

1. Commercial Motor, October 22, 1937.
2. Ibid., May 3, 1925.
3. Ibid., September 6, 1935.
4. D. G. Rhys, The Motor Industry: An Economic Survey (London: Butterworth, 1972), p. 354.
5. Ibid., p. 82.
6. Commercial Motor, November 27, 1936. At the Annual General Meeting of Humber Ltd., in 1936, the chairman stated that the Karrier business was profitable despite the enormous amount of development work that had been undertaken since the takeover.
7. Ibid., August 2, 1947.

8. Ibid., February 26, 1965.

9. Ibid., September 17, 1965.

10. Ibid., May 3, 1968.

11. Ibid., June 11, 1971.

12. Motor Transport, March 8, 1974.

13. Ibid., February 8, 1974; Commercial Motor, March 15, 1974.

14. Motor Transport, July 11, 1975.

15. For a more detailed discussion of the problem, see the article "Peter Wallace Looks at the Future for Current Models and Future Successors," Motor Transport, December 26, 1975.

16. The Guardian, January 26, 1976.

17. Commercial Motor, October 25, 1974.

18. Ibid., September 29, 1972, p. 9.

19. Motor Transport, July 11, 1975.

20. Commercial Motor, August 14, 1970.

21. Ibid., March 25, 1966.

22. Fourteenth Report from the Expenditure Committee, sess. 1974-75, The Motor Vehicle Industry, HC 617 (London: HMSO, August 1975).

23. Rhys, The Motor Industry, pp. 90-95.

24. Commercial Motor, October 9, 1964.

25. Ibid., September 17, 1965.

26. Ibid., March 7, 1969.

27. Motor Transport, July 12, 1974.

28. Ibid., February 14, 1975.

29. Weekly Hansard, House of Commons, Parliamentary Debates, no. 1026 (London: HMSO, February 20, 1976), cols. 1764-72.

30. Monthly Statistical Bulletin, March 1976. The SMMT has suggested recently that French commercial vehicles output has been overestimated by about 10 percent because of the inclusion of noncountable KDs.

31. Financial Times, March 31, 1976.

7

INDUSTRIAL
RELATIONS IN
CHRYSLER U.K.

By any measurement and from any viewpoint, the effectiveness of investment in the motor industry in the United Kingdom has been influenced significantly by the quality of industrial relations. The car manufacturers themselves have concluded at various points in time that labor issues were the most important single influence on both short- and long-term profitability. Such issues have proved vital to Chrysler, but, as in other areas of activity, the company was handicapped by the fact that it had no opportunity to make a completely new start in its relations with labor after takeover. A clearly established long-term policy for the company, and for labor, in particular, was undoubtedly a prerequisite to restructuring the U.K. investment. The end was always recognized; acceptable and realistic means were not. Some of the problems undoubtedly had their origin in the fact that Chrysler was a multinational organization with a centrally developed style of management that was not always sensitive to local conditions and that, when sensitive, was always open to the criticism of doing too much too quickly according to some ill-enunciated global strategy. In order to view the situation in which the company has operated, this chapter examines some of the implications of both the multinational dimension and of the overall labor relations environment within the motor industry in the United Kingdom. The development of industrial relations in Chrysler U.K. then can be examined in context.

MULTINATIONALS AND THE DOMESTIC
LABOR MARKET

Some of the most extensive criticisms of multinational labor relations in Western Europe have derived from a limited number of contentious issues. Of these, the most extreme has concerned the refusal of union recognition. This in turn has had the general effect of hardening union attitudes and initiating wider criticisms over recent years. While the motor industry as a whole has not been particularly affected by this issue, there have been some instances of particular problems stemming from investment in less developed areas, such as those faced by Ford with the Belgian unions in the Genk area in 1962.

On a different point, there has been some suggestion that in developed or declining industrial areas, there is a tendency for local unions to try to exploit the "superior ability to pay" of foreign subsidiaries. Where unions in such areas may previously have had little leverage in negotiations, foreign firms may appear "attractive targets for industrial action."[1] Some of the industrial action at the Linwood plant in the period immediately following 1967 may have been a reflection of this.

Another area of contention has surrounded the membership of employers' associations. While most multinationals in Western Europe are members of their respective employer associations, some notable exceptions in the motor industry have attracted attention. The feeling that many U.S. companies attempt to conduct their own industrial relations independent of local conditions was at the root of the criticism directed against Chrysler U.K.'s decision to defederate from the Engineering Employers Federation (EEF) in 1970, particularly when this appeared to be a further stage in the centralization of U.S. control. This interpretation perhaps was aided by the fact that neither Ford nor GM was an EEF member. One reason cited for Chrysler's action was that it wanted "its own management to exercise more direct control over bargaining issues."[2] Such an objective was not unreasonable in the light of the steps being taken in other directions by Chrysler U.K. toward new initiatives in labor relations, and while the company was ill-prepared for defederation, the action in itself should not have damaged industrial relations had other things been equal.

Another frequently cited cause of tension between multinationals and domestic labor stems from the transnational locus of decision making and the subsequent fear that policies concerning investment, production, and employment are established with little reference to national considerations. There is little doubt that this has been an important aspect of Chrysler's labor relations problems. It has taken the form of frequent threats to restrict investments in the United Kingdom and to rephase or reschedule investment to other European locations. Such announcements added to the friction surrounding, for example, the decisions to produce the 180/2 liter and the Alpine in France, and have also been at the root of allegations concerning machinery transfer. For many reasons, notably the absence of a European policy that was communicable to the labor force, Chrysler failed to engender any

consistent feeling of stability and purpose in the United Kingdom. The
company has been guilty at times of overplaying the threat of intercountry transfers, and has created classic insecurity symptoms when
it was not always necessary. Chrysler was not alone in this however,
as, for example, Ford employed the same tactic on several occasions.[3]

The added dimension of the "investment weapon" in the Chrysler
context was the commitment made to the U.K. government in 1967,
which, on paper at least, precluded some of the more aggressive
threats being implemented. There are as yet no signs of increasing
international contacts between labor as a response to investment
switching among countries, since national self-interest appears to
continue to motivate most of such contacts. Indeed, in Chrysler's
case, it is arguable that the post-1975 situation, by giving an increased
emphasis to the U.K. side of the corporation's European investment,
will only heighten interunion (and intergovernment?) strife between
France and the United Kingdom.

The introduction of new industrial relations practices is another
common area of tension between multinationals and labor in host countries. It is possible to attribute some of the difficulties faced by Chrysler to its desire to introduce U.S.-based methods too rapidly. On balance, however, it must be said that many of the innovations, which
were calculated to bring more standardized, companywide industrial
relations to Chrysler U.K., could reasonably be considered as in the
long-term interests of the labor force. They would have caused problems no matter who introduced them to the U.K. car industry.

One of the least tangible issues to evalute is the extent of U.S.
involvement in the detailed handling of labor problems in the U.K.
plants. As expected, there is evidence[4] of extensive contact, with
labor relations managers in Chrysler subsidiaries meeting to observe
and discuss the parent company's handling of similar situations; but
this does not in itself indicate detailed involvement in particular disputes. Some of Chrysler's problems were attributable to the employment of middle and some senior managers more in tune with practice
in the United States than in Europe. This, rather than direct intervention, created numerous initial difficulties.

In the long term, pressures seem bound to build up for the standardization of labor practices and procedures internationally. To
date, the pressures on Chrysler in Europe have not been great, perhaps because of the lack of integration of plants. On the wider scale,
some transnational contacts have been established. For example, the
International Metal Workers Federation (IMF) Chrysler World Auto
Council in 1973 considered, among other matters, that the unions should
work toward the goal of a common expiration date for all collective
agreements in Chrysler plants, regardless of country, on the grounds
that this would significantly increase union strength. As evidence of

the problems of finding a common strategy among different national
unions, this was opposed by several U.K. delegates who argued that
it would put an excessive financial burden on the unions if a strike
occurred at a common expiration date.[5]

In another context, the United Automobile Workers (UAW), in
bargaining with the Big Three car producers in the United States, has
made use of information on certain aspects of working conditions in
Europe and similar references have been made in inter- and intra-
European negotiations. Almost inevitably the greater flow of information among unions will create added pressures on labor relations in
multinationals in the future.

Insofar as generalization is possible, there is some evidence to
indicate that foreign ownership has not in itself been a major cause
of strikes in the United Kingdom. Indeed, it has been shown for one
period that labor disputes have been less of a problem in foreign subsidiaries than in domestic firms.[6] In Chrysler's case also, being a
multinational probably has served only to aggravate problems that
already existed and would have plagued whoever took over Rootes.

DISRUPTION RECORD

In order to be able to have a balanced view of the disruption
record in Chrysler, it is necessary to examine the general climate
of labor relations in the U.K. car industry and specifically to note
some of the experience of other major manufacturers. Even accepting that background, it will always be difficult to make an absolute
judgment on the best or worst disruption record among individual companies because of the complexity of strike causes and the varying
roles of internal and external factors. Emphasis is thus placed on
issues behind disputes and the postures of the bargaining parties
rather than on hours lost per worker in different companies.

The U.K. Car Industry

The record of industrial stoppages in the U.K. car industry is
poor by any standards. As Table 7.1 shows, the number of working
days lost through disputes continued to accelerate until 1974 (although
a sharp fall took place in 1975 and again in the first half of 1976), giving the car industry a much worse record than the manufacturing industry in general. With total employment around 2.1 percent of the employed labor force, the car industry in the period 1959-68 provided
on average 15.8 percent of the working days lost through strikes in
the United Kingdom.[7]

TABLE 7.1

Industrial Disputes in the U.K. Car Industry

	1964	1968	1970	1972	1974	1975
Number of stoppages	165	233	336	216	223	150
Number of workers involved	150,000	402,500	271,400	246,600	296,600	164,000
Working days lost	429,000	898,000	1,105,000	1,363,000	1,755,000	829,000
Days lost per 1,000 employees	500 to 1,000	1,800	2,000	2,750	3,550	1,800
Days lost per 1,000 employees (all manu-facturing industry)	50 to 100	200	470	1,100	650	275

Source: Department of Employment Gazette (London: HMSO), various issues. Prior to 1971, the Gazette was known as the Ministry of Labour Gazette, and the Employment and Productivity Gazette.

221

Two points have to be made to set this in perspective. First, of the total working days in the car industry, between 5 and 7 percent are lost through sickness, injury, and absenteeism compared with 2.5 percent through industrial disputes. Second, at least a proportion of stoppages are caused by factors beyond the control of the labor force in the company concerned, namely, external disputes, shortages of components and materials, breakdowns, and faulty scheduling. Table 7.2 gives some indication of the split between internal and external disputes for British Leyland. It does not include estimates for losses stemming from internal inefficiency of whatever type.

Official statistics offer only partial guidance as to the causes of stoppages. The information contained in Table 7.3 is based on employers' returns and excludes a very large number of small, disruptive stoppages, which diminishes its usefulness considerably. However, it does suggest, at least superficially, that wage claims and disputes over a variety of wage issues are the dominant reasons for stoppages. The two other major issues appear to be those related to work discipline and solidarity.

Underlying the statistics, however, are a range of interrelated variables influencing the strike record of the industry. One of the root causes lies in the large number of unions with which negotiations must be conducted, compared with the single-union situation in, say, the United States or Germany. The number of unions is decreasing through mergers, one of the most important being in 1972 when the Transport and General Workers Union absorbed the Vehicle Builders Union, but labor in the industry is still far from being represented by a single union. Ford and British Leyland, for example, have, respectively, 9

TABLE 7.2

British Leyland: Industrial Disputes

Fiscal Year	Total Man-Hours Lost by Industrial Disputes (millions)	Percent Internal
1969/70	9.0	55.5
1970/71	8.3	96.4
1971/72	13.4	74.6
1972/73	11.3	65.5
1973/74	23.8	40.3

Source: British Leyland: The Next Decade, HC 342 (London: HMSO, April 1975), p. 32.

and 17 unions with which negotiations must be conducted. The pace of
settlement is thus potentially slower and there is constant scope for
interunion disputes. Such interunion disputes are less often about de-
marcation than in the past, but a large number are variants of the comparability problem. This is a particular problem in British Leyland,
which, as an EEF member, still has 246 bargaining units in 59 plants.
At least partially related to the diffusion of formal union bargaining
power, the car industry has proved a solid base for often unofficial
shop steward and shop floor power. Independence of thought and action is still part of the U.K. car industry tradition.

As noted in evaluating Table 7.3, wage systems and differentials
have been an important source of friction. The traditional practice
in U.K.-owned car companies of paying on a piecework basis inevitably has caused many problems of differentials between grades, as has
the progressive move toward payment based on time rates (such as
through a measured day work plan). Inevitably, under the pressure
of particular disputes in different companies, and arising from the
different backgrounds of companies where merged groups had been
formed, significant pay variations developed among areas and firms.
Thus, pay parity has been a strong influence on stoppages within
plants, within firms, and among different firms. Chrysler has been
involved at all these levels, particularly between Linwood and the Midlands plants, and between firms, following its 1970 Ryton agreement
and subsequent layoff guarantees. Furthermore, while Chrysler was
working toward parity by 1976, problems have continued because of
conflicting and incompatible demands among the unions themselves.
There are few signs to suggest that such difficulties are at an end for
the industry as a whole.

It frequently has been suggested that job monotony and the general conditions of employment in car plants contribute to strike frequency, particularly to wildcat strikes. The current interest in job en-
richment is a reflection of this belief. Another psychological problem
is the instability of employment in the U.K. car industry, which has
tended to heighten tensions regarding job security and changes in work
management. Some of these problems will only be solved by the development of an efficient, more profitable, and, inevitably, smaller
U.K. industry—all of which are part of the same vicious circle.

In a recent official study of labor relations in the industry, it
was suggested that the basic cause of many of the recurring difficulties lay in communications and that "it is in the area of communications
that we see the greatest potential for improvement."[8] The absence
of effective systems and the lack of willingness to use systems that
exist are both factors contributing to the atmosphere of insecurity and
lack of trust that underlies many stoppages. Nowhere is this more
evident than in the problems connected with disputes procedures, and,

TABLE 7.3

Summary of Reasons for Stoppages in the U.K. Car Industry, 1972-75[a]

	1972	1973	1974	1975
Wage disputes[b]				
Number of stoppages	12	21	17	6
Directly[e]	10.6	28.5	18.9	2.4
Indirectly[e]	29.3	63.1	75.3	22.4
Claims for wage increases				
Number of stoppages	12	9	10	8
Directly	14.9	24.8	10.5	16.8
Indirectly	28.9	9.9	37.9	9.3
Disputes over working methods[c]				
Number of stoppages	9	7	9	10
Directly	11.5	17.6	14.6	6.5
Indirectly	22.8	23.6	21.1	29.2
Disputes over employment, dismissal, and redundancy				
Number of stoppages	10	17	6	3
Directly	22.6	34.4	4.6	2.3
Indirectly	7.8	33.4	19.4	2.8
Demarcation issues				
Number of stoppages	—	4	3	1
Directly	—	6.9	0.9	0.1
Indirectly	—	17.7	9.5	4.5
Other[d]				
Number of stoppages	3	11	5	—
Directly	2.8	19.4	2.2	—
Indirectly	3.0	63.1	17.5	—

[a]Includes only "prominent" stoppages as listed by the Department of Employment. By omitting stoppages involving less than ten workers and those lasting less than one day, it grossly understates the total.
[b]Includes disputes regarding payment systems, differentials, bargaining procedures, severance pay, and so on.
[c]Includes disputes concerning such issues as manning levels, work assignment, track speeds, methods study, interplant work transfer, and so on.
[d]Largely covering general personnel matters, for example, safety, insurance coverage, hours of work.
[e]Workers directly and indirectly involved in thousands.

Source: Department of Employment Gazette (London: HMSO), various issues.

as shall be discussed in detail later in this chapter, Chrysler shared
in this problem after leaving the EEF.

On a related point, the incidence of stoppages and types of
strikes are both affected by the quality of management in the industry.
Labor relations often have been handled by low-status, ill-trained
executives who have tended to "place greater emphasis on financial
incentives than on management-worker consultations."[9] Moreover,
top management has taken every opportunity to justify poor results
in terms of labor problems, when a more constructive approach would
be to explain the steps being taken to improve industrial relations and
to remedy other fundamental weaknesses of the industry.

One final problem area is worth noting. Many of the most protracted disruptions of car production have been caused by external
disputes in components-supplying industries. The ownership structure of the U.K. industry does not suggest an easy solution to this issue, and most of the car manufacturers, starting with Chrysler, have
introduced severance pay guarantees to reduce frustration within their
own labor forces.

In summary, the U.K. motor industry in general has been
plagued by aggressive, often politically motivated, trade unionism.
On occasion, this has produced near-anarchy with industrial action
being used as a first step in publicizing grievances. On the other
hand, management actions and reactions, reflecting a lack of personnel skill, training, and comprehension of the U.K. situation, also
have contributed greatly to the disruption record of the industry.

The Experience of Chrysler's Competitors

Table 7.4 has been included in order to give a general impression of the larger disputes affecting the industry over the 1971-75
period. There is no suggestion that the measure adopted allows accurate judgment of the relative effect strikes have had on the companies or of the quality of their labor relations. Smaller, sporadic
strikes may in fact be more damaging, since they are less easily predicted and more difficult to regulate. Even the use of the term amount
of working time lost may be an overstatement of the economic effect
of strikes; and there is the further difficulty that the figures do not
take into account the size of the labor force in each company. Bearing all these cautions in mind, Table 7.4 gives some indication of the
frequency and causes of major stoppages among Chrysler's competitors.

As would be expected in the light of its size and diversity, British Leyland suffered considerably from all the major issues during
the five-year period; while, of the other major manufacturers, GM

TABLE 7.4

Major Disputes in the U.K. Car Industry, 1971-75

Year	Company	Number of Workers Involved		Number of Working Days Lost	Comment
		Directly	Indirectly		
1971	Ford	41,370	315	1,909,300	Dissatisfaction with company's offer (in national pay negotiations) of £2 per week increase; parity demanded with other Midland car workers.
	British Leyland	8,000	15,000	208,000	Series of one-day token stoppages against the termination of a long-standing pay agreement with an employer's association.
1972	Chrysler	6,500	—	133,300	Dissatisfaction with pay negotiations: Linwood unions pushing for parity with Midlands.
	British Leyland	3,500	—	152,300	Dissatisfaction with pay offer: Bathgate unions working for parity with England.
	British Leyland	1,800	4,800	196,800	Dissatisfaction over piecework rate and pay demand.
1973	Chrysler	4,700	4,000	102,300	Protest over management's refusal to pay for lost time when track stopped because of alleged poor quality work.
	British Leyland	80	12,000	169,100	In support of a claim for upgrading.
	General Motors	6,200	3,700	170,200	Following a demarcation dispute, a demand for guaranteed employment and severance pay.
1974	British Leyland	150	12,500	110,300	Protest against layoff during other stoppages and against withdrawal of management recognition of a shop steward.
	British Leyland	450	4,200	129,400	Breakdown of annual pay negotiations.
	Ford	760	8,000	132,200	Rejection of press operators' claim for preparation and clean-up time to maintain differentials with other production workers.
	Ford	1,300	12,395	143,700	For increased shift allowances and for holiday pay to be calculated on average earnings.
	British Leyland	1,000	7,500	141,400	For severance pay during an earlier stoppage and for guaranteed week.
1975	Ford	70	5,000	115,500	Protest against reduction of number of door hangers on each shift.
	Chrysler	4,000	3,700	116,400	For pay increase.

Note: Major disputes are defined as causing over 100,000 working days lost.

Source: Department of Employment Gazette (London: HMSO), various issues.

had only one large-scale protracted dispute of internal origin in these
years. While the detailed disruption record in Chrysler will be examined later, sufficient to observe from Table 7.4 that Chrysler was
no more prone to large-scale stoppages than other manufacturers, although the effects have often been potentially more serious.

For all the manufacturers, the larger disputes have tended to
be over pay claims and general wage issues and the smaller ones are
often long running, closely interrelated disputes concerning discipline,
work management, and so on. British Leyland was plagued with many
of the latter type of stoppages, particularly in 1971 and 1973. Frequently these were caused by very small sections of its labor force.
The later introduction of the measured day work system at British
Leyland continued to result directly indisputes over pay methods and
grading into 1974 and 1975. These, combined with the frequency of
major strikes in the company, have produced a very poor overall labor
record. As far as Ford and GM are concerned, their record has differed considerably. GM has had few strikes over pay issues in recent
years and therefore few large strikes and on the whole has had a better record than the other large manufacturers. Ford's large strikes
have been particularly dramatic and attracted much attention, especially in 1971 and 1974. As with the other manufacturers, some of the
smaller disputes have led to long periods of sporadic disruption at
certain plants, for example, at Halewood in 1973 over manpower allocations and in several plants during the same year in protest against
the government's pay policy.

It is impossible to say whether or not the reduction in the number of strikes in the post-1973 recession situation has any permanence.
The new planning arrangements toward which British Leyland and
Chrysler are working should reduce their proneness to strikes, although this still has to be tested against unrestricted pay policies and
buoyant markets. Ford's record has tended to improve since 1971,
in spite of the fact that Table 7.6 notes some large strikes since that
date. This improvement is reflected in increased interest by the U.S.
parent company in investing in Ford U.K. GM workers' attitudes may
be a reflection of the doubts that have frequently been cast over the
future of the Vauxhall investment.

THE DEVELOPMENT OF INDUSTRIAL RELATIONS
IN CHRYSLER U.K.: MAJOR ISSUES
AND CAUSES OF STOPPAGES

The purpose of this section is to examine the development of industrial relations in Chrysler U.K. since 1967, highlighting the principal, and often recurring, issues of debate. The background to the

prominent stoppages is analyzed as are the relative worker and management positions in these disputes.

A highly significant component of Chrysler's inheritance from
Rootes is in the method of managing industrial relations and in the
payment systems and negotiating procedures that had been used throughout the group's 34 companies until 1967. The Chrysler takeover
brought major restructuring of staff and an extensive drive toward
centralization. In the industrial relations field, this meant the rapid
change away from the prevailing system of a Rootes personnel director with scarcely any supporting staff and almost no involvement in
the 34 companies. Immediately autonomy was removed from the companies and a start was made in the introduction of well-established
U.S. control systems to govern work measurement and payment.
Some of the latter had been under discussion previously but were only
actively pursued under Chrysler. While inevitable, and desirable, the
changes produced a general atmosphere of uncertainty that influenced
the overall climate for industrial relations, and was clearly not the
best situation to be in at the start of a long recovery program.

Court of Inquiry at Linwood

Several of these background issues underlay two of the first
major labor problems to face the Chrysler management in 1968.
Chrysler's Scottish operation consisted of two adjacent plants (Rootes
and the former Pressed Steel factory) with quite separate systems of
pay and conditions. Against a loss of £4.5 million at Linwood in 1967,
the company put forward proposals in February 1968 designed to improve productivity and eliminate the differences in grade structures
and payment methods between the two plants. These were accepted by
the National Union of Vehicle Builders (NUVB) and the Transport and
General Workers Union (TGWU), together comprising 60 percent of
hourly rated workers, but were rejected by the remaining unions.
Frustrated by the ensuing negotiations, management attempted to implement the plan in May 1968, resulting in a prolonged dispute and the
establishment of a court of inquiry[10] (to which some of the unions refused to give evidence).

The Chrysler plan, designed to provide substantial improvements
in pay and work conditions for employees at fixed intervals in return
for improvements in productivity and a common wage structure, was
considered reasonable by the court of inquiry: "We conclude that in
terms of payment and related benefits this is an Agreement which reasonable men should be able to accept without difficulty." In addition,
however, D.J. Robertson, head of the court of inquiry, recommended
that "urgent attention should now be given to creating adequate machinery

for negotiation and consultation." This was a telling comment in the light of the problems that were to be created in future years for Chrysler by the inadequacies of procedural agreements. Although the court found in favor of the company, indicated that the unions should sign the agreement, and made pointed comments on the need for unions to respond to management planning to integrate the two Linwood plants, Chrysler was not absolved of blame. Indeed, management was openly criticized for implementing the agreement when only the two larger unions involved had signed it and, the court claimed, the company had "acted with rapidity in a situation requiring patience."

The Measured Day Work Problem and
Communication Difficulties

There were some similarities in the 1968 Midlands disputes. While the Rootes Linwood plant had operated a fixed-day rate system of payment from its inception, albeit with problems on its standard fixing system, the Rootes Midlands plants had continued with an outdated piecework plan. By 1968, it was estimated that Rootes employees took between 50 and 75 percent more man-hours to produce a car than their major European competitors[11] and were still using a piecework system that had never been used by Ford in the United Kingdom and had been dropped by GM in 1942.

Attempting to break out of this system in the Midlands plants, Chrysler made a far-reaching pay and productivity offer in May 1968. After continued negotiation, management attitudes hardened and the company indicated that the plan would be introduced without agreement on August 26. Not unexpectedly, the polarization of attitudes was immediate as the workers voted against the introduction of the measured day work (MDW) system (which had by that time been under discussion for close to two years). In a series of tough statements, the company challenged the position of the unions: "We cannot continue to use outdated methods if Rootes is to be competitive. . . . This is a case of shop stewards countermanding management instructions . . . indeed it is tantamount to a suggestion that they can veto management directions. This, of course, is a situation which the company is not prepared to accept."[12]

It is difficult to assess the true situation in these initial Chrysler days. The time chosen for confrontation seemed particularly inopportune when most car plants were operating at capacity because of strong domestic and export demand. Without question, the corporation had to articulate its management style and its attitudes toward a U.K. investment that was in difficulties. On the other hand, the aggressive statements made took little account of the situation in the

U.K. car industry or of the root of the problems that lay in the uncertainty created by undeveloped communication systems. Moreover, the
unions had given ample evidence of their readiness to react oversensi-
tively to changes they did not understand.

The importance of the 1968 compromise cannot be overstressed
since it has been a recurring source of difficulty. In return for the
right to control the track speed, the company agreed on an arbitration
procedure to settle any disputes regarding the manning of the stations
on the track. This, in consequence, gave the unions in the Midlands
plants a major bargaining weapon to be used in the future, since it
maintained the opportunities for negotiation that they had held under
the old piecework system. Chrysler thus shared in some of the chronic
difficulties of the U.K. car industry in 1968, a year in which total
stoppages in car plants, either through internal or external disputes,
resulted in an estimated loss of £120 million in car production (at
showroom prices).

Several of the main problems returned in 1969 in Chrysler plants.
At Linwood, the absence of effective consultation procedures and the
ineffective use of existing procedures continued to be reflected in repeated disruptions over minor issues. In the first three months of
1969, there were 27 stoppages, costing nearly 30,000 man-hours.
The new chief executive at Linwood commented in May: "Chrysler
is extremely concerned at our seeming inability to work many conse-
cutive days without a stoppage."[13] While at Linwood, as in the other
Chrysler plants, the stoppages were usually for brief periods, the
implications for production planning and acceptable working relationships were far-reaching.

Chrysler took the initiative in an attempt to solve some of the
communication problems in the plants. In the spring of 1969, acknowledging that there were considerable problems in overdependence on
shop stewards as the link between men and management, the company
started a Foreman Training Program, initially at Dunstable. Further,
a new negotiating and procedural agreement was signed with the Draughts
men and Allied Technicians Association (DATA) at Dunstable, whereby
no problem was to take more than 20 days to pass through the disputes
procedures. A joint Works Council was introduced at Linwood, and a
trouble-shooting committee of management and shop stewards was established at the Hills Precision Plastics subsidiary.

All of these initiatives were an expression of the need for fundamen
tal reform in industrial relations and of the need for rapid progress in
areas where success could only be ensured by proceeding at a slower
pace. This was evidenced when a new pay and productivity plan was
rejected at Ryton in May 1969. The company, faced with the need to
cut back on output owing to government deflationary policies, was accused of deliberately introducing short-time working to force through

the pay and productivity deal. Gilbert Hunt described the rejection as a tragedy because "we will never reap the full benefit of our heavy investment until our Coventry plants agree to accept modern practices and modern thinking."[14] The final acceptance of this plan at Ryton in June 1969 gave workers one of the highest hourly rates in the European car industry (see Table 7.5). The crucial ingredient thereafter was to ensure that the productivity increases would follow.

Withdrawal from the Engineering Employers Federation

In many ways, 1970 was a particularly critical year in the development of Chrysler's industrial relations, with the decision of the company to withdraw from the EEF as of January 1. Convinced that a more efficient disputes procedure than that operated by the EEF could be introduced, and that the EEF was becoming too "small firm oriented," the company gave six months' notice to leave. Chrysler was caught in a position where the wage rates and conditions for its employees were better than the EEF norms, but the unions were still able to claim the costly additional benefits conceded by the federation. However, in breaking from the EEF, Chrysler had not in fact managed to negotiate a replacement disputes procedure by January 1970 and found itself ill-prepared for the consequences of its action. In retrospect, there is little question that the company handled the preparations for this withdrawal badly, and found that industrial relations over the following two to three years were influenced by the weakness of its procedural arrangements. These events were particularly significant

TABLE 7.5

Net Rate per Hour for Identical Task, 1969
(pence)

United Kingdom		Germany		France		Sweden	
Chrysler (Ryton)	86.5	Volkswagen	65.6	Renault	41.5	Volvo	44
BMC (Longbridge)	52.5	Ford	60.5	Citroen	36.5		
Vauxhall	49	Opel	66.5	Peugeot	45		
Ford	52.5	Mercedes-Benz	66				
		BMW	62				

Source: Sunday Times (London), December 21, 1969, quoted from International Metal Workers Federation, Geneva.

in view of the introduction of the Avenger range in 1970, where consistency of supply was vitally important in the extension of Chrysler's market penetration at home and abroad.

The problems for Avenger production started in the machine room and press shops at Linwood where the NUVB claimed management was giving new workers too many secure jobs and that old workers should be eligible for transfer. The resulting Linwood stoppage (June 16, 1970) halted all Ryton car assembly within two days. On several other occasions Avenger production was stopped. A Ryton dispute from June 29 to July 10 over a wage claim, for example, resulted in a stern warning from Gilbert Hunt in a letter to employees of the serious consequences that would result if the unions persisted in advising workers to walk out without notice. At this time, the company was already forecasting a loss for the year of £11 million. By early October 1970, about 22,000 Avengers (approximately 20 percent of the planned annual total) had been lost through industrial disputes. The major problem, as Peter Griffiths, director of industrial relations, observed at the time, was that most of the longest stoppages were unofficial and "in the long run unreasonable and unconstitutional disruption is self defeating."[15] Poorly developed procedures did not help the delicate situation at this time, and overall the consequences were a tragedy for the only Chrysler U.K. model launch between 1967 and 1975.

Guaranteed Severance Pay and the Parity Issue

Another 1970 pioneering initiative by Chrysler was the introduction of guaranteed severance pay, initially at Ryton in September. Paradoxically, the announcement coincided with an extensive period of disruption in the U.K. car industry when over 40,000 workers were laid off through a mixture of internal and external disputes. Unwittingly, Chrysler U.K. at Ryton was again in a pace-setting role, and "parity with Ryton" in rates and layoff provisions was a significant issue within Chrysler and between Chrysler and the industry for a considerable period thereafter. The arrangement, initially giving employees a minimum of 65 percent of their weekly earnings during layoffs or short-time working, was a considerable innovation in the U.K. industry and was a further example of Chrysler's attempts to establish a sound basis for labor relations. It was particularly ironic that it came at a time when it was clear that such efforts alone would not solve the labor problems of the company. Reviewing the year, Hunt concluded:

> In the coming year we must put the company on a firm footing. Opportunity runs out for everybody and there comes a

time when we can no longer talk about "the future" as some
vague never-never land where everything is somehow going
to be wonderful. . . . Beyond everything else we need a
year of stable industrial relations and uninterrupted production within our own plants. Another year of disruption on
the damaging scale of the past 12 months might well put us
out of business. [16]

While there were a number of Chrysler strikes in 1971, it was
a relatively dispute-free year. Toward the end of 1971, however, one
of the major issues of earlier years reemerged, namely, parity in
wage rates among plants, particularly among Linwood, Stoke, and Ryton. Linwood workers always had been paid less than their Midlands
colleagues following the Brabloch Agreement of the early 1960s when
Lord Rootes obtained the consent of the Scottish unions for a regional
rate structure as part of the deal to set up a factory in Scotland.
Tension had been building on this issue ever since the Chrysler takeover and culminated in the major parity strike at Linwood between January 7 and February 4, 1972. The strike started over a demand for
an £8 per week increase, against an initial offer from the company of
£3 per week without any alteration to existing working agreements, or
£4 per week in return for productivity improvements. After considerable acrimony and renewed controversy over this issue, the dispute
was settled with an offer of over £5 per week and the heat was taken
out of the situation by a commitment to parity by July 1976.

Once more, this strike coincided with a booming U.K. domestic
car market, cost the company an estimated £10 million in lost car
output in various plants, and led to sweeping criticisms of workers'
conduct from management. Hunt indicated that this strike and its consequences would have an adverse effect on the company's financial
health for the following two to three years and once again harangued
the unions: "There are those on the union side who have stated that
they are not interested in the company's prosperity and that it is no
part of their concern."[17] This was by no means the only dispute
where parity was an issue, but it was strongly criticized as lacking
official union support. Furthermore, the point was made that the
unions were pushing needlessly since the principle was one the company was willing to concede. Clearly, of course, some preplanned
and understood company policy might have reduced the risk of such a
prolonged stoppage on the issue.

The "Shoddy Work" Dispute

Without question 1973 was the worst year for stoppages in Chrysler U.K. in terms of available production lost, the year being domi-

nated by two highly significant disputes. The first, from May 25 to
June 25, was the so-called shoddy work dispute and the second concerned electricians staff status, extending from August 2 to November 9.

As invariably happens in major industrial disputes, the causes
are complex and the issues singled out for attention are not always
given their proper weight. This was particularly true of the shoddy
work dispute, which was in fact a culmination of many of the issues
examined already in this section. The particular circumstances surrounding the dispute occurred on May 24 when the Ryton plant manager accused the employees on the A shift of deliberately turning out
substandard work because, he alleged, they were disgruntled at being
recalled to work after a strike at Linwood. At the time, the company
claimed that 20 percent of the cars leaving the assembly line required
additional attention to bring them up to standard.

On the day in question, the whole shift was sent home. The following day the shop stewards contended that the action had contravened
agreements and that the employees should thus be paid for the whole
shift. The company refused. Thereafter the situation became highly
confused, and a series of allegations and counterallegations resulted
in industrial relations at Ryton becoming almost completely fractured.
A brief time before the dispute, in an information bulletin on April
27, the same plant manager had stated confidently: "Let me say that
by joint team efforts we have made considerable progress and that in
my view our quality and reliability is second to none in comparison
with our EEC competition."[18] It is little wonder that the contradic-
tions inherent in this situation left the employees confused on the shoddy
work allegation.

The company response to the dispute was to announce a halt to
all further capital investment and expansion until a settlement had been
reached and "until we have demonstrated over a reasonable period of
time, that we can work out our problems in a constitutional manner,
while continuous production is maintained."[19] It was as part of this
announcement that the planned investment to produce the Alpine in the
United Kingdom was halted and investment switched to France. Disputes procedures, manning levels, work quality, and substandard components all rapidly became the centers of contention as attitudes hardened. The development that attracted particular attention and scathing
comment was the action of management in attempting to remove engines
by night from the Stoke plant, which was heavily picketed by the strik-
ers. The alleged picketing violence by drivers from a firm of contrac-
tors that was handling the engines resulted in widespread criticism of
Chrysler, the company being accused of unacceptable strike-breaking
tactics on all sides. Feeling is perhaps summarized best by the Trade
Union Congress (TUC) delegation to the secretary of state for Trade

and Industry, who was advised to tell the company that the United Kingdom was not some kind of off-shore Spain where there were no trade unions.

While it is not reasonable to suggest that the Chrysler style of managing industrial relations was in keeping with the Stoke action, it gave rare opportunity for adverse comment and for concluding that there were some key managers who had an unrealistic view of trade unionism in the U.K. motor industry. Some of the parliamentary comment on the incident reflected this, one member claiming that the "Government should tell Chrysler that they welcomed their investment but expected them to take an intelligent and up to date view of industrial relations and not pursue wrecking tactics of the kind that had been seen recently."[20]

The strike lasted five weeks at a cost of 808,306 man-hours and 17,033 vehicles lost (about £10 million output at showroom prices), but clearly the indirect costs extended far beyond this. The strike itself indicated that much of the innovation in industrial relations had failed to change fundamental attitudes on both sides and that the costs of union recalcitrance and management impatience would continue to be high.

The Electricians Staff Status Dispute

The second major 1973 disruption, over electricians staff status, had some of its origins in government pay restraint policy that effectively stopped Chrysler from fulfilling a commitment. In 1972, the company had undertaken to give toolmakers and electricians staff status. But, while the toolmakers had negotiated a settlement before the Phase 2 pay policy became effective in November, the electricians were caught within the terms of Phase 2 restraint. After protracted negotiations extending into early August 1973, 150 Ryton and Stoke electricians stopped work within 24 hours of giving seven days' notice of official strike action. This immediate action was prompted by management's refusal to give unqualified guarantees that no supervisory staff would carry out electricians' duties when the planned strike began. Following the dispute earlier in the year, it was obvious that strike action would be particularly damaging to the company. Chrysler, in some undoubted desperation, was reported to be considering concession of the £250 per year claim in the knowledge that the Pay Board and Price Commission would issue a restraining order and prevent its payment.[21] The company would not confirm or deny that this strategy was under consideration, but it appeared to have the obvious merit of closely identifying the dispute as between the union concerned (Electricians and Plumbing Trades Union) (EPTU) and the government.

At this particular stage (late August), other considerations entered the dispute, including an apparent lack of support for the electricians' case. Thus, for example, on August 21, Chrysler was able to recall 5,000 workers at Ryton due to a decision by 75 millwrights to cross the electricians' picket lines. Events rapidly moved against the company, however, and led to renewed support from some other unions when Chrysler admitted (having earlier denied) using seven nonunion electricians for emergency maintenance work. This had important repercussions, including the withdrawal of labor at Linwood in sympathy from September 5 to 21, and contributed to the stopping of all Chrysler U.K. car production by September 18. Again, at least some of the problems must be attributed to management's insensitivity, which effectively gave the initiative back to the EPTU.

The company was thus forced into using what had by now become its standard tactics of making dire, albeit realistic, predictions for the future. On September 25, the management threatened to dismiss one-third of the U.K. labor force if the electricians' strike did not end that week and announced a program of progressive redundancy. Much political capital was made of the continuing dispute, an electricians' union spokesman addressing the Labour Party Conference referred to the "threatened exodus, a threat they have used repeatedly in every industrial dispute over the last six or seven years."[22] The explicit conclusion being drawn was that Chrysler was not prepared to negotiate in good faith or to "respect the customs and practices of this country."

By early October, interunion conflicts began to act in Chrysler's favor as the eight unions not directly involved strongly urged the EPTU to accept an independent committee of inquiry. Its report in late October found that the company had never given a firm commitment of £250 per year as the union contended and recommended acceptance of £190, the Phase 3 maximum. It also recommended that the company should reverse its decision of September 7 to withdraw the offer of staff status to electricians. These terms were accepted and the dispute ended on November 7. In reviewing this dispute, it is difficult to see what was gained by some aspects of company policy. At several stages singularly bad decisions were made and the company seemed to be bent on attracting criticism by its actions. One thing is certain: by the close of 1973, there was a need to build industrial relations at Chrysler almost from scratch.

The company estimated that 1.4 million man-hours and 17,033 vehicles were lost as a result of this dispute. For 1973 as a whole, the chairman's report for the year indicated that production had been affected for 18 weeks and that during the 13-month financial period, 91,129 vehicles had been lost through internal and external disruptions. In different terms, 22 percent of potential production was lost, in com-

parison with 13.8 percent in 1972 and 17 percent in 1974. Even if the
company had not been able to sell such a volume, the net effect was
still very substantial.

Although 1974 was not dominated by major strikes, the effect
of a long series of smaller disruptions kept Chrysler's industrial relations in the public eye. Interunion disagreements, manning levels,
procedural arrangements, and parity questions were among the issues
featuring. It was against this background that the management warned
senior shop stewards at Coventry in June that the company could not
sustain another prolonged strike over pay differentials and that if
pushed too hard it would consider seeking voluntary liquidation. [23]
Parity disputes brought car production to a halt in late August with
demands from components-producing subsidiaries for pay parity with
production workers at Stoke and Ryton. One of the most damaging of
the parity strikes in 1974 was by the Coventry tool room workers, a
dispute that led to further announcements early in October that the
company had decided to shelve all future expansion plans because of
the strike record. [24]

By the end of 1974, Chrysler, in common with other U.K. manufacturers, was beginning to cut its labor force in the face of declining
car sales, registrations having fallen by one-quarter in the first ten
months of the year. The company had stopped recruiting earlier in
1974, announced a program of white-collar redundancies in November,
and by the end of the year had made public a plan for a three-day week
in some plants. In a different way, thus, the events of 1974 contributed
further to the process of weakening the financial structure of the company and provided two highly unproductive years before the 1975 crisis.

Chrysler's Industrial Relations at the
1975 Crisis

Extensive government involvement in the 1975 crisis produced
a by-product of much official evidence on the labor problems within
the company. This evidence, given to select committee inquiries,
provides, albeit to a limited degree, an insight into worker and management attitudes and points to the areas requiring attention in the restructured company.

From the union viewpoint, the evidence available confirms the
known causes of disputes over a period of time. The Chrysler union
witnesses have stressed the detrimental effect of working for an overseas subsidiary of a multinational and questioned the degree to which
worker participation could be meaningful in such an organization:
"The multinational involvement creates a complete feeling of insecurity
as to the future of Chrysler U.K. and I think that is basically our prob-

lem."[25] At the same time, some of the Chrysler union representatives indicated that there were considerable overall benefits in the 1967 takeover. It was undertaken, they said, "with a very high powered management, they made some good, constructive technical changes and invested in new equipment that would allow us to be far more efficient than we have been during the period of the Rootes regime." While such statements were readily made in the dispassionate environment away from the heat of a real industrial relations situation, it was clear that in 1975 many of the detailed changes undertaken still registered as problems. In general they alleged, "the atmosphere is not there [at Chrysler] and procedures do not work,"[26] and at Ryton, it was claimed "we have lived in a vacuum in this plant for many years. There is a centralisation going on of decision making within the U.K. Chrysler company in this country. That creates many problems."[27] That this type of comment should still feature at the crisis period, after over nine years of centralizing policies, is itself a reflection of the size of the industrial relations problem faced by Chrysler in 1967. As part of the defense of the recurrence of disputes concerning procedures, union representatives from at least two of the plants accused the management of failing to operate recognized agreements. At Ryton this was alleged to be particularly true regarding frequent line changes,[28] and at Whitley the poor industrial relations record was attributed to a basic lack of communication: "This company . . . runs on tram lines. You get three lines and there is no communication amongst them at all."[29]

From these comments and from the evidence presented earlier, it is clear that as Chrysler entered the 1975 crisis, labor relations were only in difficulties for reasons fairly widespread in the U.K. industry and particularly in British Leyland. Thus, as elsewhere, industrial relations were dominated by the four related concerns of lack of long-term confidence, a history of conflict and lack of trust between the parties, poor communications, and a fragmented union structure. There is no doubt that at times the behavior of the work force had been appallingly irresponsible. Actions on some occasions had been designed specifically to push issues into the political arena, and ever since the mid-1960s, sections of the labor force had been pushing hard for nationalization as a solution to the problems of Chrysler. Management could look back and claim that some major innovations had been introduced in industrial relations policy. These were specifically viewed as including a common wage and grade policy, a common date on which agreements were negotiated with the unions, reducing the number of agreements from over 80 in 1970 to 53 in 1975, and progress on the contentious issue of parity.[30]

On the other hand, the company had failed singularly to achieve effective communications, and coming into an industry with huge labor problems, made some amazing blunders. As one comment noted, "Chrysler seems to go over the brink so often in labour relations."[31] The company actively used long-term confidence as a weapon of attack rather than defense. As such, in the context of the United Kingdom, it had behaved as a multinational that either constantly misread the situation or read it perfectly, knowing that it was assured of government support.

Even before the crisis in 1975, it was abundantly clear to management that the industrial relations situation required fundamental reform and a major new initiative. In May 1975, Gilbert Hunt indicated that "for two years we have realised that with a changing world greater participation . . . in the decision making process and in the operation of our company [by] the trade unions was something we ought to bring about."[32] However, before the company had the opportunity to discuss participation proposals informally with the unions or even to work the plan out systematically, there were renewed pressures stemming from disputes.

It was under the particular pressures of an unofficial strike at the Stoke engine plant from May 9 to June 4 over a £15 per week pay claim that the company unveiled, very prematurely, its proposals for participation. The unions were given a two-week deadline to work out mutually agreeable details on a pay and participation package. To produce such revolutionary participation proposals in such a generalized form and under such time constraints smacked of a combination of naivity and desperation, and resulted in the proposals being treated less than seriously at this stage. The unions were more interested in the settlement of their immediate pay claim, but they could hardly have responded to the participation offer when there was little, beyond the broad principle, to respond to. It was perhaps to be expected that when a return to work was negotiated in early June this took the form of accepting a pay settlement but rejecting the participation plan.

It was not until two months later, on August 21, that the company put forward its detailed plans for the Employee Participation Program to a joint working party. The proposals were far-reaching. A series of Plant Employee Representation Committees (PERC) representing the labor force were to meet weekly with the plant management to discuss and review the operation of the plant. Each PERC was to appoint representatives to key decision-making committees, including those determining production levels, manning, recruitment, quality, and so on. At a higher level, each PERC would elect representatives to the Chrysler Employee Representative Council, which would be chaired by the managing director and on which would sit senior management executives. The 24 employee representatives on this council would have functions that included appointing two directors. The final part of the proposals concerned the establishment of a pay and agreement coordinating committee to negotiate fixed-term agreements and grading structures, to deal with specific aspects of remuneration, and to approve arbitrators.

Many of these ideas were of immense potential long-term benefit in tackling the long-standing problems of the company. There is no reason to believe that they were proposed without a genuine desire to make them work, although, as could often be observed, some of the changes could have come previously. There were many pressures on Chrysler at the time, not least of which was the requirement for government finance in one form or another, which had been expressed at the time of the Stoke strike, in an application to the government-backed Finance for Industry for a £35 million loan package. It is more than likely that this pressure played a part in accelerating the proposals. However, the circumstances from August were not conducive to long-term consultations such as were obviously required and so the crisis of the winter of 1975 came with the proposals still on the table and with many of the problems they were designed to tackle, unsolved. It is worth noting, however, that the Employee Participation Scheme set the tone for the movement toward a planning agreement that was to be an important condition of government support.

THE COST OF DISPUTES TO CHRYSLER U.K.

The run-through of Chrysler's industrial relations in the previous section is important in identifying the issues that have created problems for the company since 1967 and in revealing attitudes and stances adopted by management and workers. Inevitably, this type of approach has certain limitations. It puts emphasis on the major disputes and on internal disputes, and does not provide a consistent basis for evaluating the cost of industrial stoppages to the company. It has been shown earlier, however, that quantification of disputes is complicated by poor official statistics, which themselves refer only to "prominent" stoppages; again, while it is possible to derive Linwood stoppages from official statistics, this is not feasible in the case of Chrysler's Midlands plants. Moreover, the strike statistics kept by the company are only available in a consistent and comprehensive form from 1972 onward. It is with these provisos in mind that Tables 7.6 to 7.9 attempt to quantify Chrysler's losses from industrial disputes.

The Number and Size of Disputes

Figures for the three years 1973-75 (Table 7.6) show very clearly the extent to which Chrysler has been affected by production interrup-

TABLE 7.6

Number of Disputes by Duration in Chrysler U.K., 1973-75

	Mid-lands Manu-fac-tur-ing	Lin-wood Manu-fac-tur-ing	Truck Manu-fac-tur-ing	To-tal Chrys-ler U.K.	Per-cent-age Less Than One Shift	Per-cent-age Less Than Four Hours
1973						
Under four hours	80	239	58	378		
Under one shift	46	29	22	97		
Under one week	13	5	2	22		
Over one week	2	0	1	3	95.0	75.6
Total	141	271	83	500		
1974						
Under four hours	106	261	68	435		
Under one shift	37	48	20	107		
Under one week	35	15	4	57		
Over one week	1	0	0	1	90.4	72.5
Total	179	324	92	600		
1975						
Under four hours	54	116	21	203		
Under one shift	29	29	17	77		
Under one week	10	4	1	21		
Over one week	1	1	1	5	91.5	66.3
Total	94	150	40	306		

Source: Chrysler U.K.

tions. Short stoppages, of up to four hours long, averaged one per day over the period. No comparative data were available for the other manufacturers, but there is little reason to believe that the incidence of stoppages was much different. In analyzing Chrysler's industrial relations, there is an inevitable concentration of lengthy stoppages involving large numbers of workers. This is, of course, correct. The shoddy work dispute and the electricians' strike of 1973 register as 2 out of 500 disputes for the year, but accounted for perhaps two-thirds of output lost.

In addition there is a tendency to view the multitude of short wildcat stoppages as endemic in the U.K. car industry and to that extent underrate their impact. On the other hand, the point was made earlier (Chapter 5) that even the loss of one hour's production in an eight-hour shift has a disproportionately large effect on profitability for the day. These short, usually unofficial, stoppages may have myriad causes, ranging from changes in line speeds to political demonstrations to factory temperatures. Some of management's bitterest comments have been reserved for such stoppages. The Linwood managing director described the short demonstrative strikes that plagued the plant during 1968 as "childish exhibitions of solidarity."[33] While ostensibly about trivial issues in many instances, however, the real reasons may be much more fundamental and deep-rooted. The need for clear procedural agreements and, equally important, the necessity for using such agreements is starkly obvious.

Internal and External Disputes

The high bought-out content of Chrysler cars and trucks has made the company, in common with other U.K. motor manufacturers, highly vulnerable to production disruptions in components suppliers. On the truck side, Chrysler's problems with the supply of diesel engines, for example, was discussed in some detail in Chapter 6. For the period 1972-75, company estimates reveal that 40 percent of man-hours lost resulted from external disputes or other externally derived factors (Table 7.7). Principal among the latter was the miners' strike early in 1974, which developed into a direct confrontation between the mine workers and the government and led to the introduction of a three-day week for industry. This cost Chrysler 1.2 million man-hours, and resulted in the loss of 29,000 units in the first quarter of 1974. Even excluding this once-for-all factor, external stoppages still have accounted for about one-third man-hours lost, and, as with the impact of government policy, represent one of the additional costs of operating in the United Kingdom.

The Incidence of Disputes by Plant

Both Tables 7.6 and 7.7 provide a breakdown of stoppages by manufacturing location. Differences between the plants are immediately obvious. About 60 percent of the short (under four hours) stoppages emanated from Linwood, whereas the vast proportion of disputes lasting for more than a single shift were at Chrysler's Midlands plants. This bears out a comment made by Gilbert Hunt in 1975 that labor re-

TABLE 7.7

Man-Hours Lost Due to Internal and External Factors, 1972-75
(thousands of man-hours)

	1972	1973	1974	1975
Midlands manufacturing				
Internal	1,007	1,543	639	643
External	291	138	478	353
Total	1,298	1,681	1,117	996
Linwood manufacturing				
Internal	731	731	281	73
External	330	110	462	479
Total	1,061	841	743	552
Truck manufacturing				
Internal	74	60	62	39
External	77	3	—	163
Total	151	63	62	202
Total Chrysler U.K.				
Internal	1,872	2,746	992	992
External	1,010	536	2,110	1,005
Overall total	2,882	3,282	3,102*	1,997
Internal as percent of total	65.0	83.7	32.0	49.7

*Includes 1,170,000 man-hours lost due to the national emergency
and the three-day week in the first quarter of 1974.

Source: Chrysler U.K.

lations issues in Scotland were "usually of a different character because of the difference in the nationality."[34] It is worth noting also
that the Midlands plants have lost proportionately far fewer man-hours
than Linwood because of external stoppages. With most of the components-supplying firms being located in the Midlands, alternative
supply sources are that much easier to arrange for the Stoke and Ryton
plants than for Linwood. Although a smaller operation in employment
terms, the Luton and Dunstable commercial vehicle plants have had
excellent industrial relations records, and both management and unions
have been at pains to draw attention to this in public.

One of the particularly interesting cases of disruption in the U.K. motor industry is that of Chrysler's Linwood plant. Because the data in Tables 7.6 and 7.7 refer to the very recent past, however, they do not reveal the full extent of the Linwood problems. To permit a more balanced assessment, Table 7.8, derived from official statistics, highlights the "prominent" stoppages at Linwood since Chrysler took control. The two major disputes, in 1968 when the court of inquiry was established and particularly the 1972 parity strike, stand out clearly. Such stoppages, allied with the worse than average minor disruption record of the plant, meant that up to 1972 at least, Linwood was viewed from an industrial relations standpoint as Chrysler's bete noire. The reasons for the disruption record of the plant during these years are complex and can be best understood in the context of a complete assessment of the Linwood operation and of the problems of Clydeside (discussed in Chapter 8).

The Impact of Disputes on Chrysler U.K.

Table 7.9 shows the company's estimates of the number of vehicles lost through internal disputes in the four years to 1975. Such estimates, totaling 212,000 lost units in the four years to 1975, cannot be regarded as an indicator of the true impact of production losses. The real impact would depend upon what the market at home and abroad could bear. Thus, interrupted production in periods of high demand would be more serious from the viewpoint of sales and market share than interruptions in periods of slack or falling demand. Moreover, movements in the total market might not be a reliable guide to the sales Chrysler could have achieved, since these would depend upon the attractiveness of the product range and the company's image (particularly relevant in 1975) apart from the more general factors.

There is no doubt that the U.K. market alone could not have borne these additional production volumes. The most that could have been hoped for, assuming that Chrysler had been able to maintain, say, a 10 percent market share, would have been 70,000 extra units over the four-year period.* It is doubtful whether any extra sales

---

*This assumes a 10 percent market share in each of the four years, including 1975. Such a share would only have been possible in the latter year if the speculation about the company's future in the United Kingdom had not developed. The 70,000 postulated sales, moreover, would have had to come almost entirely from the Avenger and the Arrow range, since the Imp sales actually achieved were about the maximum the market would bear.

TABLE 7.8

Linwood: Prominent Stoppages, 1967-75

Year	Began	Ended	Number of Workers Involved Directly	Indirectly	Number of Working Days Lost	Comment
1967	September 27	September 29	2,650		8,000	Increase in pay for car assembly workers following a revision of production schedules.
1968	May 13	June 7	4,600		79,000	Against certain conditions contained in a proposed new wage structure.
1969	March 6	March 11	2,010[a]	220	7,300	Complaint about supervisor being employed on inspection work while a ban in overtime was in operation.
	April 21	April 25	1,240[b]	4,340	18,800	Demand by nightshift workers for a new rotational shift plan.
	April 28	May 2	800[c]	2,500	9,700	Against the introduction of new work methods.
1970	January 7	January 12	5,500[c]		10,900	Claim for payment for time lost when labor was withdrawn because of breakdown in the heating system.
	June 16	June 22	4,000[a]	2,000	24,700	Dissatisfaction over the recruitment of new labor.
	August 21	September 4	2,000[b]		21,000	Against the speeding up of the production line.
	October 1	October 8	600[d]	2,000	12,800	Against the suspension of five workers for disciplinary reasons.
1971	June 15	June 25	145[e]	780	8,400	In protest against the dismissal of a worker for disciplinary reasons.
1972	January 7	February 4	6,500[f]		133,300	Dissatisfaction with pay negotiations: union wanted an increase of £8 per week to give parity with workers at Coventry plants.
1973	March 18	March 21	400[g]	5,000	17,600	Interunion dispute over skill status of workers installing new equipment.
	September 5	September 21	7,195[h]		79,600	Refusal to maintain or work with equipment or machinery serviced by staff employees covering electricians' duties during the latter's withdrawal of labor in sympathy with strike in Coventry plant.
1974	January 15	January 18	40[i]	6,000	19,100	Interunion disagreement over membership appropriate to new work on exhaust emission testing.
	May 30	June 7	450[b]	3,000	19,000	For an acceptable redeployment agreement when affected by a dispute in another block.
1975	October 11	October 14	700[a]	3,500	6,500	In support of two workers who refused relocation to other jobs.

[a]Production workers.
[b]Assemblers.
[c]Press shop workers.
[d]Various.
[e]Machine setters.
[f]All hourly paid workers.
[g]Maintenance workers, millwrights, electricians.
[h]Electricians, production workers.
[i]Skilled vehicle mechanics and electricians.

Note: Stoppages involving less than ten workers and those lasting less than one day are excluded except where the aggregate number of working days lost exceeded 1,000. The figures also exclude any loss of time, for example, through shortages of material, which may be caused at other establishments by the stoppages included in the statistics.

Source: Department of Employment Gazette (London: HMSO), various issues. Prior to 1971, the Gazette was known as the Ministry of Labour Gazette, and the Employment and Productivity Gazette.

245

TABLE 7.9

Production Losses in Chrysler U.K. from Internal Causes, 1972-75
(number of vehicles)

	1972	1973	1974	1975
Internal disputes	28,817	78,154	34,116	34,538
Union meetings	—	—	1,176	577
Aftereffects of disputes	4,345	8,612	763	1,898
Absenteeism	771	} 1,949	1,017	69
Mass relief and shortage of labor	—		9,484	5,436
Total	33,933	88,715	46,556	42,518

Note: Excludes production losses due to breakdowns, changed customer schedules, technical changes, and so on.

Source: Chrysler U.K.

would have been made in Europe given the distribution problems noted earlier (Chapter 5), and the Iranian contract was fixed. This leaves the U.S. market. The insecurity of supply was undoubtedly one factor leading to the replacement of the Avenger by the Mitsubishi Colt. While mere speculation, a decision in favor of the Avenger could have meant additional sales of 120,000 units to the United States. At best, therefore, about 90 percent of output lost because of strikes might have been sold; at worst, about 30 percent. The latter would scarcely have increased throughput and revenue by enough to prevent recourse to government funds, but the latter almost certainly would have, with capacity utilization being increased from under 70 to between 80 and 85 percent on average over the four years.

It is, therefore, not an understatement to say that labor problems, on top of the company's other difficulties, were a major, if not the major, contributory factor in hastening the crisis of 1975. For this, both management and the work force must bear an equally heavy responsibility. For the future, too, peace in industrial relations remains an essential ingredient for the success of Chrysler in the United Kingdom.

NOTES

1. D. J. Forsyth, "Foreign-Owned Firms and Labour Relations: A Regional Perspective," British Journal of Industrial Relations 11, no. 1 (March 1973).

2. D. Kujawa, International Labour Relations Management in the Automobile Industry: A Comparative Study of Chrysler, Ford and General Motors (New York: Praeger, 1971), p. 183.

3. See, for example, "Henry Ford and Detroit Style Poker," Times (London), March 12, 1971, and April 21, 1975.

4. Kujawa, International Labour Relations Management, pp. 97-99.

5. International Monetary Fund, "Meeting of the Chrysler World Auto Council," May 10-11, 1973, Geneva, quoted in Multinationals in Western Europe: The Industrial Relations Experience (Geneva: International Labor Organization, 1976).

6. J. Gennard and M. D. Steuer, "The Industrial Relations of Foreign Owned Subsidiaries in the United Kingdom," British Journal of Industrial Relations 9, no. 1 (1971).

7. D. G. Rhys, "Employment, Efficiency and Labour Relations in the British Motor Industry," Industrial Relations Journal 5, no. 2 (1974): 4.

8. Fourteenth Report from the Expenditure Committee, sess. 1974-75, The Motor Vehicle Industry, HC 617 (London: HMSO, August 1975), pp. 74, 75.

9. Rhys, "Employment, Efficiency, and Labour Relations," pp. 13-14.

10. Report of the court of inquiry under Professor D. J. Robertson into a dispute at Rootes Motors Ltd., Linwood, Cmnd. 3692 (London: HMSO, July 1968).

11. "Why Its 'Now or Never' at Rootes," Times (London), August 31, 1968.

12. Times (London), August 27, 1968.

13. Glasgow Herald, May 14, 1969.

14. Times (London), June 5, 1969.

15. Ibid., October 5, 1970.

16. Arrow (Chrysler U.K. house magazine), November 1970.

17. Times (London), February 8, 1972.

18. Ibid., June 8, 1973.

19. Ibid., June 7, 1973.

20. Hansard, June 25, 1973 (R. Prentice, Eastham North, Labour).

21. Times (London), August 20, 1973.

22. Ibid., October 3, 1973.

23. Financial Times, June 27, 1974.

24. Daily Telegraph, October 6, 1974.

25. Fourteenth Report from the Expenditure Committee, The Motor Vehicle Industry, HC 617, p. 117.

26. Ibid., p. 76.

27. Expenditure Committee, sess. 1975-76, Public Expenditure on Chrysler U.K. Ltd., Minutes of Evidence, HC 104 (V) (London: HMSO, February 12, 1976), pp. 192, 193.

28. Ibid., p. 195.

29. Expenditure Committee, sess. 1975-76, Public Expenditure on Chrysler U.K. Ltd., Minutes of Evidence, HC 104 (VII) (London: HMSO, February 13, 1976), pp. 233, 234.

30. Expenditure Committee, sess. 1975-76, Public Expenditure on Chrysler U.K. Ltd., Minutes of Evidence, HC 104 (XIV) (London: HMSO, March 17, 1976), pp. 363, 364.

31. The Economist, September 15, 1973.

32. Fourteenth Report from the Expenditure Committee, sess. 1974-75, The Motor Vehicle Industry, HC 617 (II) (London: HMSO, August 1975), p. 122.

33. Glasgow Herald, April 10, 1965.

34. Fourteenth Report from the Expenditure Committee, sess. 1974-75, The Motor Vehicle Industry, HC 617 (I) (London: HMSO, August 1975), p. 216.

8

THE EFFECTS OF
GOVERNMENT POLICY
ON CHRYSLER
OPERATIONS

Government action in many fields has an impact on the motor industry. Such action may be direct or indirect and include, for example, government legislation in the areas of economic policy, industrial relations, road and safety regulations, mergers and takeovers, and trade and tariffs. Some of these issues, such as government labor relations policy, have been touched upon and others concerning the social costs and benefits of transport are outside the scope of this study. The main aim of this chapter is to consider the impact on Chrysler U.K. of government policies in the fields of demand management and regional development. The former is perhaps of overriding economic importance as far as the U.K. motor industry as a whole is concerned, but the latter is also highly significant, particularly to Chrysler, since it encompasses not only economic but also social and political dimensions. To set the scene for the assessment of the 1975–76 crisis and its consequences in Chapter 9, a brief discussion is included on government support and strategy for the motor industry.

Although government regional policy influenced the location of Chrysler's Linwood plant, the subsequent performance of the Linwood operation is related to many other factors that are strictly outside the scope of this chapter. Nevertheless, since Linwood is perhaps the key to the future success or failure of Chrysler U.K., some assessment of the Linwood operation is included within the section on regional policy.

DEMAND MANAGEMENT

It is apparent from Table 8.1 and from earlier discussions that the demand for new cars in the United Kingdom has grown less overall

TABLE 8.1

Growth and Instability in Car Registrations, 1966-75

	Percent Growth per Annum	Mean Deviation in Growth*
West Germany	+3.4	8.6
France	+2.1	6.0
United Kingdom	+1.3	8.0
Italy	+0.4	6.3
Spain	+8.6	4.9

*The mean deviation is the mean of the differences (ignoring the signs) between actual growth in each year and average growth over the whole period.

Source: Derived from data in Society of Motor Manufacturers and Traders, The Motor Industry of Great Britain, various issues.

and also less steadily than in most other European countries in the last decade. Such divergences in growth rates are potentially of considerable significance for manufacturers in the countries concerned. In recent years, both Chrysler U.K. and Chrysler France accounted for about 9 percent of registrations in their respective home markets. If these market shares had been maintained in the ten years up to 1975, Chrysler sales in the United Kingdom and France would have increased by 13,000 and 25,000 cars, respectively. However, a company with a similar market share in Germany would have attained a sales growth of 54,000 units.

In the long term, the demand for cars is influenced by such factors as the different levels of car ownership (cars per 1,000 population) already achieved, the regional distribution of the population, the availability and reliability of public transport, and changes in the relative costs of either the purchase or operation of cars. But the major determinant is the rate of growth of real personal disposable income, meaning that the demand for cars is closely related to a country's general economic performance. It is significant, therefore, that the rate of economic growth in the United Kingdom usually has fallen below that of the other main car-producing countries. The purchase of Rootes gave Chrysler a poor company within a poorly performing country, emphasizing once again the need for a strategy that would have permitted the company to break out from the constraints imposed by the relative long-term decline of the U.K. economy.

The relationship between the growth of registrations in the United Kingdom and the growth of consumers' expenditure is shown in Figure

FIGURE 8.1

Changes in Car Registrations and Consumers' Expenditure

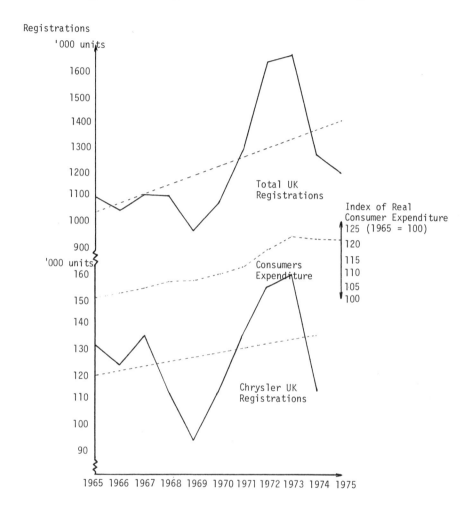

Note: The time trends estimated were R = 1004. 52 + 36.40 T and Rc = 117. 53 + 1.74 T, where R and Rc are total U.K. and Chrysler registrations, respectively (in thousands) and T is a time trend. For (1) the data refer to the years 1965-75. In the second equation, 1975 figures were omitted because of the special factors operating.

Source: Society of Motor Manufacturers and Traders, The Motor Industry of Great Britain, various issues; and Annual Abstract of Statistics (London: HMSO), various issues.

8.1. Here the long-term trends of total and Chrysler registrations
in the United Kingdom are shown in addition to the actual registration
data. The wide divergence between the two series is a reflection of
the influence of cyclical and other factors on demand. On the other
hand, the fairly close match between the long-term trends and the development of consumers' expenditure illustrates the importance of
this factor as a demand determinant.

In a mixed economy, of course, income growth can only be
partly attributed to government economic policy. Even if government
were to pursue a growth policy to the exclusion of all other objectives,
not all the determinants of growth are readily amenable to government
intervention. In the United Kingdom, moreover, conflicts between
growth and other macroeconomic policy objectives have meant that the
balance of payments, for example, often has taken priority, while
most recently the control of inflation has been the principal objective.
Be this as it may, the resulting slow and erratic rate of economic
growth has had a particularly marked effect on the motor industry and
thus on Chrysler U.K. since the income elasticity of demand is higher
than average.

While income growth is a major determinant of demand for cars
in the long term, in the short run the level of registrations is strongly
influenced by changes in hire purchase and general credit conditions
as well as by actual and expected changes in fiscal policies. Some of
these measures operate specifically on the motor industry, implying
that the industry has been used as a short-run economic regulator—
a thermostat—for the economy as a whole. It can be argued that this
has created even greater problems than those brought about by the
long-term stagnation in demand. Thus, while economic growth in the
U.K. economy has been sluggish, it has also been fairly predictable
and could be anticipated and planned for. However, a major problem
with the short-term selective controls has been their unpredictability.

In 1968, a NEDO committee under the chairmanship of Lord
Rootes came out against the use of the motor industry as an economic
regulator: "While the government must have some convenient, quick-
acting and effective way of controlling consumer demand, the use of
the motor industry for this purpose has had a detrimental effect on the
industry's sales and consequently its costs, profits and ultimately its
international competitiveness."[1] Gilbert Hunt, Chrysler U.K.'s chairman, put a similar message forward in 1975, and John Riccardo got
into the act in a letter to the then secretary of state for industry,
Wedgwood Benn, when he wrote:

> We hope . . . that the [U.K.] government will pursue
> economic, monetary and taxation policies which will stim-
> ulate the purchase of motor vehicles. Special considera-

tion should be given to reducing vehicle taxes and hire purchase restrictions. Increased sales of motor vehicles will
provide job stability and will assist us in improving Chrysler United Kingdom operations.[2]

Since the elasticity of demand for car use appears to be very low and
the price elasticity of demand for car ownership is high,[3] changes in
motoring costs have an immediate effect on the level of economic activity and thus are a good economic regulator. What needs to be established is whether or not the demand management measures employed,
in fact, have had any greater discriminatory effect on the motor industry than would more general measures.

The policy instruments that act selectively on the vehicle industry are hire purchase controls, purchase tax before 1973 and subsequently value-added tax and the special car tax, and value-added tax
and vehicle excise duty on gasoline. Not all of these measures are
specific to the motor industry, but hire purchase regulations directly
affect only a limited range of industries and the same is true of purchase tax. While the introduction of the value-added tax was a move
to a much more broadly based form of indirect taxation, a special
car tax was imposed on top of the standard rate of value-added tax.
Hire purchase restrictions were first introduced in 1952, and since
then minimum deposit rates and maximum repayment periods have
been changed frequently as a means of influencing demand. Since 1961,
for example, there have been 11 alterations in hire purchase conditions.
Although there has been some debate as to the effectiveness of such
changes in hire purchase regulations, the general opinion is that their
impact has been marked, at least in the short term.[4] More recently,
the growth of personal bank loans may have ameliorated the effect of
hire purchase regulations somewhat, although a tightening of their
controls tends to be associated with tighter credit conditions generally,
and the manufacturers themselves have been using loan facilities as
a marketing policy instrument.

Apart from their selectivity, it is the frequency of changes in
these economic controls that cause the most concern. From 1960 to
1975, there were 25 changes in government policy affecting the motor
industry; 10 were favorable to the industry and 15 were unfavorable.
Compare the changes since 1970 (Figure 8.2) in the United Kingdom
with no changes in hire purchase regulations or tax rates in either
Germany or the United States, one change in hire purchase regulations
in France, and one tax and two hire purchase changes in Japan.[5]

Figure 8.2 shows the quarterly registration figures for the United
Kingdom as a whole and for Chrysler over the period 1969-75. The
registration figures have been seasonally adjusted, but cyclical variations are still present in the data, so that the fluctuations indicated

FIGURE 8.2

New Car Registrations
(seasonally adjusted)

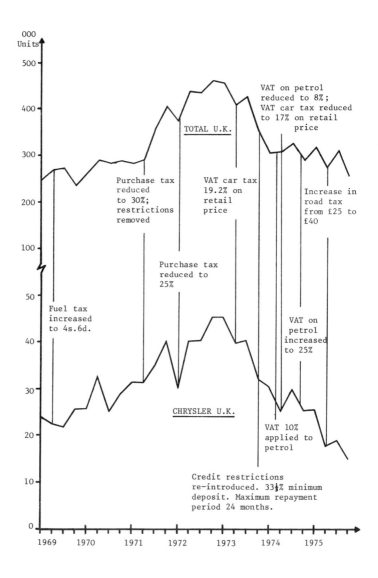

Sources: Data derived from Society of Motor Manufacturers and Traders, Monthly Statistical Bulletins, various issues. Seasoned adjustment factors for U.K. registrations provided by the Society of Motor Manufacturers and Traders.

cannot be directly attributed to government demand management policies alone. Nevertheless, the link between changes in hire purchase
regulations and tax rates and the level of demand is apparent. A
fairly close correlation exists between the pattern of total market and
Chrysler registrations. The linear regression of Chrysler registrations on U.K. registrations produces the relationship:

$$Y = -3.756 + 0.1033 \times (R^2 = 0.780)$$
$$(0.0011)$$

where

    Y = Chrysler registrations (in thousands)
    X = total registrations (in thousands), and the figure in paren-
       theses is the standard error

    The two periods when the trends differed significantly were from
the end of 1969 to the end of 1971 and 1975. In the former, Chrysler
registrations were above those for the industry as a whole in relative
terms; in 1975, conversely, Chrysler registrations declined much
more significantly than the total market. A closer relationship than
that obtained could hardly be expected given the wide variety of factors
that might affect the demand for Chrysler cars differently from total
market demand. Given the similarity of peaks and troughs, however,
the overall impression is that government demand control measures
have had a significant short-run destabilizing influence on the market
for cars in the United Kingdom. Chrysler's position, already difficult
because of problems such as low product acceptability and production
stoppages, was made that much more vulnerable by the further uncer-
tainties associated with government policy measures.
    A consideration of the rapid upsurge in demand that took place
in 1971 and 1972 is instructive in this regard.[6] In the 1971 budget,
the government introduced a wide range of tax reductions in an attempt
to reduce the then high level of unemployment. The character of a
number of the measures meant delays in their impact, and the trend
in unemployment in the months after the budget was more unfavorable
than expected. Corrective measures were taken in the minibudget of
July 19. These involved reductions in purchase tax from 36.7 to 30
percent and the removal of credit restrictions. These measures, allied to a more expansive monetary policy and a rapid rise in money
wages, set in motion the boom in car sales. A further impetus to
car buying was given in the spring 1972 budget with another reduction
in purchase tax to 25 percent. The overall reflation was "too great" or
"too late," and the stop-go policies that had plagued the U.K. economy
throughout the 1960s were being repeated with a vengeance.
    In the first eight months of 1972, car registrations increased by
35 percent compared with a year earlier. Domestic manufacturers were

unable to meet demand. Chrysler's strike-affected output, for example, was 20 percent lower during this same period, while Vauxhall's output was also reduced and British Leyland's production was only marginally higher. The U.K. manufacturers responded by switching vehicles allocated for export to the domestic market, but the market was still wide open to the importers. A formidable partnership—labor disputes and government policy—thus combined to sabotage the sales performance of the U.K. companies in both home and export markets (including Chrysler's Avenger sales to the United States) while raising unit costs significantly. With Chrysler struggling to offset its other disadvantages, the problems of operating in the United Kingdom must indeed have seemed disheartening.

The use of the motor industry as a tool of short-term demand management undoubtedly has exacerbated the cyclical fluctuations in demand to which the industry is traditionally prone. However, some observers have argued that selective economic controls have not had any greater discriminatory impact than would more general measures;[7] and given the importance of the industry in the national economy, there is no way the government could exempt the motor industry from short-term demand management measures. Nevertheless, for an industry as weak as that in the United Kingdom, and with both Chrysler and British Leyland currently in receipt of substantial sums of public money to ensure their viability, the need, and therefore the prospects, for more considered treatment for the vehicle industry are now greater than they have been in the past. In its White Paper of January 1976, the government, in accepting that it has an important role in establishing a viable U.K. car industry, stated that it was its aim to provide "as far as possible a stable economic environment for domestic sales of motor vehicles."[8] It remains to be seen what shape this new commitment will take, and what its effect on industrial structure will be in the long run.

REGIONAL POLICY

Regional policies in various forms have been operated by successive governments in the United Kingdom for almost 50 years. The main objectives of such policies have been to eliminate disparities or inequalities, particularly in employment and employment prospects, among different parts of the country. In international terms, regional inequalities in the United Kingdom are probably not great, but the major problem has been the persistence of these regional disparities. Thus, certain areas constantly have exhibited worse than average levels of unemployment, migration rates, income levels and so on, and thereby have created a nagging sore for all U.K. governments.

The causes of regional malaise in the United Kingdom have been debated at length. What is reasonably certain is that one factor, at least, is structural, emanating from the long-term decline of the coal, heavy engineering, and shipbuilding industries.

Government's first recognition of the problem came at the end of the 1920s with the establishment of an Industrial Transference Board. In the following decade, the Special Areas acts came into force, with northeast England, West Cumberland, South Wales, and Clydeside being assisted through the establishment of industrial estates and the provision of factories and financial assistance to firms moving there. Legislative changes have been introduced at frequent intervals since the 1930s. At present, only central and southern England, less part of the southwest, remain entirely unassisted areas, although incentives vary according to the classification of the area. The most-favored special development areas are the Clyde Valley, northeast and northwest England, and South Wales—little different from 40 years earlier. The financial incentives consist of a range of grants and loans, to which was added a wage subsidy (regional employment premium) in 1967, and advance factories are also available.

Aside from these incentives, an important component of U.K. regional policy is the Industrial Development Certificate (IDC). Introduced first in 1947, the United Kingdom is the only country in Western Europe with a wide-ranging IDC policy. Under its terms, the government can refuse permission for a firm to locate or expand a project in the area of its choice; and as will be shown the refusal of an IDC has been the major factor in determining the siting of new motor vehicle manufacturing capacity since 1960.

Chrysler's Linwood plant is located in the special development area of the Scottish Clyde Valley. While Scotland as a whole has been regarded as backward for many years, the problems of Clydeside, centering on the Glasgow conurbation, have been and continue to be particularly severe. Despite many years of active regional policy and of comprehensive urban redevelopment, Clydeside's economic and social difficulties remain more comprehensive and intransigent than those of any other region in the United Kingdom, or indeed the EEC as a whole. In this situation, the size of the Linwood facility in employment terms makes it immensely important politically.

The Dispersal of the Motor Industry

The motor industry has not been the only industry affected by the U.K. government's regional policy, but the expansion of the vehicle industry into Scotland, Merseyside, and South Wales in the early 1960s was the largest piece of industrial dispersal that has ever been attempted in the United Kingdom.

Traditionally, the U.K. motor industry was concentrated in the West Midlands and, to a lesser extent, in the southeast of England. The predominance of the former area can be explained in terms of the original concentration of the trade there before 1914, the easy access of the region to all parts of the United Kingdom, and the external economies and supply of skilled labor developing from the numerous light engineering firms located in the area. Its population concentration, which provided both labor supplies and markets, was probably the principal reason for the concentration of the industry in this region. Together, by 1960, the two areas accounted for 88 percent of employment in the motor industry (Table 8.2).

In the postwar period, the first major phase of expansion in the motor industry began in 1954. For the most part, these developments took place in existing locations. In 1960, a further major round of expansion commenced, but the new factor was close government involvement in the locational decisions of the motor firms. By wielding stick (the refusal of IDCs) and proferring carrot (the loans and grants available under the 1960 Local Employment Act), the Board of Trade steered the companies toward the development areas. Ford announced plans in 1960 for an integrated car plant at Halewood on Merseyside, and in the same year Vauxhall outlined plans for a new factory at Ellesmere Port, also on Merseyside. To complete the moves to the northwest of England, Standard-Triumph announced proposals for a new plant at Liverpool. Given that the motor manufacturers were being refused IDCs for expansion in or near existing locations, Merseyside had the advantage of being the nearest development district to other group plants, components suppliers, and markets; in addition, Liverpool was an important port of export, and a fairly concentrated supply of spare labor was available.

Apart from the establishment of components factories in South Wales, the other major developments took place in Scotland, a location very much farther removed from suppliers and markets. BMC established a tractor and truck manufacturing operation at Bathgate, near Edinburgh in 1961-62, while earlier, on October 1, 1960, Lord Rootes announced plans for the Linwood factory. It is difficult to convey precisely the enthusiasm that Rootes' statement generated. The Times commented on the day of the announcement: "Thus one of the main aspirations of native economists, industrialists and trade unionists . . . has been fulfilled in Scotland which has not had a car factory since 1928"[9] (Argyll cars).

Undoubtedly, one important reason for the decision of BMC and Rootes to expand in Scotland was an earlier announcement to establish a steel strip mill at Ravenscraig. Moreover, Lord Rootes stated that additional reasons for choosing Linwood were the availability of transport and dock facilities and labor supplies, and particularly the fact

TABLE 8.2

U.K. Motor Industry: Regional Employment[a]
(thousands of employees, midyear)

Area[b]	1960	1965	1970	1975
South	184.8	201.5	192.3	157.3
Midlands	199.3	203.7	215.5	190.1
North	35.8	57.6	86.3	79.8
Wales	8.9	12.5	18.5	19.9
Scotland	6.1	20.5	22.5	20.3
Total United Kingdom	434.8	495.8	535.2	488.1[c]
Scotland as percent of total	1.4	4.1	4.2	4.2

[a]1960 and 1965 data refer to minimum list heading (MLH) 381 of the 1958 Standard Industrial Classification. Later data refer to MLH 380 and 381 of the 1968 Standard Industrial Classification. Data over time are not exactly comparable because of changes in classification and collection methods.
[b]South-southeast, East Anglia, and southwest; Midlands = East and West Midlands, Yorkshire, and Humberside; North = northwest, northern.
[c]Total includes 26,200 employees in MLH 380 not classified by region because the number of firms was too small.

Sources: National Economic Development Office, Motor Industry Statistics, 1959-68 (London: HMSO, 1969); National Economic Development Office, Motors: Industrial Review to 1977 (London, 1973), p. 66; Department of Employment Gazette (London: HMSO, July 1975).

that Pressed Steel, which was to supply car bodies to Rootes, already had a plant on an adjacent site in the village.

The overall effect of the motor companies' expansion programs was to produce a very significant employment transfer (see Table 8.2). According to the Board of Trade, 41,000 jobs were made available in the development areas as a result of movement of firms in the Vehicles category of the Standard Industrial Classification between 1960 and 1965. In Scotland and the northwest, employment attributable to the industry rose by 36,000 in this period. Developments in the motor industry post-1965 have also benefited employment in the development areas, particularly in Wales and the north, but in Scotland total employment in vehicle manufacturing has remained very constant. As will be shown, this reflects both the failure to attract ancillary industries to the region and the generally unhappy experience of both British Leyland and Chrysler with their Scottish operations.

The Costs and Benefits of Regional Policy

As noted earlier, perhaps the principal aim of regional policy has been to improve employment prospects. Work covering the period 1963-70 suggested that, overall, about 220,000 jobs were diverted to development areas as a direct consequence of regional policy, at an exchequer cost per job of something like £6,000.[10] For the motor industry specifically, it has already been shown that in 1960-65 over 57 percent of the industry's total increase in employment took place in the northwest and Scotland, virtually all of which can be attributed to the successful operation of regional policy. What is important is the extent to which the policies pursued have maximized employment creation. The view was constantly expressed in the early 1960s that the motor industry as a "location leader" would attract much supporting investment and thereby lead to increased employment in ancillary and components industries.[11] In Scotland, at least, this never occurred and the Linwood and Bathgate plants are frequently quoted as examples of the misguided application of growth point philosophy. Even if the dispersal of the motor industry had had a greater multiplier effect on employment, there are grounds for arguing that the vehicle industry was not ideal for the development areas because of its instability. The industry's well-known susceptibility to booms and slumps and therefore the associated uncertainty in employment prospects were not required in areas that had suffered high unemployment for so long.

In considering the impact of regional policy, inevitably this section must concentrate on the effects on the motor firms themselves and particularly the effects on Chrysler. The motor manufacturers have claimed that the operation of government regional policy has served the national interest at the expense of corporate interest. Thus, they have argued that while geographic dispersal might achieve its immediate aim of job creation, this could be at the expense of company competitiveness and profitability and therefore long-term employment prospects. As Chrysler's Gilbert Hunt remarked: "I think there is a true dichotomy here, because the social aspects of the policy of successive governments . . . are in true conflict with the economic aspects."[12] And "if the Government wanted to take work to people as a social requirement [with which I agreed] and if at the same time we had to be efficient and produce at unit costs in order to trade around the world in competition with everybody . . . those two things were in conflict."[13]

In a comprehensive memorandum produced for the Expenditure Committee inquiry into Regional Development Incentives in 1972-73,[14] Chrysler attempted to quantify some of the additional costs and benefits of operating at Linwood (Table 8.3). Regarding the financial benefits, Rootes received three government loans in 1961-62 under the terms of the Local Employment Act amounting to £9.6 million, and the company also inherited three outstanding loans from Pressed Steel when the latter's Linwood plant was purchased in 1966. These loans were for periods of between 15 and 20 years at interest rates between 1 and 1.5 percent lower than market rates, thus providing a continuing financial benefit until the dates of maturity. Additionally, from 1966 the company benefited from the higher investment grants paid in the development areas, and from 1968 regional employment premiums were received under the government plan to encourage the use of labor in the assisted areas.

The company also identified a number of financial penalties in operating at Linwood.

Additional Manufacturing Costs

The isolation of Chrysler's Scottish operation from the company's Coventry plants and from the generally Midlands-based components suppliers meant increased transport costs. As Figure 8.3 indicates, nearly 80 percent of Chrysler's total purchases of vendor-supplied parts were obtained from the Midlands and south of England, while, since the Linwood plant supplied substantially all the pressings for the U.K. company and the Stoke plant all the engines, inevitably significant transshipments were involved (see Figure 3.1). The company estimated that the cost of launching the Linwood plant and the Hillman Imp in 1962-63 amounted to £2 million, £1.2 million greater than the equivalent cost if expansion had been centered in Coventry. Initially, at Linwood, the available labor, whose background was shipbuilding and dock working, was not accustomed to or trained for the regulated form of work and mass production techniques of the car industry. Thus costs were increased because of greater training requirements and lower productivity. Chrysler, however, estimated that higher labor costs were offset by wage differences among its manufacturing locations.

Additional Operating Costs

Key personnel had to be transferred to Linwood to set up and operate the required systems and methods of operation in the new

TABLE 8.3

Estimates of Some Additional Costs and Benefits of Chrysler's Linwood Operation[a]
(thousands of pounds)

	1963-70	1971	1975[b]
Benefits			
Investment grants	2,880	121	167
Government loan interest	1,380	165	Not stated
Regional employment premium	1,500	804	1,119
Total	5,760	1,090	1,286
Additional costs			
Manufacturing costs			
Transport costs	3,800	1,100	958
Launch costs	1,200	—	—
Operating costs			
Relocation	300	20	48
Travel and communications	1,000	150	300
Duplication of services	3,000	500	1,130
Costs of additional inventories	700	200	158
Effect on distribution costs			
Home market	1,600	400	416
Export market	400	100	46
Total	12,000	2,470	3,056
Excess of costs over benefits	6,440	1,380	1,770

[a]Excludes, for example, receipt of regional development grants on capital expenditures and continuing benefit from servicing of government loans at noncommercial interest rates. Also takes no account of differences in labor efficiency, although Chrysler estimated that lower productivity at Linwood was offset by wage differences. Figures shown are gross cash and benefits and do not take account of the effects of taxation, although this is not relevant in Chrysler's case.
[b]Estimate as of March 1975.

Sources: Expenditure Committee, sess. 1972-73, Regional Development Incentives, HC 327 (London: HMSO, June 1973), p. 44; and Fourteenth Report from the Expenditure Committee, sess. 1974-75, The Motor Vehicle Industry, HC 617 (I) (London: HMSO, August 1975), p. 226.

FIGURE 8.3

Percentage of Total Purchases of Vendor-Supplied Parts
by Distance from Linwood, 1972

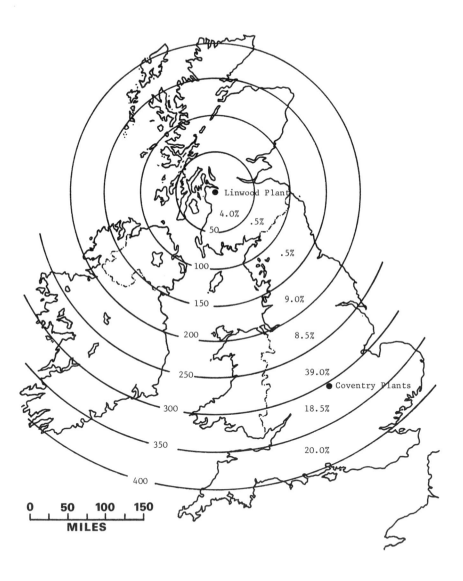

Source: Expenditure Committee, sess. 1972-73, Regional Development Incentives (London: HMSO, June 1973), p. 45.

plant. These relocation expenses were estimated to cost £200,000 (net of government assistance) in 1963–67. Once employees recruited locally were ready for promotion, the additional relocation costs were reduced substantially. Costs of travel and communications included time spent in traveling between Linwood and the other plants and administrative offices, travel costs, and additional telephone and Telex charges. The physical existence of the Linwood plant and its isolation meant a duplication of certain service and management functions.

Additional Inventories

Chrysler calculated that at Linwood it was necessary to hold an additional two days of parts bought from suppliers to ensure against transport time and anticipated delays. Furthermore, an additional one day's stock was held of all company-manufactured parts delivered to and from Linwood. Extra stocks of nonproductive parts were also held.

Additional Distribution Costs

As Figure 8.4 shows, at the time Chrysler submitted evidence, only 15 percent of domestic sales of cars produced at Linwood were to dealers within 150 miles of the plant. Similarly, 85 percent of all export vehicles were shipped from either Merseyside or ports in London and the southeast. Thus, in both the home and export markets, extra distribution costs were incurred as compared with those incurred by production in the Midlands.

In total, it was estimated that the company incurred additional costs from its Linwood operation amounting to approximately £800,000 annually during 1963–70, rising to £1.4 million in 1971 and an estimated £1.8 million in 1975. In 1975, this excess represented £8 per car when spread over total Chrysler U.K. output.

In evidence to the same Expenditure Committee inquiry, the other three major motor firms confirmed that there was some net continuing cost to them in operating in the assisted areas.[15] As of 1972, British Leyland estimated the net cost as about £4.7 million per year, whereas Ford and Vauxhall calculated the excess of costs over benefits at only £150,000 approximately. Such estimates need to be treated cautiously because of the absence of any common methodology (see the footnote to Table 8.3) and in some cases the different items included. A significant part of the difference between the extra costs attributable to British Leyland as compared with Ford or Vauxhall, nevertheless, is accounted for by differences in transport costs, reflecting the more isolated locations of some of the Leyland plants. As the ever-quotable Lord Stokes, then chairman and managing direc-

FIGURE 8.4

Percentage of Domestic Sales of Linwood-Produced Vehicles
by Area, 1972

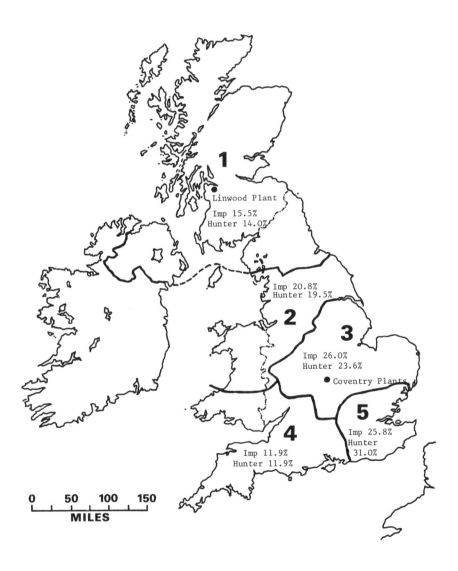

Source: Expenditure Committee, sess. 1972-73, Regional Development Incentive, HC 327 (London: HMSO, June 1973), p. 47.

tor of BLMC, stated: "We have a motor industry scattered around as if somebody had thrown some confetti on the ground."[16] In evidence to the Expenditure Committee inquiry into Public Money in the Private Sector in 1971, Lord Stokes estimated that it cost his company £18 to transport the component parts of each 5-ton truck from England to its assembly factory at Bathgate in Scotland and then (with 75 percent of the market in southern England) another £40 to ship the assembled truck back again.[17] The extra costs represented between 3 and 4 percent of the price of a truck at that time.

In making any such calculations, of course, the assumption is that expansion could have been undertaken in existing locations without any noticeably adverse effect in costs. But, as the Department of Trade and Industry has pointed out,[18] unrestrained expansion by firms in the Midlands during periods of acute labor shortage such as ruled there through much of the 1960s could have been expected to lead to higher wage costs because of increased competition for labor, higher training and working costs through shortages of suitable skilled labor, higher costs to the community through congestion, and additional requirements for housing, schools, and so forth.

Furthermore, in other European countries, motor firms on occasion have deliberately chosen to decentralize, even if the manufacturers have not been subject to IDC controls. A report made this point firmly: "British car manufacturers, grumbling at having to emigrate from the Midlands, should look at their competitors on the map. The Americans have component plants scattered across a thousand miles of the mid-West . . . the French have moved far from Paris: VW have deliberately decentralised 200 miles or more away from Wolfsburg."[19] The U.K. problem is more one of having too many plants to achieve economies of scale and/or organizing production such that complete bodies, which are metal with air inside and very expensive to transport, are moved over long distances. It is arguable also that the U.K. manufacturers were spoiled by the sophistication of their Midlands workers, such that they tended to underestimate the need for training as production was expanded in the new locations. Such mistakes were not made by the continental car firms. The French, for example, "automatically assumed that the people of Rennes . . . at Le Havre, were rustic fellows unused to production lines."[20] The claims made by the U.K. motor firms of lower productivity in their new locations, therefore, could merely reflect lack of investment in training.

In considering the impact of government regional policy on the industry, the motor manufacturers can be accused, not for the first time, of protesting too much. Don Lander, in his new role as executive vice-president, Europe, of the Chrysler Corporation, provided a much more balanced assessment when he declared: "I do not believe

that in any country . . . plants are always going to be well situated
in relation to geography. I think that is a cost . . . recognised by
most countries in relation to producing any product."[21]

Chrysler's Linwood Operation and the Motor
Industry in Scotland

Chrysler's Scottish operation undoubtedly contributed significantly to the company's difficulties after its takeover of the Rootes
Group, but it would be incorrect to relate the poor performance of
Linwood merely to the peripheral location of the plant. The aim of
this section, therefore, is to review the reasons for the failure of
Linwood to perform up to expectations over the years since the com-
mencement of manufacture in 1963. This is important since under the
terms of the new agreement with the government, Linwood will occupy
an increasingly important role in the activities of Chrysler U.K.

The village of Linwood itself is situated just outside Paisley,
about 12 miles west of Glasgow, and owes its origins to iron ore mines
opened during the Crimean War but subsequently abandoned. A major
employer in the immediate postwar years was Pressed Steel Company
Ltd., which acquired a factory at Linwood from the government in 1947.
This was converted for the manufacture of railway rolling stock and
began with a labor force of about 250. By the beginning of the 1960s,
the plant had expanded to produce railway carriages, and car bodies
for BMC and Volvo.

In 1958, the government announced a plan to build a wide strip
mill at Ravenscraig in Scotland, and, as it was apparent that much of
the output would have to be sold south of the border, pressure increased
for the establishment of local sheet-using industries. Rumors of negotiations with motor manufacturers crystallized into plans for a tractor and commercial vehicle plant for BMC at Bathgate and a Rootes
factory at Linwood, directly across the road from the Pressed Steel
Fisher plant, which was to extend its pressings to supply the necessary car bodies. The BMC plant was opened in 1961, and the £23.25
million Rootes factory began manufacture of the Hillman Imp at the beginning of May 1963. The village of Linwood became one of the biggest
reception areas for the Glasgow overspill, with nearly 2,000 new homes
being built by the local authority to meet the needs of the factory, and
road and rail links and shopping facilities were all improved. Aside
from the economic benefits that would accrue from the plant, it was
hoped that in the social field the project would "contribute to curing
the cancer of Glasgow housing."[22]

In spite of the high hopes, as early as February 1965 the Glasgow
Herald was calling the Linwood operation a "running sore,"[23] and by

1969 the London Times had virtually written off Linwood and the entire
Scottish motor industry: "The outcome [of Bathgate and Linwood] to
date points to the conclusion that the experiment ought never to be repeated."[24] While there is no simple unique explanation for the lack
of success of the Linwood operation, a number of related factors seem
to be of sufficient weight to justify discussion.

Inability to Attract Components Suppliers

In Chrysler's calculations of the additional costs of operating
at Linwood, the company estimated a recurring penalty of £500,000
per year from the purchase of components from Midlands-based suppliers. In the summer of 1963, 20 percent of the components used in
the Imp were Scottish. This proportion dropped sharply with the Rootes
purchase of the Pressed Steel plant and, as Figure 8.3 shows, was as
low as 5 percent by 1972. As well as increasing Chrysler's costs,
there is no doubt that the inability to attract components manufacturers
has been a major disappointment to all concerned with the development
of the Scottish economy. At the time of the decision to build the Linwood car plant, it was being suggested that for every job inside the
factory there might be two jobs outside, with a major stimulus being
given to the development of tire, paint, interior trim, and general engineering supply industries in Scotland. Yet a year before the Linwood
factory was opened, planners in West Lothian (Bathgate) were already
reappraising industrial prospects following the failure of the BMC
factory to attract ancillary industries. The lack of the necessary labor
skills, doubts about being in a "miners' area," and business psychology
were the main reasons put forward for the absence of components suppliers.

The first of a series of exhibitions to give Scottish engineering
firms an opportunity to tender for the supply of components for Linwood was held in the late summer of 1963. The first response was an
agreement between Rootes and Rubery Owen for the supply of gas tanks
for the Imp, but, as was to prove usual in such cases, the overall reaction proved disappointing. One explanation given for the slow growth
of local components manufacture was the traditional structure of Scottish industry with its emphasis on large and heavy engineering products
rather than the light, precision engineering requirements of the motor
industry. But the small scale of most Scottish manufacturers and,
conversely, the economies obtained from large-scale components
manufacture in the Midlands proved crucial. These, plus a central
location, better market knowledge, and a sharing of external economies
gave the Midlands firms a decisive advantage. With the stagnation of
domestic demand from 1963 through to 1970, and the widely publicized
labor and product problems of Bathgate and Linwood, the components

suppliers were reluctant to duplicate investment in Scotland. This
was particularly so when there were increasing suggestions that transport costs were of diminishing importance to the performance and
economics of the components industry.[25]

Thus the widely anticipated motor manufacturing satellite area
did not come into being in Scotland. As noted earlier, Chrysler on occasion has expressed alarm at the dependency of the U.K. company on
outside suppliers, and one of its earliest actions was to try to increase
the degree of in-sourcing. The purchase of the Pressed Steel factory
from BMC in 1966 was a move in this direction, but there were few
other effects as far as Linwood was concerned. While Gilbert Hunt
was still expressing the hope in 1972 that more suppliers would move
to Scotland "to help my unit costs and my competitiveness,"[26] the
problem of the Scottish vehicle industry, together with the entry of
the United Kingdom into the EEC and its effects on location policy,
were making that increasingly unlikely. Even under more favorable
circumstances it would not have been possible to create overnight an
agglomeration of manufacturers, since such conditions had taken many
decades to evolve elsewhere. For the future, thus, the best hope for
increasing components manufacture would seem to lie with the company itself.

Problems with the Product Range

Comments have been made elsewhere about the problems that
have been created for Chrysler U.K. overall by the failure of the Imp
to capture a large enough market segment—and Linwood was the Imp
plant. The theoretical capacity of Linwood was 150,000 cars a year,
but, as Table 8.4 reveals, it was not until 1971 that car assembly was
operating at even 50 percent of capacity (by which time the product
range had been extended considerably).

The reasons for the lack of success of the Imp have been discussed widely. The under 1,000 cc market segment was contracting
throughout the 1960s (see Table 4.1), and BMC Mini was well established within this segment. Inevitably there were startup troubles
with the Imp, as with any new car, but the early problems, particularly with the clutch and water pump, were such as to give the Imp a
continuing unreliability tag. There also have been suggestions that
the quality of the car suffered as a result of a raw labor force and
the frequency of industrial stoppages. The unconventional nature of
the Imp and the large number of body panels in the design made it
costly to produce.

The target set initially was an annual sales rate of 100,000 cars
by the end of 1963, but this was constantly rescheduled. By early
summer of 1964, Rootes was still waiting. While "target dates . . .

were being changed as regularly as a new born baby,"[27] the company's resources were being strained, thereby hastening the Chrysler link with Rootes. By the end of the year it had become clear to all that a wider range of vehicles would have to be produced if Rootes was ever to get its Scottish venture on to a profitable basis. But the company's response of introducing new variants on the Imp was not the answer. The political significance of Linwood was to prove its savior. The government extracted from Chrysler at takeover in 1967 an "undertaking" concerning a major development involving a substantial increase in employment at Linwood in a year in which the Scottish operation lost £4.5 million.[28] Linwood (including the former Pressed Steel plant) took over the bulk of Hillman and Singer body production, until then being carried out by Pressed Steel Fisher Ltd. at Cowley. At first car bodies were sent south for assembly, but from the autumn of 1969 the assembly of the complete Arrow range was transferred to Linwood. Part of the reason for the move clearly was to permit Avenger assembly to go ahead in the Midlands, but the Linwood plant also benefited to the extent that the Avenger pressings, transmission, front suspension, and rear axle were scheduled for manufacture in Scotland.

With the changes introduced in the late 1960s, it is not possible to discuss the Linwood product range in terms of complete vehicles as such. However, the Scottish operation was becoming increasingly important to Chrysler U.K., whatever the evidence the company provided on the additional costs of operating there. From being the Imp plant, Linwood had been developed into an integrated facility with a complex product mix and responsibilities across the entire Chrysler U.K. range. As such, the fortunes of the Scottish operation were closely related to those of the U.K. subsidiary as a whole. Thus, when it was decided early in 1970 to postpone U.K. production of the Chrysler 180/2 liter, Linwood suffered along with the rest of the U.K. operation, since the Scottish plant was to have produced body panels for the new car. Similarly, the decision in June 1973 to shelve U.K. production of the Chrysler Alpine affected Linwood, which would have been responsible for stampings for the new model.* In the context of the outcome of the government rescue and the claims that Linwood gained most from the deal because of its political importance, it is worth remembering, therefore, that "the Linwood complex is a more integrated car manufacturing plant than Coventry" and "to make a complete motor car company, as it were, Linwood lacks the engine production only."[29]

---

*It is worth noting that Linwood was also to have built the transmissions for the subcompact that Chrysler Corporation had planned to launch in the United States in January 1972.

TABLE 8.4

Chrysler U.K.: Annual Production of Passenger Cars by Plants

Year	Built-Up		Knockdown		Total Passenger Cars
	Ryton	Linwood	Ryton Type	Linwood Type	
1960	120,830	—	23,142	—	143,972
1961	84,845	—	11,172	—	96,017
1962	123,138	—	19,830	—	142,968
1963	118,400	23,382	19,099	4,656	171,537
1964	120,743	69,420	17,436	12,480	220,079
1965	104,452	47,342	17,349	4,118	173,261
1966	109,875	43,748	13,332	3,684	170,639
1967	112,019	45,240	24,772	2,212	184,243
1968	106,006	43,256	38,964	876	189,102
1969	89,879	31,768	49,344	1,656	172,647
1970[a]	88,761	67,902	5,360	57,212	219,235
1971	129,280	75,630	8,950	51,420	265,280
1972	111,311	87,717	7,280	57,144	263,452
1973	115,664	80,717	6,710	62,322	265,413
1974	97,291	72,160	7,750	84,600	261,801
1975	58,933	34,649	16,960	119,460	230,002[b]

[a] Arrow production transferred to Linwood during the year, partly produced at Linwood and Ryton.
[b] 1975 data supplied by company slightly different to those from published sources.

Source: Fourteenth Report from the Expenditure Committee, sess. 1974-75, The Motor Vehicle Industry, HC 617 (I) (London: HMSO, August 1975), p. 194.

Labor and Labor Relations

It is a regrettable fact that the subject of labor relations in the
U.K. motor industry is so emotional as to make objective comment
almost impossible to obtain. Linwood has had its fair share of difficulties, that much is certain. But, on the other hand, conditions,
particularly in the early days, were hardly conducive to good industrial relations. A number of points can be noted in this regard. Following the high hopes that the establishment of the Linwood plant aroused,
the introduction of a four-day week at the factory as early as August
1964, and the prospect of 400 redundancies at the end of that year were
hardly an auspicious introduction to a new livelihood for the work force
concerned.

In the early days of the plant, middle management, foremen,
trade union officials, and the work force all were inexperienced, but
were being called upon to produce a new car in a new factory. Inexperience on the part of middle management, for example, was evidenced
at the beginning of June 1964 when 270 assembly workers were dismissed for operating a go-slow after they had decided to return to normal working.[30] Again, research by Strathclyde University suggested
that labor relations improved as the trade union structure grew stronger. Initially, before there was a proper union organization and shop
stewards who knew what they were doing, "people would start march-
ing out at the drop of a hat."[31]

Another factor that has been postulated as contributing to the
difficult labor situation at Linwood initially was the background of the
labor force. Many of the workers came from the declining shipbuilding and coal-mining industries, which had a tradition of militancy and
industrial strife. Similarly, the very different production techniques
in the motor industry and the necessary retraining and reorientation
of workers' attitudes have been suggested as causes of potential friction. While both of these points have been mentioned in relation to
the poorer industrial relations record of U.S. firms in Scotland as a
whole,[32] as well as to Linwood, the actual evidence is very scanty.

In a similar vein, the lesser degree of autonomy enjoyed by
foreign-owned firms in backward regions such as Scotland has been
suggested as a factor of relevance. It can be argued that where bargaining is undertaken by plant management but the ultimate decisions
are taken by headquarters management, misunderstandings and incon-
sistencies can arise that exacerbate industrial relations difficulties.
This is not a problem specific to Linwood, but with the administrative
headquarters of Chrysler U.K. in England, the Scottish plant is one
step farther removed from the main center of decision making. As
an example of such a problem, the dismissal of the 270 workers quoted
earlier could be viewed not only as the result of inexperience on the

part of middle management but also as "the price Rootes paid to have the doors in Detroit opened for them."[33] The announcement of Chrysler's acquisition of a stake in Rootes came only a few days after the dismissals, the implication being that the desperately needed Chrysler finance was only forthcoming after Detroit management had received some evidence of a change to a tougher line in negotiations.

Other industrial relations issues that have posed problems at Linwood, such as the merging of the Pressed Steel and Rootes plants, the parity issue, management brinkmanship, and so forth, have been considered at length in previous chapters. Only one other factor will be discussed here, namely, the disturbing tendency for so many industrial relations issues to be discussed openly in public by both management and workers independently. This could hardly simplify subsequent face-to-face bargaining. It is again not a problem specific to Linwood, but, given the reputation for militancy that Clydeside as a whole had gained, deservedly or undeservedly, Linwood has had more than its fair share of media bargaining. A classic example of this occurred in October 1970 when Gilbert Hunt wrote to the editor of the Glasgow Herald criticizing labor relations in Scotland as a central factor in determining the high level of unemployment prevailing in the region. Hunt went on: "Industrial relations at Linwood have never been good and are far worse than at the company's other plants. The response of John Carty, the convenor of the shop stewards at Linwood was: "The management keep telling us that industrial relations should be conducted inside the factory and not in the newspapers."[34]

Given these problems and the long history of conflict dating back to the very earliest days of the Linwood plant, it is obvious that peaceful industrial relations will never come easily to Chrysler's Scottish operation. On the other hand, the signs of improvement since 1973 at least give grounds for cautious optimism for the future.

Conclusions

In assessing government regional policy from the viewpoint of the Scottish motor industry, it is unreasonable to completely write off the decision to bring a vehicle industry to Scotland as a ghastly mistake, as many commentators have done. A motor industry complex has never come into being, but only a small part of the blame for the lack of success of Linwood (or Bathgate) can be laid at the door of regional policy.

From Chrysler's standpoint, Linwood consistently has failed to make any money, except perhaps in 1972, and in the early years in particular, the plant was a heavy drain on company resources. The additional costs of operating at Linwood are very real, at the scale at which the company has been operating. This is the crucial point. The Imp, for example, was a car for the U.K. market and as such failed to achieve the sales volume necessary for viability. In an integrated Chrysler Europe, the Linwood facilities, which make it, on management's admission, among the top manufacturing plants in the Community, may yet be utilized fully. In such circumstances the political maneuvering that has increased the importance of Linwood may yet turn out for the best in economic terms, particularly if Chrysler concentrates on components manufacture in Scotland to minimize the impact of higher transport costs. And yet the social and political aspects of Linwood's position remain important assets. T. R. H. Godden, secretary of the Scottish Economic Planning Department, made this point clear in April 1976, when, in referring to the rescue of Chrysler, he stated: "Our approach was clearly that the closure of the Linwood factory would have been an economic disaster of the worst magnitude for the West of Scotland."[35]

GOVERNMENT SUPPORT AND STRATEGY
FOR THE MOTOR INDUSTRY

It is fair to say that, until the fundamental rethink forced by the events of 1974-76, the British government did not have a strategy for the motor industry comparable to those of some continental European governments. The industry was viewed very much as part of the private sector and its funding as a private sector responsibility. This was so in spite of government involvement in mergers and takeovers among motor firms in the 1960s; and a more interventionist approach to economic and industrial development in general, reflected in the establishment of the National Economic Development Council in 1962 and the setting up of the Labour government's IRC after 1964.

The final merger between British Motor Holdings and Leyland Motors in 1968 was actively encouraged by the government. The IRC acted at times as an intermediary and loaned £25 million on favorable terms to assist the merger. The major motor industry takeover referred to the Monopolies Commission was the BMC acquisition of Pressed Steel in 1965. The Board of Trade did not however hold up the takeover pending the Monopolies Commission report, and the latter subsequently declared that it was not against the public interest. Chrysler Corporation's acquisition of an interest, and subsequently controlling interest, in Rootes were the other major issues in which the government and the IRC became involved. Otherwise, government left individual companies well alone, although its demand management measures at least contributed to the fast deteriorating competitive position of the motor firms during this period.

The watershed in government relations with private industry did not stem from the vehicle manufacturers, however, but rather from

the collapse, first, of Rolls-Royce early in 1971, and then Upper Clyde
Shipbuilders later in the same year. Only a few months after the formulation of a strategy for applying greater stringency in requests for
state support, the so-called lame-ducks policy was dead. But this was
only the beginning of a period in which other famous names in U.K.
industry came close to insolvency. As has been shown, the oil crisis
and the dramatic slump in car demand hastened the decline of the
weakest firms in the U.K. motor industry, the crunch coming first
for British Leyland toward the end of 1974.

The next 12 months saw the publication of three reports that,
while probably a decade too late, may yet provide the basis of a coherent strategy for the motor industry in the United Kingdom. In April
1975, the Ryder Report, recommending massive financial aid for
British Leyland was published; in August, the Fourteenth Report from
the Expenditure Committee on The Motor Vehicle Industry appeared;
and in December, a CPRS study, The Future of the British Car Industry, emerged. The actual decision to support Leyland was necessarily
piecemeal and crisis-oriented. While it was based on the recommendations of the Ryder team (whose report took only three months to pre-
pare), any decision other than that of supporting the only indigenous car
manufacturer would have been unthinkable. EEC Commission approval
was required under the competition rules of the EEC treaty, but this
could hardly have been refused given the existence of state-owned
and -supported vehicle firms in other Community countries. The two
subsequent reports contained damning indictments of the whole motor
industry.

The immense publicity that was sparked and subsequently stoked
by the crisis in the affairs of Chrysler, forced a government response
in its White Paper of January 1976.[36] The government agreed with
the Ryder conclusions that vehicle production "ought to remain an essential part of the UK's economic base and if the UK were to opt out,
it would be difficult to see where this would end." In comparison with
most previous situations, including those of British Leyland and Chrysler, where the government was merely responding to events, there
was for the first time the suggestion of the initiation of action:

> The next step will be for the Government to discuss and
> seek to agree with each company and representatives of
> its employees plans for the improvement of productivity,
> quality, continuity of production and efficiency. As part
> of this process companies will be asked to undertake
> jointly with representatives of their employees a plant by
> plant study of these problems.[37]

It is against this background that the 1975-76 events and the future of Chrysler U.K. will be examined in Chapter 9. Sufficient to

observe at this stage that the government had not evolved a coherent policy toward the industry when the Chrysler crisis developed.

NOTES

1. NEDO, The Effects of Government Economic Policy on the Motor Industry, 1968, p. 3.

2. Letter from John J. Riccardo to A. Wedgwood-Benn, dated February 18, 1975, quoted in Fourteenth Report from the Expenditure Committee, sess. 1974-75, The Motor Vehicle Industry, HC 617 (I) (London: HMSO, August 1975), pp. 221, 223.

3. D. G. Rhys, The Motor Industry: An Economic Survey (London: Butterworth, 1972), p. 243.

4. See M. A. Ali, "Hire Purchase Controls and the Post-War Demand for Cars in the UK," Journal of Economic Studies 1, no. 1 (1965).

5. Central Policy Review Staff (CPRS), The Future of the British Car Industry (London: HMSO, 1975), p. 124.

6. Information for this section was derived from the National Institute Economic Review, nos. 55-62 (London: National Institute of Economic and Social Research, 1971 and 1972); and Economist Intelligence Unit, Motor Business, no. 72, October 1972.

7. "The Government and the Motor Industry in the UK," EIU, Motor Business, no. 60, October 1969.

8. Department of Industry, The British Motor Vehicle Industry, Cmnd, 6377 (London: HMSO, January 1976).

9. Times, October 1, 1960.

10. B. Moore and J. Rhodes, "Evaluating the Effects of British Regional Economic Policy," The Economic Journal, 83, no. 329, March 1973. See also the evidence of Moore and Rhodes to the Expenditure Committee: Expenditure Committee, sess. 1972-73, Regional Development Incentives, HC 327 (London: HMSO, June 1973), pp. 161-75.

11. For example, R. C. Estall, "New Locations in Vehicle Manufacture," Town and Country Planning, vol. 32, 1964.

12. Expenditure Committee, Regional Development Incentives, HC 327, p. 48.

13. Fourteenth Report from the Expenditure Committee, The Motor Vehicle Industry, HC 617, p. 49.

14. Expenditure Committee, Regional Development Incentives, HC 327, pp. 40-47.

15. Second Report from the Expenditure Committee, sess. 1973-74, Regional Development Incentives, HC 85 (London: HMSO, December 1973).

16. Sixth Report from the Expenditure Committee, sess. 1971-72, Public Money in the Private Sector, HC 347 (I) (London: HMSO, July 1972), pp. 194 ff.

17. Ibid.

18. Expenditure Committee, Regional Development Incentives, HC 327, pp. 413-15.

19. "Cars: The Continental Divide," The Economist, July 9, 1966.

20. Ibid.

21. Expenditure Committee, sess. 1975-76, Public Expenditure on Chrysler UK Ltd., Minutes of Evidence, HC 104 (xii) (London: HMSO, March 3, 1976), p. 330.

22. Norman Buchan, "Linwood Story," New Statesman, December 4, 1964.

23. Glasgow Herald, February 12, 1965.

24. Times, May 23, 1969.

25. A view expressed in Chapter 10, in G. Manners et al., Regional Development in Britain (London: Wiley, 1972).

26. Expenditure Committee Inquiry, Regional Development Incentives, p. 54.

27. Glasgow Herald, June 5, 1964.

28. Quoted by George Cattell, Linwood director of production, in Glasgow Herald, June 18, 1968.

29. Expenditure Committee, Public Expenditure on Chrysler UK Ltd., HC 104 (xii), p. 330.

30. Glasgow Herald, June 2, 1964.

31. Scotsman, August 4, 1966.

32. D. J. C. Forsyth, U.S. Investment in Scotland (New York: Praeger, 1972), chap. 7; and Forsyth, "Foreign-Owned Firms and Labour Relations—A regional Perspective," British Journal of Industrial Relations 11, no. 1 (March 1973).

33. Glasgow Herald, June 2, 1964.

34. Ibid., October 28, 1970.

35. Expenditure Committee, sess. 1975-76, Public Expenditure on Chrysler UK Ltd., Minutes of Evidence, HC 104 (xviii) (London: HMSO, April 27, 1976), p. 442.

36. Department of Industry, The British Motor Vehicle Industry, p. 3.

37. Ibid., p. 6.

9

THE 1975 RESCUE
AND PROSPECTS FOR
FUTURE VIABILITY

THE BACKGROUND TO THE CRISIS

The crisis in the affairs of Chrysler U.K. during 1975 was not unexpected. What perhaps was unexpected was the starkness with which the choices of government ownership or withdrawal suddenly emerged after having been rumored for so long. It is difficult to pinpoint a date or an event from which it could be said that Chrysler U.K. would not recover. Early 1970 and the Avenger launch probably represented the highpoints of optimism about the future of the U.K. company. In February of that year the reestablishment of Chrysler International headquarters in Geneva was announced, and a new product strategy to launch one new model a year in Europe was unveiled. In introducing the news, the U.K. managing director stated: "The rationalisation programme we have been working on with Chrysler, Simca . . . and Barreiros . . . has now reached the stage where we can take full advantage of our membership of the Chrysler organisation."[1] For the fiscal year July 1969/70, a loss of £11 million was recorded, but the company returned to the black in the following year when output reached a peak of nearly 308,000 cars and commercial vehicles.

The year 1973 was probably crucial in the buildup to the crisis, in spite of the fact, ironically, that the company made record profits and increased its share of both output and registrations. During that year a series of events combined effectively to seal the fate of Chrysler in the United Kingdom. The decision to halt investment in June and the huge output losses from labor disputes led The Economist to comment on September 29: "The company [Chrysler] has made net losses of £32 million in the last decade. There is a time when you have to cut such losses and concentrate on profits in countries . . . where people actually want to build cars."[2] The onset of the oil crisis late in 1973 and the miners' strike and three-day week early the following year brought further massive problems, and speculation on the lines of "When will Detroit start closing Britain down?" was rife.[3] In a declining market Chrysler had no models to take advantage of the switch to smaller cars, a switch that was of major advantage to the importers. On the commercial vehicle side, the Commer Commando was launched under the most inopportune circumstances imaginable.

From late 1974, Chrysler Corporation was having to prop up its U.K. subsidiary. U.K. banks, concerned about the motor industry in general, began to refuse to renew short-term loans and, in addition, for Chrysler U.K. specifically, the banks were requiring Chrysler Corporation guarantees on any loans that were made. In December, the U.S. parent company injected $12 million into Chrysler U.K., followed by additional infusions of $13 million in both January and February 1975. The corporation, meanwhile, was having its own problems, closing five out of six assembly plants for up to six weeks from November 1974, and recording a loss of $52 million for the year as a whole (after profits of $255 million in 1973). In the end, it was perhaps this more than anything that heralded the drama of the winter of 1975.

THE EVENTS OF 1975

Since the events leading up to the government rescue have been documented in considerable detail elsewhere,[4] this section merely catalogs the critical dates leading up to the press conference held in Detroit on October 29, 1975 by John Riccardo, chairman of the board of Chrysler Corporation, and Gene Cafiero, president of the corporation. Becuase of the implications for the future, rather more detail is included on the negotiations conducted between Chrysler and the U.K. government.

January: The secretary of state for industry, following further speculation, wrote to Chrysler Corporation regarding its future intentions about operations in the United Kingdom. Riccardo subsequently discussed the problems of Chrysler U.K. with the prime minister, Harold Wilson.

February 18: Riccardo replied to the letter from the secretary of state. The reply, described as "delphic by the members of Parliament investigating the rescue,[5] hinted at further production cuts, painted a fairly gloomy picture for investment, and gave no definite commitment to stay in the United Kingdom. The prime minister, at least in public, took Riccardo's letter as a clear understanding that Chrysler would continue its operations in the United Kingdom. But, possibly as a precaution, Wilson also asked Lord Ryder, industrial adviser to the government and at that time heading a team of inquiry into the affairs of British Leyland, to look at the Chrysler situation.

March 18: Chrysler Corporation made an application on behalf of Chrysler U.K. to the Finance for Industry (FFI)* for a £35 million loan. The loan was to be used to restructure the company's financial base by replacing short-term borrowings with medium-term loans, and to provide additional export finance. Inconclusive discussions continued between the parties over a period of time, but while there was never any formal rejection of the application, it ultimately became clear that the conditions attached to any loan would be unacceptable.

May-July: Early in the month, Chrysler U.K. opened discussions with the Department of Industry regarding the possibility of financial assistance under the Industry Act of 1972 for the development and introduction of new models—specifically a replacement for the Arrow range to be built at Linwood, costing £25 million. This application was quite separate from, and in addition to, that made to the FFI. It was not until July 23 that a Chrysler team met Department of Industry officials with a formal application, the terms of which by then had been altered following the failure to arrange the FFI loan. In the weeks thereafter, numerous meetings were held at various levels to discuss the Chrysler proposals and financing requirements.

July 29: The half-yearly results for Chrysler Corporation were announced, showing a loss of $153 million for the six months. During January and February, the corporation had taken steps to improve its credit facilities in the United States by over $1 billion, while costs were being slashed by a 30 percent reduction in fixed manpower levels and cutbacks of $100 million in capital spending. The possibilities of further financial support for Chrysler U.K. from its parent company were remote.

August: Following a strike at the Stoke engine plant in May, the effects began to work through into the cash position of Chrysler U.K. This, together with three demand factors that emerged during August, meant that earlier estimates of financial support required substantial upward revision. The three factors were a downgrading of volume estimates for the industry; a deterioration in Chrysler penetration of the U.K. market, emanating primarily from a lack of confidence on the part of consumers; and a shortage of assembly capacity in Iran affecting the demand for CKD kits.

September-October: In the light of the deteriorating market situation, intensive discussions were reopened between Chrysler Cor-

---

*FFI was formed in November 1973. Eighty-five percent of its equity is owned by the English Clearing Banks and the Scottish Banks. It makes medium-term loans for commercially justified projects at commercial interest rates.

poration and its U.K. subsidiary. In the United Kingdom, the Department of Industry had almost completed its assessment of Chrysler's application for assistance under the terms of the Industry Act, when the company requested that this be deferred pending a reassessment of the figures. According to Sir Peter Carey of the Department of Industry, this was "the first hint we had that they might be contemplating something more drastic."[6]

October 28-30: Hunt and Lander, then chairman and managing director respectively of Chrysler U.K., were invited to attend a Chrysler Corporation board meeting on October 30 to present the U.K. case. Two days before this, however, Chrysler Corporation's Report to Shareholders was released, showing an overall loss of $232 million for the nine months to end September. The report stated: "We are exploring with the British Government various alternatives, but the continuing economic crisis there makes any solution most difficult."[7] More ominously, the report ended: "In operations where the probability of continued losses remains, extraordinary actions, which could result in non-recurring losses, may be necessary to protect the company's interests and improve its long-term profitability."[8]

On October 29, Riccardo and Cafiero held a press conference in Detroit. Questioning homed in immediately on the meaning of "extraordinary actions" and the possibility of disposing of the corporation's U.K. subsidiary, its "biggest single problem." Riccardo stated: "Obviously the United Kingdom situation is a very grave one. The economic situation in the U.K. is not good and unfortunately it seems to be getting worse rather than better . . . we have a number of alternatives but no final decision has been made."[9] While Riccardo was unwilling to discuss the alternatives in detail, it was clear that the possibility of disposal of Chrysler U.K. was a serious proposition, and equity involvement by the British government was not ruled out.

The use of a press conference in Detroit to make fairly explicit suggestions of such magnitude, without first consulting the U.K. government, sets a highly disturbing precedent in relations between multinational corporations and national governments, smacking, as it does, of modern-day imperialism. Without doubt, it was a distasteful episode. Apart from the U.K. government, the work force of Chrysler U.K., its dealers and customers were being openly sacrificed as a negotiating stance.

The Chrysler board meeting in New York on October 30 merely ratified the decisions that had already been taken. The chairman and president were given authority "to take any actions necessary with the British Government to solve the then unsatisfactory position."[10]

November 3: Riccardo met with the prime minister, secretary of state for industry, and the paymaster general in London. Three possibilities were mentioned by Chrysler's chairman: liquidation of the U.K. operation in three months beginning at the end of November; Chrysler would give the U.K. company to the government; or Chrysler would transfer a majority interest (of more than 80 percent) to the government, retaining only a minority stake. Speaking in the House of Commons on November 6, the prime minister said of the meeting "the Government [were] presented with a pistol to their head."[11]

The options presented at the meeting should not have been unexpected. The writing had been on the wall for at least two years: the Department of Industry had been having detailed discussions with Chrysler over a period of months and Lord Ryder had reported to the prime minister that Chrysler U.K. was not big enough to be viable as a mass producer. In addition, the members of Parliament's report on the Motor Vehicle Industry and the CPRS report were available. Both emphasized the weaknesses of Chrysler U.K. and were quite explicit in their suggestions that the company was in a long-term loss situation and that Chrysler could shut down at least one assembly plant in Europe. And yet the government seemed genuinely taken by surprise. Eric Varley, the secretary of state for industry, said later: "The stark choice developed suddenly. I do not think anybody in the Government . . . expected Chrysler Corporation to come and say: 'we are prepared to transfer the ownership of Chrysler U.K. or pull out.'"[12]

The unpreparedness of the government, the sustained hysteria and resentment of the media, the accurate leaks of confidential information, and the tight time schedule implied by the multinational's ulrimatum meant that the next six weeks were to be some of the most embarrassing and inglorious ever faced by a U.K. government.

The Government's Position

From the U.K. government's viewpoint, the options put forward by Chrysler represented a "fearsome choice."[13] Chrysler ownership or an 80 percent shareholding were not attractive propositions. It was estimated that the immediate liabilities—redundancies, losses, and development costs—would have amounted to about £170 million, for which all the government would receive would be a small company that was not viable on its own. The situation was somewhat reminiscent of that of 1967 when nationalization was rejected because the government would have been left "with a company which in technological terms, was not of a scale which could survive" and was not believed to be "a viable organisation with or without Government money."[14] The extra ingredient in 1975 was a government-funded British Leyland, which was to be run on a holding company basis by the newly established National Enterprise Board (NEB). This offered two possible solutions: that the NEB might operate Chrysler U.K., in addition to Leyland; and that Chrysler could be integrated with British Leyland. Given Chrysler's size problems, only the second of these alternatives was feasible, but the view of all parties was that Leyland's reorganization problems were so large on their own as to preclude any possibility of also taking Chrysler on board.

The Department of Industry had discussions with both Ford and Vauxhall to investigate the possibility of the acquisition of all or part of Chrysler's facilities, but neither company had any interest in "taking over more than one or two isolated parts of the operation."[15] For the government, therefore, the choice rapidly narrowed into liquidation or some form of pruning or reorganization of Chrysler U.K. (assuming that the latter would be, or could be made, attractive to Chrysler Corporation).

Commentators in the United Kingdom, almost unanimously, were opposed to any form of government aid to Chrysler and therefore, by implication (although this was not spelled out so clearly), were in favor of allowing Chrysler to go to the wall:

> A "market solution" would no doubt be anathema to some sections of the Labour Party, but the Government must surely be wary of increasing its commitment to the motor industry; in this business with its high risks and uncertain future, one lame duck is enough.[16]

> Any policy artificially to keep the fourth manufacturer in existence must now make even less sense than it did in 1966. . . . If the Government truly believes in investing in success, Chrysler is the last place it should choose to put money.[17]

> Do we, say next week, double the price of school meals and package the cash to Detroit for Christmas? Chrysler . . . is a brutal test of this Government's credibility.[18]

In the end, however, after much backtracking and considerable political infighting, the government was not prepared to let Chrysler go out of business. The factors that were primarily instrumental in producing this decision seem to have been as follows.

Unemployment

Direct job losses resulting from liquidation would have numbered 25,000, but in total the government estimated a loss of 55,000 jobs. The exchequer cost, in terms of social security payments, direct and indirect taxation losses, and so on, was calculated at £150 million.[19] Nationally, unemployment at the time of the crisis was higher than at

any time since the 1930s, with 6 percent of the working population on
the basis of the U.S. definition[20] out of work, and was being forecast
to increase in 1976. Additionally, while only a small proportion of the
job losses would be in the west of Scotland, the problems of Clydeside
merited special attention. On this occasion the social aspects of unemployment resulting from the closure of Linwood were probably less
important than the political aspects. The Scottish National party had
won 11 seats at the previous general election and were second to
Labour in 35 out of its 41 seats. The question could well be asked:
"whose pistol at whose head?"[21]

The Iranian Contract

The importance the Iranian government attached to the continued
fulfillment of the contract has been noted earlier in Chapter 5. The
contract to supply CKD units for the assembly of Peykans was a prestige project, and a cessation of supply undoubtedly would have had serious implications for future ventures. The maintenance of the contract, per se, would not, of course, have required a government rescue operation on the scale of that ultimately agreed upon, or indeed
a rescue at all. Thus, Iran might have been supplied by other Chrysler
Corporation subsidiaries or other U.K. manufacturers. But even if
any of these possibilities had been feasible, crucial time delays would
still have been involved, which might have had equally prejudicial effects on trading relations with Iran as would the termination of the
contract. The alternative solution of the government allowing the
liquidation of Chrysler U.K. except for the Stoke plant, which services
the INIM, would only have saved 3,000 jobs; and this would not have
taken account of Iran's requirements for technical assistance, model
development, and so on.

Balance of Payments

The government estimated that the shutdown of Chrysler U.K.
would have an adverse effect on the balance of payments of £200 million per year over the period 1976-79. This loss to the balance of
payments was calculated by a comparison between a no-Chrysler situation and a Chrysler continuing to operate on the basis of the plan
agreed with the government. Items in the calculation included some
estimate of the loss of exports, including exports to Iran, and an estimate of the proportion of domestic Chrysler sales that would be taken
up by U.K. manufacturers as opposed to importers. Of major importance to the latter was the extent to which Chrysler dealers switched
to foreign franchises. The Chrysler Dealer Association considered
that up to two-thirds of dealers would have gone over to other fran-

chises, and since the U.K. manufacturers were in the main still rationalizing their own networks, major opportunities existed for the importers.

Inevitably, such calculations are fraught with difficulties, particularly when the very different circumstances of 1976-79 are used
as a base for comparison. Nevertheless, an annual loss of £200
million, even as an order of magnitude, would have created further
major problems for government economic policy. Import controls,
which probably should have been imposed on motor vehicles in any
event to allow time for British Leyland to rationalize, would have
become a near certainty with a Chrysler closure.

The economic arguments for saving Chrysler possessed considerable merit, assuming that the company had the potential to be viable,
but in the last resort the political and social arguments won the day.
As has happened frequently in the past in the United Kingdom, government blanches at the prospects of unemployment and social conscience
overrides economic reality. Once government had reached this position, and in spite of the antics that reportedly took place within the
cabinet before it was reached,[22] the only solution was to come to some
agreement with Chrysler.

Chrysler's Position and the Progress
of Negotiations

There seems little doubt that Chrysler was serious in its ulti-
matum. Although the company worked through the costings of a series
of options on behalf of the government from early in the negotiations,
Chrysler was still unwilling to have any financial responsibility for a
U.K. operation. Chrysler's position in the negotiations did not alter
until the November 26, when Riccardo stated that if the government
were to take over Chrysler U.K. completely, Chrysler Corporation
would make a payment of £35 million. Alternatively, if Chrysler
were to retain an equity holding of under 20 percent, they were prepared to contribute £13 million. In addition Chrysler expressed willingness "to enter into a management contract covering future technical, marketing and managerial needs of the U.K. company."[23]

The government, meantime, was under increasing pressure
from all sides, and with the negotiations dragging on inconclusively,
Chrysler ultimately was more or less asked to state its terms. The
secretary of state reported to the investigating members of Parliament:
"It was not until very late in the negotiations [December 5] that we
asked Chrysler Corporation again whether they could foresee a continuing commitment, that is Chrysler Corporation having a subsidiary
here, bearing the whole responsibility, and in what way could the

British Government help; could it be by covering losses and making good any future potential losses; what kind of guarantees could we give for loans and that kind of thing. That is how the negotiations were finally agreed."[24] Chrysler's reply that "Yes, provided the Government helped,"[25] ensured that it was then only a matter of time before an acceptable settlement was achieved.

The reason for Chrysler's apparent change of heart seems to have been directly associated with the offer of government finance. The company has stressed on occasions since the deal that "by June this year [1976] France will be producing to maximum output while in Britain we will continue to have considerable excess capacity."[26] Without the U.K. operation, extra capacity would have had to be installed elsewhere. But the corporation's view appears to have been that the extra risks of operating in the United Kingdom—labor relations, government policy, and all—offset the advantages of ready-made capacity, without government aid to finance these additional risks.

THE DEAL

Chrysler had considered a number of options on behalf of the government, including the Stoke, Linwood, and Truck SLT) plan: This plan would have involved the closing of the Ryton assembly plant, with 10,000 redundancies. The forecast cost to the government, covering capital spending, losses, and redundancy payments, was £96 million over the four years 1976-79.[27] This excludes social security payments and so on that subsequently would have had to be paid to the 10,000 redundant employees. The Linwood plan: All operations except Linwood would have been closed. Volume car production would cease, and Linwood would supply spares, manufacture commercial vehicles, and handle the Iranian contract. Nineteen thousand redundancies were involved at an estimated cost of £83 million. The Stoke plan: All operations would be closed except Stoke, from where the Iranian contract would be supplied. The estimated cost was £32 million with 22,000 redundancies. The Linwood (Iranian contract) plan: Here, again, only the Iranian contract would be retained, but the work would be transferred from Stoke to Linwood. Twenty-two thousand job losses were involved at an estimated cost of £59 million.

The only option that "identified positive capacity,"[28] that is, viability, over the four-year period was the SLT plan. This formed the backbone of the agreement that was eventually achieved. However, before the final agreement was signed on January 5, 1976, two fairly crucial extensions were added to the basic SLT plan: first, an additional £55 million was included for the development and introduction of new models; and second, Chrysler Corporation proposed that assembly of the C6 Alpine should be transferred from Poissy to Ryton with a capital contribution of £10 to £12 million for its introduction. This extension prevented the closing of Ryton, as envisaged by the SLT plan, and was a psychological boost since it meant that Chrysler U.K. would be relaunched with a model voted European Car of the Year in 1975.

Discussions on technical aspects of the plan and on the relative financial commitments of the parties continued during the first two weeks of December. Finally, the secretary of state announced the terms of the agreement to the House of Commons on December 16, a solution, as he put it, to the "fearsome choice we have been wrestling with."[29] In his statement, Eric Varley emphasized the need for "the fullest cooperation of the work force in accepting redundancies . . . and in collaborating to improve productivity."[30] A Christmas Eve letter from the Department of Industry to Chrysler confirmed that the government would require assurances that "satisfactory progress is being made in these matters"[31] before the main agreement was signed. The trade union's acceptance of the plan on January 3 was taken as evidence of such progress. The final deal among the government, the Chrysler Corporation, and Chrysler U.K. was thus signed on January 5, providing "the basis for a continuing operation into the 1980s."[32] Essentially, the plan envisages a pared down, reorganized, and more productive Chrysler U.K. and provides the funds for a start to be made on the badly needed new model program.

Financial Arrangements

The Appendix summarizes the financial arrangements agreed betwen Chrysler and the U.K. government to facilitate the reorganization and development of Chrysler U.K. The potential government commitment over the period 1976-79 is £162.5 million, broken down into £72.5 million for possible losses, £55 million in loans for capital development, and £35 million as a guarantee for a medium-term loan to be raised in the private banking sector. Of the £55 million, £28 million is unconditionally guaranteed by Chrysler Corporation and the remaining £27 million is secured on the assets of Chrysler U.K.; the £35 million medium-term loan is counterguaranteed by Chrysler Corporation.

The Chrysler Corporation potential commitment consists of £32.5 million for possible losses, £19.7 million for the waiver of loans (and interest)[33] made earlier to Chrysler U.K., and £10 to £12 million for the introduction of the C6 Alpine. This latter sum is to cover the introduction of the model to Ryton and to bring the U.K. content up to 57 percent by the middle of 1977. During that year, a decision will be taken on whether to spend a further £23 million to source the Alpine completely in the United Kingdom.

Chrysler has argued that the corporation's financial commitment under the terms of the agreement is not far short of the government's. It arrived at this conclusion by adding into the items mentioned above the £90 million in loans on which Chrysler guarantees or counterguarantees have been obtained. If losses during 1976 do not exceed £40 million and the planned small profits are achieved in the three following years, then Chrysler Corporation will have no loss-funding liability. This is because the U.K. government has sole responsibility for the first £40 million of losses in 1976; the equal sharing arrangement only applies on losses in excess of £40 million in 1976 and on losses in subsequent years. Don Lander, the vice-president elect, Chrysler Europe, commented to the press at the end of March 1976 that the arrangements provided financial stability and meant that Chrysler U.K. was "much less likely than in the past to be blown off course."[34]

Redundancies

The rescue plan provided for 8,200 redundancies (–33 percent) by August 1976 (Table 9.1), with Stoke and Ryton being hardest hit. Linwood, by comparison, came off fairly lightly, and very few redundancies were incurred at the Luton and Dunstable commercial vehicle factories, chiefly because the closing of the Maidstone plant involved the transfer of work to Luton.

Facilities

Ryton, beginning with the Alpine, was to become a center for assembling front wheel drive cars, with rear wheel drive car assembly concentrated at Linwood. This immediately involved the transfer of Avenger assembly to Linwood and the transfer of the Alpine assembly from Poissy to Ryton. The Stoke plant remained as the major machining operation for Chrysler U.K., with Iranian contract work also to be continued there. Aside from the capital expenditure on new models, half of the finance made available was to be spent on improving manufacturing facilities.[35] For example, £4.6 million was to be spent on improving the Dunstable and Linwood paint shops, thereby increasing both capacity and quality. At Stoke, £4.24 million was planned to be spent to modernize and increase the capacity of the foundry, and a major machine tool refurbishing program was to be started. That this investment program at Stoke was long overdue is evidenced by the fact that between 1969 and 1975 only £811,000 had been spent on capital equipment at the plant. In addition, the internal layout of the Dunstable truck plant was to be completely rearranged at a cost of £1.7 million.

TABLE 9.1

Chrysler U.K. Rescue Operation: Plant and Employment Forecast

Plant	Employment December 1975	Employment Planned, August 1976
Linwood	7,000	5,500
Stoke, Coventry	6,300	4,000
Ryton, Coventry	4,300	1,600
Whitley, Coventry	1,700	1,400
Birmingham	1,000	800
Luton and Dunstable	2,800	2,600
Maidstone	500	—
Other small plants	1,500	1,000
Total	25,100	16,900

Source: Eighth Report from the Expenditure Committee, sess. 1975-76, Public Expenditure on Chrysler UK Ltd., HC 596 (I) (London: HMSO, July 1976), p. 92.

New Models and Production and Market Planning

As part of the agreement with the government, Chrysler Corporation provided a Declaration of Intent (see the Appendix) outlining its intentions in relation to the long-term future of Chrysler U.K. While this is not a legally enforceable document and smacks suspiciously of some of the commitments made in 1967, a clear indication is at least given of the "new" models to be introduced by Chrysler U.K. over the four years up to 1979. The plan envisaged the early phase out of the Imp and Arrow range (except for the Iranian contract), but in fact continuing demand for Hunters led the company to defer the withdrawal of the latter. Then, apart from an improved Avenger and the Alpine, Chrysler is to launch a new, small, light car, code named the 424, from Linwood in 1977. On the commercial vehicle side, the Walk-Thru range (including the Bantam) is to be replaced by a new light van-truck in 1978; and, while not included in the Declaration of Intent, the U.K. company also has indicated that much-needed changes to the PB vans (first launched in 1960) are also liable to be made. Finally, in the last year of the four-year program, a new light car is to be introduced.

The crucial component of the rescue deal for Chrysler U.K., of course, concerns the production and marketing plans for the company, particularly the degree to which these fit into the overall European strategy of the Chrysler Corporation. The Declaration of Intent states that Chrysler U.K.'s products will be planned as an integral part of Chrysler's overall product plan, so that the products of the U.K. subsidiary will be complementary to, and have a specific position within, Chrysler's worldwide product offering. The need for integration on at least a Europewide basis has been stressed at various points in this book. Integration can mean many things. It is by no means clear from the agreement between Chrysler and the government, which is a plan for Chrysler U.K. in isolation, what is actually meant by integration. On the one hand, Don Lander has stated, "the policy on Product Development is to introduce commonality on a world-wide basis wherever this is possible."[36] On the other hand, the possibility of the complete in-sourcing of the Alpine is in prospect, which could be viewed as the antithesis of production integration. Again, Gwain Gillespie has argued that because "Chrysler France paid for and developed" the Alpine that was then being introduced into the United Kingdom, this was "integration in its true form."[37] This important issue will be considered in detail later in this chapter.

Control and Monitoring

A number of controls were noted in a memorandum submitted on behalf of the secretary of state to the committee of inquiry investigating the public expenditure on Chrysler. Some of these are reproduced in the Appendix, and include, for example, the right of the government to appoint two directors to the board of Chrysler U.K. and the requirement for Chrysler to provide quarterly management accounts and other financial information. But other elements are involved as well. Chrysler U.K. is forbidden from making any substantial alteration to the nature of its business, from making loans to outside companies, and from disposing of any subsidiary companies without the agreement of the secretary of state. Also, transfer prices are required to be determined on an "arm's-length basis"; dividends and other payments to Chrysler Corporation may not exceed the amount of government loans repaid; and the company has agreed to negotiate a planning agreement[38] with the government and the unions, one of the provisions of which will be employee participation.

The monitoring process will be the responsibility of government departments, but, in spite of the laudable (if naive) sentiments expressed above, it remains to be seen how effectively this can be implemented in a multinational corporation, particularly if at last Chrysler U.K. is integrated within Chrysler Europe. The logic of integration, after all, would be for Chrysler U.K. to lose its separate identity.

Monitoring of Chrysler U.K. in these circumstances would be point-
less and meaningless.

REACTION TO THE DEAL

Press Reaction

Given the hostile press reaction that followed Riccardo's ulti-
matum to the British government, it was fairly predictable that the
subsequent agreement with the government would also be treated with
disdain. The antagonism was expressed in various forms. The agreement made nonsense of government industrial strategy: "It is . . .
only six weeks since a brand new industrial policy was agreed. . . .
That policy, among other things, declared a more hard-headed attitude
to claims on the government's (and the taxpayer's) resources, even
stipulating that candidates for help ought to be able to show clear
potential for success."[39] Chrysler as "the lamest duck in the pond"[40]
hardly came into that category. The argument was that if Chrysler
was to be supported, where would it all end?: "Then there are all the
other deserving cases who could well claim priority of treatment. If
Chrysler is to be aided, why not Vauxhall, even Ford—now faced
with competition from two separate state-backed rivals?   (Rolls-
Royce, significantly was already yesterday seeking a further £100
million.) "[41]
A related point, that the government would be unable to resist
further requests for finance from Chrysler itself: If Chrysler was
"ready to go broke in the next recession, what then? The Government will not easily be able to cut it off without a further penny (where
have we heard those not-a-penny-more sentiments before? Upper
Clyde-cum-Goven, Harland & Wolff, Rolls-Royce, Alfred Herbert,
British Leyland)."[42] Britain had been left with too many car firms
and too much capacity in an industry that would have worldwide over
capacity for the next ten years: "A Chrysler rescue will leave
Britain with four producers of mass-market cars, as against West
Germany's three, France's three . . . and Italy's one. . . . Britain's
new car market in 1972-74 averaged 1.55 million, against 1.65 mil-
lion in France, 2 million in West Germany, and 1.4 million in Italy.
And Britain's economic growth is less than elsewhere."[43]
There was also resentment over the way in which U.K. taxpay-
ers' money was being used to support a multinational corporation, ef-
fectively, it was argued, subsidizing U.S. shareholders of Chrysler
Corporation. This was exacerbated by the view taken in the United
States toward the agreement, as summed up by oft-quoted remark of

the Wall Street Journal, that public money in the United Kingdom had turned Chrysler U.K. from a "financial albatross" into a "financial angel."[44]

Political Reaction

In the political arena, the deal was pushed through Parliament with lightning speed. The secretary of state announced the terms of the agreement to the House of Commons on the afternoon of December 16, 1975, only hours after the CPRS report had been made public. A one and a half hour debate took place on the proposals the following evening (although in fairness a lengthy debate had been held on the motor vehicle industry as a whole the previous afternoon and evening), and parliamentary approval was obtained at 11:45 p.m. Threats of a revolt on the government side proved, as usual, to be insubstantive. Many of the same arguments expressed by the press were repeated in parliamentary debate. Calls for nationalization or at least for the government to take an equity stake in the company were heard from the left wing members of the Labour party. The well-rehearsed anti-multinational argument was expressed as, for example, "how does he [Eric Varley] equate his largesse to this American multinational firm with his refusal to help Norton Villier's Triumph, for example, and the crisis facing the railways."[45] Less emotionally, concern was expressed over the reconciliation of cuts in health, education, housing, and road programs with the expenditure on Chrysler, and over the relative effectiveness of the two as employment stimulants. Some resentment emerged from English members of Parliament over the apparent favoritism shown to Scotland in the deal, and accusations that the government action was based on political fear of Scottish nationalism were heard: "The real reason for the motion is to enable the Government to pay Scotgeld. That will prove as futile a policy as paying Danegeld."[46]

In detail, Conservative member Michael Heseltine queried how the sums of money allocated for new products in the agreement could possibly be adequate. Only £55 million was allotted for the development and introduction of four new models, whereas, on the basis of the CPRS estimates of costs, Heseltine calculated that a minimum of £125 million would be required. Varley replied in correspondence that the £55 million was realistic because all of the models "will draw to a greater or lesser extent on existing models and developments planned to take place in other Chrysler companies as well as in the UK. Integration of this kind is good economic sense . . . just because it enables heavy development, tooling and investment costs to be spread over a wider area."[47] Another member of Parliament, Eric

Moonman, expressed concern over the way in which Chrysler Corporation referred to the new models in its Declaration of Intent. Only in the case of the Avenger was reference made to "production" in the United Kingdom; for the other models, the term used was either "assemble" or "introduce." Unless the government had this clarified, Moonman feared that Chrysler U.K. would end up as merely "an assembly shop for the rest of the Chrysler organisation," since no one could "take the trust and goodwill of the Chrysler company too seriously."[48]

Other Reactions

Subsequent to the debates in the House, the Trade and Industry Sub-Committee, which had earlier in 1975 published its report on the Motor Vehicle Industry, announced an inquiry into Public Expenditure on Chrysler U.K Ltd. The committee took evidence from Chrysler itself and its employees and dealers, from the secretary of state for industry, civil servants, and other interested and involved parties. Their report made the following conclusions. Chrysler U.K. (CUK) was unlikely to be viable in the long term:

> CUK must be able not only to show profits, but to be able to generate sufficient funds after 1979 to finance a continuing model programme as well as repaying their loan. We do not think that CUK will be able to generate such funds. . . . If the funds available to CUK are inadequate, and if CC [Chrysler Corporation] is unwilling to help, then the thrice postponed collapse of the company (1964, 1967 and 1975) might occur.
> The integration of CUK with CC's continental operations ought to be an important part of the UK company's future, but it is not one guaranteed by the agreement with the Government.[49]

On the other hand, the redundancies in the plan made it possible for Chrysler to reduce its unit costs and increase its labor productivity.

Chrysler Corporation had gained significant benefits for a relatively small financial commitment. There were also benefits for Chrysler France. The shift of Alpine assembly to Ryton removed the capacity constraint under which the company had been operating, and any integration of Chrysler's European activities would be of equal benefit to both the French and U.K. subsidiaries. The committee regretted that because of the government's unpreparedness, it was "forced to think in terms of one company rather than of the effect on a whole section of manufacturing industry." In addition, it considered that while the rescue was not wholly inconsistent with some aspects of the government's industrial strategy, in the main it could "by no stretch of the imagination . . . be said to form a glorious chapter in the history of the Government's industrial policy."

Although there was little comment from Chrysler U.K. itself at the time of the rescue, Don Lander sharply denied the committee's suggestion that Chrysler would have to ask the government for more money. This, Lander said, was "irresponsible speculation"; and of the committee's call for greater integration, he said "our new model program for cars and commercial vehicles is a coordinated one, for all our European operations, including those models to be built in Britain, and the funding of the programme has been carefully planned. Indeed we are already looking as far ahead as 1985."[50]

The CPRS study of the U.K. car industry was completed, although not made public, before the events of November 1975. This report had made pointed remarks about Chrysler U.K., but more generally had argued that there were too many manufacturers with too much capacity and too many models in the United Kingdom to sustain a viable industry. When questioned before the Expenditure Committee on the rescue operation, Sir Kenneth Berrill of the CPRS did not completely write off the prospects of a successful recovery for Chrysler U.K.[51] Berrill felt, however, that a number of major changes would have to occur: communications improvements, major increases in productivity, and, most important, the development of an integrated model range. On balance, it was felt that these required changes would not take place to the extent required, and that as a consequence the odds against viability after 1980 were rather greater than the odds in favor.

Much the same conclusion had been reached by the Industrial Development Advisory Board (IDAB),[52] the government's formal advisers under the terms of the Industry Act of 1972. Some members of the IDAB felt that assistance would be warranted if greater financial commitments could be obtained from Chrysler, if the government's commitment could be curtailed or varied in light of events, and if binding arrangements could be obtained with the work force concerning manning levels and productivity. The final agreement with Chrysler went some way to meeting these conditions, but, in spite of this, the IDAB as a whole reaffirmed its earlier conclusion that the arrangements did not offer prospects of viability.

In total, therefore, virtually all authorative opinion was of the view that the government rescue of Chrysler U.K. was unlikely to enable the company to achieve long-term viability. It was in the face of such conclusions and a general atmosphere of hostility that the company set about activating its reorganization during 1976.

PROGRESS DURING 1976

Inevitably there are difficulties in trying to assess progress made, as at the time of writing only eight months had elapsed since the agreement had been signed between Chrysler and the government. But it is also true to say that any assessment will be nearly as difficult for perhaps two or three years. The reason for this is that both Chrysler Corporation and Chrysler U.K. will benefit from the cyclical upturn in the world economy and in the demand for cars and commercial vehicles. As a result, for the first quarter of 1976, Chrysler Corporation turned in a profit of $72 million against net losses of $94 million for the same period in 1975.

In regard to reorganization, it is fair to comment that substantial progress has been made in Chrysler U.K. The moves of the Alpine from Poissy and the Avenger from Ryton were completed on or ahead of schedule, and the modernization of facilities was proceeding as planned. After running down employment in line with the government plan, the company was recruiting additional workers for its Stoke, Ryton, and Linwood plants during August 1976. How far this merely meant that productivity targets were not being met was not known. Increased employment at Ryton was brought about by higher demand for the Alpine as compared with target sales; at Linwood, extra orders for body panel sets from Iran and the decision to continue output of the Hunter sedan indefinitely have meant additional employment. The Stoke plant has been given some work on machining engines for Chrysler France, and the company has now disclosed plans to use Stoke to supplement Simca's capacity in other areas, beginning with water pumps, con rods, and suspension items.

Industrial relations in the "new" Chrysler got off to a bad start with a dispute at Linwood at the end of January. As part of the rescue plan, 57 packers of car parts were moved from a plant 4 miles away in Johnstone into Linwood, but the company refused to pay the men the Linwood rate, which would have involved an extra £1 and 10 pence per week. According to the shop stewards, basic trade union rights were at stake that had implications for the shift of the Avenger line to Scotland, and the entire work force came out on strike. After the usual withdrawal threats from Chrysler management, the company conceded the entire claim. The strike cost the company 173,000 man-hours in lost output. The implications of the strike for the future are undoubtedly very serious, but subsequently at Linwood and at the other plants, losses through disputes have been substantially reduced. In June 1976, Peter Griffiths, Chrysler's deputy managing director (industrial relations) was prepared to say: "I am very satisfied that there is a general improvement in the industrial relations climate in the plants."[53] Discussions on a planning agreement got under way

in the middle of March 1976, and the worker participation proposals
were to be discussed in this forum. In addition, the company has been
making strenuous efforts to improve communications through new
channels of information and through training courses for managers and
representatives of the work force. How far these innovations will
solve Chrysler's crucial industrial relations problems remains to be
seen. The test will not come until government pay restraint begins
to ease and Chrysler (hopefully) returns to profitability.

PROSPECTS FOR FUTURE VIABILITY

Having outlined the events leading to the government rescue of
Chrysler and the terms of the rescue plan, the aim of this concluding
section is to analyze the prospects for the future viability of Chrysler
U.K. This is to be done initially by drawing upon earlier chapters
to assess the factors that were of prime importance in Chrysler's
downfall. These conclusions will then be used to evaluate how far
conditions have been changed by the injection of government and Chrysler Corporation finance, and what still remains to be done if the company is to be viable in the 1980s. In addition, since it is important
from a policy-making viewpoint to be made aware of potential problems
well before they arise, some measures are provided against which
the progress of Chrysler U.K. can be gauged between 1976 and 1979.

The Causes of Failure

Earlier chapters have identified a wide range of factors that
cumulatively made it impossible eventually for Chrysler to continue
its operations in the United Kingdom without major financial assistance.
This is a critical point. The problem is multidimensional. The determinants of Chrysler's decline can usefully be categorized into three
groups: strategic, environmental, and operational. Even to attempt
such a classification runs the risk of the very oversimplification it is
hoped to avoid. However, where areas of overlap and interdependence
exist, these will be indicated as the discussion proceeds, and the model
can be defended as being clear and unambiguous.

Strategic Factors

Although the Chrysler Corporation was late in moving into Europe, probably no one would quarrel seriously with the eventual decision of the corporation to establish a manufacturing base on the Continent. Certain strategic decisions made consequently, however, can

be considered in retrospect as being seriously wayward. These include, first, the policy of buying into Europe through the acquisition of failing national companies; second, the view taken that these companies were first and foremost individual firms whose performance and profitability would be judged on this individual basis; and third, that U.S. managerial experience and expertise, together with an initial capital injection, would be sufficient to permit the acquired firms to achieve self-sustenance.

Chrysler Corporation policy from the beginning either should have involved developing an integrated car and commercial vehicle facility for the whole of Europe or, less ambitiously, entering Europe experimentally by taking over or acquiring an interest in profitable European firms from where U.S. management could observe the different environment and market characteristics of Europe. The end result of both strategies should have been an integrated Chrysler Europe. This would have entailed the manufacture of a European product range, with components production and assembly centralized so as to maximize output at any one location, and alongside this a European marketing and distribution network.

As of 1975, Chrysler, by contrast, had a Simca range sold in continental Europe and belatedly in the United Kingdom, and a Rootes range sold essentially in the United Kingdom (apart from the Iranian contract). By chance rather than design, there was some complementarity in the ranges, but the Simcas were manufactured and assembled in France and the Rootes models were manufactured and assembled (at two centers) in the United Kingdom. Yet, Chrysler must have known that in acquiring Rootes in 1967, it was taking control of a company that was too small to be successful. Perhaps some of the problems lay with the financial difficulties of the corporation itself. By 1969, operations were being cut back severely and company stock was under serious pressure (see Chapter 2), and after only two good years subsequently (1972 and 1973), the corporation slumped into a loss situation in 1974 and 1975.

In fairness to Chrysler it can be argued that only after many decades in Europe has Ford, for example, finally reached the stage of complete production and marketing integration. With its first mini model, the Fiesta, engine blocks will come from Dagenham in England, transmissions and axles from Bordeaux, carburetors from Northern Ireland, and engine machinery from Valencia in Spain; assembly of the car had been split among the United Kingdom, Spain, and Germany. Effectively the integration process began when Ford of Europe was set up in 1967 and it has taken ten years to reach the present stage. This is understandable. Integration can only realistically be developed with new models, major investment and/or rationalization is involved, and the progress of manufacturing integration was necessarily constrained by the speed of EEC integration. All these points are relevant to the Chrysler Corporation, which, in a European sense, as management has argued, is still only ten years young.

Moreover, Chrysler Corporation's strategy toward Europe has not been completely inflexible over these ten years. From 1970, the corporation's strategy appeared to be evolving toward the establishment of a common identity for its subsidiaries in Europe and toward the introduction of a European model range and a common distribution network. But this was never pursued very far or with sufficient determination, and by being sidetracked by environmental and operational problems, ultimately collapsed. As Lander has stated with reference to Chrysler U.K.: "The labour climate, the consistency of supply, whether it be machined parts of built-up cars, did give us difficulty in convincing people that we were a good base to be integrated with."[54]

For Chrysler U.K., the effect of the corporation's strategy was to limit the size of the market within which the company could sell its products, inevitably, therefore, affecting the potential viability of the U.K. organization. It has been argued that, realistically, Chrysler U.K. did not have the models to sell in Europe, and that since the relatively simple rear wheel drive cars were better suited to the needs of the less developed countries, Chrysler U.K. became the main cneter for CKD kits. But this is scarcely convincing. The failure to sell the Avenger in Europe from 1970 was a reflection of strategy (and of supply problems) rather than a fault of the car.

Environmental Factors

It would be impossible to undertake an analysis of a company manufacturing in the United Kingdom or of a sector of U.K. industry without relating performance in some way to the existing environment, that is, the performance of the U.K. economy as a whole. It is far from coincidental that the top three motor manufacturers in Europe in terms of returns on capital (Table 1.15) were located in West Germany. Equally, by whatever criterion used, none of the U.K. motor manufacturers achieved minimum rates of return during this same period. Government, management, the unions, the Civil Service, the City, attitudinal factors, the level of taxation, and so forth all have been blamed at one time or another for the persistent, intransigent problems besetting the U.K. economy. Whatever the cause, the environment has an important bearing on company performance.

Macroeconomic problems, such as the rate of economic growth, the level of employment, inflation and currency instability, and, equally important, the measures employed by government to influence these variables, have had real effects on Chrysler. Since an integration strategy was not pursued, the company was restricted from broadening its production and marketing base to cover the whole of the European continent. Its performance, therefore, became locked into that of the U.K. economy. The discussion in Chapters 5 and 8 revealed some of the ways in which the company was affected: a stagnant domestic market increased competition for available volumes, at a time when the break-even level of capacity utilization was rising; and the instability of demand, exacerbated by government demand management measures (some specifically directed at the motor industry), adversely affected manufacturing costs and cash flow. Government regional policy was considered by all the motor firms (and by Chrysler in particular) to have increased operating costs. But the companies' cost calculations assumed that expansion in existing locations would have been costless, and, in general, the concern expressed by firms was shown in Chapter 8 to have been exaggerated. For Chrysler, the main problem was that the company was producing an unsuccessful car in a peripheral location.

Other environmental factors had an important influence during this period. The oil crisis had a dramatic effect on car demand. The United Kingdom, as first a potential and then an actual member of the EEC, was subject to greatly increased international competition. Concurrently, the much more rapid rate of inflation in the United Kingdom, in comparison with the rest of the developed world, greatly increased the price competitiveness of imports until the downward float of sterling halted this trend during 1975 and 1976. The general labor relations situation in the United Kingdom can also be considered as an environmental variable in the sense that union conventions, practices, and structures are mostly outside the control of the individual firm. Similarly, any firm in the car industry, for example, being dependent upon a large number of components suppliers, is obviously vulnerable to the impact of production stoppages in such supply industries. Also, political disputes, such as the national dock strike in 1970 and the miners' strikes of 1972 and 1974, have repercussions at the individual firm level. Such disputes are symptomatic of a period when successive governments, realizing the contribution of poor industrial relations to the country's economic malaise, were attempting unsuccessfully to introduce legislative reform and wage controls.

There is no reason to believe that Chrysler would have been affected more adversely than any other U.K. motor firm by the environmental factors, had other things been equal. However, given the corporation's strategy, the environment became of considerable significance to the U.K. subsidiary. Environmental factors have another dimension in a multinational corporation. When European investment decisions are being considered in Detroit, the performance of the respective subsidiaries would be considered, but, in addition, the investment climate of the competing countries would be assessed, involving the broad economic variables that make up the operating environment. For the Chrysler Corporation, comparisons between France and the United Kingdom would have been as significant as comparisons between the French and U.K. subsidiaries.

Operational Factors

In assessing the contribution of this group of factors to Chrysler's downfall in the United Kingdom, it is clear that many of the company's operational difficulties were a function of the strategic and environmental variables already mentioned. Thus, for example, some of the problems of making Chrysler U.K. into a profitable company were a direct result of the strategic decision to buy Rootes. On the other hand, the view must have been taken that Rootes had the potential to be profitable, utilizing corporation managerial expertise to improve production and marketing efficiency, financial control, labor relations, and so forth. Decisions taken within all of these areas post-1967 come within the scope of operational management.

Chrysler's inheritance from Rootes is a useful starting point for this analysis. The Rootes family managed a rambling, ill-controlled, laissez-faire empire that cried out for rationalization and centralization. In the marketing field, Rootes was selling a large number of brands, but few models, through a dealer network that, while loyal, was in need of reorganization. The company's traditional quality image had been sacrificed when it took the decision to move into the big leagues with the launch of the Hillman Imp, but the Imp and the Linwood plant were consistent loss makers. Above all, the company was in need of a winning model. In the industrial relations sphere, the Rootes' management philosophy had produced a completely uncoordinated system of wage structures, bargaining procedures, and payment systems that required fundamental reorganization if productivity levels were ever to be raised to a satisfactory level. Investment was required in manufacturing facilities and plant restructuring was essential. On top of this, the management structure, the quality of management, and financial control were all in need of change and improvement.

In spite of the formidable task facing it in Europe as a whole, Chrysler set about the reorganization of its U.K. subsidiary with considerable vigor. The problem was that the company was having to act quickly in some relatively unexplored areas, particularly labor relations, where time was the essence of success. By and large, Chrysler was successful in reorganizing management and management control systems and production facilities. The company would probably have preferred to dispose of the Linwood plant at this time, if a buyer could have been found, but it was prevented by the agreement with the government. The rationalization of the dealer network and the simplification of the product line were, on balance, moves in the direction of greater efficiency; and, with the general reorganization under way, the launch of the Avenger was designed to provide the company with the profits from which new models could be financed.

However, the failure of Chrysler to handle industrial relations in the company was a key factor, and had a number of important consequences. Labor productivity, while fairly good in a U.K. context, only reached about 60 percent of that in Chrysler France. Labor relations affect productivity not only through the influence of disputes but also through manning levels and track speeds since these are subject to management-union negotiation. On the other hand, output per worker is affected by other variables outside the labor relations area, including the level of investment and the organization of production. Negotiated wages in certain Chrysler plants were higher at certain times than those in other U.K. manufacturers. Without commensurate productivity gains, this clearly would have had an adverse effect on hourly labor costs. The introduction of guaranteed severance pay by Chrysler had a similar effect in the sense that it did not lead to an offsetting improvement in labor relations.

While disputes seriously affect profitability at any time, some of Chrysler's stoppages came at particularly unfortunate periods, such as when the market was booming or when the company was running losses for other reasons. The disputes at the time of the Avenger launch were singularly inopportune and were an important factor in the decision to replace the Avenger on the U.S. market with the Mitsubishi Colt. Quality problems, another reason given for the cancellation of U.S. imports of the Avenger, can also be related to some extent to the incidence of disputes.

Labor relations issues seem to have been perceived by Detroit as the crucial factor affecting the performance of Chrysler U.K. This being so, it is irrelevant whether or not industrial relations was actually the most significant profit-loss determinant. With better labor relations, therefore, Chrysler Corporation may have been prepared to assist the U.K. company with its investment plants, in spite of the declared policy of self-sustenance.

It is important, however, not to go too far in emphasizing the role of labor relations in Chrysler's problems of slow productivity, output variability, and product quality. To do so would fall into the trap of oversimplification, and, for example, both quality problems and low productivity are partly a function of lack of investment.

Chapter 7 showed how difficult it is to try to apportion responsibility for the company's industrial relations record among the parties concerned. Some of management's actions were far-reaching and innovative and deserved a better response than they actually obtained, but against this, management showed an astonishing ability "to set fire to the oil it had previously poured on troubled waters."[55] The depressing point is how little seemed to have been learned by 1975.

Chrysler's industrial relations initiatives were undoubtedly part of its planned program of reorganization and rationalization, which was successfully implemented in other areas. In the case of labor relations, however, there was a need to sell reform, which did not apply in these other areas. This appears to have been underestimated, on the somewhat naive assumption that reform was in the interests of labor and therefore would be acceptable, per se. The company's actions at times suggested strongly that it did not understand the environment of industrial relations in the U.K. motor industry, a function both of the role of Chrysler Corporation in decision making and of the inexperience of U.S. middle management in the handling of Chrysler U.K.'s affairs. In addition, Chrysler's multinational status, as evidenced by the presence of U.S. executives at the negotiating table, could not have helped labor relations. An inheritance of good industrial relations management would have been a considerable asset.

Aside from the labor relations situation, Chrysler's reorganization plan for Rootes laid too much investment emphasis in the early years on the improvement of plant facilities to the detriment on investment in new models. Another new model, probably a replacement for the Imp, should have been a prerequisite in market planning to consolidate the company's position, since in 1969 Chrysler's U.K. market penetration was 2.5 percentage points lower than it had been at takeover. Even so, for a small company such as Chrysler U.K., success with the Avenger alone might have been enough to see the company through the short term. The marketing policy of Chrysler U.K. can be criticized in a number of other respects. For example, price cutting, heavy advertising (in the early years after takeover), and warranty extensions meant low profit margins on sales. As a result of these and other factors, Rootes' quality image, which had enabled it to avoid head-on confrontation with larger competitors, was lost. Rootes, in fairness, had gone some way to destroy this image when the Imp was launched, but the charisma remained with some of the other brands. On balance, Chrysler probably undervalued Rootes' goodwill.

Moving into the 1970s, the shortage of finance proved an insuperable problem, at a time when investment was required not only for new models but also to update plant and replace aging machine tools. It was at this time that the parent corporation's policy and decisions proved the key. The corporation's policy of subsidiary self-sustenance, its perception of the U.K. situation, its own volatile financial state, and the relative success of Chrysler France were all factors militating against the U.K. subsidiary.

In summing up the impact of operational factors on the performance of Chrysler U.K., it must be concluded that the Chrysler Corporation's view of what was required to transform Rootes into a viable enterprise proved to be inadequate. The analysis of the problems as applied to most areas of the company could hardly be faulted, but in implementing the necessary changes, the approach appeared rigid and inflexible and revealed a lack of understanding of the U.K. car market and its workers and customers. The effectiveness of any reorganization ultimately depends on people, and the management methods employed appeared at times to disregard this vital ingredient.

The Contribution of Strategic, Environmental, and Operational Factors to Viability

Drawing together the various strands of the discussion, the overall conclusion with respect to Chrysler U.K. is that long-term viability could not have been achieved within the European strategy of Chrysler Corporation as it appeared to have been laid down in the 1960s. Viability in this sense would mean that taking one year with another the company would be capable of generating sufficient profits to finance all or a substantial proportion of the funds required for investment in facilities and new models. While a correct strategy would have been a necessary condition for long-term viability, it would not be a sufficient condition. Viability would require, in addition, success at the operational level. The influence of the environment is the most difficult to assess. In the period since 1967, environmental factors would have created serious problems in particular years, for example, 1974, but taking the nine years to the end of 1975 as a whole, the environment would probably not have precluded viability for an integrated and well-managed organization. On the other hand, within the context of the U.K. environment, it would be difficult, if not impossible, to achieve performance comparisons on a par, say, with the West German vehicle manufacturers. Again an unstable operating environment greatly increases the risks associated with integration. This important issue will be discussed further in the context of the postrescue situation.

The management of Chrysler U.K., for its part, consistently has argued that the environment within which the company operated was the key to its unsatisfactory performance. In a statement after the crisis, Lander commented: "The difficulties the Company experienced were not of its making."[56] Undoubtedly, in Chrysler U.K. as actually constituted, with its emphasis on the U.K. market, the environment in the United Kingdom was a significant factor in performance. Even then, environmental variables were probably less significant than the operational factors. If Chrysler U.K. had solved its operational problems and specifically its labor relations difficulties, even given the hostile environment and a strategy that precluded integration, the company may well have been able to attain short-term viability. That is, a reasonably consistent profit performance. Such a level of profits, however, while normally adequate to fund the company's debt burden, would have provided insufficient surplus for financing a continuing model program from internal sources.

Prospects for the Future

Since the Chrysler problem is multifaced, the remedy will not be found in simple solutions. That more than anything is the fundamental conclusion to emerge from this book. The company itself seems to accept this. Thus, Don Lander, in a speech at the end of March 1976, listed eight factors as being important in determining the future success of Chrysler U.K.[57]

By using the criteria developed in previous paragraphs, the aim of the present section is to consider how far the Chrysler U.K.-government agreement alters the potential viability of the company as compared with the pre-1976 situation; to assess whether any new factors might emerge to assist or hinder the attainment of viability; and, finally, to consider what problems remain to be solved if a repeat performance of the 1975 crisis is to be avoided.

Integration Strategy

It was suggested earlier that an integration strategy, encompassing the three Chrysler subsidiaries in Europe, was an important prerequisite for the success of Chrysler U.K., while, of course, offering equally attractive prospects for Chrysler France and Chrysler Espana. The requirements of such a strategy, however, are by no means unambiguous. A number of possibilities exist.

Design and Development Integration. Subsequent manufacture may or may not be specialized or subsidiaries may jointly manufacture a standardized product range.

Marketing Integration. Here, as a minimum, a common dealer network in Europe would sell the range of vehicles produced by fellow subsidiaries, utilizing brand names that disregard supply sources. Where competing or similar products are produced at two locations, a decision is made on the market area to be allocated to each subsidiary. Marketing integration could be extended to cover pricing policies, promotions, warranty plans, and so forth.

First-Stage Production Integration. This is where a planned and complementary European product range exists and subsidiaries are each responsible for the manufacture of a part of that range. Strictly speaking, if production volumes were great enough, similar products could be produced in more than one location; for example, the Ford Escort is built in both the United Kingdom and Germany.

Second-Stage Production Integration. Here components are sourced among subsidiaries so as to maximize the utilization of capacity in each location. But only limited progress has been made on the standardization of components, and vehicles assembled in each subsidiary primarily utilize components manufactured by that subsidiary.

Third-Stage Production Integration. In this plan, manufacturing facilities are reorganized and components manufacture for the whole of Europe is sourced from single plants. The number of major components, for example, engines, axles, and body shells, is reduced to maximize output and production runs. The association between subsidiaries and complete vehicles is thus removed.

Essentially, among the U.S. subsidiaries in Europe, only Ford with its new car, the Fiesta, has reached the third stage of true production integration. This entails with it, of course, both design and development integration, as well as marketing integration. This third stage is the key area for potential cost reduction. Although it is the most expensive and time consuming to organize and involves painful choices on production locations, it is essential that Chrysler strategy be directed firmly toward this goal. Third-stage integration for Chrysler will involve concentration of output in larger plants of efficient size so as to take full advantage of economies of scale.

Naturally, there are risks in this strategy for Chrysler. The concentration of supply greatly increases risks for the whole European operation. Production disruption in a single plant producing a particular component would very soon bring the entire European output to a halt. This point was referred to when discussing the impact of environmental variables on viability. Lander commented that problems in the United Kingdom made it difficult to convince the corporation's and Chrysler France's management that Chrysler U.K. was a company worth integrating with. If integration goes ahead in Chrysler and subsidiaries become interdependent for supplies, difficulties in Chrysler U.K., for example, will be reflected not only in the balance sheet of the U.K. company but in those of the French and Spanish subsidiaries as well. Having said this, only this strategy offers the prize of a viable Chrysler Europe if the gamble pays off. Any other strategy would be more likely to see a complete termination of Chrysler's presence in Europe within a decade.

The rescue plan agreed between the government and Chrysler does not guarantee that the necessary integration between Chrysler U.K. and the corporation's continental operations will take place. The Declaration of Intent speaks of planning Chrysler U.K.'s products and model ranges as an integral part of the corporation's overall worldwide product plan. In announcing the agreement to the House of Commons, the secretary of state mentioned that Chrysler U.K. would be integrated into the corporation's "overseas market structure."[58] All that would be required to satisfy these conditions would be marketing integration. On the other hand, Chrysler's comments and actions subsequently seemed to indicate acceptance of the need for closer integration than that necessitated by the rescue plan. In a company document, Lander expressed the need to integrate the key elements of manufacturing on a European basis, the overall aim being to get "the match of products and facilities right so that we can benefit fully from the economies of scale available and utilize all the manufacturing capability."[59]

While the corporation's ultimate goal may be assumed to be true manufacturing integration, it seems to be aiming initially for second-stage production integration so as to maximize capacity utilization. The decision taken during the summer of 1976 to have certain components for Chrysler France machined at Chrysler U.K.'s Stoke plant is a first step in this direction. Similarly, the possibility of in-sourcing the Alpine in the United Kingdom, which could be seen as the reverse of integration, is a means of utilizing excess capacity in the United Kingdom. Even such limited steps involve fairly difficult decisions, but, by themselves, they do not go far enough. As the Expenditure Committee report on the rescue commented: "The use of the entire U.K. operation simply as spare assembly capacity might mean parts of CUK effectively being peripheral to the French facilities."[60]

To achieve true integration and with it the possibility of long-term viability, facilities must be reorganized so that individual plants become the sole European source of supply for certain items. This is a long way off and could scarcely be achieved within the four years of the support program. Even if it were possible, the corporation could be forgiven for being wary of committing itself to full European integration until it had some indication that the U.K. situation was more stable. The fact that fundamental decisions on where these sole supply sources will be located have yet to be made (or at least expressed publicly) is an indication of the potential problems that could still exist for Chrysler and the U.K. government (and, indeed, the French or Spanish government).

It is difficult, moreover, to see at this stage how the new car program for Chrysler U.K. fits in with the corporation's integration strategy. As things stand, Chrysler U.K. in 1979 will be producing four models (assuming that the Avenger is still in production but that the Hunter has been phased out). In 1978, the corporation is proposing "to strengthen our [Simca] 1100 range with a new product which is currently being developed in conjunction with our North American product programme"[61] and will be manufactured presumably in France. Together with other French models this indicates a large number of products for Chrysler in Europe in comparison with other manufacturers. How far these will use common components is unknown, but the Expenditure Committee's comment regarding a Chrysler Europe model range is worth repeating:

> Because Chrysler will be smaller than most other European mass producers even when it is integrated it must reduce the number of major items (such as power trains, axles and body shells) much more drastically than Ford or GM, and source them from single plants. For example, the UK and French operations could make two cars each of a four-model integrated range, and one engine could be manufactured entirely at Stoke, and another at Poissy. Only this sort of tight integration will overcome the problem of scale, which, in comparative European terms, will not have been banished entirely."[62]

Much of the discussion in this section is inevitably speculative. All that can be said in summing up is that the rescue program, while accepting the need for integration, is a program for Chrysler U.K., not for Chrysler Europe. The corporation's strategy appears to be directed toward integration, but it is doubtful how much can be or would want to be achieved in the four years up to 1979. The most painful, most politically sensitive, and most financially draining decisions are unlikely to be taken within this period of time. How far they are ever taken depends on the environmental and operational factors.

Environmental Influences

The rescue plan for Chrysler, while concerned primarily with operational issues, must inevitably have some indirect influences of an environmental nature. With both Chrysler and British Leyland about to receive substantial sums of public money, it could be argued that the U.K. government is likely to be more reluctant than in the past to use the motor industry as a short-term regulator for the economy as a whole. However, this depends upon the balance of conflicting objectives within government policy. The United Kingdom's

TABLE 9.2

Estimates of U.K. Passenger Car Registrations, 1976-79
(millions)

	Plan with Government	Chrysler U.K. Forecasts
1976	1.03	1.17
1977	1.25	1.35
1978	1.35	1.45
1979	1.40	1.50
Percent growth 1976-79	+36	+28

Source: Building the New Chrysler, presentation made to members of the U.K. press by Chrysler U.K., March 29, 1976.

rate of economic growth will continue to be the major factor determining the expansion of registrations and here the prospects are no more favorable than in the past. Even if the expected rapid expansion in sales between 1976 and 1978 is achieved, this will be deceptive and may tend to give a false impression of Chrysler's long-term prospects. This market growth largely affects a pickup in the economy following the severe recession and slump in sales between 1973 and 1975. Chrysler estimates of U.K. passenger car registrations are given in Table 9.2

The forecasts for inflation in the United Kingdom are uncertain, but the annual rate is unlikely to fall significantly below double figures during the remainder of the present decade, and an acceleration in the rate of price increases is a strong probability if there is a return to free collective bargining. This, in turn, together with the continuing balance of payments deficit, has implications for the exchange rate.

Having said this, the integration strategy, as applied to the marketing of cars and commercial vehicles, should facilitate a better balance between sales in the United Kingdom and continental Europe than in the past. Chrysler U.K., therefore, should be less restricted by the vagaries of the U.K. market, although the manufacturers' argument of the need for a strong home market as a base for exporting is still relevant. In Western Europe as a whole, overcapacity is the one new environmental factor that may play an increasingly important role as compared with the prerescue period in the achievement of both home and export sales.

From an output viewpoint, the labor relations environment in the United Kingdom is obviously important. As at 1976, the signs were promising, but the apparent stability has yet to be proved. The pay policy, the forecast of a continuing high level of unemployment throughout the period of the rescue, the forthcoming general election, and inflation are just four factors against which the permanence of this stability will be tested over the next few years.

Operational Influences

Models and Marketing. The rescue agreement mainly concerned operational matters. Arguably, the most important part of this agreement covered financial aid for the introduction and development of new models, enabling the company to make a start for the first time on a significant product program. It is impossible to assess the contribution these models will make to viability without details of the vehicles themselves—design, specification, performance, price, and so on. Then, too, the initial impression a model makes on the market seems to be an important factor, and Chrysler will want to ensure that some of the early problems that were experienced, for example, with the 180/2 liter and the K382OP heavy truck, are not repeated.

It is not clear how new the models will be, from either marketing or production viewpoints. It is apparent from the expenditure allocations that the products must draw substantially on existing models. This is valuable to the extent that a greater commonality of components among models means longer production runs, and where components are tried and tested, risks are thereby reduced. One potentially important point concerns the design of the models. The new products are designs brought off the shelf when the government and Chrysler Corporation cash became available. If funds had been available in the early 1970s, some of the models might have been marketed for over two or three years by now. There must be some worry, therefore, that by the time the products actually appear on the market, they will be too late either in design package items or in terms of market saturation.

Both of these points concern, for example, the new, small, light car—the 424. The growth of this supermini market was a by-product of the oil crisis. Most of the major European manufacturers now have current or planned models to cater for this segment, the latest entrant being Ford (with a maximum output potential of 500,000 units). Ford expects the European market for minis and superminis to grow from 25 percent of the total market in 1975 to 30 percent in 1980, meaning perhaps between 800,000 and 900,000 extra units.[63] The latest information from Chrysler is that the 424 will be made at a rate of between 70,000 and 90,000 vehicles a year. At such a small scale of production, it might be considered relatively easy to find a niche in the market to accommodate the 424. On the other hand, the 424 will appear on the U.K. market just after the Fiesta and may suffer by comparison. Again the 424 is a rear wheel drive car, which is cheaper to produce, but probably less acceptable to the market, particularly in Europe, than front wheel drive models. Ford is forecasting this market segment in the United Kingdom alone to increase by between 110,000 and 130,000 cars,[64] and with its own Fiesta likely to take a substantial chunk of this, Chrysler will have to sell up to perhaps 50 percent of its output abroad to meet planned production targets.

Taking Chrysler's figures for its model program for the immediate future, it should not be too difficult to fill plant capacity. The Alpine will be made at the rate of about 40,000 units a year. Assuming Avenger sales of at least 50,000 units (and Avenger output in the autumn of 1976 was being raised to an annual rate of about 80,000 units), CKD output of 125,000 Hunters for Iran in 1977, and sales of the 424 at the lower rate of 70,000 units gives a total of 285,000 cars. With an assembly capacity in the United Kingdom of 320,000 cars, utilization on the basis of the crude figures quoted would be about 89 percent. This, moreover, excludes the sale of any Hunters, other than those to Iran, and the Avenger figures quoted are probably on the conservative side. Thus, the Avenger sold nearly 40,000 units in the United Kingdom alone in the depressed market conditions of 1975. With a revamped 1976 model and greater efforts to sell the car in continental Europe, sales of well over 50,000 cars should be possible.

Turning to commercial vehicles, the model designed to take over from the Walk-Thru/Bantam range, scheduled for 1978, is undoubtedly late. This is particularly so in the context of the suggestion that was made in Chapter 6 that a replacement for this model was rumored as long ago as 1969. The PB van is also in need of more radical alteration than the mere cosmetic changes that the company appears to be planning. Since even these changes are not incorporated into the Declaration of Intent, presumably they are that much less certain.

Given that Chrysler U.K. has been granted the opportunity to make a substantially fresh start in terms of models, it is obviously necessary to ensure that other aspects of marketing policy are pursued in such a way that will capitalize on the opportunities provided. The rescue was not concerned with this level of detail, but models do not bring profits without effective pricing, promotions, and distribution. In assessing the contribution of operational factors to Chrysler's downfall, criticism was directed at the company's discount pricing policy and its introduction of costly unlimited mileage warranty plans. Even in an integrated situation, Chrysler will still be a small produ-

cer in European terms and therefore cannot afford to achieve sales
via higher marketing costs and lower margins. Yet the company's
marketing policy seems to foresee a continuance of this. Chrysler's
director of sales and marketing stated during its spring 1976 press
conference: "It has always been Chrysler policy to offer very keen
pricing and our action in holding prices when most other car manufacturers increase theirs, earlier this year, has given us an even greater
price advantage."[65] This and associated policies will make the attainment of viability that much more difficult.

Iranian Contract. A major reason for the rescue was, of course, the
Iranian contract. Its importance to Chrysler is obvious. The planned
1977 volume of 125,000 units represents 40 percent of the company's
assembly capacity. Even if the contract is barely profitable to Chrysler, this is a very substantial volume of sales to replace by May 1981,
the earliest date the contract can be terminated.* Since Chrysler's
problems are going to be difficult enough, some renegotiation of the
contract must have a high priority. The rescue says nothing on the
subject, but some direct approach from the United Kingdom to the
Iranian government seems an obvious possibility.

Production Operations. Aside from the finance for new models, the
rescue provided a substantial sum of money for the improvement of
plant facilities, which will help to raise productivity and alleviate
some of the quality problems that were experienced prior to the rescue. As on the marketing side, however, the rescue plan was very
inadequate in terms of detailed production operations. There was
clearly an important need for the inclusion of binding arrangements
on productivity and manning levels and for the incorporation of a no-
strike clause. Chapter 5 showed that productivity would have to be
raised by over 50 percent if output per worker in Chrysler U.K. was
to match that of Chrysler France. If output levels could have been
raised within the planned 33 percent fall in employment, such an increase in productivity was obviously feasible, but the fact that Chrysler was recruiting again in the late summer of 1976 is hardly a very
encouraging sign for the future.

On labor relations, the Declaration of Intent made suitably acceptable noises on employee participation, and the company, in fairness, has been moving rapidly to improve communications. Virtually
nothing new can be said. Whether management or worker inspired,

_____

*The contract between Chrysler U.K. and INIM runs for an indefi-
nite period, although after May 1980 it is subject to termination at one
year's notice from either side.

labor relations could still make or break the company. This being so, the rescue plan should have gone much further, perhaps insisting that disputes should not be accompanied by work stoppages, but that both management and workers should have the right to appeal to some independent tribunal whose findings would be binding on all parties.

Conclusions and Recommendations

It is difficult to say, in conclusion, whether or not Chrysler U.K. will be viable in the long run. It has the potential to be viable, but that is not quite the same thing. Short-run viability, as defined earlier, is possible, and, given the performance of the U.K. car industry as a whole, that is no mean achievement. On balance, the failure to obtain detailed operational guarantees makes it likely that the profit performance of Chrysler U.K. will be too volatile to attain long-run viability. In addition, complete integration is necessary for long-run viability and this could hardly be achieved within the four years of the rescue program. The profit performance of the Chrysler Corporation, moreover, is unlikely to be either sufficiently stable or sufficiently strong to fund European integration.

The rescue itself could be defended as a laudable attempt to maintain a motor industry in the United Kingdom. However, with Chrysler, as with Leyland, it was wrong to put public money at risk with so few guarantees. Since the government probably has a breathing space before the next recession and the next bout of industrial collapse, there is time to remedy this situation. A new, much more detailed agreement, incorporating binding commitments on operational issues and including a planned program leading to complete integration by the mid-1980s should be negotiated in return for further government financial support. It is naive to recommend that no money should be forthcoming for Chrysler after 1980. If similar circumstances to those in 1975 arise in the 1980s, the conclusions would be identical—but the intervening time would have been wasted. If a detailed renegotiation takes place on these lines, there is every opportunity for Chrysler to be viable in the long run. Under such circumstances, too, there would be much clearer criteria against which Chrysler's progress could be monitored, given that this is going to be particularly difficult anyway in an integrated multinational enterprise. Similarly, if these criteria are not met, the government has a defensible means of withdrawing support.

GUIDELINES FOR EVALUATING PERFORMANCE
IN CHRYSLER U.K.

While it has been suggested that long-term viability is not in prospect with the terms or period of the 1975 plan, between 1976 and 1979 the U.K. government and the public will inevitably be looking for signs of progress and recovery in Chrysler U.K. The tempation may be to over emphasize what could be essentially short-term, superficial signs of improvement rather than await a consolidation of trends before claiming victory or defeat. Accepting the need for a view over the period as a whole, a growing volume of evidence will emerge within the next two or three years that inevitably will be used to judge the future prospects of Chrysler U.K. The guidelines set out in this section are not comprehensive. Indeed, they may be criticized for being oversimplistic. Nevertheless, taken collectively, favorable performances on most of these measures would be at least a sign of the possibility of long-term prosperity. For a government looking on anxiously and from the viewpoint of the wider public interest, they will provide an early indication of the likely outcome of the 1975 plan.

Market Share

The U.K. market share attained by Chrysler U.K. cars will need to be built up consistently to approach 10 percent by the end of 1978, and increase further with the launch of the new light car in the following year. From the viewpoint of the profitability of the U.K. dealers, and bearing in mind the desire to integrate France and the United Kingdom, the Chrysler France share of the U.K. car market should increase to between 2.5 and 3 percent by 1979. In order to provide guidelines that are easily monitored, these market share data (and the export figures following) refer to cars only, but equally similar signs of improvement must be evident in the commercial vehicle side.

Exports

There will have to be signs of the extension and successful renegotiation of the Iranian contract by 1978–79 to provide the required volume of business. Alternatively, a major source of substitute business will have to be on the horizon by that year. U.K. production will have to become more oriented toward the EEC and up to 20 percent of U.K. car output should be so allocated by 1979.

Strike Losses

If it is accepted that there is no single effective measure of the true losses from strikes, then the guidelines cannot be fully expressed in terms of maximum annual output losses or maximum numbers of strikes of a particular duration. However, there will be justified cause for concern if the strike record does not improve dramatically. For the management and work force, the target must be to avoid man-hours lost exceeding 500,000 per year from internal causes. This would constitute a reduction in man-hour losses of 50 percent as compared with even the exceptionally good 1975 record.

Productivity

To achieve the necessary cost savings, the target for the U.K. company must be to make significant progress toward the productivity achieved in Chrysler France. An output level of 15 vehicles per employee by 1979 would show that such progress was being achieved.

Financial Performance

From a profit viewpoint, the U.K. company should be averaging annual pretax profits of £10 million by 1978–79. While this is not a figure that would necessarily fund investment development, it would be an indication that the rescue plan had begun to produce tangible results and would give future confidence in the company in a firmer footing. While profit must be the long-run criterion, the government could find satisfaction with some evidence of improvement in the financial structure of the company within the plan period. This would be expressed in a changing balance between long- and short-term debt, improved returns on capital employed, and so on. More important, from the monitoring viewpoint, the signs required in the management accounts will have to include minimum variances in cost and sales budgets, maintenance of production targets, and sustained improvements in cash flow.

The guidelines here refer to operational variables only. Success in achieving these will be particularly noteworthy if accompanied by positive signs of integration. Such evidence would be available if, for example, at least one major component for the new 1100 car to be assembled in France and the 1979 U.K. light car was common and was sourced solely in the United Kingdom.

APPENDIX

Financial Arrangements Agreed Between the U.K.
Government and Chrysler Corporation

Potential Government Commitment

£50   million maximum share of loss in 1976
£10   million maximum share of loss in 1977
£12.5 million maximum share of loss in 1978
          and 1979

Funding of
possible
losses[a]

£28   million loan for capital development
          (guaranteed by Chrysler Corporation)
          in 1976-77[b]
£27   million loan for capital development
          (secured on Chrysler U.K.) in 1978-79[b]

Loans to
finance
specific
capital
projects

£35   million medium-term bank loan facilities guaranteed by gov-
          ernment (and counterguaranteed by Chrysler Corporation)[c]

_____

£162.5 million

Potential Chrysler Corporation Commitment

£10   million maximum share of loss in 1976
£10   million maximum share of loss in 1977
£12.5 million maximum share of loss in 1978
          and 1979

Funding of
possible
losses[a]

£10 to 12 million for the C6 (Alpine) model introduction[d]
£19.72 million waiver of loans (and interest) made to Chrysler U.K.[e]

Summary of Declaration of Intent by
Chrysler Corporation[f]

Chrysler U.K. will be viewed by Chrysler in the same manner
and in all respects on a par with other Chrysler subsidiaries throughout the world and it will continue to play an important and expanding
role within the total Chrysler Group.

Chrysler U.K.'s products and model ranges will be planned as
an integral part of Chrysler's overall worldwide product plan so that
Chrysler U.K.'s products will be complementary to and have a specific
and definable position within the total Chrysler worldwide product offering.

Chrysler U.K. will embark on a program of modernization and investment in new models that will help it to grow and prosper in the United Kingdom and specifically to provide continued employment at Chrysler U.K.'s principal plants.

Chrysler U.K. will move forward quickly, starting in 1976, to introduce as new models: a new improved Avenger (autumn of 1976), the Chrysler C6 car (to be assembled within the United Kingdom in 1976), a new small conventional drive car (1977), a new van-truck (1978), and a new light car (1979).

Chrysler will support Chrysler U.K.'s efforts to the full extent of Chrysler's managerial, product planning, engineering, design, and worldwide distribution facilities in the same manner as it support its other subsidiaires.

Chrysler U.K. will work with its employees on the basis of expanding employee participation to improve the long-term productivity of Chrysler U.K.

Control

The government will have the right to nominate two directors to the board of Chrysler U.K. (which will continue to have a majority of U.K. directors). Under the loan agreements, Chrysler U.K. will be required to provide quarterly management accounts and any other financial information reasonably requested by the government. As long as any loans are outstanding, Chrysler Corporation will not be allowed to reduce its shareholding in Chrysler U.K. below 80 percent. Chrysler U.K. also has agreed to negotiate a planning agreement.

EEC Consultation

The commission of the EEC concluded that the proposals did not threaten competition to such an extent that they would seriously affect trading conditions to an extent contrary to the common interest.

---

[a]Government responsible for first £40 million of losses in 1976. Equal sharing of further losses in 1976 and possible losses in 1977–79 up to maximum figures shown.

[b]Both government loans repayable in ten semiannual installments between 1985 and 1990; second tranche to be repaid first.

[c]Loan facilities provided by a consortium of banks to fund short-term borrowings.

dChrysler Corporation will consider by the end of 1979 the provision of additional funds—estimated at £23 million—to enable the Alpine to be totally sourced in the United Kingdom.

eSee comment in Chapter 5.

fThis is not a legally enforceable commitment.

Source: Expenditure Committee, sess. 1975-76, Public Expenditure in Chrysler U.K. Ltd., Minutes of Evidence, HC 104 (I) (London: HMSO, January 14, 1976).

NOTES

1. Glasgow Herald, February 11, 1970.

2. The Economist, September 29, 1973.

3. Ibid., February 23, 1974. The new general director of GM in Europe was quoted as saying: "The oxygen is going out at such a rate you don't know how close to death you really are."

4. Eighth Report from the Expenditure Committee, sess. 1975/76, Public Expenditure on Chrysler UK Ltd., HC 596 (I) (London: HMSO, 1976), from which most of the following section has been drawn.

5. Ibid., para. 75.

6. Eighth Report from the Expenditure Committee, para. 87.

7. Ibid., para. 89.

8. Ibid.

9. Ibid., para. 90.

10. Ibid., para. 91.

11. Weekly Hansard, House of Commons Parliamentary Debates, no. 1014 (London: HMSO, November 6, 1975), col. 607.

12. Expenditure Committee, Minutes of Evidence, January 14, 1976, HC 104 (I), para. 66.

13. Weekly Hansard, House of Commons Parliamentary Debates, no. 1019 (London: HMSO, December 16, 1975), col. 1165.

14. Ibid., no. 739, January 17, 1967, col. 39.

15. Eighth Report from the Expenditure Committee, para. 134.

16. Financial Times, October 30, 1975.

17. The Economist, November 8, 1975.

18. The Guardian, December 11, 1975.

19. Eighth Report from the Expenditure Committee, para. 164. The assumption was that the 55,000 people made redundant would remain unemployed for an average of a year.

20. Quoted in Department of Employment Gazette 84, no. 7 (London: HMSO, July 1976): 714.

21. The Economist, November 29, 1975.

22. For details, see Sunday Times (London), December 14, 1975.

23. Public Expenditure on Chrysler U.K. Ltd., para. 141.

24. Expenditure Committee, Public Expenditure on Chrysler U.K. Ltd., Minutes of Evidence, HC 104 (I) (London: HMSO, January 14, 1976), para. 46.

25. Public Expenditure on Chrysler U.K. Ltd., para. 145.

26. Building the New Chrysler, presentation made to members of the British press by Chrysler U.K. Ltd., March 29, 1976.

27. Eighth Report from the Expenditure Committee, para. 135. The cost of each option was calculated on the basis of the forecasts involved being met, and, unlike the figure of £162.5 million associated with the final agreement, did not include a margin to cover any possible shortfall.

28. Ibid., para. 142.

29. Weekly Hansard, December 16, 1975, col. 1165.

30. Ibid.

31. Expenditure Committee, Public Expenditure on Chrysler U.K. Ltd., Minutes of Evidence, p. 54.

32. Weekly Hansard, December 16, 1975, col. 1168.

33. Expenditure Committee, Public Expenditure on Chrysler U.K. Ltd., Minutes of Evidence, p. 3. In a memorandum submitted to the Expenditure Committee on behalf of the secretary of state, this item was omitted from the financial details provided. From the government's viewpoint, this is correct since the loans had been made already and if Chrysler U.K. had gone into liquidation, then the £19.7 million would have been written off in any event.

34. Building the New Chrysler.

35. Public Expenditure on Chrysler U.K., Ltd., para. 209.

36. Building the New Chrysler.

37. Expenditure Committee, Public Expenditure on Chrysler U.K., Ltd., Minutes of Evidence, HC 104 (III) (London: HMSO, January 28, 1976), para. 667.

38. For a discussion on planning agreements, see Public Expenditure on Chrysler U.K., Ltd., chap. 10.

39. The Guardian, December 17, 1976.

40. Ibid.

41. Ibid.

42. The Economist, December 20, 1975.

43. Ibid.

44. New York Times, December 17, 1975.

45. Weekly Hansard, December 16, 1975, col. 1175.

46. Ibid., December 17, 1975, col. 1544.

47. Expenditure Committee, Public Expenditure on Chrysler U.K., Ltd., Minutes of Evidence, HC 104 (I), p. 53.

48. Weekly Hansard, December 17, 1975, col. 1543.
49. Public Expenditure on Chrysler U.K., Ltd., paras. 151-53.
50. Sunday Times, August 1, 1976.
51. Expenditure Committee, Minutes of Evidence, HC 104 (XVI) (London: HMSO, August 7, 1976), para. 3434.
52. Eighth Report from the Expenditure Committee, paras. 151-53.
53. Ibid., para. 269.
54. Ibid., para. 231.
55. The Economist, September 15, 1973.
56. Building the New Chrysler.
57. Ibid.
58. Weekly Hansard, December 16, 1975, col. 1168.
59. Building the New Chrysler.
60. Public Expenditure on Chrysler U.K., Ltd., para. 241.
61. Building the New Chrysler.
62. Public Expenditure on Chrysler U.K., Ltd., para. 240.
63. The Financial Times, June 17, 1976.
64. Ibid.
65. Building the New Chrysler.

CHAPTER
10

**NATIONAL AND
INTERNATIONAL
IMPLICATIONS OF
THE CHRYSLER CASE**

The extensive public interest in the affairs of Chrysler U.K.
both in the United Kingdom and abroad is an acknowledgment of the
many fundamental and wide-reaching implications of the case. These
extend beyond the actual justification for and mechanics of the rescue
operation. Nor are they confined to the United Kingdom, since one of
the unique facets of the problem is that the U.K. government was forced
into supporting a crippled branch of a major multinational without participation in its equity. This inevitably raises related questions regarding government responsibility for transnational companies operating
within its country; for example, whether the government objective of
of sustaining employment overrides the method by which this has to
be accomplished and how accountability for public investment in such
an instance can be defined, let alone implemented, when global decision
making is involved. The purpose of this chapter is to stand back from
the detail of the recovery program for the company and to assess some
of the implications of the whole case. These will be examined from
the overlapping viewpoints of the U.K. government, the motor industry in Europe, the EEC, and the Chrysler Corporation. Thereafter,
some of the wider issues regarding multinational investment decisions
and the control of transnational companies will be studied.

U.K. GOVERNMENT

From the perspective of the U.K. government, some of the most
significant implications are as follows. The government was forced
to support Chrysler at a time when its total approach to industrial

strategy was in an embryo stage.* The method of rescue, and the way in which the emergent guiding principles of that policy were applied, did much to erode confidence in the viability of the strategy as a whole in the eyes of domestic and foreign observers.

While government policy earlier had anticipated involving the U.K. holdings of multinational companies in the consultation process of three-year planning agreements, [1] the spirit of the 1974 White Paper was directed to the regeneration of domestic industry. Both of the major tools of policy—planning agreements and the National Enterprise Board—were designated to operate in a systematic way and within criteria of effectiveness that could not have been readily applied to Chrysler. The Expenditure Committee observed that the question of whether or not the rescue of Chrysler U.K. was consistent with government policy "must be to a large extent a matter of interpretation." [2]

On the other hand, the Chrysler case did little to aid the credibility of the regeneration program considered to be so vital to economic recovery, since it suggested that the strength of resolve to restructure the U.K. industry did not exist. By any measure, Chrysler was an unfortunate precedent for the whole industrial policy. Whereas there was nothing unusual or necessarily improper in allowing social considerations to outweigh economic logic, the timing of the rescue coincided with an apparently serious attempt to enunciate wider support principles within which it would have been difficult to make a case for funding Chrysler U.K.

The general credibility of the industrial policy was not aided by the evident lack of detailed knowledge of the company's affairs in the responsible government departments—a point that did not escape criticism from the Expenditure Committee. [3] Nor did the findings of the government's own policy advisers on the industry, as expressed in the CPRS report, suggest any case for extending financial support to another U.K.-based producer.

One of the principal implications for the U.K. government was the apparent erosion of its strategy toward the car industry inasmuch

---

*The crisis meeting between Riccardo and the prime minister in November 1975 occurred before the publication of the government document "An Approach to Industrial Strategy" (Cmnd 6315, 1975) and days before the 1975 Industry Bill was finally approved. It also predicated the formation of the National Enterprise Board on November 20, 1975. Although all of these were anticipated and had been under discussion for an extensive period, they were largely in terms of principle rather than practice. Neither had the Criteria for Assistance (Industry Act 1972) been tested against a case parallel to that of Chrysler.

as it was difficult to reconcile support for Chrysler with the British
Leyland plan. The declared objective of government policy for the
U.K. industry was "to bring about an improvement in the efficiency
of the motor vehicle industry."[4] It is difficult to conceive of realizing
this objective without significant rationalization, which would more
than likely reduce overall capacity in the U.K. industry. This being
so, the government had already taken on more than enough in the long-
term rescue of British Leyland, based on the most fundamental of
premises, that "vehicle production is the kind of industry which ought
to remain an essential part of the U.K.'s economic base," and "therefore that BL should remain a major vehicle producer, although this
means that urgent action must be taken to remedy the weaknesses
which at present prevent it from competing effectively in world markets."[5] From the narrow viewpoint of restructuring the car industry,
therefore, Chrysler should not have been supported.

Among the consequences of the Chrysler support exercise, the
continuing issue of accountability is likely to prove one of the most
contentious. The way in which the government handled its initial responsibilities of accountability to Parliament while negotiating the
deal will continue to be cited as a completely inacceptable precedent.[6]
The deliberate delays in publication of the CPRS report and the speed
with which the eventual agreement was pushed through Parliament are
other points of disquiet.

Regarding the control of government finance in Chrysler U.K.,
the fundamental question is whether it is at all realistic to talk about
monitoring a multinational subsidiary. Even if it is, will the very
process of monitoring not in itself result in a too ready acceptance
of the need for future funding? The system of monitoring being operated under the 1975 rescue falls very short of even limited accountability since the rescue operation has been undertaken without a long-term
guiding objective. Thus, while it is possible to ensure that the money
is spent as per the agreement, the absence of a detailed control program designed for a long-term goal is critical. This is made more
important by the existence of an externally determined strategy for
Chrysler Europe.

Thus, while both Chrysler and the U.K. government may both
see the solution in terms of "integration," this policy declaration
needs to be broken down into subobjectives that can be measured and
controlled so that the two parties are talking in the same language.
Clearly, the implications of such a significant support exercise within
the context of the known problems of the car industry make it vital to
extend accountability far beyond management accounts and the like.

Even if the development of effective monitoring targets is assumed, there remains the question of whether Chrysler U.K. can ever
effectively ensure cooperation while being responsible to its parent

company. It may be possible to accept (reluctantly) that there was a coincidence of objectives between the government and the company at the time of the rescue in recession-struck Britain, but it is not difficult to see these separating. Some of the problems over which this could occur could be employment, industrial relations, management, model policy, and integration of U.K. and French facilities and corporation investment policies in other locations. All of these issues have featured in political debate over Chrysler in the last ten years and were by no means solved by the new arrangements.

It is already clear that, although the U.K. government had more warning of the impending collapse of Chrysler than it would ever likely get in most cases, the balance, in terms of bargaining power, was tipped strongly against the government at the precise time of the rescue, inevitably affecting the outcome of the negotiations. The Chrysler case will not have gone unnoticed by other multinationals. As a country, the United Kingdom is highly dependent on U.S. investment, especially in some of the sensitive regions[7] (such as Scotland). This could result in convincing arguments for assistance being advanced by other multinationals (and by labor in these multinationals), albeit on a smaller scale and without the fallback that Chrysler aid is really aid to tackle the unsolved problems of a former U.K. company.

Apart from the likelihood of the Chrysler affair sparking off further requests for aid, there is the additional point of resentment among other multinational (and domestic) firms at the preferential treatment accorded to Chrysler. For Ford and Vauxhall, facing two government-backed rivals, this is a particularly sensitive issue.

One interesting aspect of the whole Chrysler affair is the degree of responsibility that has been given to management and the work force of the company. At the very root of the plan is the assumption that the new participatory management style in a government-backed operation will bring both stability and maturity to the industrial relations situation in the company. On the basis of the past track record, this is a brave assumption and would not be made by a dispassionate observer. While the first eight months of 1976 were generally characterized by cooperation[8] and the claimed emergence of a completely new atmosphere, only time will tell whether this is a valid assumption. If it does demonstrate even a measure of success in industrial peace, Chrysler will prove to have been one of the most rigorous test beds for industrial democracy in the United Kingdom. Clearly, if such a policy can pay dividends in a crisis situation, there is more than likely to be increased pressure for legislation.

A further aspect of the Chrysler case concerns the "social accounting" employed to justify supporting the company, and in particular whether there is anything new in this that could set a precedent for future public expenditure. Among a number of issues is that of whether the government was maintaining employment or maintaining Chrysler. It would not be unusual to find a government concluding that on a cost-benefit basis it would be more expensive in terms of direct and indirect redundancy costs to close an operation rather than to support it. This argument was indeed convincingly advanced. On the other hand, senior officials in the Department of Industry argued that the most important single factor, in fact, was the maintenance of Chrysler.[9]

Whatever is postulated in theory, the reality of the situation is that neither the employment nor the import-saving objective could be attained without a company, in this case Chrysler, no matter how unacceptable such a solution might appear on other grounds. Since this is so, any thorough cost-benefit study would have to take into account the benefits of actually having a company to support as well as the cost of not achieving the employment and other objectives, the costs of lack of accountability, and so on. The outcome of this type of analysis, properly discounted, would be likely to lead to all rescue projects above a certain size and with a minimum number of agglomeration links being supported almost by definition.

Clearly, this is a form of accounting that a government committed to industrial reconstruction cannot afford to live with. Indeed, that it cannot be applied meaningfully is already obvious in the car industry by the government's refusal to provide limited funding to revitalize Jensen Motors, a case where it was severely criticized by the liquidator.[10] Thus, while the government may argue that Chrysler poses no precedent because the circumstances were special, the case for support could not readily be interpreted as such. This is so particularly when it appears that one of the reasons for supporting the U.K. company was that it was part of a multinational.

Many of the implications for the U.K. government examined in this section stem directly from the transitional character of Chrysler U.K. The transitional problem extends to many areas of company activity. At the time of the 1975 crisis, it included model policy, marketing strategy, labor relations, and financial structure. In none of these fields had the U.K. company arrived at an operational equilibrium, let alone an optimum. To a degree, the uncertainty is increased by the need to view the solutions to some of these problems as European, implying adjustments to the operations of both Chrysler U.K. and Chrysler France.

By identifying Chrysler as going through a fundamental transition, the company is in effect being viewed as a microcosm of the U.K. economy. Thus, some of the microaspects of policy adopted toward Chrysler have a macrodimension for overall economic management. The spirals of decline that Chrysler U.K. was experiencing regarding models and market share, labor relations and worker participation, profitability, and productivity are all symptoms of the "British disease." For Chrysler, government rescue action has given the company no more than an opportunity to break out of the spiral. The lessons for the government lie in the dramatic action required to ensure such an opportunity for just one large company. How much more, therefore, is required for large sections of a whole economy? From this perspective, the lessons of the Chrysler case demand a complete reappraisal of what is really required to regenerate growth in U.K. manufacturing.

EUROPEAN MOTOR INDUSTRY

Viewed with the future of the European car industry in mind, the Chrysler rescue has a number of implications. These concern, for example, the maintenance of Chrysler capacity in the face of expected overcapacity in the industry as a whole; the attitudes of national governments, particularly that of the French government to an integrated Chrysler Europe; and the issue of the comparative styles of management adopted by European governments toward vehicle producers operating in their respective countries.

Although detailed forecasts vary considerably, most estimates suggest continued overcapacity in the European industry. Some of these forecasts were presented in Chapter 1, when it was suggested that by 1980 in Europe capacity could exceed demand by about 25 percent. Clearly, this depends on demand forecasts, import penetration, price competition in the face of capacity surplus, and so on. In any event, it would have been difficult for the U.K. government to conclude from the evidence available that capacity problems in Europe would be aided by supporting Chrysler. This was by no means the only parameter to be considered of course, and even if it had been, it must be said that the continued positive balance of trade achieved by the industry could be an important factor in deciding that U.K. capacity should not be volunteered for cuts too readity.

Against a background of very tough competition in Europe for at least the next decade, the CPRS report concluded that in the U.K. car industry "there are too many manufacturers with too many models, too many plants and too much capacity."[11] The government, however, argued that the Chrysler agreement was in line with the CPRS conclusions on the industry.[12] The underlying assumptions behind this belief must have been that an increase in efficiency and international competitiveness would stem from the Chrysler rescue, making it a part of capacity that would no longer be readily identifiable as "excess." Interpreted in this way the government backing of Chrysler was a vigorous attempt to preserve U.K.-based capacity regardless of the consequences for other U.K. and European producers. Inevitably, the Chrysler support program involves the launch of new models and penetration into sectors in which the European industry faces intense competition. In the short term, and even more so in the long term, if the company is successful, this must have implications for the profitability of the European industry.

Since the other U.K. manufacturers are among the weakest in Europe, it is tempting to suggest that a successful Chrysler would have particularly adverse effects on profitability in the U.K. motor industry. On the other hand, neither British Leyland, Vauxhall,[13] nor Ford expressed any great concern about the impact of Chrysler's survival upon their own respective positions. These views, however, may have reflected that fact that in the past Chrysler was not a threat because it was out of step with the market. As the Chrysler product range is brought nearer to the long-term thrust of the market, there must be implications for the other U.K. producers.

The overcapacity situation in the European industry is almost bound to have some effects on the marketing and pricing policies of the companies involved. It is difficult to predict whether the Chrysler plan, per se, introduces an additional element of price competition in Europe and whether the Chrysler policy of actively using price as a major competitive weapon has any particular implications. The fact that the scale of the company's U.K. output is relatively small, and therefore its effect limited, may be offset by the general tightness of margins that is likely to prevail in the near future.

In evidence to the Expenditure Committee,[14] the chairman of Vauxhall, referring to the support program for Chrysler, expressed his concern as to "how the money is used in marketing areas of business." Clarifying this point, he argued that there would be disadvantages, "if we have to [and we would have to] combat marketing practices that were not geared to the attainment of viability." Undoubtedly, the last has yet to be heard of this.

The fact that Chrysler continues to operate in both the United Kingdom and France has some potentially important implications. While relatively successful in the past, Chrysler France is still well below optimum size for a mass market manufacturer, and even as a smaller specialized manufacturer, it would be extremely difficult for the French firm to survive in the market sectors now so successfully dominated by Volvo, BMW, and others. The demise of Chrysler U.K. could thus be followed by the emergence of problems for Chrysler France. Unless the company was capable of being absorbed into a French firm, the government in France on "le defi americaine" model would probably have little hesitation in allowing the Chrysler subsidiary to go to the wall. An integrated Chrysler Europe thus is only slightly less important to the French subsidiary than to Chrysler U.K., and therefore Chrysler France will tend to become more dependent on success in the U.K. operation than previously.

The attitude of the French government will be extremely interesting to observe over the next few years. What might be expected is to see the French government defend Chrysler France if it becomes obvious that Chrysler U.K. is benefiting at the expense of the French company. On the other hand, the French government might not be keen on an integrated, more competitive Chrysler Europe because of its effects on Renault and so on. The rescue of Chrysler U.K. was not patently anti-Chrysler France, but both the French company and government could justifiably feel aggrieved if any permanent change in roles begins to take effect.

Tight integration between the companies, on the lines discussed earlier, is probably not a feasible proposition before 1980. However, such integration will require intergovernment agreement between the United Kingdom and France as well as government finance. In theory at least, depending largely on the rationalization of British Leyland, the U.K. government might find such an intergovernmental solution attractive on the basis that a problem shared is a problem halved. But what happens if the French government refuses to cooperate? For both governments, thus, the period at the end of 1979 will be important in reaching conclusions on their future commitment both to Chrysler and to their indigenous car industries. From the viewpoint of industrial structure, a forced marriage between the two companies is not likely to prove particularly successful when many of the past intercompany agreements in Europe have run aground even with initial goodwill on both sides.

As yet within the European motor industry, intergovernmental problems emanating from competition for the investments of Ford, Chrysler, and GM have not yet arisen to any great extent. However, the difficulties that seem likely to arise for the U.K. and French governments (and possibly also the Spanish government) over Chrysler may yet be repeated in other European countries over Ford and GM as these companies' own integration policies become progressively tighter.

At its root, the Chrysler rescue raises the issue of the style of management adopted by European governments toward their respective motor industries. As observed in Chapter 1, governments in all major producing countries have accepted, and appear committed to increasing, their role in the future direction of the industry. Management styles, however, have differed. The French long-run strategy—through Renault and by loan support for Peugeot to rescue Citroen—seems to be aimed at centralization within one or two companies, actively directed under the indicative planning system. The Germans with significant participation in Volkswagen/Audi-NSU confirmed in 1975 that their approach to crisis situations is based on a rejection of short-term job protection. Recognizing the logic of Volkswagen's need to shed in excess of 20,000 employees after the $300 million losses in 1974, the government concentrated on major efforts to offset the dislocation caused by redundancies. There is little indication in German policy of any willingness to either preserve capacity or employment in spite of worker participation. In Italy, the public sector (in Alfa Romeo) is technically very small, relative to the dominance of Fiat in a two-company industry. Long-term strategy is thus difficult to predict but will probably include more direct participation in Fiat, thus supporting its dominance of the domestic market.

In each of these cases, there appears to be a fundamental principle directing government interest in the industry: French centralization, German efficiency through participation, and Italian home market contról. In contrast, U.K. policy toward the industry was late in emerging but could perhaps have been characterized by rationalization and a strategy of recouping domestic market shares through British Leyland, had the need to help Chrysler not arisen. From this viewpoint, willingness to support Chrysler is against all precedent in Europe and, at the least, delays the development of a national U.K. policy toward the industry.

EUROPEAN ECONOMIC COMMUNITY

Looked at objectively, the scale of the Chrysler problem and the nature of the ultimate solution would both point to the involvement of the EEC. It is arguable that the 1975 rescue program would have been more integrative in intent if it had been viewed as a Community problem at that stage. Unfortunately, the relative underdevelopment and underfunding of the EEC would have precluded any real weight being brought to the problem. Neither is the situation likely to change significantly during the 1976-79 phase of the program, although the prospect of Community involvement will remain an important aspect of the solution for several reasons. In the first place, if the European motor industry remains with overcapacity, the importance of developing a pan-European strategy will increase, in which the EEC will have an important role to play. Over the integration of Chrysler, too, there are many potential areas of dispute between the United Kingdom and France for which the EEC is the obvious source of initiative and arbitration.

The regional aspect of the Chrysler problem represents an additional area for EEC involvement. Accepting that there will be, as evidence suggests,[15] a continuing and increasing problem of peripheral area development in the EEC, Chrysler's Linwood plant is likely to continue in its role of political counterweight. This will only be heightened both by Scottish devolution and by the new importance that Linwood has assumed in the 1975 plan for the company. Given that regional development policies will probably increase in importance within the Community, Chrysler may feature in EEC programs because of the consequences for the west central Scottish region.

Of course, the EEC attitude to the initial rescue scheme might well influence any future support from Brussels. While little official comment was made, the EEC reportedly did not favor the 1975 agreement because it appeared to create additional difficulties for long-term planning for the industry. Evidence given by the European Commission to the Expenditure Committee[16] before the Chrysler crisis gives some indication of the way in which it has viewed such a situation. While it appears that the commission found nothing wrong with government assistance for modernization, provided that the aim was eventual profitability, the indications were that it would oppose the noncommercial preservation of excess capacity. Its view that competitive forces would produce specialization and functional mergers in the European industry could hardly be applied to the Chrysler case.

CHRYSLER CORPORATION

The 1975 plan for the U.K. company also has certain implications for the corporation as a whole. The mechanism by which the rescue was accomplished removes little strategic flexibility from the corporation, although inevitably it has led to a consolidation of the corporation's position in the United Kingdom. Similarly, few of the items in the Declaration of Intent limit the corporation in adjusting future policy. The one area in which the corporation policy might possibly have been influenced beyond its intent is in the relative investment in United Kingdom and France. It is difficult to imagine any corporation investment program, even excluding the immediate crisis, showing such a preference for the United Kingdom. The responsiveness of the U.K. government changed that and implied much backtracking by Chrysler on previous remarks regarding the relative efficiency and profitability of the two companies.

The rescue does introduce a new dimension to the corporation's overall planning because of government involvement. Different types of association with governments have been formed in the past, however, as, for example, in Peru, and government loan support in the United Kingdom is not unique. Whatever the corporation's original intention might have been regarding the role of the government in operations such as the United Kingdom, the corporation had made it clear for a considerable period before the crisis that a government approach of-

fering support would not be spurned. As one senior executive put it,
"We're the most flexible company in the world when it comes to who
has what stake."[17] In the end, the deal perhaps has done more to lock
the government into Chrysler than vice versa, and in that sense it has
given the corporation's European strategy a reprieve.

     The net benefit of the rescue is heavily weighted in the corpora-
tion's favor over the next four years, even taking into account the undertakings and guarantees given by Chrysler as part of the 1975 package. Also, since capital restructuring was required in any event if
the company was to continue, the loan terms[18] and profit support commitment give considerable advantage to Chrysler after 1979. The
corporation, given success, will have gained a regenerated subsidiary
on preferential terms and at a bargain basement price.

     From the viewpoint of the corporation, there is an inherent
paradox in the type of agreement reached with the government. Too
general to involve much detailed monitoring, it was simultaneously
too general to ensure that many of the detailed conditions of success
could be achieved. Thus, for example, while there were advantages
in a quick, pressurized treatment of the U.K. government, less rapid
and more specific bargaining on details concerning manning levels,
productivity, and so on might have given the corporation an opportunity
to use the investment in a way that was more in keeping with its own
interests. Such an item-by-item negotiation would have taken time and
would have involved lengthy joint discussions among management,
unions, and government. Together, nevertheless, the parties involved
might have been able to achieve sufficient agreement on an investment
in exchange for productivity basis to tackle some of the fundamental
problems of Chrysler U.K. The government and the company implicitly
seemed to consider that extended worker participation would be the sine
qua non of future cooperation. While this may be so, detailed bargaining against a time limit might have given a focus to participation and
put it to the test at the rescue period. As things stand at present, the
company is not guaranteed any concrete changes in productivity in
areas that are vital for long-term recovery.

MULTINATIONAL INVESTMENT DECISIONS
AND HOST NATIONS

     Some of the important longer term lessons of the Chrysler case
are in areas concerning the strategy of multinational enterprise and
in the methods of control adopted by host countries toward multinational
corporations. While there is always an inherent danger in generalizing
from one case, the scale of the Chrysler operations in Europe and
Chrysler's recurrent difficulties raise some issues that are of wider

relevance to other multinationals investing abroad. It is particularly pertinent in instances where, like Chrysler, the investment in a major growth industry is being undertaken late and at a higher risk in light of strong local competition. There are inevitably many aspiring multinationals in a similar position. When the market growth potential appears attractive and the invested confidence is high, considerations on modus operandi could tend to become secondary to the perceived long-term gain. As has been observed in Chapter 9, this often resolves round the gap between identifying the real problem and being able to implement the correct solution. Chrysler failed to recognize the real overall problem of European strategy, and hence valid operational decisions were often undertaken in a vacuum.

Investment Decisions

Chrysler is not the first corporation to discover the difficulties of finding a formula for achieving profitability in its European acquisitions. As a late entrant, the corporation had little alternative than to enter by acquisition and minority participation. This immediately put it in a high risk area. To balance this, however, it was making a horizontal move into Europe, staying within its own area of expertise, and thus was more likely to achieve success. Moreover, there is evidence to indicate that the vehicles industry has been one of the more fruitful areas for multinational acquisition[19] and that the United Kingdom and France have been among the more profitable host countries.

Within this overall picture, Chrysler has had an experience counter to the trend. There may be several reasons for this. First, there were few willing European partners and finance was limited. Thus, it was not possible to make an objective choice. Second, developing from this, the corporation bought into relatively small unsuccessful companies, none of which might have been chosen on the basis of a strict managerial audit.[20] Inevitably, reorganization and reinvestment were simultaneously required on all three European fronts. Third, excessive confidence was placed on the ability to transfer U.S. management experience to Europe. The assumption was made, incorrectly in the case of Rootes, that the European companies would be receptive to managerial inputs, and that the known control techniques employed in the United States would resolve any deficiencies.

Fourth, the only terms of entry attainable were based on converting minority holdings to majority over a period of time. While this brought the advantages of being able to assess developments before achieving control and before making further financial commitment, it also brought the disadvantage of not being in complete control in a fast-moving market situation. Fifth, the very different environments of France, Spain, and the United Kingdom required different management approaches. From the viewpoint of Detroit, Europe may have been seen too much as a single entity and the necessary flexibility of approach may have been lacking. There are, of course, other factors, some of which would be ranked as of greater importance by the corporation. These might include the size of the market share purchased in Europe. Although there were problems in the U.K. company arising from its declining market share, there is no reason to believe that at the time either the U.K. or French operation was below a viable size by definition. Indeed, had they been consistently perceived to be so, steps presumably would have been taken to integrate the two operations.

While there is little encouragement in the Chrysler case for any multinational wishing to enter late into a key market, there is less for one that intends to do so without a policy that reflects the realities of that market. It is on this issue above all else that the Chrysler European investment has found difficulties. Chrysler, as with many others, appears to have found it difficult to develop a unified policy to guide international activities, without which even the most efficient operational management could not be guaranteed success. To some extent, this reflected a failure to evolve a type of organization for Europe that was sufficiently strong and stable to develop such European policies. But, of course, a strategy that conceived of semiautonomous European units as the basis for operations made a European organization virtually superfluous.

One important lesson of the Chrysler case, emerging from the acquisition of a respected if failing national firm and from U.K. government involvement in the investment process, is the need for considerable sensitivity in company actions. In such circumstances the sensitivity required goes well beyond that necessary for any multinational operating abroad. Chrysler has operated in the United Kingdom under the constant attentive gaze of public opinion, and the company frequently has suffered from overexposure in the press and media. Much of this was brought on by the actions of management itself, for example, in dispute situations; and Chrysler must have wished on frequent occasions to have had a lower profile in the United Kingdom.

An acquisition strategy that involves continued government support of one type or another may seem an attractive and low risk route, but it has consequences. Some of these lie in public interest but, more fundamentally, they involve the multinational coming to terms with government in a way that goes beyond accepting government loans in the balance sheet. Thus, while Chrysler frequently has pledged its flexibility of approach in its relationship with government, a more positive acceptance of continued government involvement in, for example, earlier commitment to worker participation, more extensive prior consultation in finance, and so on, would have dampened down much of the public hostility the company has attracted in the United Kingdom. The 1975 rescue was probably assisted by public interest in the United Kingdom, so that public attention has been a double-edged weapon. However, Chrysler's cavalier treatment of the U.K. government at the time of the deal may prove to have done incalculable harm to the long-term interests of the company in the United Kingdom. Moreover, it would be naive to conclude that 1975 Chrysler-like circumstances occur sufficiently regularly to be employed as a technique of planning for ailing European subsidiaries.

Host Nations

There are many aspects of Chrysler's investment in Europe, particularly in the United Kingdom, that touch on important issues of relationships between multinationals and host nations. These are especially significant in the light of the efforts of the European Economic Community, the Organization for Economic Cooperation and Development, the United Nations, and other bodies to develop codes of conduct to regulate multinational enterprises. The external formulation of policies with major social implications, the "pistol to the head" conditions faced by the U.K. government in 1975, the lack of accountability at national level as the Chrysler policy in Europe becomes more international, and the effectiveness of any planning agreements or similar contributions to national economic management are among the many-sided dimensions of this issue.

Current developments in the area of evolving controls in practice tend to fall into the trap of either being so widely defined as to be ineffective or to be so stringent as to require the company to cease to operate effectively as a transnational corporation. Accepting that there is a need for balance in any such policy, it would be reasonable to expect that a corporation would tend to become more considered in its actions the more dependent it is on domestic capital. The fact that Chrysler U.K. has continued to receive favorable consideration from the U.K. government should heighten the need to come to terms with close government scrutiny and intensified public interest in the company's fortunes.

It has already been made clear that Chrysler has been in a position to influence some aspects of national economic policy, especially as regards industrial strategy. This, however, is only one dimension of the wider problem that has attracted particular attention in recent years.[21] For example, Chrysler, primarily through its Iranian contract, is making an important positive contribution to the U.K. balance of payments. Indeed, should subsequent financing be required by the U.K. company, the optimum strategy would appear to be to maximize exports and thereby maximize leverage. Problems within this whole area have been classified in terms of harmonies and tensions between the company and host nation. In Chrysler's case, tensions arising from uncertainty about the corporation's future plans for Europe, industrial relations management, and so on have had serious disbenefits for the United Kingdom but have proved to be ultimately beneficial to the corporation. If anything, Chrysler, in its dealings with the U.K. government, has traded in tension.

One of the major allegations of tensions between multinationals and host nations concerns the existence of restrictive export franchises on national subsidiaries. As has been indicated in earlier chapters, Chrysler's export record in general is not in itself open to criticism, nor is it proportionately worse than Ford and GM in the United Kingdom. It has, however, caused tension at various times, especially over the substitution of the Colt for the Avenger in the U.S. market. Depending on the way in which future integration is actually defined and implemented, export market allocations for the United Kingdom and France might continue to be a source of tension, and further tensions will be likely to arise when decisions are made on components sources.

Various attempts have been made to assess the impact of the multinational firm on actual industry performance in the host nation. Clearly, it is impossible to do this comprehensively without comparisons of interfirm efficiency. The overall performance of Chrysler certainly has not exceeded industry norms, so to that extent there has been no particularly beneficial effect. The company, however, introduced some significant reforms that have had an impact beyond Chrysler itself. Opinion is widely divided as to their effect. For example, the guaranteed working week arrangements, while desirable, were introduced without an effective productivity payoff. The plan acted as a model for other groups of workers and probably raised costs in the industry. The question as to whether this system would have been introduced in any event under pressure of labor withdrawal in other companies must remain an open one. The Chrysler rescue, as a whole, on the other hand, can be said categorically to have had an adverse effect on industrial structure and on attitudes toward efficiency, although the effects were as much a function of government's response as of Chrysler's action.

It is perhaps within the area of regional policy that Chrysler has had most effect in the United Kingdom. Its inherited presence at Linwood, as has been noted, has proved critical. Chrysler might on occasion not have wished to be holding such a pawn from an operational point of view, but from the perspective of strategic relations with the U.K. government, Linwood has proved an important asset.

There is little doubt that the move toward devolution in Scotland will only serve to increase the bargaining power vested in Linwood, perhaps far beyond the wishes of Chrysler.

NOTES

1. The Regeneration of British Industry, Cmnd 5710 (London: HMSO, August 1974), para. 17.

2. Eighth Report from the Expenditure Committee, sess. 1975–76, Public Expenditure on Chrysler U.K. Ltd., HC 596 (I) (London: HMSO, July 1976), para. 47.

3. Ibid., para. 39.

4. The British Motor Vehicle Industry, Cmnd 6377 (London: HMSO, January 1976), para. 2.

5. British Leyland: The Next Decade, HC 342 (London: HMSO, April 1975), para. 13.

6. Public Expenditure on Chrysler U.K. Ltd., para. 290.

7. For a discussion of some facets of this, see N. Hood and S. Young, "U.S. Investment in Scotland: Aspects of the Branch Factory Syndrome," Scottish Journal of Political Economy 23, no. 3 (November 1976).

8. Public Expenditure on Chrysler U.K. Ltd., chap. 9.

9. Expenditure Committee, Public Expenditure on Chrysler U.K. Ltd., Minutes of Evidence, HC 104 (II) (London: HMSO, January 21, 1976), para. 278.

10. Financial Times, August 19, 1976.

11. Central Policy Review Staff, The Future of the British Car Industry (London: HMSO, 1975), p. v.

12. Public Expenditure on Chrysler U.K. Ltd., HC 596 (I), para. 27.

13. Expenditure Committee, sess. 1975–76, Public Expenditure on Chrysler U.K. Ltd., Minutes of Evidence, HC 104 (XXI) (London: HMSO, May 4, 1976), para. 4174. But the Vauxhall reply was qualified somewhat.

14. Ibid., paras. 4139, 4172.

15. For some evidence on this point, see S. Young and N. Hood, "The Geographical Expansion of U.S. Multinationals in Western Europe: Some Survey Evidence," Journal of Common Market Studies 14, no. 3 (March 1976).

16. Fourteenth Report from the Expenditure Committee, The Motor Vehicle Industry, HC 617 (London: HMSO, August 1975), para. 307.

17. Ed Doyle, The Economist, March 15, 1975.

18. Expenditure Committee, <u>Public Expenditure on Chrysler U.K. Ltd.</u>, Minutes of Evidence, HC 104 (I), para. 11.

19. J. Kitching, "Winning and Losing with European Acquisitions," <u>Harvard Business Review</u>, March–April 1974.

20. See, for example, W. A. Dymsya, <u>Multinational Business Strategy</u> (New York: McGraw-Hill, 1972), p. 74.

21. For a review of the issue, see T. G. Parry, "The International Firm and National Economic Policy: A Survey of Some Issues," <u>Economic Journal</u>, December 1973.

A.E.C., 63
Alfa Romeo, 13, 41; and Saviem, 201, 202, 328
Allegro, 123
A.M.C., 47
Arrow range, phase-out, 289; replacement for, 280
Austin-Morris, 65
Auto Union, 10
Avenger: development of, 110; and industrial relations, 232; investment in, 99-100; and Mitsubishi Colt, 133, 246; pricing, 116; and 1975 rescue, 288-89; sales prospects, 310

Berrill, Sir Kenneth: and Chrysler U.K. recovery, 294
Big 3 U.S. producers: expansion strategy, 29-34
BMC, 12; early commercial vehicle trade, 175; origins, 87; and regional policy, 258
BMW, 10, 22; and EEC, 27; and Rootes, 180
Board of Trade, 258
Borgeward, 10
Brabloch Agreement, 233
British Leyland: and anti-dumping, 28; commercial vehicle trade, 186, 195; costs in assisted areas, 266; 1974 demand, 275; disputes, 227; and EEC, 223; and ENASA, 63; market share, 137; origins, 12, 77, 275; pricing, 38, 116; rationalization, 285, 291; and Rootes rescue, 81; Ryder Report on, 275, 282; scale economies, 149; principles behind support of, 322, 326

Cafiero, Gene, 279
Callaghan, James, 80
capacity utilization: U.K. car industry, 151
Carey, Sir Peter, 281
Carty, John, 273
Central Policy Review Staff: and Chrysler U.K., 294; report on future of car industry, 275, 282, 292; on European competition in cars, 325; conclusions summarized, 137
Chrysler Alpine, 108, 123; transfer of development to France, 234, 270; transfer to U.K., 287, 295
Chrysler Corporation: commercial development, 175; dividend policy, 160; European expansion strategy, 29-30, 54, 297; and European governments, 307, 326-27; European integration, 297, 304; European production and market shares, 30-31; versus indigenous European producers, 35; interpretation of European strategy, 67; potential financial commitment post-1975, 287-88; investment in subsidiaries, 157-58; and Iran, 145, 284, 311, 313; losses in 1975, 280; marketing policy, 129-30; 1975 negotiations, 285; profits, 45; Rootes reorganization, 97-98; Rootes takeover, 77; transfer pricing, 140; U.K. labor, 218; loans to U.K. company, 279; management of labor in the United Kingdom, 302; U.K. rescue implications, 329-

STEPHEN YOUNG is a Lecturer in Economics in the Department of Economics and Management at Paisley College of Technology, Scotland. Before joining the Paisley staff, he worked with the Ministry of Agriculture in Tanzania and was manager of the International Economics Department of the Milk Marketing Board in London.

A graduate of the University of Liverpool and Newcastle, he has researched and published widely in the areas of agricultural economies, international trade, and multinational enterprise. The present Chrysler study emerged directly from joint work between the authors on the impact of multinational enterprise on U.K. industrial and regional strategy.

He is author of a number of papers in journals including Journal of Agricultural Economics, Scottish Journal of Political Economy, Journal of Common Market Studies, Management Decision, and European Journal of Marketing.

NEIL HOOD is a Senior Lecturer in Economics in the Department of Economics and Management at Paisley College of Technology, Scotland. Before joining the Paisley staff, he was employed by British Steel and came directly from research work in the export efficiency of the U.K. textile industry. His undergraduate and graduate studies were at the University of Glasgow. He has wide consultancy experience with bodies in the public and private sector, and has researched and published extensively in the areas of managerial economics, marketing, and the economics of multinational enterprise.

He is author of a number of papers in journals including Scottish Journal of Political Economy, Journal of Business Policy, European Journal of Marketing, Management Decision, and Journal of Common Market Studies.

MULTINATIONAL CORPORATIONS AND GOVERN-
MENTS: Business-Government Relations in an International Context

> edited by Patrick M. Boarman
> and Hans Schollhammer

*ECONOMIC ANALYSIS AND THE MULTINATIONAL
ENTERPRISE

> edited by John H. Dunning

†THE MULTINATIONAL CORPORATION AND SOCIAL
CHANGE

> David E. Apter
> Louis Wolf Goodman

†MANAGING MULTINATIONAL CORPORATIONS
> Arvind V. Phatak

THE MULTINATIONAL CORPORATION AND SOCIAL
POLICY: Special Reference to General Motors in
South Africa

> edited by Richard A. Jackson

INTERNATIONAL LABOR AND THE MULTINATIONAL
ENTERPRISE

> edited by Duane Kujawa

DEPENDENT INDUSTRIALIZATION IN LATIN AMER-
ICA: The Automotive Industry in Argentina, Chile,
and Mexico

> Rhys Owen Jenkins

*Available in the United States and the Philippines only.

†Also available in paperback as a PSS Student Edition.